JUS ET SOCIETAS

PROFESSOR WOLFGANG FRIEDMANN (1907-1972)

JUS ET SOCIETAS

ESSAYS IN TRIBUTE TO WOLFGANG FRIEDMANN

with an introduction by
PHILIP C. JESSUP

GABRIEL M. WILNER
Principal Editor

1979
MARTINUS NIJHOFF PUBLISHERS
THE HAGUE / BOSTON / LONDON

The distribution of this book is handled by the following team of publishers:

for the United States and Canada

Kluwer Boston, Inc.
160 Old Derby Street
Hingham, MA 02043
USA

for all other countries

Kluwer Academic Publishers Group
Distribution Center
P.O. Box 322
3300 AH Dordrecht
The Netherlands

ISBN 978-94-009-9323-5 ISBN 978-94-009-9321-1 (eBook)
DOI 10.1007/978-94-009-9321-1

Library of Congress Cataloging in Publication Data CIP

Main entry under title:

Jus et societas.

'A bibliography of the writings of Wolfgang Friedmann': p.
1. International law – Addresses, essays, lectures. 2. International economic relations – Addresses, essays, lectures. 3. Friedmann, Wolfgang Gaston, 1907-1972 – Addresses, essays, lectures. I. Friedmann, Wolfgang Gaston, 1907-1972. II. Wilner, Gabriel M.
JX3091.J87 341 79-11626

PREFACE

When Wolfgang Friedmann died there was a great outpouring of grief, affection and admiration from his friends all over the world. These deeply felt sentiments were soon channelled into a number of projects to honor him.

The initiative towards the preparation of this volume in tribute to Wolfgang Friedmann was taken by his colleague, Hans Smit, of Columbia University, who also arranged for its publication. Judge Philip C. Jessup was the chairman, and Professors John N. Hazard, Louis Henkin, Oliver Lissitzyn, Willis L. M. Reese and Hans Smit of Columbia University Law School, A. A. Fatouros of Indiana University Law School (Bloomington), and Gabriel M. Wilner of the University of Georgia Law School were members of the editorial committee.

The authors of the essays are a group of distinguished legal scholars from many countries and who hold widely diverse views. All of them had many ties with Professor Friedmann, including those of friendship and shared interest in problems that were of the greatest concern to him. The number of eminent jurists from countries around the world, and particularly from the United States, who would have wished to participate in this tribute to Wolfgang Friedmann is large; however, several important considerations made it necessary to limit the number of contributions. Thus, for example, the work of several members of the editorial committee is not represented in the volume.

The essays are appropriately preceded by an introduction, written by Judge Philip C. Jessup, which evokes the unique personality and accomplishments of Wolfgang Friedmann. The diversity of the essays with respect to subject matter is entirely consistent with the universality of Friedmann's interests in the law. This is why it has not been possible to place the articles in a few limited categories; the contributions appear in alphabetical order by author.

The volume includes articles that are generally addressed to the future of the international community, its structure and rules (Gregory Tunkin, Richard Falk). There are essays on methods and institutions for the creation of conventional international law (R. Y. Jennings, Louis B. Sohn) and an article on certain aspects of the practice of the International Court of Justice (Rosalyn Higgins). The essay contributed by the late C. Wilfred Jenks, whose imaginative perspectives on the future of international law were very much appreciated by Professor Friedmann, deals with the International Court of Justice's treatment of the concept of *actio popularis*.

An analysis and critique of political change in the United Nations is offered by Julius Stone in his article entitled, "Conscience, Law, Force and the General Assembly."

Several essays focus on questions of international economic and social justice for the developing countries (Oscar Schachter) and the structuring of regional political and economic organizations in Latin America, Africa and the Middle East (B. Boutros-Ghali, F. V. García-Amador).

Professor Friedmann's innovative thinking on the subject of the international law of cooperation is reflected in the article on the impact of the World Bank on international law (A.A. Fatouros) and the essay by Joseph Gold on the "International Monetary System and Change." Two other contributions—one concerning *force majeure* and international supply contracts (Philippe Kahn), and a second on international and multinational enterprises (Roger Pinto)—deal with subject areas that Friedmann considered to be among the new fields of international law.

The strong and enduring interest Wolfgang Friedmann maintained in legal philosophy is represented by an essay on the jurisprudence of contracts (Harry W. Jones). Still other articles focus on comparative aspects of areas of municipal law in which he had done much thinking and writing. O. Kahn-Freund has contributed an essay on comparative labor law entitled, "Strikes and the Law"; the relationship between administrative tribunals and courts are explored in A. Abel's article. An essay on Canadian constitutional law as it relates to the treaty-making power, by R. St. J. MacDonald, brings together a number of elements which were of lively concern to Professor Friedmann.

The final section of the volume contains a bibliography of the published writings of Wolfgang Friedmann. In addition to books, articles and reviews it was considered appropriate to include letters and articles published in the *New York Times* in which he came to grips courageously and lucidly with the immediate problems of the day.

The editor has been inspired by the support that Mrs. May Friedmann has given to the preparation of this volume. Mrs. Friedmann, whose close collaboration with her husband is exemplified by her work as editor of an abridged edition of the *Changing Structure of International Law,* provided many insights and much practical assistance for which the editor is most grateful. The editor also wishes to recognize the able assistance rendered to him by Mr. Kenneth Klein, *J.D.*

A final note of appreciation is due to the Parker School of Foreign and Comparative Law, Columbia University School of Law (Professor Willis L. M. Reese, Director) for the financial support given toward the publication of this volume.

GABRIEL M. WILNER
Principal Editor

CONTENTS

INTRODUCTION – ABOUT WOLFGANG FRIEDMANN

PHILIP C. JESSUP

The passage of five years—or of decades more to come—can not cushion the shock or begin to fill the gap created when Wolfgang Friedmann was slain on the street near the campus of the University which he served so well. The sorrowful memorials have long since been eloquently spoken and it is not the purpose of this volume to repeat them. Nor can even the distinguished contributions to this one book compete with his voluminous writings which remain as a living monument to his memory. The contributors whose valued thoughts are to be found herein, on behalf of a multitude of others, bear witness to the enduring forward reach of Wolfgang Friedmann's keen and sympathetic understanding of the ever-changing pattern of the problems of mankind.

Wolfgang Friedmann's versatility was untainted by superficiality. Perhaps the quality of his contributions to an understanding of man and the society in which man exists, is best exemplified by the posthumous award of the Phillips Prize by the American Philosophical Society. It was a particularly appropriate award since the founder of the Philosophical Society, Benjamin Franklin, would have recognized Friedmann, in Europe or America, as a worthy and worthwhile correspondent or conversationalist, whether in philosophy, international affairs or many other topics.

Let me quote from the Report of the Society's Committee which recommended the award of the Phillips Prize:[1]

> The major works to which the Phillips Prize would accord the Society's recognition are *Legal Theory* (5th ed., 1967) and *Law in a Changing Society* (2d ed., 1972). In these as in his other writings Professor Friedmann brilliantly surmounted the walls within which legal scholars (like others) seek to confine their

1. The report was written by the chairman of the Committee, Professor Walter Gelhorn of the Columbia University School of Law.

PHILIP C. JESSUP has been Judge of the International Court of Justice (1961-1970); Hamilton Fish Professor of International Law and Diplomacy, Columbia University 1946-1961; and is a member of the Institut de Droit International.

> disciplines. He was, in Justice Frankfurter's phrase, an expert in relevance. More than most, he was able to perceive the connections between things whose relationships had not previously been clearly seen. Dubious about the utility of "a theory of justice based on abstract philosophical postulates," he squarely faced the perennially difficult "conflict of values" which he deemed "inherent in the solution of any legal problem, whether on a national or an international scale."[2]
>
> *Law in a Changing Society* developed the theme that the legal order is both a reactor to and an initiator of social change. It reexamined, in diverse contexts, the relation between the individual on the one hand and public power on the other. A man of compassion and courage, Professor Friedmann in this work as in others showed himself able to distinguish between what the once called "theoretical freedom" and the social realities which too often prevented the development of moral and intellectual responsibility.
>
> *Legal Theory* surveys the impact of various ethical theories on the development of legal philosophy, carrying forward scholars' ceaseless consideration of law's relation—or lack of relation—to morality. The most recent edition considers also the impact of modern scientific thought upon legal theory. It enlighteningly examines the judicial function in effecting change, bringing to bear on this question the author's rich learning about foreign legal systems. And it explores new conceptions of international law, a topic Professor Friedmann developed more full in his *The Changing Structure of International Law* (1964).

Wolfgang Friedmann was a man of many countries. Born and educated in Germany, he was a student and teacher in England, professor in Australia, Canada, and the United States, lecturer in Holland, India, France, Iran, Tanzania. Disregarding the implied attribution of agency, it could be well said that if one invokes the maxim *qui facit per alium facit per se,* his cosmopolitanism was literally global as his research teams and students carried on work he inspired.

The devotion and enthusiasm which he aroused in his students is witnessed by the issue of the Columbia Journal of Transnational Law dedicated to him on the occasion of the tenth anniversary of the founding of the Journal. He was responsible for the Journal's foundation and for advising on its development. The issue, the first copy of which was presented to him, contains tributes from colleagues as well.[3]

2. Friedmann, A Theory of Justice: A Lawyer's Critique, 11 *Colum. J. Transnat'l L.* 369, 371, 379 (1972).

3. The issue of the *Columbia Journal of Transnational Law* is Vol. 10, No. 1, Spring 1971. The tributes, especially of Dean Michael Sovern of the Columbia Law School (pp. 5-8), contain more biographical and bibliographical data than can be included in this introduction to a volume which is a further tribute.

It was on January 25, 1907 that Wolfgang Friedmann was born in Berlin, Germany, so that he was too young to have personal experience of World War I although he grew up in the economic distress of the post-war era. His mother was French by birth and Wolfgang was enrolled in the *Franzosiches Gymnasium* where part of the teaching was in French. He went on to the Law Faculty of the *Universitat Berlin* where his teachers included Arthur Nussbaum and Ernst Rabel; Rabel supervised his thesis entitled *Die Bereicherungshaftung im Anglo-Amerikanischen Rechtskreis in Vergleichung mit dem Deutschen Bürgerlichen Recht* which was published in 1930 under the auspices of the *Institut für Auslandisches und Internationales Privatrecht* and which is still cited as authoritative in comparative studies of the doctrine of unjust enrichment.

After a year in a German law firm, he went to England where he worked in a solicitor's office and taught German in an English school. But he returned to Germany in the following year and at the Labour Court in Berlin showed his characteristic courage in standing up against the mounting Nazi terror. He was summarily dismissed and escaped to England.

> In England, Wolfgang did not immediately return to the law, but instead anticipated some of today's students by organizing a commune in Welwyngarden City, a city honored by the Quakers who provided a house for the purpose at nominal rent. There political and racial refugees from Germany, together with a number of sympathetic Englishmen, lived in a community emphasizing agriculture and manual labor, in which each contributed all his efforts to the whole. Wolfgang, who had resumed his high school teaching of German, was one of the few who was gainfully employed and who also gave his earnings, instead of only personal labor, to the commune.[4]

With the encouragement of a life-long friend and now an equally eminent jurist, Otto Kahn-Freund, Friedmann resumed his legal studies in evening courses at the College of Law of the University of London. He was appointed Reader in law at that University in 1938 and held the post until 1947, teaching courses in public and private international law, torts, contracts and jurisprudence.

The year before his appointment as Reader, he married May Lewis; they had four sons. In 1939 he became a naturalized British subject and in 1943 joined the British intelligence service. He was sent to Germany in 1945 and attached to SHAEF, the Allied High Command, where he became Head of the Office for Economic Reconstruction in the British Sector of Germany. These experiences led to his publishing in 1947 *The*

Allied Military Government of Germany which characteristically reflected his independent point of view, critical of several aspects of Allied policy. In the same year he accepted the chair of Public Law at the University of Melbourne where he stayed for three years before going on to be Professor of Law at the University of Toronto from 1950 to 1955. Each change of scene, so to speak, involved heart-rending decisions and the breaking of fond ties, although his English, Australian and Canadian contacts were always kept fresh and vital. The last move came in 1955 when he yielded to the pressures and the challenges of Columbia University which appointed him Professor of International Law and Director of International Legal Studies. The Dean of the Columbia Law School testifies to Wolfgang Friedmann's accomplishments in this his last academic post:

> This [International Legal Studies] Program, of which he is both the originator and the guiding hand, has produced remarkable results on a variety of levels. First, it has produced a series of studies on legal problems in underdeveloped countries, a subject in which Wolfgang had become interested as a consultant to the United Nations. The most important of these are *Legal Aspects of Foreign Investment* (with Pugh, 1959), *Joint International Business Ventures* (with Kalmanoff, 1961), *International Financial Aid* (with Kalmanoff and Meagher, 1965), *The Role of the State and the Rule of Law in the Mixed Economy* (Tagore Law Lectures, 1971), and *Joint International Business Ventures in Developing Countries* (with Béguin, 1971). Second, the Program has greatly stimulated and financially facilitated, Columbia's graduate program for foreign lawyers. Indeed, lawyers all over the world are in its debt for its initiative and assistance. And third, the program has supported—intellectually, morally and financially—the *Columbia Journal of Transnational Law* which in this issue so appropriately commemorates Wolfgang's vital role.[5]

Thus at Columbia, Wolfgang Friedmann's interests were more and more concentrated on international legal problems, always with an acute awareness of their interrelationship with economics. These interests were focussed in his contributions to the Hague Academy of International Law. He chaired and inspired a Study Group appointed by the Curatorium of the Academy in 1965. The result was an almost revolutionary improvement in the teaching procedures of the Academy and the broadening of its activities through the new External (or Overseas) Programme which has included the sending of teams of professors to Africa, Latin America and Asia to conduct courses and seminars, largely for young professors and civil servants, in international legal problems with special regional interest. In instant recognition of his contributions, the Curatorium invited Friedmann to deliver in 1969 the prestigious General Course in international law; those lectures supplemented his 1964 volume on *The Changing Structure of International Law*. Through the Hague Academy also, Wolfgang Friedmann in numerous ways displayed his keen personal interest in individual students.

His emphasis on international economic and social problems, particularly of the developing countries, was grounded in a continuing appreciation of all aspects of international relations as revealed in his *Introduction to World Politics,* which went into its Fifth Edition in 1965 and which was adopted by Commonwealth Governments for distribution to their embassies throughout the world. While at Toronto, he was a frequent commentator and debator on international politics in the programs of the CBC. Later at Columbia, he contributed, through letters to the New York *Times* and in various forums, to vigorous discussions of the international issues of the day.

One must examine the Bibliography in this volume for an adequate appreciation of the breadth and depth of Wolfgang Friedmann's legal writings, beyond the few already mentioned. I merely list a few additional titles: *Principles of Australian Administrative Law,* (1950), *Law and Social Change in Contemporary Britain* (1951), *The Public Corporation* (1954), *Matrimonial Property* (1955), *Antitrust Laws* (1956), *The Future of the Oceans* (1971).

I would close this modest introduction by again recalling Wolfgang Friedmann as a warm human being rather than as the eminent scholar that he was. That concern for his students to which reference has been made, also inspired what became almost a traditional institution at Columbia. Dozens of young men and women cherish the memory of the annual springtime picnic at the Friedmann's home in North Salem, New York. There they experienced the warm hospitality and delicious outdoor lunches of May Friedmann among her skillfully cultivated flowers and shrubs. None could outdo Wolfgang in gymnastics or games on the lawn. There was a camaraderie which embraced even those European students brought up in the strict tradition of the revered *Herr Doktor Profesor*; but for them and their more unconventional American fellow-students, admiration for physical prowess and informal friendship never diminished their respect for the scholar, who was so young in spirit and so mature in wisdom.

COURTS AND TRIBUNALS: PARTNERS IN JUSTICE

A.S. ABEL

> [C]ourt and agency are not to be regarded as wholly independent and unrelated instrumentalities of justice, each acting in the performance of its prescribed statutory duty without regard to the appropriate function of the other in securing the plainly indicated objects of the statute. Court and agency are the means adopted to obtain the prescribed end . . . Neither body should repeat in this day the mistake made by the courts of law when equity was struggling for recognition as an ameliorating system of justice; neither can rightly be regarded by the other as an alien intruder, to be tolerated if must be, but never to be encouraged or aided by the other in the attainment of the common aim . . .[1]

In the legal unlike the physical order two bodies can occupy the same place at the same time. They do in countries where courts and administrative authorities share the task of adjudication.

An institutional equivalent of the territorial imperative unhappily has blighted the relationship. The obsessive concern of participants and observers has been to establish a subordination, tending asymptotically to outright attrition of one of the cotenants of the decisional function. Still conditioned by, however much they disavow, Blackstonian and Diceyan notions about the rule of law, those with a common law formation have been so preoccupied with judicial review of administrative determinations as to let it absorb their whole attention.[2] In a different setting, the very title *Tribunal de Conflits,* of a most ingenious mechanism for specifying the accomodations between judicial and

A.S. ABEL is Professor of Law, University of Toronto.

1. United States v. Morgan, 307 U.S. 183, 191 (1939) (per Chief Justice Stone)

2. Both the legislation (see, *e.g.,* Administrative Procedure Act, 5 U.S.C. Ts. 1001 *et seq.;* 1971 Ont. Stat. c.48) and the scholarly writing (see not only S.A. de Smith, *Judicial Review of Administrative Action* (1959) and L. Jaffe, *Judicial Control of Administrative Action* (1965), but also the more broadly titled works of, for example, Davis, Griffith, Dussault and Street, and Reid) have little or nothing to say about aspects of interaction other than review by the courts.

administrative organs, likewise reflects an attitude that holds that at least opposition, if not hostility, is the dominant feature of the relationship. That may inescapably be so; yet there are occasions for and have been instances of reciprocal recourse between them which merit exploration and indeed expansion. The focus of this discussion will be on the ways available to courts and to administrative agencies for employing each other's capacities. Materials on the one hand from the United States and Canada, and on the other from France will furnish illustrations of the development of a common potential under the differing legal systems of the common law and the civil law.[3]

I. DEFERENCE TO OTHER COURTS

The phenomenon of co-existing spheres of judicial competence can be found in contexts other than judiciary and administration; brief preliminary note may be made of some of these. A common pattern will be found; it is a pattern generally of jealous competition in the assertion of jurisdiction but mitigated by occasional deference and reference to the parallel legal order.

The memory of the squabble between law and equity, culminating in the confrontation of Coke and Ellesmere[4] is still fresh, as Chief Justice Stone's remarks demonstrate. It has obscured their admittedly sporadic resort to harmonizing devices such as directions by: Common Law judges to seek in equity relief beyond their own power;[5] Chancery to Common Law to settle a point of law;[6] and both Chancery and Common Law to the Exchequer Chamber of proceedings separately brought in each where the facts and issues were the same.[7] Typical instances were the Common Law's reliance on equity procedures for discovery[8] and the use of temporary injunctions against prejudicial changes of position pending determination of legal actions,[9] and by contrast equity's availing itself of a feigned issue to obtain the verdict of a jury[10] and, perhaps most notably of its discretionary declining of relief

3. The wording in the text is unavoidably inexact, what with an important part of Canada not a common law regime (although public law is throughout) and what with administrative law not being a part of but apart from civil law in France. No better terms seem to exist though to signal adherence to different legal systems.

4. A full account of the incident may be found in 2 J. Campbell, *Lives of the Lord Chancellors and Keepers of the Great Seal of England* 386-90 (J. Mallory ed. 1874).

5. See Arguments Proving from Antiquity the Dignity, Power, and Jurisdiction of the Court of Chancery, 21 Eng. Rep. 577, 581.

6. See *id.* at 596 (discussion of Throgmorton's Case, 1597).

7. Calvin's Case, 77 Eng. Rep. 377, 379 (K.B. 1609).

8. Abbott, "The Co-operation of Law and Equity," 7 *Harv. L. Rev.* 76 (1893) gives many instances.

9. See, *e.g.*, Ireby v. Gibone, 21 Eng. Rep. 44 (Ch. 1579), Harmon v. Jones, 41 Eng. Rep. 505 (Ch. 1841).

10. See, *e.g.*, Clayton v. Meadows, 67 Eng. Rep. 11 (Ch. 1841); Goodyear v. Providence Rubber Co., 10 F. Cas. 712 (No. 5,583) (D.R.I. 1864).

on issues of tort or contract suable at law.[11]

In a more remote semi-forgotten past is the era when the royal courts co-existed with a welter of other jurisdictions such as courts merchant, manorial, municipal and, most conspicuously, ecclesiastical courts. Their relations with the incipient royal courts like those of common law and equity seem to have been characterized in general by endemic antagonism tempered by recognition of necessary accommodation. This is not the occasion for nor indeed are materials readily available to permit a survey of this interplay. But, to indicate only the chief case, the courts of State and of Church, while they often antagonized each other, worked out patterns of mutual aid[12] both in England and on the Continent.[13]

This is historical; but separate judicial hierarchies having authority within a given body politic continue to exist and new ones continue to emerge.

The American dual structure of federal and state courts is a prominent example of such a structure. In federations like Australia[14] and, until very recently,[15] Canada[16] where, except for special subject matter areas, courts of first instance are found only at the state (provincial) level and, what is probably of more critical importance, where the content of state (provincial) law is not independently determined but is settled by the federal supreme court, there is less of a basis for differentiating their functions and no traces have been found of a practice like that of abstention which has developed in the United States.

Stated broadly, without entering on its refinements, the practice in the United States is one by which a federal court seised of a cause whose disposition hinges on the application of unresolved doubtful points of state law may or should abstain from undertaking to settle such points and withhold decision to permit their determination by the state courts.[17] Its rather recent articulation,[18] stimulated perhaps by greater

11. Todd v. Gee, 34 Eng. Rep. 106 (Ch. 1810); *cf.* McClintock, "Discretion to Deny Injunction against Trespass and Nuisance," 12 *Minn. L. Rev.* 565 (1928); Note, "Public Convenience and Injunctions Against Torts," 36 *Harv. L. Rev.* 211 (1922).

12. See *Introduction of the Curia Regis Rolls, 1199-1230 A.D.* ch. 9, 62 Selden Soc. Ser. (C. Flower ed. 1944).

13. See P. de Remi, *Coustumes de Beauvoisis* Ch. XII (A. Salmon ed. 1900).

14. Z. Cowen, *Federal Jurisdiction in Australia* ch. 5 (1959).

15. B. Laskin, *Laskin's Canadian Constitutional Law* 793-96 (4th ed. rev. 1975).

16. It is too soon to tell whether the Federal Court Act, *Can. Rev. Stat.* c. 10 (2d Supp. 1970), which gives a wide range of concurrent jurisdiction in matters involving federal legislation thereby giving an opening for the abstention doctrine, will effectively lead to its introduction. To date there is no indication of it.

17. Kurland, "Toward a Co-operative Judicial Federalism: The Federal Court Abstention Doctrine," 24 F.R.D. 481 (1959).

18. It was first explictly propounded in Railroad Comm'n v. Pullman Co., 312 U.S. 496 (1941).

attention given to state law following *Erie Railroad Co. v. Tompkins,*[19] has been reiterated and developed so that it is now firmly established.[20] The practice as now established in the United States relates not to the jurisdiction but to the discretion of the court in which suit is instituted;[21] in that context it has provided a technique of collaboration through recourse to the other interested system in the course of the litigation. There is, it is true, no reciprocal arrangement for withholding state proceedings pending a federal court ruling; but there is no occasion for one since state and lower federal courts alike have the opportunity to apply federal law in appropriate circumstances,[22] subject always to potential ultimate determination by the Supreme Court. An offshoot,[23] strengthened by considerations of harmonious federalism, of the more general concept of *forum non conveniens* counselling self-denial in the exercise of a possessed competence, abstention is one modern instance.[24]

A mirror image is found in European Community law, reversed as is the nature of mirror images. Article 177 of the European Economic Community Treaty is to the effect that when the interpretation of a Treaty provision or of a measure emanating from agencies of or established under the Community is involved in a proceeding before a tribunal of a member state, such tribunal *"peut, si elle estime qu'une décision sur ce point est nécessaire pour rendre son jugement"* ask the Court of Justice of the Community to rule on the question; if it is a national court of last resort, it is its duty so to do. Only genuine and serious problems of interpretation are contemplated.[25] As to national lower courts, their power and duty to decide and to pay heed to Community law strikingly parallels that of American federal courts with relation to state law. The same is true with respect to the discretion to withhold permission for the Court of Justice to make its interpretation. Although only some use has been made of the option, the very spelling

19. 304 U.S. 678 (1938). *Erie* did not touch directly on the abstention problem, but it did invite attention to the importance of state law in the federal system.

20. See, *e.g.*, Lake Carriers' Ass'n v. MacMullan, 406 U.S. 498 (1972); Kaiser Steel Corp. v. W.S. Ranch Co., 391 U.S. 593 (1968); Louisiana Power & Light Co. v. Thibodaux, 360 U.S. 25 (1959).

21. Meredith v. Winter Haven, 320 U.S. 228 (1943).

22. Second Employers' Liability Cases, 223 U.S. 1 (1911).

23. "On substantially *forum non conveniens* grounds we have required federal courts to relinquish decision of cases within their jurisdiction where the court would have to participate in the administrative policy of a state." Gulf Oil Corp. v. Gilbert, 330 U.S. 501, 505 (1947) (per Justice Jackson).

24. For discussions of *forum non conveniens* see Blair, "The Doctrine of Forum Non Conveniens in Anglo American Law," 29 *Colum. L. Rev.* 1 (1929); Braucher, "The Inconvenient Federal Forum," 60 *Harv. L. Rev.* 908 (1947) (original said to be law of Scotland); *cf.* 28 U.S.C. s.1404(a) (1970).

25. See T. Mathiesen, *Guide to European Community Law* 163-66 (1972).

of it out in a provision of the Treaty manifests a sense of the potential fruitfulness of such a device.[26]

These are illustrations of deference by courts to other courts. As such they do not bear directly on reciprocity between tribunals of unlike types. They do, however, show a recognition that it is permissible and on occasion wise to forego the full exercise of jurisdiction and instead to seek the participation in the course of decision of extraneous tribunals with special competence.

II. EFFECTS GIVEN TO DECISIONS BY OTHER TRIBUNALS

Once a judicial or administrative decision is made, tribunals of the other type do attach some operative consequences to it. Respect for what the other has done cannot be equated with reliance on it as an auxiliary in making the decision; this is the central theme of this paper. Nevertheless, as an example of court-agency cooperation or at least co-ordination, it calls for brief preliminary discussion, both to define by exclusion the field of main concern and to rebut any notion that there are separate universes functioning in total isolation.[27]

A decision may be urged as relevant to the disposition of a distinct proceeding. Or it may be the basis for invoking certain means of enforcement. Whether consequential effects or implementation be involved, it is clear that there is some recognition of decisions of the other hierarchy and thereby some harmonized integration.

When authoritative rulings on matters which are constituent elements in suits before them are made, both courts and administrative tribunals[28] in France accord to the other's decisions the full force of *chose jugée* where there is an *effet positif* as well as in cases of an *effet négatif*.[29] The two concepts correspond approximately to the notions distinguished in American terms as collateral estoppel by judgment and merger and bar, as sub-divisions of the broader concept of *res judicata*.[30] The *effect négatif* can be traced to Article 1351 of the Civil Code, the satisfaction of whose conditions is required;[31] the *effet positif*

26. Fougère, "Les Incidences de Communautés Européenes sur le Contetieux Administratif Français," in *Les Communautés Européenes et le Droit Administratif Français* 401 (1972).

27. Nothing that follows deals with challenges to decisions by appeal or other direct review procedures, as to which decisions the effect of privative clauses, the respect accorded the presumption of regularity, etc., are pertinent. Instead, only decisions not subject or at least not presented for supervision by the second tribunal are contemplated.

28. See *Encyc. Dalloz, Droit Administratif, tit. Chose Jugée*, paras. 25-35.

29. For a very full analysis see C. Durand, *Les Rapports entre les Juridictions Administrative et Judiciare* (1956) [hereinafter cited as Durand].

30. *Restatement of Judgments* ss. 61-72 (1942).

31. 3 J. Auby & R. Drag, *Traité de Contentieux Administratif* para. 1257 (1962) [hereinafter cited as Auby & Drago].

rests partly at least on a broader base, *séparation des pouvoirs* which is a fundamental constitutional principle.[32] The question of when a determination is to be regarded as *chose jugée* presents many complexities but its effect is the same between the two jurisdictional orders as within each of them.

The United States position is less clear and the Canadian situation is an enigma. That agencies may and indeed must[33] accept as being settled matters which a court has decided seems to be taken for granted and has attracted little discussion.[34] The converse situation as to the *res judicata* effect of administrative determinations upon court proceedings, presents problems. In the United States, suggestions that there is no such effect have been repudiated by the highest authority.[35] At least some have even been regarded as qualifying for treatment in the same manner as "judicial proceedings" under the Full Faith and Credit Clause of the Constitution.[36] Yet most writers have summed up with a sometimes yes and sometimes no, accompanied by illustrative instances but little critical analysis.[37] In Canada it has been blankly asserted that administrative decisions can not be *res judicata* in court,[38] but the assertion is at odds with the results of some actual holdings,[39] although not cast in *res judicata* terms.

The American position probably approximates the French in substance, despite its equivocal statement. Denials of *res judicata* effect have been directed to avoiding the freezing of a ruling disposing of existing claims into a rule controlling future cases, as contrasted with the particular matter which is commonly taken as concluded once it is no longer reviewable. This attribute of attachment to a concrete claim is a conditioning circumstance for giving the effect of *chose jugée*[40] which

32. See Durand, *supra* note 29, at 323.

33. *Cf.* Drysdale v. Cominion Coal Co., 34 S.C.R. 328 (1904); Rumble v. Rowlin, [1935] 2 D.L.R. 402 (Man.).

34. K. Davis, *Administrative Law Treatise* s.18.11 (1958) [hereinafter cited as Davis] states this as the general principle but subject to qualifications. *Cf.* Note, "A Judgment as Evidence in a Later Proceeding," 33 *Harv. L. Rev.* 850 (1920).

35. "Occasionally courts have used language to the effect that *res judicata* principles do not apply to administrative proceedings, but such language is certainly too broad." United States v. Utah Constr. Co., 384 U.S. 394, 421 (1966).

36. Magnolia Petroleum Co. v. Hunt, 320 U.S. 1 (1943); see Abel, "Administrative Determinations and Full Faith and Credit," 22 *Iowa L. Rev.* 461 (1937).

37. See *Restatement of Judgments* s.2 (1942); Groner & Sternstein, "Res Judicata in Federal Administrative Law," 39 *Iowa L. Rev.* 300 (1954); "Developments in the Law of Res Judicata," 65 *Harv. L. Rev.* 818, 865-74 (1952).

38. Donnaconna Paper Co. v. Cannon, 63 Que. K.B. 525, 531 (1937) (per Justice Rivard); R. Reid, *Administrative Law and Practice* 175 (1971).

39. *Cf.* Northern Ry. v. Robinson, 43 S.C.R. 387 (1910); Zone Tp. v. McDowell, 61 S.C.R. 360 (1921); Re Zorba's Food Service, [1970] D.L.R. 618 (Alta.).

40. See 1 G. Jéze, *Les Principes Généraux du Droit Administratif* 254-56 (1925) [hereinafter cited as Jéze].

pertains only to an *acte juridictionnel,*[41] that is, to an exercise by administrative authority of the *fonction juridictionelle* rather than the *fonction administrative.*[42] American administrative actions denied *res judicata* effect ordinarily seem to be cases that in France would be assigned to the *fonction administrative.* In Canada the respect occasionally mandated for administrative decisions[43] has been only in situations which would qualify in France or the United States, though even then not always.

Invoking the services of the other jurisdictional order for implementation of decisions is a special case. Many court and many administrative determinations, notably those which by rejecting claims simply continue a *status quo* as also many of those where the only issue is attribution of a status categorizing a party as coming within a legally significant class,[44] are self-executing and do not call for supplementary recourse in order to be operational. Others do. Then, a basic structural difference as to the execution of judgments in the French and the common law systems comes into play.[45] The former remits the judgment by way of the *formule exécutoire,* expressing a command addressed to law enforcement officials in the name of the Republic, to the administrative apparatus and also to the *droit public.*[46] The common law practice, reflecting the historic development of that law through the writ system which prevailed in connection with execution as elsewhere, leaves it to the parties to realize on judgments in their favor by using them as a basis of claim in court proceedings.[47] Hence, whether one starts with the decision of a judge or of an administrator, if compulsion is needed to implement it, in France one turns to administrative tribunals, and in Canada and the United States to judicial tribunals for that purpose.

When, as is normally the case, the *huissier,* and any other officials

41. P. Duez & G. Debeyre, *Traité du Droit Administratif* 219-25 (1952) [hereinafter cited as Duez & Debeyre].

42. For the distinction between these two functions, specifically at the *Conseil d'Etat,* see 1 Auby & Drago, *supra* note 31, at 220 *et seq.*

43. See Wallace Tp. v. Canadian Nat'l Ry., [1936] Ont. W.N. 431; Davidson v. The King, [1945] Ex. C.R. 160; references cited note 38 *supra.*

44. Declaratory actions in which a court "may make binding declarations of right, whether or not any consequential relief is or could be claimed," see the Judicature Act, [1970] *Ont. Rev. Stat.* c. 228, s. 18(2) are a conspicuous though by no means the only or even a representative instance.

45. For a comparative discussion of execution in several legal systems see R. Pound, *Jurisprudence* s. 149 (1959).

46. 2 R. David, *Le Droit Français: Principes et Tendances* 290 (1960). For a detailed analysis of the foundations and distinctions of the law in this area see Hébraud, "L'Execution des Jugements Civils," 9 *Revue Internationale du Droit Computé* (1957).

47. *Cf.* W. Blackstone, *Commentaries* 412-26 (discussion of the particular writs appropriate for various types of judgments).

whose assistance may be required, act as directed by the *formule exécutoire,* that ends the matter; but, if they do not, as seems to have happened notably where courts have ordered evictions of occupants, to induce enforcement of civil judgments recourse must be had to the administrative tribunals. They no more than the courts can order the relevant officials to do what the court prescribed; that function falls within the domain of hierarchical administration and not of a tribunal.[48] However, the classical decision *Couiteas*[49] established that, in staying its enforcing hand, the administration subjects the public to pecuniary liability for the resultant damage except as long as considerations of *ordre public* justify inaction. The determination of that liability falls within the competence of the administrative tribunals.[50] Both for cases having no other administrative law incidents and for those of civil judgments competently rendered against a governmental defendant, the recalcitrance of the official duty bound to honour the judgment's terms is a form of *excès de pouvoir* and, as such, is an issue left to the administrative tribunals. The administration can and occasionally does by regulation, amendment or lack of action frustrate even an administrative judgment. Yet, it is through application to the administrative tribunal that official duties relating to enforcement of court judgments are authoritatively imposed. The tribunals have been the faithful and necessary midwives of court judgments in cases of difficult deliveries.[51]

Under English law, courts have no need to look outside for help since the status of sheriffs, constables and other such officials was, as respects writs of process, that of officers of the court.[52] They are not within the agency establishment which, when it must depend on them for implementation of its decisions, ordinarily must rely on outsiders to institute enforcement proceedings before a court. The matter has attracted almost no attention in the literature[53] which is preoccupied with modes of resistance to rather than the effectuation of administrative

48. R. Chapus, *Responsabilité Publique et Responsabilité Privée* 538 (1954); Petot, "Quelques Remarques sur les Notions Fondamentales du Droit Administratif Français," 81 *Revue du Droit Publique et de la Science Politique* 369, 388 (1965).

49. C.E., 30 Nov. 1923, S. 1923, 3.57; D. 1923, 3.59. See also La Catonnerie et Imprimerie St. Charles, C.E., 3 June 1938, S. 1939, 3.9; D. 1938, 3.65.

50. Auby & Drago, *supra* note 31, section 427.

51. See Durand, *supra* note 29, tit. 3, for a careful and exhaustive discussion of the execution of judgments.

52. W. Tidd, *Practice of the Court of King's Bench* 33 (2d Am. ed. 1807); Regina v. Wyatt, 92 Eng. Rep. 286 (K.B. 1704).

53. The three volume treatise of Davis, *supra* note 34, has only a single brief section, 23.07, dealing with it. L. Jaffe, *Judicial Control of Administrative Action* (1965) [hereinafter cited as Jaffee] does not index "Enforcement," but does index "Enforcement Orders" and refers to portions of the book examining the machinery for court enforcement of orders of particular agencies. Mullan, *Administrative Law* 1 C.E.D. (3d ed.

determinations. Exceptionally, as in immigration matters, an administrative warrant to the law enforcement officers is authorized[54] or, as in tax collection, levy and distraint by the revenue authorities.[55] Sometimes indeed an order duly filed is made the full equivalent of a court judgment.[56] But "most administrative action depends for enforcement either immediately or ultimately upon sanctions imposed by courts."[57] The administrative decision is the potential gravamen of an appropriate court proceeding - for a fine, conviction, or the establishment of private claims as the case may be - to be commenced by a competent complainant, usually either a person asserting rights derivative from the decision[58] or the regular prosecuting authority as representing the public interest in law observance.[59] The administrator whose decision is involved cannot pursue the matter unless particularly authorized so to do.[60]

Ordinary prosecutions and private suits do not bear on the question of court-agency collaboration, but agency proceedings to enforce, when

---

1973) says nothing about enforcement. R. Reid, *Administrative Law and Practice* (1971) commences Chapter 10, "Appearances by Tribunals in Courts," by stating "The question dealt with here is the right of a tribunal to [*inter alia*] pursue . . . actions on its own behalf," but deals only with standing to appear in support of its decisions. There is nothing relevant in the federal Administrative Procedure Act, 5 U.S.C. ss.551 *et seq.* (1970) and the Model State Administrative Procedure Act, while providing in section 12(3) that "the filing of a petition [for review] shall not stay enforcement of the agency's decision," confers no enforcement authority and evidently contemplates only consequential effects on self-executing decisions not needing compulsion. Parker, "The Execution of Administrative Acts," 24 *U. Chi. L. Rev.* 292 (1957) is a rare if not indeed a lone instance of extended examination.

54. See, *e.g.*, *Can. Rev. Stat.* c I-2, s.14 (1970).

55. See Internal Revenue Code, 26 U.S.C. s.6331 (1970).

56. See, *e.g.*, the Statutory Powers Procedure Act, *Ont. Stat.* c. 47, 19(1) (1971) (certified tribunal order may be filed with Registrar of Supreme Court "and, if it is for the payment of money . . . enforced at the instance of the tribunal or of [*a*] party in the name of the tribunal in the same manner as a judgment of that court"). 1 Dussault, *Traité de Droit Administratif*, Canadien et Quebecois 697-700 (1974) [hereinafter cited as Dussault).

57. Davis, *supra* note 34. See also F. Goodnow, *Principles of the Administrative Law of the United States* 352-56 (1905).

58. See Brown, "Administrative Commissions and the Judicial Power," 19 *Minn. L. Rev.* 260, 295 (1955). The claimant must satisfy the requirements of standing to challenge. United States v. S.C.R.A.P., 412 U.S. 669 (1973).

59. *Cf.* E. Freund, *Legislative Regulation* ch. 11 (1932).

60. British Columbia Interior Vegetable Marketing Board v. Kamloops Produce Co., [1938] 1 W.W.R. 773 (B.C.); *cf.* Stern, " 'Inconsistency' in Government Litigation," 64 *Harv. L. Rev.* 759 (1951). Such authorization is not however, uncommon. See, *e.g.*, Labor Management Relations Act, 29 U.S.C. s.160(a) (1970) (NLRB suits on unfair labor practice orders); Federal Water Pollution Control Act, s.309, 33 U.S.C. s.319 (Supp. II, 1972) (Environmental Protection Agency Administrator suits against violators of water pollution abatement orders); Statutory Powers Procedure Act, *Ont. Stat.* c. 47, s.19(1) (1971).

so authorized, are essentially like the French practice noted above, save that, while the gist of the enforcement proceeding is compliance with the antecedent decision in Canada and the United States, an administrative decision does not have *res judicata* effect immunizing it from court scrutiny of its validity.[61]

Administrative subpoenas deserve brief special mention. Besides seldom used statutory provisions making criminal the flouting of a tribunal order to produce evidence in the course of a hearing, a variety of techniques have been tried, most of which involve processing the matter through a court to compel obedience. The simplest possibility, that of allowing the tribunal to treat contumacy as contempt just as a court might, has seemed unpalatable,[62] and in the United States this might perhaps be considered unconstitutional.[63] Therefore, court collaboration has been invoked in various forms and at various stages: (a) by application to the court for an original subpoena; (b) by application for aid in effectuating an agency subpoena followed if needed by a second application to commit for contempt of the court's order; (c) by application for commitment pursuant to agency determination of contumacy respecting its subpoena.[64] This may or may not entail court assistance in implementing a tribunal decision depending on whether and how far the matter is crystallized by an agency ruling preliminary to the application made. All the procedures have the common feature of vouching the court in aid of the agency, whether that aid be viewed as going to the enforcement or to the development of an agency decision.

III. MUTUAL ASSISTANCE

Courts and tribunals have found it appropriate and feasible to assist each other by giving operational effect to decisions of the other order as well as helping each other make decisions. The considerations supporting these exercises of mutual respect intersect to support the position that there are situations where it is appropriate and feasible that courts and tribunals lend each other a hand in making decisions.

61. Rex v. Merner, [1945] 2 W.W.R. 33 (Alta.); Jaffe, "Judicial Enforcement of Administrative Orders," 76 *Harv. L. Rev.* 865 (1963); 2 Dussault 1064-1067.

62. See, *e.g.*, 1 McRuer Report, *Royal Commission Inquiry into Human Rights* ch. 32 (1968). But see Note, "The Power of Administrative Agencies to Commit for Contempt," 35 *Colum. L. Rev.* 578 (1935).

63. This view rests on dictum in Interstate Commerce Comm'n v. Brimson, 154 U.S. 447 (1894).

64. For variants of the procedure see W. Gellhorn & C. Byse, *Administrative Law: Cases and Comments* 621 (1954); Note, "Use of Contempt Power to Enforce Subpoenas and Orders of Administrative Agencies," 71 *Harv. L. Rev.* 1541 (1958); Administrative Procedure Act s.6(c), 5 U.S.C. s.1005(c) (1970); Statutory Powers Procedure Act, *Ont. Stat.* c. 47, ss.12-13 (1971).

An examination of instances where it has been found appropriate and feasible may encourage more frequent use of the potential for mutual assistance.

In France involvement of one jurisdictional order in an action commenced before the other is in principle not dependent on the discretion of the latter but on observance of rules of law worked out for accomodating co-ordinate organs of adjudication within a single legal order, each of which has its particular and distinct range of competence. The nature of that accommodation is reasonably well defined, the authorities being in general agreement on its main outlines.[65]

Claims are classified into those which are for court and those which are for administrative tribunal determination. But a dispute coming within one of these categories may hinge upon a component circumstance belonging to the other. A maxim of procedure, *le juge de l'action est juge de l'exception,* would call on the judge whose basic jurisdiction was properly invoked to deal with and rule on all elements of the case. The principle of separation of powers forbids courts to intermeddle with the workings of the administrative process and also prohibits administrators, including their adjudicatory component, to intermeddle with the application of private law, as well as penal law.

The solution has been to relieve both courts and tribunals of the constraint of the maxim when it is considered to clash with the principle. In a case presenting a *question préjudicielle,* or indeed in the more inclusive category which one writer[66] calls *question sollicitée,* the judge before whom a proceeding within his competence is instituted, but who discerns in it a critical issue that belongs in the other system, may stay the proceeding (*surseoir*) to give an opportunity for that issue to be passed on by the other system. He cannot indeed *ex proprio motu* submit the question for decision to the other system since for either jurisdiction to make a demand on the other would itself infringe upon the notion of separation of powers. He must rely on a party in the action before him to pursue the matter, although he may note the presence of the alien issue and order the stay on his own initiative as well as at the instance of a party. The order will formulate the question about which a ruling is needed. Often a time is fixed within which the initiator of the action must proceed or risk dismissal.

While administrative tribunal deference to courts and court

65. The text discussion that follows rests largely on Auby & Drago, *supra* note 31, especially paragraphs 804-09, 946-74; Duez & Debeyne, *supra* note 41, at 281-85; Durand, *supra* note 29 especially paragraphs 228-58; 1 Jéze, *supra* note 49 ad 329-332; 1 Labaudère, *Traité Elémentaire de Droit Administratif* 396, 407-12 (1963); M. Waline, *Traité Elémentaire de Droit Administratif* 148-51 (6th ed. 1951). As it is a synthesis and summary of generally similar expressions, specific attributions will seldom be made.

66. See Durand, *supra* note 29, para. 227.

deference to administrative tribunals are both possible, less difficulty arises with respect to the former because of the more specific content of questions that are typically before the courts; marital status and nationality status, ownership and forgery are examples of such questions. What matters the courts should refer to tribunals is less clear. The interpretation of administrative directives is open to them, but not the interpretation of particular administrative actions. But, challenges to validity should be dealt with by tribunals except that in penal prosecutions and where *voies de fait* are involved, courts may properly act independently.

Any element beyond the competence of the body before whom the main proceeding is rightly initiated in order to maintain the separation of powers must be referred to the appropriate outside organ of decision. The treatment of *questions préjudicielles* does not therefore presuppose a purely voluntary exercise of comity. There has not been, however, and perhaps cannot as a matter of common sense be rigid insistence on that. Thus, if the threshhold issue is one whose answer is clear or one of little materiality to the main dispute it can be dealt with by the *juge de l'action,* thus leaving him some say as to whether a stay is called for. Conversely, in cases such as challenges to validity in penal actions, the court which could itself decide may choose not to, with the same effect as though it lacked competence. So, while collaboration is in a sense commanded, the command is flexible enough to leave some leeway for appraising the usefulness of obtaining the opinion of the other jurisdictional order.

A judge to whom a question is brought following a stay can decline to answer if he deems the question not to come within the competence of his jurisdictional order in which case there might arise a *conflit négatif* that may go to the *Tribunal des Conflits.* He can withhold responding to a muddily framed question pending clearer formulation by the first judge. Otherwise it is up to him to resolve the matter submitted, even though he believes that his participation should not have been needed or that the question is inept. His decision has the force of *chose jugée* even on matters properly not in his competence.

This well-developed technique greatly resembles the cooperative mechanisms of law and equity in their heyday as separate systems. It is strengthened, however, by the fact that it is considered to be a norm of interaction instead of a merely available procedure. It is the only way by which French courts and tribunals accommodate their respective jurisdictions.[67] Two other things are, however, so closely related as to deserve brief mention.

67. For both courts and tribunals there are also statutory extensions in specific situations, the existence of which should be noted; but their recital would unduly complicate this summary account.

The *Tribunal des Conflits,* with joint representation from the *Conseil d'Etat* and the *Cour de Cassation,* definitively settles attribution of jurisdiction claimed to have been either wrongfully exercised or wrongfully refused, to either the administrative or the judicial institutions. A *renvoi* brings, before the *Tribunal,* the propriety of the exercise or a refusal. This is not collaboration in the task of decision making, except for the infrequent case of a *conflit négatif* about a *question préjudicielle,* because the whole issue is whether the first step toward a decision has effectively been taken. It is rather collaboration in deciding on clearance for entry into a decisional stream. Its special feature is its structure which associates the two orders instead of depending on separate unilateral determinations. While self-abnegation manifests an impulse by court or agency to respect the other's domain, the *Tribunal des Conflits* determines the domain entitled to respect.

Administrative tribunal case law in France does not recognize the doctrine of *lis pendens.* On the other hand, the courts do recognize the doctrine within the rather narrow limits prescribed by the Code of Civil Procedure.[68] In those few cases whose circumstances admit of framing a claim alternatively, within either order of jurisdiction, a tribunal will take no account of an existing court action, but a court will take such account of an action pending before a tribunal if it would do so were the action pending before another court.[69]

In the United States and Canada, the picture is more confused. The genius of the common law for development by litigation in virtual neglect of doctrinal writing is partly responsible. Another aspect of the confused picture is the tendency of both judges and scholars to limit their awareness of administrative law to judicial review and control of agencies, leaving all else to be dealt with haphazardly and *ad hoc.* These habitual approaches have compounded a difficulty posed by the fact that the ground of division between administrative and court adjudicating competence differs fundamentally from that in France. In France the division is vertical; the substance of what is to be decided governs who may decide. This contrasts with a horizontal division, where almost everything is open to eventual court examination, with the main problem being the timeliness of involvement in the decisional process. Multiform collaborative techniques have emerged, for the most part episodically. Their potential sets one hoping; their development leaves one groping.

Corresponding to the situation of the *question préjudicielle,* the structured but unique occasion in France for the involvement of court

68. *Code de Procédure Civile,* art. 171.
69. Auby & Drago, *supra* note 31, para. 808.

and tribunal, one finds Canadian and American examples of suits with an administrative component, and alternatively of agency hearings with a jural element. In a number of such cases, utility of a reference by the jurisdiction initially invoked has been recognized.

In the United States, court abstention from deciding matters falling within a regulatory scheme which it is an agency's responsibility to administer is a generally accepted principle.[70] The concept of primary jurisdiction,[71] and occasionally but less accurately that of exhaustion,[72] is assigned as the basis; these concepts find application though not expression in Canada as well.[73] Simple dismissal of the suit, either as prematurely brought or on the equitable notion of a comparable remedy at law, manifests respect for the other jurisdictional order but it does not enlist its aid in the decisional process except perhaps indirectly and awkwardly. That can only be done neatly, and is in fact regularly done by the court's staying the proceeding,[74] as in France, to permit recourse to the tribunal and even, as is not possible in France, by direction or reference to the administrative tribunal[75] in appropriate cases.[76] Allowing for differences in the contours of competence, in the underlying rationale for abstention and in the content of the order which may be made, an American court's dealing with a threshold administrative component very closely approximates the French position. Canada, probably because of the more rudimentary state of the relevant doctrine, has been backward in this respect but there too isolated examples in limited categories of cases have recognized the

70. See, *e.g.*, Ricci v. Chicago Mercantile Exchange, 409 U.S. 289 (1973); Port of Boston Marine Terminal Ass'n v. Rederiaktiebolaget Transatlantic, 400 U.S. 62 (1970); Texas & Pacific Ry. v. Abilene Cotton Oil Co., 204 U.S. 426 (1907).

71. Davis, *supra* note 34, ch. 19; Jaffe, *supra* note 53, ch. 4.

72. Davis, *supra* note 34, ch. 20; Jaffe, *supra* note 53, ch.11.

73. The terms are not used either by Canadian courts or Canadian writers, an omission which both reflects and occasions the comparatively minor role of the concepts in Canadian administrative law where, nevertheless, both are used. See, *e.g.*, Davidson v. The King, [1945] Ex. C.R. 160 (exhaustion); United Amusement Corp. v. Kent Theatres, [1944] Que. K.B. 736 (primary jurisdiction).

74. See, *e.g.*, Chicago Mercantile Exchange v. Deaktor, 414 U.S. 113 (1973); Thompson v. Texas Mexican Ry., 328 U.S. 134 (1946).

75. See, *e.g.*, United States v. Western Pacific R.R., 352 U.S. 59 (1956); J.M. Huber Corp. v. Denman, 367 F. 2d 104 (5th Cir. 1966). The court should not, however, specify the procedure to be followed in submitting the matter to the administrative agency. Michigan Consol. Gas Co. v. Panhandle Eastern Pipeline Co., 173 F.2d 784 (6th Cir. 1949).

76. There is, as in France, no occasion for a stay if the incident issue is one that is clearly settled (see Strickland Transp. Co. v. United States, 334 F.2d 172 (5th Cir. 1964); Ratner v. Chemical Bank New York Trust Co., 309 F. Supp. 983 (S.D.N.Y. 1970)) or is not material to the disposition of the particular litigation (see Slick Airways, Inc. v. American Airlines, Inc., 107 F. Supp. 199 (D.N.J. 1952).

propriety of a stay.[77] The practice of a statutory requirement of ministerial clearance as a condition to suit,[78] which is special to Canada and which may be traced to the historic need of a fiat for a petition of right,[79] is a substitute in the sense that it too restrains resort to the courts. It is, however, a crude and imperfect substitute whereby the administrative tribunal makes no substantive contribution to the decision but only exercises a veto over whether a matter may be brought on for decision. This veto is purely discretionary[80] and so has no necessary relation to any issue in the case.

What about tribunal proceedings that have jural elements? The Federal Court Act[81] provides that "a federal board, commission or other tribunal . . . may at any stage of its proceedings refer any question or issue of law, of jurisdiction or of practice and procedure to the Court of Appeal for hearing and determination."[82] In advancing beyond a mere stay to an actual reference, the Act generalizes a practice that as the case law demonstrates is followed in a variety of situations.[83] Generally, however, the practice has had an express statutory basis so that how such a reference or even a stay would be regarded in the absence of one is obscure. Clearly there is no duty to direct a stay.[84] In the United States there is no equivalent legislative pattern clearly[85] treating court consideration of issues presented in proceedings before administrative

77. Dominion Canners v. Costanza, [1923] S.C.R. 46; Re British American Oil Co., 33 D.L.R.2d 162 (Alta. 1962); Re Donald Bye Excavating Co. v. Peterborough, [1973] 1 O.R. 139 (1972); Forget v. Mack Trucks Mfg. Co., [1971] 1 O.R. 682 (1970); *accord* Lethbridge v. Canadian W. Natural Gas Co., [1923] S.C.R. 652 (court equally divided as to whether statute gave Board "exclusive" jurisdiction); *cf.* Imperial Inv. Corp. v. Newman, 29 D.L.R.2d 176 (Alta. 1961) (matter not to be noticed by court *ex mero motu*); Koenig v. Figol, [1941] 2 W.W.R. 33 (Alta.) (with parties' consent); see Hughes v. The King [1948] 1 D.L.R. 276 (B.C. 1947) (statute specifically directing transfer held constitutional). Compare Warren v. Union Gas Co., [1943] 4 D.L.R. 688 (Ont.) (stay held proper) with Re Russell, [1942] O.R. 466 (Wkly. Ct.) (like stay held improper).

78. See, *e.g.*, Poitras v. Attorney-General of Alberta, 7 D.L.R.2d 161 (Alta. 1965); Rex v. Safeway Stores Ltd. (No. 3), [1938] 2 W.W.R. 488 (Alta.).

79. See H. Immarigeon, *La Responsabilié Extra-contractuelle de la Couronne au Canada* sec. 20 (1965); Jamieson, "Proceedings by and Against The Crown in Canada," 26 *Can. B. rev.* 373 (1948).

80. Ballantyne v. Duplessis, 76 Que. S.C. 448 (1938).

81. *Can. Rev. Stat.* c. 10 (2d Supp. 1970).

82. *Id.* s.28(4).

83. See, *e.g.*, Le Vesconte v. Administrator, Motor Vehicles Accident Claims Act, 52 D.L.R.2d 430 (Alta. 1965); Re Thorne, 33 D.L.R.2d 167 (N.B. 1962); Re Milton, [1942] 2 D.L.R. 329 (N.B.).

84. Re Cedarvale Tree Services, [1971] 3 O.R. 832 held that there was no duty to withhold decision pending a reference to court remarking that "it is for the Board itself to decide how it shall proceed," language apparently broad enough to support a discretionary stay.

85. The provision of the Administrative Procedure Act (5 U.S.C. s.705 (1970) that pending judicial review, any agency is authorized where it finds that justice so requires, to "postpone the effective date of action taken by it" might be so construed, but a more

tribunals. The reasoning in *California v. F.P.C.*,[86] that courts and tribunals stand on the same footing as to the use of stays in deference to the competence of each other, is less helpful than it seems because it was uttered in a context of simultaneous independently instituted proceedings. Other than in situations having such a *lis pendens* aspect, there is in American law an absence of judicial authority just as there is of statutory direction for administrative *renvoi* to obtain a court ruling.

A North American development[87] with no French counterpart[88] finds the administration acting as moving party, complaining witness or petitioner, in a formally distinct suit. The aim of the suit may be either to gain some advantage from a court judgment on the substance of a matter where a tribunal order would be a less suitable alternative, or to invoke court assistance in creating or maintaining conditions on which the effectiveness of a prospective tribunal decision depends.

Ordinary prosecutions seeking a penalty for violation of agency prescriptions contribute only to compliance, not to decision. However, *pro forma* prosecution has been usefully employed to elicit court interpretation, which has precedential force, in lieu of the less exalted ruling the agency could give or of regulatory formulation.[89] The effect is to obtain a declaratory judgment by way of the criminal process.

It is not obvious why in cases in which suits for a declaration are authorized by statue, as is almost universally true with respect to the United States and Canada, the roundabout procedure noted in the last paragraph is used by the administration instead of a direct application for a declaratory order. The facts remains that, although declarations respecting administrative conduct are familiar enough,[90] instances of administrative application for clarifying declaratory judgments to aid

natural reading seems to be that it deals with agency action not preliminary to but following an administrative decision crystalized to a condition of reviewability. The legislative history is unenlightening; the comment on this section deals almost entirely with its extension to the courts of the authority to stay. See Sen. Doc. 248, 79th Cong., 2d Sess. (1946), at 38, 277, 369. All cases decided under the section appear to have involved court stays. There is no pertinent language in the Model Act.

86. 369 U.S. 482, 490 (1962).

87. In other countries of the common law too, however, see D. Benjafield & H. Whitmore, *Principles of Australian Administrative Law* 241 (1971).

88. Administrative officials, normally the prefects, can of course bring suits in court—and indeed only there—to enforce civil law claims of public bodies against individuals (see L. Rolland, *Droit Administratif* secs. 81-82, 328), but the clear differentiation of the *"tribunaux administratifs"* from the *"administration active"* (see *id.* secs. 315-20) means that the former are in no way involved in such activity.

89. The King v. May, 17 M.P.R. 461 (P.E.I. 1944).

90. See E. Borchard, *Declaratory Judgments* ch. XIV (2d ed. 1941) [hereinafter cited as Borchard]. Borchard discusses a wide range of applications in none of which does it appear that the agency was seeking Court direction in aid of tribunal adjudication.

tribunal decision are lacking. This may be because of several reasons including: apprehended difficulties as to the agency's standing as a party; [91] the prospect of discretionary refusal because the court deems the agency's own process to be adequate remedy; [92] or, problems involved in shaping a *lis* with appropriate adverse parties, which conceivably in the United States might prevent there being even a "case or controversy."[93] The closest resemblance seems to be the occasional Canadian practice of the statement of a case by the tribunal for court determination.[94]

This reticence about suing to settle legal interpretations incident to cases arising for tribunal decision eschews collaboration where it might have been expected. It is measurably offset, however, by flexible ingenuity shown in presenting to courts situations falling within the tribunal's own competence, thus where a potential conflict of interest would color any decision the tribunal might make,[95] where the contempt power of the court is a clearly more effective control than the tribunal's supervisory devices[96] or than its necessarily protracted license revocation proceedings,[97] where assets of a regulated company have to be taken over and preserved pending its dissolution,[98] and where orders for trustee compensation or mandamus, injunction or receivership have been applied for and granted. A court will reject as an abuse of its functions, a spurious suit concerned with obtaining not the exercise but

91. The declaratory judgment proceeding like others requires parties capable of suing and being sued (Borchard, *supra* note 90, at 15); whether a public authority is a legal entity in that sense depends on the functions confided to it by its basic statute. See Parker v. Unemployment Compensation Comm'n, 358 Mo. 365, 214 S.W.2d 529 (1948); Samuels v. A.-G. for Canada, 1 D.L.R.2d 110 (Alta. 1955). Such a provision as section 9(2) of the Judicial Review Procedure Act, 2 *Ont. Stat.* c. 48 (1971) ("the person who is authorized to exercise [a statutory] . . . power may be a party") may well suffice independently of any particular delegation.

92. Alternative remedies as a ground for refusing a declaration, see Borchard, *supra* note 90, ch. VI.

93. On the "case" or "controversy" test in declaratory judgment proceedings see *The Constitution of the United States of America: Analysis and Interpretation* 532 (E. Corwin ed. 1953).

94. See Re Thorne, 33 D.L.R.2d 167 (N.B. 1962); Re Milton, [1942] 2 D.L.R. 329 (N.B.); Re Treasurer of York Tp., [1938] Ont. W.N. 191; *cf.* The Federal Court Act, *Can. Rev. Stat.* c. 10 s.17(3)(b) (2d Supp. 1970). To be distinguished is the use of the stated case as a review technique.

95. See Re Hamilton Harbour Comm'rs, 65 Ont. L.R. 151 (1930) (compensation for services of commissioners having authority to determine "cost of management").

96. See Procureur Général v. Princeville, [1942] Que. S.C. 18 (mandamus to municipal officials to comply with water pollution abatement orders instead of diverting departmental resources to execution of required works).

97. Civil Aeronautics Bd. v. Modern Air Transport, Inc., 179 F.2d 622 (2d Cir. 1950).

98. Krueger v. American Christian Mut. Life Ins. Co., 43 N.W.2d 676 (N.D. 1950) (may sue without prior Administrative Procedure Act hearing).

only the effect of its judgment, a situation which is indeed a mere parody of collaboration.[99]

The job of courts being to take what comes to them and not to operate regulatory programs, it is not in their nature to set things in motion. Thus, it is not surprising that there are no examples of proceedings initiated by them before tribunals. The nearest analogy is in one atypical setting, namely, bankruptcy. Bankrupcy calls for general and continuous supervision of an administrative nature; in such cases, in the United States, Chapter X of the Bankruptcy Act directs court reference of plans of reorganization to the Securities and Exchange Commission for comment.[100]

Historically, through use of the interlocutory injunction,[101] courts could order parties to pending litigation to refrain from changing any circumstances that affect the subject of the suit, in order to prevent the parties from frustrating the determination which might be reached by the court.[102] The original and usual exercise of this auxiliary service has been to maintain the *status quo* preliminary to court judgments. But there is no intrinsic reason for excluding courts from extending similar protection to pending tribunal proceedings. In the United States, orders of miscellaneous types, varying with the nature of the case and the posture of the parties, have been issued with some frequency, though refusals by other more reluctant courts blur the picture.[103] Relevant reported Canadian cases are too few and too devoid of analysis to constitute a body of law. While there seem to be no cases where the tribunal took an initiative to claim such assistance,[104] and there are cases where the court withheld action in aid of jurisdiction which it might appropriately have extended,[105] other decisions including one of the Supreme Court of Canada[106] manifest a disposition to employ the

99. See The King v. Hooper, [1942] Ex. C.R. 193 (suit aimed at circumventing government budget practices).

100. See L. Loss, *Securities Regulation* 447 (1951). While the analogy to agency suits in court is not very close, the practice nevertheless seems to deserve Professor Loss' characterization of it as "an experiment in judicial administrative collaboration."

101. 2 E. Daniell, *Chancery Practice 1516-1518* (5th ed. 1871).

102. See Hovey v. McDonald, 180 U.S. 536 (1901); Hendrie v. Beatty, 29 Gr. Ch. 423 (Ont. 1881).

103. Compare Board of Governors of the Federal Reserve System v. Transamerica Corp., 184 F.2d 311 (9th Cir. 1950) with Federal Trade Comm'n v. International Paper Co., 241 F.2d 372 (2d Cir. 1956). For an excellent discussion of the American position see L. Jaffe, *Judicial Control of Administrative Action* ch. 17, and especially 662-686.

104. But *cf.* Re Graham, 56 D.L.R.2d 420 (Sask. 1966) (application to court for order of substituted service instead of exercising tribunal's own power).

105. See McLaughlin v. Westward Shipping Co., 21 D.L.R.2d 770 (B.C. 1959) (Labour Board substitution of successor employer); Re Cambrian Realty Corp., 37 D.L.R.3d 516 (Ont. 1973) (broker withdrawal of registration pending investigation).

106. Fortier v. Longchamp, [1942] S.C.R. 240 (temporary postponed effectiveness of a mandatory injunction to allow application for a commission permit to legalize maintenance of dam).

court's process to hold matters in suspense for the time needed for administrative decision-making.[107]

IV. CONCLUSIONS

This article has been written in the hope that the bringing together of the scattered materials illustrative of the division of labor between courts and administrative tribunals will make all those concerned with the subject more conscious of the potential of such a division of labor and may stimulate its use.

Although not always appropriate, rules would be helpful and are in some respects needed as to procedures for invoking the aid of the other jurisdictional order.

Control of the docket would allow cases of which a court or a tribunal is seised, at the instance of its partner in the business of the rendering of justice, to be given priority in being heard. Such priority could and probably should be embodied in the rules of practice. This would go some way toward reducing delay which has been a prime argument urged against facilitating resort to the *question préjudicielle*[108] or to abstention.[109] The argument of delay seems exaggerated since even a stay to await proceedings elsewhere must result in less delay than the alternative of outright dismissal; this is particularly the case where the stay is for a stated time, subject to dismissal if action is not taken within that time.[110]

If, instead of a stay to permit party action, there were a direct transfer by the initial forum to the auxiliary forum, the matter should move even more smoothly. That might require legislation[111] for which there is ample precedent: in the American arrangements for transfer by federal and acceptance by state courts in abstention situations;[112] in Canadian statutes for filing of extraprovincial provisional family maintenance orders[113] or for administrative statement of a case for

107. Lethbridge v. Canadian W. Natural Gas Co., [1923] 2 D.L.R. 1; *cf.* Reece v. Manufacturers Life Ins. Co., [1942] 2 D.L.R. 760 (Sask.) (reversal on appeal where conditions inserted at trial to preserve Board jurisdiction had opposite effect, continuing jurisdiction needing court inaction); Jack's Enterprise Ltd. v. Saskatchewan Liquor License Comm'r, 17 D.L.R.3d 370 (Sask. 1970) (accord).

108. See Durand, *supra* note 29, at 252.

109. Note, "Inter-jurisdictional Certification: Beyond Abstention toward Cooperative Judicial Federalism," 111 *U. Pa. L. Rev.* 344 (1963).

110. *Cf.* 2 Auby & Drago, *supra* note 31, at 272.

111. But *cf.* Kearney Lake, Land & Reservoir Co. v. Lake DeSmet Reservoir Co., 487 P.2d 324, 328 (Wyo. 1971) (calling on Board to make appropriate practice rules).

112. The initial Florida legislation has provided a model for similar statutes elsewhere. Lillick & Mundy, "Federal Court Certification of Doubtful State Law Questions," 18 *U.C.L.A. L. Rev.* 888 (1971).

113. *Que. Stat.* c. 56, arts. 2, 7 (1951-1952).

court decision of an issue of law or jurisdiction;[114] in the European Economic Community Treaty provision[115] authorizing member nation courts to ask for a ruling by the Community Court of Justice. The particular technique to be used, whether it should be any of these or some other ones, must be determined by the legislature after full study. However, some such arrangement seems desirable. The obstacle suggested in France, that the separation of powers doctrine inhibits a direct approach by an administrative organ to a judicial organ, or vice versa, might perhaps be surmounted by channeling actions through the *ministère public* as is done by prefects.[116] Constitutional questions aside, the whole question of party standing presents problems calling for legislative treatment by extending the capacity to sue, by creating a new class of *ex parte* proceedings, or in some other suitable manner.

However, the removal of impediments to implementation of a policy under which courts and administrative tribunals will work together is a proper subject for another and a more detailed study. The stress in this article has been placed on basic policy considerations.

Les agents de tout ordre, the tout rang, de toute catégorie, ont le devoir juridique de se prêter un mutuel appui, de fournir avec zèle et devouement leur collaboration à l'effet de faciliter la marche du service public de justice.[117]

114. See, *e.g.*, *N.B. Rev. Stat.* c. 255, s.34(8) (1952).

115. Treaty Establishing the European Economic Community, *done* March 25, 1957, art. 177, 298 U.N.T.S. 11 (unofficial English version).

116. See P. Cuche, *Précis de Procédure* 146 (10th ed. 1951). I suggest this with utmost diffidence, since my understanding of the implications of the French version of *séparation de pouvoirs,* like that of virtually all *étrangers,* is by no means complete.

117. Jéze *supra* note 40, at 258.

TWO INTERNATIONAL ORGANIZATIONS OF THE THIRD WORLD

BOUTROS BOUTROS-GHALI

What always struck me, in the many years during which I had the privilege of Professor Friedmann's friendship, was his lively and imaginative understanding of the Third World and his remarkable knowledge of its problems. It is then surely appropriate that this study of two of the most important regional organizations of the Third World, should be one of the ways in which a tribute to the late Professor Friedmann can be made. I should like to begin by posing a number of questions, some of which were the constant theme of our unrelenting inquiries in friendly conversations that always seemed to develop into exchanges of questions and more questions.

How does an international organization function when all its members are underdeveloped countries? How is the balance of power established in a community of poor countries within the framework of an international organization? These are just two of the questions which will be examined in this comparative study of the Arab League and the Organization of African Unity.

In the first part of this article we shall examine the role of both organizations regarding the decolonization process; in the second part we shall deal with their part in the settling of international disputes; and, in the third part we shall study their action in favor of economic cooperation.

I. DECOLONIZATION

The Arab League was created in March 1945, but the Organization of African Unity (O.A.U.) was only established in May 1963, that is,

BOUTROS BOUTROS-GHALI is Professor at Cairo University and Director of the Department of Political Science; Associate Member of the Institut de Droit International; and, a member of the International Commission of Jurists.

This paper, in somewhat different form, was presented to the sixteenth annual meeting of the African Studies Association held in Syracuse, N.Y., U.S.A. (October 31 – November 3, 1973). It does not take into consideration the basic changes that have occured in and to these organizations since 1973.

some eighteen years later. Both organizations have, however, many characteristics in common. Initially, both are anticolonial organizations created to accelerate the decolonization of their respective regions. However, the eighteen years separating the birth of the two organizations are crucial to their different interpretations of the concept of colonialism.

In 1945 the decolonization of the Arab world was not explicitly mentioned among the aims pursued by the Arab League. The Arab world had not yet become fully aware of the scope or the nature of the colonial phenomenon. The only independence of which it could conceive was political independence within the narrow framework of an economic and cultural interdependence with the former colonial powers.

Moreover, since they were militarily occupied and economically enslaved, the Arab states could not afford to openly antagonize the colonial powers. In the aftermath of the war, these powers seemed to be in a position to indefinitely maintain their domination over Africa and Asia. Thus, colonialism is not mentioned, either in the Pact of 22nd March 1945 or in the Collective Defense Pact of 17 June 1950, and the anti-colonialist struggle is only mentioned indirectly.

In contrast the Organization of African Unity was born immediately after the completion of the decolonization of North and Central Africa and after the colonized states had attained their political maturity either through liberation or in the arena of the United Nations. Moreover, the African states were fully aware of the colonial phenomenon; they realised that political independence was only one step forward in the search for national liberation, and that such a step had to be followed by economic independence. Thus not only is "the eradication of all forms of colonialism from Africa" mentioned in the Addis Ababa Charter, but neocolonialism is emphasized by the Charter.

Economically, neocolonialism appears as an attempt by foreign investors to maintain a territory's dependence on the former colonial power. On the diplomatic level, neocolonialism takes the form of bilateral agreements and the existence of military bases. This theme, with variations, has since been taken up vigorously by Africans of many shades of political opinion.

The Ghanaian Representative to the United Nations called neocolonialism "the practice of granting a sort of independence with the concealed intention of making the liberated country a client-state, and controlling it effectively by means other than political ones . . . ." For Kwame-Nkrumah, the multiplication of artificially created African mini-states—in other words the Balkanization of Africa—was a perfect instrument of neocolonialism.

At Addis Ababa in May 1963, President Nasser discussed the effects of neocolonialism in greater detail when he said: "There exists that insistence on making of the continent a mere warehouse for raw materials at prices which fail to satisfy the hunger of its people while the total benefit goes to the importing countries which try to make of their industrial and scientific progress a quasi-colonialism of a new form, that of unjust exploitation of the wealth of others without a fair share."[1]

It has been recognized that any relationship between an ex-colonial power and a former colony is inevitably colored by its past history. However, while the O.A.U. emphasizes neocolonialism, the Arab League seems much less preoccupied by this phenomenon. Two explanations may be proposed in order to account for this difference of attitude.

Firstly, the common Arab Cultural heritage offers a better defense against foreign cultural assimilation and linguistic domination. Consequently, the Arab World is less afraid of the cultural impact of neocolonialism than the African world which does not have the benefit and defense of a common culture and language of its own.

Secondly, Zionist colonialism was at the outset the immediate preoccupation of the Arabs in their struggle against colonialism. The League went as far as to give this struggle priority over the decolonization of its own founding members and thus Zionism overshadowed all other forms of colonialism.

In spite of these differences of attitude toward the colonialist phenomenon, the two organizations established similar programs of action in order to realize the total national independence of all Arab and all African countries still subject to foreign domination. These programs included: (a) an invitation to the colonial powers to take the necessary measures for granting immediate independence to the colonial countries and peoples; (b) the sending of delegations to the Security Council whenever the affairs of Arab or African territories under foreign domination were being discussed; (c) the severance of diplomatic relations between Arab and African states and those governments giving support and assistance to colonial governments; (d) the non-recognition of new colonialist states such as Israel, Rhodesia; (e) the total economic boycott of Israel, Portugal, South Africa and Rhodesia taking the form of prohibiting the importation of goods from these countries, the closure of ports and airfields to their ships and planes and the refusal to grant permission to fly over Arab or African countries; (f) the unification of the different liberation movements; and (g) the creation of liberation armies and volunteer corps on the territories of different independent Arab and African states.

1. SCIAS/GEN/INF/26, at 2.

As an example of similar types of diplomatic action one can compare the vast campaign undertaken by the Arab League to oppose the payment of compensation by Germany to Israel in 1952 with the diplomatic campaign undertaken by the O.A.U. to obtain British intervention in Rhodesia in 1966. Both campaigns unfortunately resulted in total failure.

To conclude, the fight for the decolonization of Palestine has been marked by a series of defeats with the Zionist state occupying more Arab territory or strengthening its domination in the region. The decolonization of southern Africa has equally been marked by stagnation and regression with the apartheid state strengthening its domination. Nevertheless, the decolonization of all other Arab and African states has been very successful.

It could be argued that the decolonization of the Arab World and Africa would have taken place regardless of the League's action or the O.A.U.'s intervention. Such an assumption should be corrected. The League as well as the O.A.U. provided a framework for the claim of dependent Arab states and independent African states. Once such a framework was created, the intervention of the Arab States for the decolonization of Arab territories or the intervention of the African states for the decolonization of African territories could no longer be condemned as a form of Arab intervention or African intervention in the affairs of other Arab or African States.

Moreover collective Arab intervention or collective African intervention, prepared and carried out within the framework of an international organization and supported by the system and the ideology of the organization, gave legitimacy to Arab collective action or African collective action in the face of colonialist dialectic which views all liberation movements as seditious.

The Arab League and the O.A.U. have largely contributed to making decolonization a doctrine and a principle of international law. This principle was later adopted by the United Nations. Had this, in fact, been the only contribution made by the Arab League and the O.A.U. it alone would have been a very significant one indeed.

II. PEACEFUL SETTLEMENT OF DISPUTES

In 1946, the ideology that prevailed in the Arab World was "the rule of law." The ruling elites were filled with Western constitutionalism and believed that inter-Arab conflicts could be settled by an international judge or by an arbitrator. One needs only to read the minutes of the preparatory meetings which preceded the drafting of the Pact of 22nd March 1945 to realize the emphasis certain delegates placed on the principle of compulsory arbitration. However, as a result of the opposition of the delegates from the Lebanon—who wished to preserve as much as possible the sovereignty of the future members of the League—a compromise solution was reached. It appears in the Pact under article 5, which stipulates that:

> It is forbidden to have recourse to force in order to settle conflicts which may arise among Member States of the League. Should a dispute arise between two such States, in no way concerning the independence, the sovereignity or the territorial integrity of these States, and if the parties to the conflict request the Council of the League to settle the dispute, the Council's decision shall be binding and executory.

And, in order to satisfy those delegates who were in favor of compulsory arbitration, Article 19 of the League's Pact states that: "The present Pact can be amended by a majority of two-thirds of the Members of the League. In particular it can be amended to establish . . . an Arab court of arbitration. . . . " In fact, the creation of this Arab court has been the subject of numerous discussions and even more numerous resolutions. Seldom has there been a session of the Council of the League at which the matter of a future Arab Court of justice has not been raised. Despite all these resolutions, the Court has not yet materialized.

Eighteen years later the same problem arose in relation to the O.A.U. Article 19 of the Addis Ababa Charter stipulates that:

> Member States pledge to settle all disputes among themselves by peaceful means and, to this end decide to establish a Commission of Mediation, Conciliation and Arbitration the composition of which and conditions of service shall be defined by a separate Protocol to be approved by the Assembly of Heads of State and Government. Said Protocol shall be regarded as forming an integral part of the present Charter.

The August 1963 Council of Ministers which met at Dakar set up a special committee to work out a separate protocol for the Commission. The protocol was adopted in Cairo in July 1964 by the Council of Ministers[2] and by the Council of the Heads of State[3] and became an integral part of the Addis Ababa Charter, as stated in Article 19 of the Charter and Article 32 of the Protocol. The twenty-one members of the Commission were nominated during the third Session of the Heads of State at Accra in October 1965. However, the Commission did not meet

2. Resolution CM/Res 42/III.
3. Resolution AHG/22.

until December 1967 at Addis Ababa, and this was its first and last meeting.

In a different manner we reach the same result, namely, the failure of judicial settlement of disputes both in the Arab League and in the O.A.U. On the other hand, whenever inter-Arab and inter-African disputes were settled the results were achieved by diplomatic negotiations under the auspices of the League and the O.A.U.

How can this similarity between the two organizations be explained? First, the lack of an international Arab Court forced the Arab States to settle their disputes within the Council of the Arab League. In the same way the long period taken by the African states to set up the Commission of Mediation, Conciliation and Arbitration compelled the African States to revert to *ad hoc* commissions for the settlement of Inter-African disputes. Second, the Arab as well as the African world has a certain distrust for international law which both have come to know mainly through its colonial aspect which is interested invariably only in legitimizing European acquisitions and privileges. This mistrust of Western-oriented general international law has been transposed to the regional level. Furthermore they have still not developed a regional international law which could help them in solving their disputes. Third, judicial settlement is a lengthy and costly process which only wealthy and developed states can afford.

In conclusion, in their regional disputes the Arab and the African world are still at the stage of diplomatic negotiations which are more in line with their experience and traditions. More elaborate or technical procedures would run the risk of never being implemented, or, even worse, they might embitter inter-Arab of inter-African conflicts.

At this point, however, the similarities between the Arab League and the O.A.U. in the peaceful settlement of disputes cease. In conformity with the principle stated in Article 52 of the United Nations Charter which provides that Members of the United Nations entering into regional organizations shall make every effort to achieve pacific settlement of local disputes through such organization before referring them to the Security Council, both the Arab League and the O.A.U. have repeatedly stated that Arab disputes should be settled in an Arab context and that African disputes should likewise be settled within a purely African framework. But, whereas the African states have respected this principle in most of their conflicts, such as in the case of the boundary between Algeria and Morocco or the dispute between Ethiopia and Somalia or Kenya and Somalia, the Arab States have rarely observed it. They have always gone directly to the Security Council, bypassing the Arab League, as in the case of the dispute between Egypt and the Sudan in February 1958 or in the conflict between Lebanon and the United Arab Republic, in August 1968. Such also was the case in the conflict between Kuwait and Iraq in June-September 1967.

How can this important difference between the attitude of the Arab States and the African states regarding their respective organizations be explained? How can one explain the inadequacy of the League in solving the conflicts that arise among its members and the success of the O.A.U. in settling inter-African disputes? Finally, how can one account for the lack of confidence of the Arab states in their own organization as an instrument for the peaceful settlement of their disputes and, on the other hand, the confidence of the African states in their own organization?

Some have claimed that this situation has its origin in the archaic and obsolete nature of the machinery set up by the League to deal with conflicts. If a court of arbitration existed, then Arab states would be less reluctant to turn to the Arab League. In reality this lack of confidence has nothing to do with the system set up by the League. The Commission of Mediation, Conciliation and Arbitration set up by the O.A.U. has also never functioned but in spite of this the African organization has managed to settle inter-African disputes "within a purely African framework."

We believe that this crisis originates in the profound contradictions inherent in the Arab world, contradictions which lead Arab states to prefer intervention by a non-Arab third party (be it a state or an international organization) rather than by an Arab one. This crisis has its origins in the predominant role played by Egypt within the League. It is worth noting that in most cases, the Arab states that have submitted disputes to the Security Council or other institutions, rather than to the League, were in conflict either with Egypt itself, or with one of Egypt's allies. A similar phenomenon can be seen in inter-American practice; those states that are in conflict with the United States or with a state that has close ties with Washington prefer to turn to the Security Council rather than to the Organization of American States where the preeminence of the United States is unquestionable.

Within the O.A.U., no one African state has a preponderant role. The African states participate in the various forms of collective action and share equally in the decision-making process. Although the Charter of Addis Ababa does not go as far as to state explicitly its nonacceptance of any "leadership," it does in effect bar any single African state from playing the role of leader by stressing the principle of absolute equality. President Habib Bourghiba of Tunisia has said: "The desire for supremacy is the worm in the bud. When one partner wishes to dominate the group, sooner or later that group will fall apart."[4] In

4. SCIAS/GEN/INF/8, at 5-6.

other words the nonacceptance of leadership by any particular state and the non-existence for the time being at least of any leadership in the O.A.U. is the main cause of the success of this particular organization in settling inter-African disputes.

One may say therefore that a comparative study of different disputes in the Arab League and in the O.A.U. leads one to two conclusions. If the leadership of a particular state in a regional organization is open to doubt, then the member states which are involved in a dispute can afford to reject the competence of the regional organization if they so prefer and appeal directly to the United Nations. This appears clearly in the Arab League. For the sake of comparison, we note that if the leadership of a particular state in a regional organization is total and unchallenged, the member states will always settle their disputes within the framework of this organization. An example of this is the case of the Soviet regional system in which disputes among the member states are always settled within the system itself and never reach the United Nations. If the regional organization is not dominated by a single state or a group of states and all states have equal influence within the organization then the states involved in a dispute will have more confidence in their own regional system for the settlement of their disputes, as in the case of the O.A.U.

III. ECONOMIC COOPERATION

The major problem facing the Arab world and the African continent today is that of underdevelopment, and it is likely to remain so for a long time to come. What are the policies for development and integration which have been adopted by the Arab League and the O.A.U. to remedy this state of affairs?

It may be recalled that the General Assembly of the United Nations discussed the factors of classification for those countries which it considers as being "economically underdeveloped." Two criteria of underdevelopment were proposed; one based on per capita national income and the other on each country's utilization of the technical assistance received from the United Nations.[5]

According to these criteria every African state, without exception, must be considered as being economically underdeveloped;[6] however, not every Arab state is underdeveloped, and some Arab states are

5. This second criterion was adopted on December 20, 1961 (Resolution 1733) in order to allow certain states to reduce their contributions to U.N.O.C. (United Nations Operations in the Congo).

6. South Africa is an exception, but it is not, in fact, an African state within the definition of the Charter of Addis Ababa since it does not conform to the requirement of African legitimacy as established by that Charter.

among the richest countries in the world. Thus the question of Arab underdevelopment has never been posed as a regional problem while African under-development which is ever present in Africa has been mephasized with lucidity and courage by more than one African head of state. At the Addis Ababa Conference in May 1963, Leopold Senghor, President of the Republic of Senegal, said: "We have also in common our situation as underdeveloped countries, characterized by a certain number of traits that can be summed up as under-nourishment and under-productivity because of lack of capital and technically trained personnel . . . "[7] In the same spirit Abmadou Ahidjo, President of the Cameroun declared: "It must be recognized that, in what one calls the 'Third World,' we are among the most disinherited . . . ."[8]

The fact that Arab underdevelopment has never been a major preoccupation of the Arab League does not mean that Arab economic cooperation was not one of the aims of Pan-Arabism. After first mentioning political cooperation, Article 2 of the Pact establishing the Arab League adds that the League "also has the objective of assuring, within the framework of the respective regimes and situations of each state, close cooperation between member states in the following matters: Economic and financial matters . . . Communication . . . Social welfare . . . Health."

In fact, the anti-colonial struggle and particularly the anti-Zionist fight forced the pursuit of this objective into the background. It was only after the first Palestine defeat that problems of economic cooperation came to the forefront of the League's activities. Four procedures, common to all international organizations, were used in order to lay the foundations of Arab economic cooperation: (1) the adoption of resolutions inviting member states to initiate integration in given fields; (2) the encouragement of meetings, congresses, conferences, colloquia and seminars devoted to the various fields of economic, social and cultural cooperation; (3) the creation of relevant specialized agencies attached to the League; (4) the encouragement of the conclusion of technical agreements aimed at institutionalizing Arab cooperation in specific fields such as the transit trade, oil and communications.

The first procedure was used extensively by the Council of the League which passed a great number of resolutions concerning the most diverse aspects of cooperation, but these resolutions remained for the most part ineffective. Use of the second procedure resulted in an incredible number of conferences, congresses, and seminars at all levels and covering the widest range of subjects. One positive aspect of these

7. SCIAS/GEN/INF/9, at 2.

8. Sommet CIAS/GEN/INF/10, at 7. This paragraph was omitted in the English translation of the speech. See SCIAS/GEN/INF/10, at 6.

meetings was that they allowed the Arab elites to become better acquainted with each other. But all too often, the recommendations drafted and adopted at these meetings have been ratified by the appropriate organs of the League, then referred to the Governments of member states, then sometimes submitted again by these states to the Council of the League and once more referred to member states in the form of recommendations from the Council. This has been a vicious circle, one unlikely to lead to any progress in promoting Arab cooperation and integration.

Use of the third procedure gave rise to the establishment of various specialized agencies, namely, The Arab Postal Union, the Arab telecommunications and radio-communications union, the Arab International Institute for the defense of Society against crime, the Arab International Institute for Public Administration, the Arab Organization for education, culture and science called the Arab "U.N.E.S.C.O." These agencies operate within the framework of the Arab League but very often compete with the League. On the other hand, many specialized agencies, such as the Organization of Arab World Airlines[9] or the Arab Maritime Company,[10] never came into being at all.

The fourth procedure brought about the conclusion of various international conventions. Chronological priority belongs to the Cultural Convention approved by the Council of the Arab League at its second session on 27 November 1945 (Resolution 14/2). The Convention on Writs and judicial Commissions of inquiry, the Convention on the Execution of Judgments and the Convention on the Extradition of Criminals approved by the Council on 14 October 1952 represent a second group of conventions aiming at improving Arab integration in the legal domain. In the economic field several conventions have been proposed for signature and ratification including: the Convention to promote and organize trade among the Arab states; the Convention on the settlement of payments and the transfer of capital between Arab States; and the Convention on the economic union of the Arab states.

It should be pointed out that the procedure adopted for the conclusion of these conventions is a particularly slow one. A draft convention is first prepared by the competent Department in the Secretariat of the League; then it is approved by the appropriate permanent commission which often holds a special meeting in order to give a more solemn character to the convention. At the next stage the convention is approved by the Council of the Arab League or by the

9. Created by virtue of Resolution 18, passed by the Economic Council of the League on April 1961.

10. Created by virtue of Resolution 23, passed by the Economic Council on December 1963.

Economic Council. The convention is then signed by an *ad hoc* meeting of plenipotentiary envoys. It then still has to be ratified by the various Arab States, and finally the instruments of ratification must be deposited with the Secretariat of the League which in turn notifies the Arab states when the convention enters into force.

The pointless complexity of such procedures has been to a certain extent responsible for the delays incurred in the coming into force of these conventions. Moreover, due to the interval between the drafting of the convention and its application, the convention once ratified must almost immediately be amended to make it correspond to new situations. As the procedure established for amending these conventions is as intricate and time-consuming as that for ratification, the present usage is therefore incapable of keeping pace with the Arab world's economic evolution.

It thus seems that this whole structure of conventions is nothing more than a facade intended to hide the crisis of Arab cooperation. It appears that Arab states do not really wish to bind themselves with other Arab states through conventional or institutional obligations. At the same time however, they wish to show public opinion that they are resolutely heading towards integration. The Arab League is used as a frame for this equivocation, which is deliberately perpetrated with the complicity of its member states. This institutional demagogy results in a continuous pretense of activity at various levels and masks the stagnation of Arab cooperation.

Having reviewed the economic cooperation in the Arab world, let us now see whether African cooperation in the economic fields has been more successful or better managed. The principle of African economic cooperation is mentioned in the third paragraph of the Preamble and reaffirmed in Article 2 of the Charter of Addis Ababa which puts among the objectives of the O.A.U. the desire "to coordinate and intensify their cooperation and efforts to achieve a better life for the people of Africa." The O.A.U. however has not created a special body entrusted with economic cooperation. Whereas the Arab treaty of joint defence and economic cooperation has provided for an Economic Council distinct from the other major organs of the Arab League, the Charter of Addis Ababa has given to its various directing bodies (*i.e.*, the Summit Conference, the Council of Ministers, the Secretariat) the task of directly dealing with economic questions. It should nonetheless be noted that, among the five special commissions created in conformity with the stipulations of Article 20 of the Charter of Addis Ababa, the foremost is the Economic and Social Commission, charged with the promotion of Pan-African economic cooperation.

At the special session of the African Summit Conference held in Addis Ababa in May 1963, the delegates were so anxious to bring forward this whole question of economic cooperation that they decided, in Point Four of the Agenda, to press for the immediate creation of a "Preparatory Economic Committee" while waiting for the creation of the actual Economic and Social Commission. The Preparatory Economic Committee never actually met, but the Economic and Social Commission did hold its first meeting in Niamey in December 1963 and considered the major objectives envisaged by the first African Summit. The Commission also considered the problem of coordinating its own work with that of the Economic Commission for Africa. Finally the Commission decided to hold its next annual meeting in Cairo in January 1965. This second meeting was actually to be the last because the majority of African states refrained from sending delegations and did not even reply to the invitations for further meetings, sent by the Secretariat of the O.A.U.

In order to find some way out of this situation, the Secretary-General proposed to the Council of Ministers in Kinshasa in September 1967 that the Economic Commission should be bypassed in favour of a direct move to examine economic cooperation. As the Secretary-General's Report indicates, this move is only a makeshift one which presents two major problems. First of all, it is difficult for the Council of Ministers to deal with the technical details involved in the problems of African economic cooperation. Secondly, the Council of Ministers of the O.A.U. is primarily a political body, more concerned with the questions of decolonization and of international politics than with questions of economic cooperation.

The second move was to increase cooperation between the O.A.U. and the Economic Commission for Africa (E.C.A.). An agreement was concluded between the United Nations and the O.A.U. on November 1965.[11] Different methods of collaboration between the two institutions were afterwards implemented, among them being reciprocal representation and participation at meetings, reciprocal provision of suggestions, recommendations and comments through resolutions, inter-secretariat consultants, exchange and joint use of information, and joint sessions of expert bodies. Several factors have combined to facilitate O.A.U.—E.C.A. collaboration. In the first place, both organizations are situated in Addis Ababa. The O.A.U. working alone had been hampered in its functioning by the grave lack of qualified staff and personnel in its Secretariat, and this was remedied by the close cooperation with the E.C.A. Finally, a new division occurred in the work done by the O.A.U. and that done by the E.C.A. The former is concerned with the political aspects of economic cooperation, the latter with the technical and practical aspects.

11. U.N. Doc. A/6174 (1965).

In particular, when reviewing the net results achieved in the field of economic cooperation after ten years of work within the O.A.U. framework, one must stress: the failure of the Economic and Social Commission; the weakness of the different specialised agencies working with the O.A.U.; the lack of interest on the part of the Heads of State Conference and the Council of Ministers of the O.A.U. concerning economic problems; the multiple difficulties encountered by the Secretariat in its attempts to establish a research and study center; and finally, the dominating position of the E.C.A. in the whole field of economic cooperation in Africa.

These conclusions indicate the failure of the O.A.U.'s attempts at economic cooperation in Africa, a failure which seems to appear at various levels. First, at the institutional level the organizations created for the purpose of promoting economic cooperation have never functioned properly. Second, at what may be called the normative level these organizations have shown themselves incapable of establishing the necessary basic standards from which to formulate programs concerning cooperation, and also incapable of agreeing on common policies to be put into practice. Finally, there is a failure on the level of diplomatic psychology in the sense that the African countries have little or no confidence in African organizations. In fact, this attitude is the principal reason for the lack of success of O.A.U. activity concerning economic cooperation.[12] The report of the O.A.U. Secretariat is explicit on this point:

> Unless the O.A.U.'s Member states wish now to give up to non-African organizations their rights to discuss and decide questions concerning their own social and economic development, unless they wish to transfer their rights and controls to other non-African hands which could make such use of them as would not be in the interest of the majority of Africa's citizens, then it is perhaps imperative that we study the situation as it actually is at present, and that we resolve yet once more to allow the specialised commissions to function with certainty. . . .[13]

It would, however, be a grave mistake to underestimate the importance of the O.A.U. for Africa, and the role which it could play in connection with economic and social development. First, the O.A.U. is the only African organization which deals with economic development

12. The Secretariat's Report notes with bitterness that meetings attended by non-African States receive the full support of the Members of the O.A.U. while meetings dealing with the same problems but held by the O.A.U. cannot be held for lack of quorum.

13. CM/169, at 3.

on a continental basis. All the other organizations in this area deal with the question from a point of view which is either regional and isolated or from one which is not specifically African. The Secretariat's Report refers to "those forces of destruction which are aimed at demolishing this fragile structure of unity which the African states have laboured to build . . . ."[14] The O.A.U. wishes and rightly so, to be the one and only spokesman for Africa since it is the only organization under which the African states have been able to unite. "It is through the O.A.U. and through it alone, that Africa can choose and effect her own desires."[15] Second, the O.A.U. enables the African states to present a common front in the Specialised Agencies and at international conferences on economic development; Geneva in 1966, Algiers in 1967, New Delhi in 1968 and Santiago in 1970. Most African states have neither the means nor sufficient experts to allow for the proper preparation which such conferences necessitate. The O.A.U. gives them the technical and diplomatic assistance which allows them to adopt a common policy and attitude in facing the rich countries and the non-African partners from the Third World. Third, the O.A.U.'s activities in the field of economic cooperation have enabled a stronger, more mobile cooperation between the African states on the one hand, and the United Nations and its Specialised Agencies on the other. The O.A.U. acts as the halfway house between the world organizations and the new African countries. It permits the diplomats and the experts from these countries to work in these organizations in the interest of Africa.[16]

One is thus confronted by a paradoxical situation. The O.A.U. has failed to promote economic cooperation within the African continent, but it has, on the contrary, succeeded in reinforcing the position of Africa in the outside world by successfully promoting economic cooperation between Africa and the outside world. This must be compared with the Arab League which has failed to promote economic cooperation both within the Arab World and between the Arab World and the outside world. The principal explanation for this contrast may be found in the attitude of the United Nations and the majority of its member states toward the Arab League and the O.A.U. While the League organization was never really admitted in the world community neither as such nor as the principal organ for Arab cooperation, the O.A.U. was accepted both by the United Nations and its member states.

The domain of conjecture is sometimes rewarding in the search for causes and motives. It is not a field where the scholarly mind should advance with intrepid steps, but it is, nonetheless, an uncharted region

14. CM/169, at 3.
15. CM/169, at 18.
16. CM/157, at 16.

of the mind where the truth may be stumbled over almost by accident. It could be suggested that there is an explanation for the difference of world attitudes to the organizations. This explanation might include a suggestion that the Arab League was created at a time when the principle of decolonization was considered to be seditious and incompatible with the aims and early ideals of the United Nations. On the other hand, the O.A.U., a more recent creation, was founded when the policy of decolonization was not only accepted but also legitimized and encouraged, in conformity with the newer philosophies of the United Nations. For Western public opinion, the Arab League, however, was stained with the original sin of sedition and continued to be regarded in this light, regardless of changing attitudes towards decolonization. Another hypothesis, perhaps a secondary consideration, is that the Arab League can be thought of as representing the heirs of the traditional enemy of the world of Christendom and the West, an attitude inherited from the Crusaders and which has not decreased with the passing of the centuries. It could be argued that this racist, anti-Arab and anti-Moslem movement has culminated in a shift of sympathy on the part of the West in favour of the establishment and development of the Israeli State. Whereas, the O.A.U., while it includes a number of Arab states, is nevertheless generally regarded as an organization of black peoples. The attitude of the West may be tinged with a feeling of guilt, harking back to the slave trade. This guilt complex could be one of the motive forces militating in favour of sympathy towards an African Revival and any Pan-African movement which might advance the cause of this revival. Moreover, the struggle of the Arab League against Zionism is not acceptable to Western opinion, which is as pro-Zionist as it is unavowedly anti-Semitic. Pan-Arab anti-Zionism is considered incompatible with the aims and principles of the United Nations, since Israel was first officially created by the U.N. and then admitted to its membership. The struggle of the O.A.U. against apartheid is viewed in a different light, and the campaign against racial discrimination in Africa has become an international article of faith which allows the O.A.U. to take coercives measures against South Africa, in spite of the disturbing fact that South Africa herself is a founding member of the United Nations Organization.

IV. CONCLUSIONS

The Arab League and the O.A.U. have contributed towards improving the situation of the poor countries within the United Nations and other specialized agencies rather than promoting regional action or continental cooperation.

The Arab League was the nucleus of the Afro-Asian group in the

United Nations, the first institutional voice speaking for the poor nations, face to face with the rich world. Later on, the O.A.U. came on the scene to reinforce the League when the latter began to lose its youthful dynamism. However, the Arab states and the African states have obtained more support and aid in their struggle against colonialism from the World Organization than from their own organization. The intrinsic weakness of the Arab and African states themselves remains the main cause of the weakness of the Arab League and the O.A.U. We must add to this weakness the increasing power of Israel and South Africa. Those two dynamic, advanced and domineering states accentuate the internal contradictions of the Arab world and the African world respectively by creating a situation with which neither the Arab League nor the O.A.U. are capable of dealing. A situation which has unfortunately pushed the real economic and social problems of the Third World into the background.

And yet even if the weaknesses of the Arab League and the O.A.U. are further aggravated, these organizations will retain their prestige and their symbolic value because they are the first two organizations created and directed by the poor nations for the poor nations of the world. Having said this, however, let us not forget that the inability of the Arab and African worlds to make full use of modern scientific developments and establish a communications network allowing cooperation and awareness of common Arab and African problems is a phenomenon shared by all the underdeveloped countries.

This inadequacy explains the attitude of the Arab League and the O.A.U., an attitude which is characterized by disillusioned impotence and sterile anger. It is responsible for the distorted vision that the Third World has of contemporary history which leads it to prefer the magic of incancation and imprecation to a technological and realistic approach. Only an organization which will successfully encourage and spread a politically mature culture—and not simply repeat endlessly partisian propaganda—will make the Arab and African peoples capable of dealing adequately with the regional and worldwide tasks that await them.

Nevertheless, the oil weapon which has been used so recently by the Arab countries in a singular movement of genuine unity of purpose, not only against the industrialised countries but also against South Africa, Rhodesia and Portugal, adds a new dimension to the anti-colonial struggle. It offers new possibilities for a dialogue from a position of strength which the underdeveloped countries can engage with the developed world. Bandoeng was a turning point in the struggle for the political independence of the Third World and the October 1973 war of the Arabs against Israel is perhaps the turning point of the struggle of the developing world for a minimum of economic independence.

It can be said therefore, with a measure of emphasis, that the developing countries have undergone a qualitative change from being the objects of international law and politics to becoming the subjects of a dynamic new relationship with the world of the industrialised rich. The time has come for the regional organizations of the Third World to burst into the political arena of this age of accelerated change.

THE FUTURE OF WORLD ORDER

RICHARD A. FALK

Perhaps more profoundly than any international lawyer of our time, Wolfgang Friedmann combined a deep humanistic commitment to an improved system of world order with a lively awareness that proposals for global reform must first pass tests of political feasibility to warrant serious attention.* It is a great tribute, I think, to the strength of Professor Friedmann's vision that he could accept the harsh realities of international relations, especially given the persistence and intensification of the war system, without over the years growing either sentimental or cynical, that is, without succumbing to the easy advocacy of either instant world government or the facile endorsement of what was once called *realpolitik,* but which might now be more easily recognized if identified as Kissingerism or for that matter, Brzezinskiism.

It is within this intermediate zone of what I would call practical idealism that Friedmann's many notable contributions were made. He saw clearly, and far earlier than most of his colleagues, that the mixture of nuclear weapons technology, demographic and ecological pressure, and massive poverty were overwhelming the problem-solving capacity of a fragmented system of sovereign states. In this sense, his pioneering work in the 1960's on a series of functional issues anticipated the current emphasis on "the management of interdependence."[1] Having ruled out both utopian blueprints of a new world order and dysutopian visions of decay, Friedmann believed that the best hope for genuine, substantial progress in world affairs arose from the functional logic of international cooperation based on mutual advantage in the many areas of proliferating interaction. This hope rested on the conviction that governments would become more cooperative with one another as they

RICHARD A. FALK is Milbank Professor of International Law, Woodrow Wilson School of Public and International Affairs, Princeton University.

*A portion of this essay was initially delivered as a part of the Yencken Lectures at Australian National University on September 10-11, 1974.

1. See especially W. Friedmann, *The Changing Structure of International Law* (1964); Friedmann, "General Course in Public International Law," 127 Académie de Droit International. *Recueil des Cours* 39 (1969).

came to realize that territorial interests could be protected in an interdependent world only by entering into an ever-expanding web of cooperative international arrangements.

In this spirit, the future of the oceans was an appropriate test case of the reformist potentiality of the state system. Wolfgang Friedmann, characteristically, sensed ahead of most, the pivotal significance of the rush to exploit the mineral wealth of the oceans for the future of world order.[2] As was also characteristic he tried to lend support to as progressive a legal solution as was consistent with the political framework of the state system, perhaps pushing expectations slightly beyond the horizon of what others deemed realistic but still analyzing options in terms that were sufficiently politically relevant to influence serious debate.

It is alarming, but not surprising, that Wolfgang Friedmann's death, left an intellectual vacuum in international legal studies that has not been filled. Friedmann's particular brand of functionalism-searching for areas of convergent state interest as the building blocks of a burgeoning international law of cooperation—is peculiarly relevant in this period of resource diplomacy and of a broad call for "a new international economic order."

My essay does not even pretend to fill this vacuum left by Friedmann's departure in the slightest, but it does draw inspiration from his abiding concern with understanding what opportunities for creative human action existed within a given set of political constraints. Friedmann was very aware of the tension between freedom and necessity in relation to the work of global reform. His emphasis was upon the opportunities for action once the elements of necessity—that is, the practical constraints—are taken into account. Friedmann's work and life are a ringing testimonial to the reality of freedom, and hence, the responsibility it entails: "The first and most fundamental principle is the moral necessity to accept freedom of choice and a sense of individual responsibility in the future of mankind. The historian may well regard political developments as conditioned by laws of growth and decline, or record helplessness in the face of circumstances. But the essential factor in such development has always been human behavior, and only the conviction that we are enchained by the events of the past can compel us to believe in the inevitability of developments in our own time."[3] In the spirit of this affirmation, I seek in this essay to clarify the way students of world order might think about the prospects for global reform. Implicit in this inquiry is my belief that existing frameworks are partially outmoded because the premises of the state system have been

2. W. Friedmann, *The Future of the Oceans* (1971).
3. W. Friedmann, *An Introduction to World Politics* 21 (5th ed. 1965).

eroded to a large extent. In view of this situation it is difficult to take the traditional framework for granted in considering what kinds of incremental changes are feasible and desirable. As Wolfgang Friedmann clearly understood, it is the structure itself that is changing, and yet elements of continuity persist. My effort, then, is to identify a framework appropriate for a period of structural transition.

Alfred North Whitehead suggests that it is the mixture of blind historical forces and powerful moral visions that combine to destroy old modes of order and create new ones. For the European society of this time, it was steam and democracy that had displaced the old order of privilege and status, whereas looking backwards in the history of the West it was the barbarians and Christianity that mounted their successful assault upon the Roman Empire. Whitehead observes that "The well-marked transition from one age to another can always be traced to some analogues to Steam and Democracy, or—if you prefer it—to some analogues to Barbarians and Christians. Senseless agencies and formulated aspirations cooperate in the work of driving mankind from its old anchorage. Sometimes the period of change is an age of hope, sometimes it is an age of despair."[4]

I believe that human society is now undergoing such a transition from one age to another, but not on the level of an empire or civilization—such as Rome or the West—but a transition of greater magnitude, encompassing the planet and the entire human species. To grasp this unprecedented process of transition it is initially necessary to depict both the "senseless agencies" and the "formulated aspirations" that are driving the human species beyond its separated condition of fragmentation and deadly sub-species rivalry.[5]

It is also necessary to consider whether grounds for hope exist. Whitehead's dichotomy of hope and despair in an age of transition would, as of the moment, lead most of us to identify ours as one of despair. Whitehead observed that "When mankind has slipped its

4. A.N. Whitehead, *Adventures of Ideas* 7 (1933) [hereinafter cited as Whitehead].

5. This formulation with references to Freud by Erik Erikson at a session of the Wellfleet Discussions of Psychohistory held in August 1974.

cables, sometimes it is bent on the discovery of a New World, and sometimes it is haunted by the dim sound of the breakers dashing on the rocks ahead."[6] The connections between constructive and destructive energies seem more dialectical than Whitehead's comments suggest. That is, it is "the dim sound of the breakers dashing on the rocks ahead" that may summon the vital forces needed to embark on the perilous journey to "a New World;" it is the challenge of the future that summons the response in the present.

Proceeding from this orientation I propose to consider the political life of the human species in relation to its impending transition to a form of order beyond the state system, and to the unresolved character order that awaits. Within this indeterminate future lies forever locked beyond full disclosure the answer as to whether it is plausible to be hopeful about the future of the planet.

The mood of despair rises out of an interpretation of basic international trends, and interpretation that was discredited as alarmist as recently as five years ago but is now almost an ingredient of conventional wisdom on the part of almost all informed observers who are not government officials. This despair results from the realization that "the senseless agencies" are posing grave threats to the stability of political relations, and even to the survival and well-being of the human species and the habitability of the planet. Nuclear hazard, resource depletion, population pressure are the barbarians at the gates. The search for equity, the spreading awareness of deprivation and exclusion, and intense demands for justice and redistribution of wealth and influence constitute "the formulated aspirations" of the age, often blandly described as "rising expectations," "revolutionary energies," or "the development imperative." Put simply, the planet is too crowded, its resource base too constrained, its social structure too hierarchical, and its political structure fragmented and overly responsive to the concerns and interests of dominant groups to allow for an easy transition to a global community where the needs of the species for survival with dignity could be satisfied. As such, the pressures are mounted against mechanisms ill-conceived for such global integration, and the options narrow to various frantic efforts to stave off disintegration by refusing to heed the formulated aspirations of peoples. Can this holding operation of the state system succeed? Do we as citizens of a given time and place and members of a species want such a strategy to work during our lifetime? Are there alternatives for the future that transform world order without breaking it asunder?

Despite "the dim sound of the breakers dashing on the rocks ahead" the statist logic proceeds more rigorously than ever. No organized

6. Whitehead, *supra* note 4, at 7.

society has yet seriously proposed a new basis of organization for human affairs. Political leaders seem particularly obtuse about planning for the future; they seem occupationally committed to projecting an attitude of hope, especially when the case for despair is overwhelming. Why is this the case? Because the legitimacy of government rests, even in non-democratic societies, on its capacity to cope adequately with the basic problems of its peoples. But suppose these problems can't be solved? Then it is tempting in the extreme to deny their existence, or more plausibly, to underestimate their seriousness. As matters now stand, the great challenges facing humankind are approached, if at all, with the most effusive tact whenever national sovereignty is in issue. Why is this? The answer is relatively simple. The constructive forces trying to fashion some kind of world order response to the dangers posed by these senseless agencies are trying to devise some way to entice governments to tiptoe up to their edge. So like luring to the water a child who cannot yet swim, the need to offer national leaders constant reassurance is intense. Hence, those who work with or for bureaucracies on these problems are caught up in a terrible dilemma—either governments will do nothing at all or they must be told that nothing will encroach upon their traditional prerogatives if they display the good faith to consider them. Therefore, sovereignty, at once, the root enabling and disabling attribute of the world order system, must be uncritically reaffirmed in the very context in which its traditions are incompatible with reaching real solutions.[7] Good illustrations of this prevailing mood were the statements made in the summer of 1974 at the opening session of the U.N. World Population Conference held at Bucharest. Even relative optimists about international prospects, such as John P. Lewis, consider recent population growth as "inexorably ominous," a "clearly non-sustainable" surge.[8] Overcoming this situation by a continuing reliance upon the traditional *laissez faire* approach in which governments are asked to do no more than to celebrate the dire conditions that exist in the world seems totally unrealistic. But it is precisely this sanctimonious tone of concern without any movement toward accountability that was struck at Bucharest, which was, indeed, the unavoidable price of holding a meeting of governments on world population policy at this time. The 1974 meeting in Bucharest on population policy could be held because governments were reassured that they would not be asked

7. This observation applies mainly to the post-industrial sector of world society. For less economically evolved societies the stress on sovereignty may have mainly positive effects. There is great unevenness of position in the international system among states with respect to problem-solving and, hence, it is not possible to make satisfactory system-wide generalizations.

8. Lewis, "Oil, Other Scarcities, and the Poor Countries," 27 *World Politics* 63, 64 (1974) [hereinafter cited as Lewis].

to cede their sovereign control over the subject-matter, nor even expected to abandon pro-natalist postures toward the future.[9] Note that it is not being argued here that the state system is incompatible with a responsible world population policy, but only with a Hegelian view of sovereign prerogative, a view that was dangerous and romantic in the worst sense even at the moment of its utterance.

The Hegelian view of state sovereignty was endorsed at Bucharest. Nicolae Ceausescu of Rumania, leader of the host country, assured the delegates in his welcoming remarks that every country "has the sovereign right to promote that demographic policy . . . that it considers most suitable, consonant with its national interests, without any outside interference," Even the Secretary General of the United Nations, Kurt Waldheim, felt obliged to say that whatever action is proposed at Bucharest "emphatically recognizes the prerogatives of national sovereignty."[10]

In the background, of course, are countries like Brazil, Argentina, Czechoslovakia, and many others which pursue avowedly or operatively pro-natalist or *laissez faire* policies. Indeed, the Brazilian government announced only weeks before sending its delegation to Bucharest that it seeks a doubling of its present population by the end of the century so that it might cross the 200 million threshold by the year 2000.[11] Her leaders, probably correctly, regard population size as one critical credential for access to superpower status. Even further in the background, is the deteriorating world food situation, the deepening pockets of starvation, and the growing belief that mass famines in the Indian Subcontinent and elsewhere in Asia, Africa, and Latin America are virtually inevitable in the years ahead.[12] World food reserves have been steadily falling over the past decade or so. The most trusted indices of food security are the per cent of reserves as a share of annual grain consumption and the number of days at present consumption levels that the reserves would hold out. The figures in 1961 were 26% and 95, whereas the estimates for 1974 are 7% and 27 days; even in absolute deterioration is evident the reserve stock in 1961 was 154 million metric tons, whereas the estimated figure for 1974 is 89 million.[13]

9. Some observers, nevertheless, regard such a conference as valuable because delegates are educated to an appreciation of the magnitude of the problems posed and transmit their appreciation to national leaders. In effect, beneath the conference polemics a real learning experience occurs.

10. As quoted in *N.Y. Times,* Aug. 20, 1974, at 9, col 1.

11. The open question is whether Brazil will have 400 million in 2025. The present fertility pattern virtually assures 200 million Brazilians by the year 2000.

12. See Brown & Eckholm, "Food: Growing Global Insecurity," in *The United States and the Developing World: Agenda for Action 1974,* at 66 (J. Howe ed. 1974) [hereinafter cited as Brown & Eckholm].

13. These figures are taken from tables compiled in *id.* at 74; also, in 1962 the United States had the equivalent of 81 million metric tons of idle cropland, whereas in 1974 it has none.

Taken in conjunction with the increases in world population, the decline in the stock of food reserves indicates a dangerous vulnerability to mass starvation for the world as a whole.

Also in 1974 the Executive Board of UNICEF issued a Declaration of Emergency because of the dangerous situation confronting 400-500 million children in Asia, Africa, and Latin America. In the words of the Declaration, "The Board concludes that an emergency situation faces many of those children and believes that it is the Board's duty to call this danger to the attention of the world community."[14] The tragic situation in Sahel, Africa is already familiar, afflicting some 25 million people with the danger, now fortunately somewhat alleviated, of starvation. A tribe in northern Chad, suffering through eight years of drought, all its cattle dead and most of its camels gone, was faced by an outbreak of diptheria among its undernourished children who were too weak to resist its effects. When Morse Pensah, an FAO administrator for West Africa offered to send drugs, the tribal leaders begged him not to do so. "Starvation, they told him, would be too slow a death. Let diptheria rage."[15]

If the dangers posed were to other sectors of world society than to those Fouad Ajami has referred to as "those who do not matter," to "the marginals" as the more neo-Darwinian commentators often put it, then we would also share the UNICEF atmosphere of emergency.[16] These problems will remain abstract, as do all questions of justice, until the victims pose threats that are perceived as dangerous and credible by those with the power to change the situation. It remains uncertain whether the hungry masses will allow us to forget them, whether they will die politely and quietly, or will strike back in some way at the cruelty of their destiny.

At a gathering in the United States not long ago, the novelist Bernard Malamud reacted to this kind of question: "If it's true what you're saying, then what do we do about it. I don't want to live in a world where 400 million children are in danger of either dying from starvation or growing up deformed by malnutrition." In a sense Malamud is saying that the moral question is prior to the political question—that even if millions will starve in peace it is not in our interest as human beings to let this happen. Can we prevent this? Whose decision shall it be? It is, of course, true that the task of formulating a common world population policy to be uniformly applied is vastly complicated by the unevenness of national situations and their official

14. U.N. Doc E/ICEF/CRP/74-21, 21 May 1974.

15. Quoted *N.Y. Times,* Feb. 24, 1974, s.4 at 2, col. 3.

16. Well-expressed by Fouad Ajami, "The Global Populists—Third World Nations and World Order Crises," Princeton University Center of International Studies, Research monograph No. 41, May 1974.

perception. Thus, some governments sense different priorities about the relative importance of inhibiting population growth, have different ideas and traditions about the normative costs of doing so, have different views as to why population growth is a menace and, therefore, what to do about it. This condition of unevenness is so fundamental that it virtually precludes the formation, even in years ahead, of a global consensus on what should be done at national levels. The most that can be expected, as the bad effects of continued population growth become more widely appreciated, is that governments might try to strike a world order bargain of the sort that is being attempted at present with respect to ocean resources. Here, too, unevenness of situation and perceptions preclude a consensus; hence, to reach agreement it is necessary to strike a bargain through compromise and tradeoff. Even if governments negotiate an agreement that commands wide assent it would not be assured that it could be implemented in a context of rapidly shifting perceptions as to what is reasonable and fair.

The American Secretary of Agriculture, Earl Butz, has spoken of food as power, and so it is. Food experts report that ". . . North America today 'controls' a larger share of the world's exportable surplus of grains than the Middle East does of current world oil exports."[17] Because of geopolitics Egypt will receive large grain exports from the United States, because of geoeconomics other Middle Eastern countries will also receive preferential treatment. Lester Brown said, at Bucharest, because of physical factors such as drought and climate changes cutting into North American food output, the United States "might soon become the arbiter in decisions as to which nations starve and which survive" as "American surpluses, if any, will be insufficient to feed all those demanding food."[18]

It is significant that Brown's comments were made at a nongovernmental forum organized at Bucharest to compensate for the insufficiency of governmental perspectives. It was the same at the U.N. Conference on the Human Environment held at Stockholm. To find out what is needed to be and should be done about the environment it was necessary to attend nongovernmental counter-conferences and heed voices like those of Barry Commoner, Paul Ehrlich, Dai Dong, and the Oi Committee; but to find out, alas, what could be done it was necessary to attend the desultory and ritualistic intergovernmental sessions.[19]

But even this distinction is not without difficulties. After Lester Brown spoke at Bucharest he was challenged by an African delegate in the audience: "You in the developed countries have the paper, and we

17. Brown & Eckholm, *supra* note 12, at 75.
18. N.Y. Times, Aug. 21, 1974, at 2, col 4.
19. T. Artin, *Earth Talk: Independent Voices in the Environment* (1973).

have to read what you put on it. You want us to go back to our villages and take your pills. You over-intellectualized everything. Why don't you listen to us for a change?" In reporting the incident Malcolm Browne tells us that "She was applauded as she stalked out of the hall."[20] There are no wise men from the rich, white, dominant part of the world who have any moral authority with the poor and weak of the world. And reverting for a moment to Lewis' analysis of population pressure we should recall that he linked it to "widening international income disparities" and regarded both tendencies as "even more inexorably ominous than the appearance of worldwide wars, the invention of nuclear weapons, or the galloping hegemony of the automobiles."[21] There are two points here: first, the need to listen to spokespeople from the victim societies and secondly, the insufficiency of the sort of technocratic quick-fixes that appealed even to genuinely concerned individuals and governments in the favored portions of the world. In this crucial sense, current world order challenges are overwhelmingly political and moral. What changes are needed in social, economic, and political organizations at the national and global levels to deal with world poverty? How can such changes be brought about?

In the quite different context of energy policy the results of pressure on the state system are the same: namely, not less, but more statism. The United States under Richard Nixon initiated Project Independence to assure the country of national self-sufficiency in energy supplies by the 1980's. Gerald Ford in his first major speech as President told a joint session of Congress that "We must not let last winter's energy crisis happen again. I will push Project Independence for our own good and the good of others."[22] Side effects of Project Independence represent a boost for the nuclear power industry, a further relaxation of safety standards, and a growing unwillingness to impede resource development for reasons of environmental protection. Similarly, the main response to the new wealth of the oceans and to the problems of fisheries from overfishing and pollution is to increase, not decrease, the role of sovereign prerogatives. Instead of international management for human benefit, the probable new line of development is a carving up of the most valuable portions of the oceans into quasi-sovereign coastal zones of 200 miles or more.

The same story is evident with regard to the multinational corporation. The principal response to its great power and penetration capacity is not what we might have expected or hoped for, namely, the creation of an effective framework of international regulation of business to serve the general welfare, but rather an enhancement of the

20. *N.Y. Times,* Aug. 21, 1974, at 2, col. 2.

21. Lewis, *supra* note 8, at 64.

22. Quoted *N.Y. Times,* Aug. 13, 1974, at 20, col. 5.

economic role of national governments so as to enable a greater statist capability to strike a better national bargain.[23]

We find the same pattern evident elsewhere. The protection of the world environment provides yet another illustration of the pattern, a poignant one because of the extent to which the planetary coherence of the biosphere is the most fundamental expression of the inability of artificially demarcated political actors to cope with ecological decay.[24]

Perhaps, the most telling context of all is the evolution of the war system in the 32 years since the Hiroshima explosion. Increasingly, we find an abandonment by the superpowers of any commitment to disarmament or even denuclearization. Arms control goals increasingly do little more than place high ceilings on arms spending that justify increasing defense budgets rather than the reverse. Indeed, we find an opposite tendency. Superpower status and respect do seem to follow from the acquisition of nuclear weapons. China understood this. India's nuclear explosion was a further testimony to this wisdom. Brazil seems to grasp the relevance of nuclear status to its superpower aspirations, a natural complement to its unabashed pronatalism. And Richard Nixon, in perhaps his most dubious diplomatic initiative, promised nuclear power plants to several governments in the Middle East during his visit in the Spring of 1974; the Soviet Union has, in the meantime, stepped forward with its own offers of nuclear generosity. Instead of gilded bird cages or sculptured ivories imperial ceremonies of ingratiation involve the bequest of nuclear reactors, which bring the recipient to the very edge of a nuclear weapons capability. With increased oil prices raising import costs the pressure on several key governments to earn foreign exchange by arms sales is greater than ever before. Several key industrial countries are virtually locked into a major arms sales program—in 1973 estimated at $8.5 billion for the United States alone—to avoid economic collapses. In the Western press India was lectured about its irresponsible decision to walk across the nuclear tripwire at the very time Richard Nixon was engaged in his Middle Eastern nuclear diplomacy. Again, the impulse toward collective self-destruction is evident: instead of initiating a process of denuclearization through, for instance, a formal declaration of no first use of nuclear weapons, the strong and powerful nuclear actors pointlessly censure and

23. See Gilpin, "The Politics of Transnational Economic Relations," in *Transnational Relations and World Politics* 48 (J. Nye & R. Keohane eds. 1973); also R. Barnet & R. Müller, *Global Reach: The Power of the Multinational Corporations* (1975) [hereinafter cited as Barnet & Müller].

24. Recent disclosures of the extent to which SST technology, aerosal spray chemicals, and atmospheric nuclear explosions may be depleting the ozone shield that protects earth from the lethal rays of the sun illustrates both the problem and the unresponsiveness of principal institutions of authority to considerations of planetary well-being.

even punish the weak and poor for their failure to impose on themselves a regime of nuclear self-denial.[25] The irony of the posture is not lost, but neither are the dangers of accelerated proliferation abated.

This double standard of nuclear powers is resented especially by states with the potential to acquire nuclear status, and it parallels the more diffuse anger felt by poorer countries when told to limit *their* populations for the sake of humanity. This resentment was effectively expressed by M. Anandakrishnan, an India diplomat: "In the last few weeks there have been reports of seven nuclear explosions (only two underground), each several times more powerful than India's. The Nuclear Nonproliferation Treaty provided unlimited license for a handful of nuclear-weapons countries to proliferate their weapons while tying the hands of other countries even on reserach for peaceful uses. India would not sign such a discriminatory treaty."[26] On such an issue of reciprocity and equity the governments are more restrained than their peoples. According to a poll conducted among highly educated Indians some weeks after this explosion, two-thirds of the respondents wanted India to make the bomb despite Indira Gandhi's repeated pledges to the contrary.[27]

Even reactionary, pro-Western governments acknowledge the impropriety of the industrial rich telling the developing poor to exercise self-restraint for the sake of the planet. Aranjo Castro, Brazil's Ambassador to the United States, put the point as follows, in a letter to the *New York Times:* "I have never seen in your editorial policies any sign or any inkling of a suggestion to the effect of the non-desirability of further expansion of the U.S. economy, although this nation has attained unheard of levels of development and industrialization .... And we are likewise puzzled by the fact that those who propose some 'limits to growth' fail to propose any rational limit to underdevelopment and poverty."[28] Of course, there is a double irony present, because whereas Ambassador Castro is absolutely correct in his indictment, it applies even more directly to his own government, which has subordinated the claims of its poor so as to further satisfy the greed of its native rich.[29] Besides, the foreign investor and multinational corporation, that is, the rich sector of world society, has been a main

25. See K. Subrahmanyam, "The Indian Nuclear Test in a Global Perspective," India International Centre, 1 August 1974; R.V.R., Chandrasekhara Rao, "Proliferation and the Indian Test," 26 *Survival* 210 (1974).

26. Letter (dated July 17, 1974) from M. Anandakrishan to the Editor, *N.Y. Times,* July 24, 1974, at 40, col. 3.

27. Reported *N.Y. Times,* August 3, 1974, at 2.

28. Letter (dated August 13, 1974) from A. Castro to the Editor, *N.Y. Times,* Aug. 19, 1974, at 24, col. 5.

29. For a range of serious assessments of the Brazilian experience since the coup of 1964 see *Authoritarian Brazil* (A. Stepan ed. 1974).

benefactor of Brazil's refusal to heed "the limits to growth." These comments on current developments exhibit a mixture of genuine concern and deliberate confusion that is emanating from the dominant portions of world society, those that are at once somewhat attentive to "the breakers dashing on the rocks ahead" and often responsible for sustaining the dangerous situation.

The case of India is, perhaps, the most ominous. The size and population of India, the commitment of its leaders to building a decent society, the relative absence of repression, the major effort by the government to deal with population growth and food shortages, the strength of Gandhian ideas of non-violence and the recent nuclear explosion combine to make India a critical arena, one that is very discouraging at the moment.[30] The celebration of Independence Day on August 15, 1974 was the grimmest in the 27 years since India regained political independence. Indira Gandhi could tell her people nothing better than that "Losing courage has never helped. . . . The people of India have never been crushed under any burden." An economist, Prem Shankar Jha, writing in The Times of India, observed that "After a quarter century of effort, the goals the country set for itself seem actually to have receded from view." Mrs. Gandhi finished her speech at Red Fort by assuring her people that "the shortages are not of an extent as to make them unbearable." She told her audience that "We may have to modify our habits, change traditional ways and we may also have to suffer a bit." But she concluded "To believe that nothing is getting done or can be done, and to get utterly dismayed would be truly a dangerous thing."[31] Such an assurance was set forth at a time when at least 200 million Indians are reliably reported living below the very low poverty line of $40 earnings per year. Mrs. Gandhi was right to fear the political consequences of a sense of hopelessness—it sharpens the prospects into a choice between undesirable extremes: repressive violence from the elite or the mass. Put differently, such conditions invite the choice between the Brazilian solution and the Chinese solution to the challenge of development in a context of misery and inequity. The resurgence of Naxalite terror in Calcutta and the nuclear explosion in Rajasthan are among the indications that India, as now constituted, is moving in the direction of adopting drastic strategies. What possible bargain could be struck on a global level that could allow India to find a way out that did not presuppose repression at home and danger abroad? And what governments would have any incentive to reach such a bargain?

Bitter struggles in many parts of the world suggest a human

30. For a probing depiction of the Indian failure see Morris, "India: Ripe for Revolution," 10 *WIN* 4, 17 (1974).

31. Reported *N.Y. Times,* Aug. 16, 1974, at 6, col. 3.

willingness in situations where deprivation is acutely sensed to resort to the politics of desperation. The pervasive threat posed by terrorism is part of the critical context of danger. Governments unable to meet the needs of their people and unwilling to embark on the difficult kind of reforms that might change the situation are also unable and unwilling to abide by the dynamics of political self-determination. A dreadful cycle of violence ensues, the terror of insurgent factions being abetted by the repressive regime of incumbent governments. In a transnational setting, the desperation of militant Palestinians is suggestive, as well, of the extent to which the politics of desperation is not curtailed by a "law and order" calculus of the relation among forces. The Olympic killings of Israeli athletes at Munich in 1972 and the Maalot Massacre of Israeli school children in 1974 bears grim witness, not so much to the fanatical acts themselves or to the depravity of the perpetrators, as to their effectiveness in piercing the veil of public indifference. The point here is that various forms of terror arising from situations of extreme discontent provide a pretext and rationale for militarized civic life throughout the world, an atmosphere that is antagonistic to all efforts to unfreeze the *status quo,* even efforts that are designed to conserve what is most valuable about it.

What I am saying by way of diagnosis, then, is suggestive of what that archetypal American soldier said of a destroyed South Vietnamese village: "we have had to destroy the village in order to save it." Put into the rhetoric of world order—"our leaders are destroying the state system in order to save it." In neither context is it mindless destruction—it is just a matter of carrying a serviceable logic in one historical setting into a new setting where it becomes unserviceable. As Erik Erikson observed, "the facts are getting out of hand." Or reverting to Whitehead, the senseless agencies are not being neutralized by the formulated aspirations and so, indeed, the sound of the breakers dashing on the rocks ahead seems closer, more ominous. It is in this historical situation that I think we need to face questions about whether we can construct a system of world order capable of sustaining life on earth in a manner that does not violate our elemental sense of decency. I think these questions need to be posed with all the seriousness at our disposal, by citizens in all parts of the world, and not just by those with paper enough to write books. New sparks of political consciousness must be struck if we are going to be able to effectuate a world order solution that serves the interests of the human species as a whole; the only viable moral premise for politics in the ecological age is an anthropological one.

The confusion now current may be a prelude to clarity. The biblical parable of the Tower of Babel is acquiring an uncomfortable aptness; the Lord said "Come let us go down, and there confuse their language, that they may not understand one another's speech . . . and they left off building the city." Part of our deficiency concerns the knowledge at our disposal, especially for those of us interested in global reform. In this sense, it is necessary to find a means to transcend the confrontation between a food expert like Lester Brown and an angered African delegate who wants to hear about solutions, not problems. Obviously, knowledge tempered by humility is needed; obviously, also a holistic outlook that is integrative in stance is called for to overcome the angle of vision appropriate for a world organized into sovereign parts. My central proposition is that for better or for worse, for richer and for poorer, the world will be organized as a whole. It is a matter of making the most of the free play that still exists within such a constrained prospect. Before advancing a positive perspective of my own, I would like to consider briefly the mainstream dialogue on the direction of global reform.

Not so long ago Hedley Bull has described "the construction of a viable international order" as "the central issue of international relations in our times." To achieve this result it will be necessary, Professor Bull tells us, to form a consensus among "the deeply divided groups of which world society today is composed." And Professor Bull warns, and I agree, that "No consensus is possible that does not take account of the demands of African and Asian countries for political, economic and racial justice, and these cannot be satisfied without drastic change in some of the traditional attitudes of the Western powers."[32]

In a sense, Professor Bull's call for consensus is conceptually, but not normatively, equivalent to a similar call that has been voiced from time to time by Henry Kissinger. But the equivalence is deceptive. What Kissinger seems to have in mind is moderating Great Power relations and ignoring, or at most placating, Third World demands for a more equitable internal order. It is a consensus, if at all, only among a few critical actors and it seeks to achieve order without first satisfying justice demands.[33] Professor Bull's solution looks toward what is, in effect, a new social contract of global scope whereby governments cooperate over time in creating a reasonably fair and equitable world system where the

32. Hedley Bull, "Australia's Perceptions of our Role in the World" 14 (July 1974) (mimeographed text).

33. Even Kissinger seems recently aware of the precariousness of his own vision of world order. In a long interview with James Reston, Kissinger revealed this new concern: "I would like to leave at least the beginning of a perception of a structure that goes beyond these centers of power and moves toward a global conception. There is no question in my mind that by the end of the century this will be the dominant reality of our time. I believe we have to move toward it now." See "Secretary Kissinger Interviewed for New York Times," 71 *Dep't State Bull.* 629, 638 (1974).

stake in stability is high all around.[34] The political foundation for such a new order appears to derive, in part, from an appeal to self-interest (without such a consensus "the center cannot hold" and "the blood-dimmed tide of anarchy" will result) and, in part, from our sense of decency (many people do care about the sufferings of others enough to help with their elimination especially if the alternative is to face a hostile, dangerous challenge).[35]

It is a momentous question to ask whether the governments of the world are, under any set of conditions, capable of achieving and acting upon the enlightened awareness presupposed by such a consensus, as well as to determine with as much precision as possible the extent of dislocation that would be required to give it effect. Before the realities of resource scarcity, and the wider constraints embodied in the phrase "the limits to growth," were assimilated, there existed a widely shared and politically convenient conviction that the proliferation of dynamic growth models from the rich industrial countries could gradually cut the shackles of world poverty without requiring painful adjustments or sacrifices by rich and powerful countries; on the contrary, such self-serving Western pundits as Herman Kahn argued that the greater the growth of the rich the quicker would the plight of the poor be alleviated. But now, as the world teeters on the brink of mass famine and economic collapse, there is also a growing realization that growth dynamics are unlikely to provide the material basis for an equitable international order. Indeed, the stark realizations caused by the 1973-74 world crisis, with its sharply higher oil prices, has brought poorer countries (and even advanced industrial states such as Italy) closer than ever to a condition of chronic bankruptcy. The hopes of just a few years ago kindled by foreign aid, developmental economics and "the green revolution" have faded, and it now seems that a combination of economic and physical factors will make it increasingly difficult to keep the world food supply growing fast enough even to meet highly inadequate current per capita consumption standards.

It is within this setting that my disagreements with Secretary Kissinger on the one side and Professor Bull on the other take shape. These disagreements can be formulated in a simple way:

-it may be possible, but it is highly undesirable to achieve the kind of solution that Secretary Kissinger appears to favor;

34. Various ideas leading in the direction of a global social contract are gaining currency recently. See Gardner, "Report of the Seminar" and "A Postscript," in *The World Food and Energy Crises: The Role of International Organizations* 49 (Conference at Institute of Man and Science, Rensselaerville, N.Y., May 1974).

35. A very perceptive discussion of these tendencies and their practical limits can be found in Stone, "Approaches to the Notion of International Justice," in *The Future of the International Legal Order* 372 (C.E. Black & R.A. Falk eds. 1969).

—it would be desirable, but it seems virtually impossible to achieve the sort of solution that Professor Bull proposes.

Such an assessment follows from the discussion of the global setting that has already been made. For the Kissinger type of consensus to take hold requires an agreement on moderation among the main centers of state power that presently exist in international relations; the cement for such an agreement would be mutual respect for a favorable *status quo*, the need for coordinated efforts to maintain political order and economic viability, and a shared renunciation of any serious effort to gain position or power at the expense of other governmental participants in this directorate of the rich and powerful. Implicit in this scheme is a large role for the multinational corporation (and its socialist equivalent) which inclines both politics and economics in a regressive direction, but not necessarily rightwards. What the multinational corporation requires is order and predictability. Therefore, it is not surprising that big businessmen return home to America enthusiastic whether they have been to Peking or Rio de Janeiro. Either China or Brazil is a positive model as they share in common a capacity to provide domestic order. What is intolerable is uncertainty, especially of a sort associated with popular discontent. Therefore, Argentina is a disfavored economic setting, not because its government is antagonistic to business enterprise, but because the leaders and police have not yet preempted all the political space and succeeded in suppressing political dissent, terrorism, and kidnapping. What I am suggesting is that the multinational corporation perspective is, or at least pretends to be, increasingly non-ideological, demanding from host governments only a high degree of order with respect to its economic operations. To achieve such order is almost certain to entail coercion, and such coercion will be needed through time if no social transformation at the bottom is involved.

Thus the China and Brazilian models are not really equivalent at all either in effect or in the mind's eye of the multinational corporate elite. China, by means of a long revolution, reconstituted state power to promote a new economic order for its people, eliminating the widest income disparities and, seemingly, dealing with poverty, although not without inflicting hardships on a significant portion of its population. Brazil, in contrast, has experienced a counter-revolution dominated by a conservative military elite, its economy has been organized around considerations of GNP and profitability, with very little of benefit accruing to the bottom 75% of its population. A continuing brutal program of repression has been institutionalized without even the compensating benefits of social transformation. This Brazilian strategy is centered upon development under the aegis of the multinational corporation, which by the nature of its operation is heavily focused on servicing the top layers of a mass economy—that is, electric appliances, cars, middle class luxuries, rather than clothes, schools, medical facilities. Until recently it could at least be said that the Brazilian model was easier to shake off than the kind bureaucratic socialism associated with the Communist world. But I am afraid this is no longer the case. Advances in the art of counterinsurgency politics have included the development of bureaucratic and para-military efficacy that make it exceedingly difficult, if not impossible, to organize an effective opposition even if mass discontent exists.

Given the extent of world poverty and the degree of dissatisfaction with inequities, such a Kissingerian consensus at the top would not succeed in sustaining order and stability at the bottom without brute force and efficient bureaucracy, especially depending on authority being delegated out to repressive intermediate regimes. In essence, the implication of the Kissinger approach, it hardly matters whether the goal is witting or not, is to vie for a post-Allende Chile solution or, what is the same, but in a less spectacular mode, the Brazil solution, *i.e.* alliances with highly repressive governments that rule and impose their will without either soliciting the consent or meeting the needs of the governed. And more than just alliances. Disclosures show a pattern of CIA interventions to help tip the balance of domestic forces so as to allow Brazilian solutions to prevail in the domestic play of forces. The militarization of politics already is accepted as normal within the Soviet bloc and therefore its extension to non-Communist poor countries would not create any serious ethical problems for political managers in Moscow. Quite the contrary. Whether this solution would be stable would depend very much on the extent to which the mutual respect and perceived shared interests at the top were sufficient to generate the central guidance procedures needed to manage the complex interdependencies of the world economy and of the global ecosystems.[36] It would also depend on sustaining the counterinsurgency postures of many governments over a long period of time. For reasons that I have already suggested this stability model is likely in the future to require more comprehensive and harsh methods and to spread its tentacles to many additional societies. In the United States we are still, despite the Nixon demise, wrestling with the structural problems of what has come to be called "the imperial presidency," which involves in its most extreme manifestations the adoption by the government of a counterinsurgency stance toward the American citizenry, although fortunately, still of a mild variety. In several other liberal democracies in Europe and Asia polarizing moods are unfolding as the mounting

36. For elaboration of what sort of central guidance procedures are needed and possible see R.A. Falk, *A Study of Future Worlds* ch. IV (1975).

inability of moderate, consensual government to solve a lengthening agenda of problems grows manifest. Rather than a reversal of international traditions of selfishness so far as the needs of others are concerned, I notice mainly gathering neo-Darwinian storm clouds in which scarcity on many sides (oil, food, money, space, clean air and water) makes the choice between "us" and "them" even easier than in the past to make on purely selfish grounds. Liberal ideology, supported by the industrial revolution and the credibility of an idea of progress, was premised on evading or overcoming the neo-Darwinian issue altogether by saying "us" first and then "them," with enough for "all" in due course. The United States has been and, I suppose, remains the principal testing ground for this ideology, and hence, Kissinger's repudiation of its ethical premise of human solidarity is especially significant at a time when such a premise no longer seems sustainable. I would emphasize not only Kissinger's repudiation of the politics of empathy but the extent to which his diplomatic stance seems widely admired even by foreign statesmen.

I am led to the pessimistic conclusion that Kissinger's solution – the so-called structure of peace – might work for the world in the same perverse sense that South Africa's or Soviet Russia's structure of peace has "worked." It is this form of "peace" that is being plotted on the geopolitical drawing boards of the powerful, perhaps not in the conspiratorial spirit these words imply, but as a natural expression of convergent assessments as to what is desirable and what is possible by leaders in the critical states of the world.

In opposition to this kind of imposed world order Professor Bull proposes a consensus that is wide enough to satisfy the minimal needs, at least, of voices of discontent. Such a proposal, especially, coming as it does from such an influential and realistic student of international relations as Hedley Bull, deserves our most careful and sympathetic attention. Of course, Professor Bull, so far as I know, has not yet spelled out what he has in mind, what kinds of adjustments would be appropriate and necessary to strike that historic social contract which would be the vital expression of a new international order. In my view, governments cannot hope to effectuate such a consensus without prior social and economic transformations on a national level – the domestic disparities are too great, the scarcities too pronounced, the capital surplus too restricted, the capacities for disruption too dispersed and potent, the erosion of economic viability too evident, and the energies of the entrenched elites too formidable to reach any kind of workable consensus among governments as to what is fair and just in the world. Furthermore, the proliferation of centers of national decision make it impractical to establish the central guidance mechanisms that are needed to cope satisfactorily with the growing challenges of economic and ecological interdependence, challenges that range from assuring that currency transactions don't upset the delicate balance of the world economy to gaining confidence that increases in world population don't overwhelm the material and social basis of decency in human relations. On this general level of analysis, then, I am making two kinds of contentions:

—first, the evidence available suggests a monumental absence of *will* on the part of leadership groups to achieve a redistributive consensus that is premised on justice for all sectors of global society;

—secondly, to the extent that such a redistributive consensus could be reached as to goals, it could not be successfully implemented by the state system.

I am suggesting in this second contention that Professor Bull does not express the crisis in broad enough terms to capture economic and ecological factors and, therefore, the kind of solution proposed, at most, keeps conflict within bounds of moderation and makes satisfactory progress toward the elimination of mass poverty and foreign economic exploitation from the international scene.

I believe, along with Professor Bull, that we need at this stage of history to shape a consensus about the character of global reform. However, I do not think that governments are now in a position to shape such a consensus, but are concentrating upon the task of providing reassurances of their capacities to deal with national problems. In its most extreme form, this reassurance involves the unwillingness of governments to face unpleasant facts. For instance, recently several African governments have been reported reluctant to acknowledge even domestic starvation because of an evident fear that it would reflect unfavorably on their governing capacities. But such an extreme instance is but a grotesque caricature of a general situation of unacknowledged ineptitude. Whether the preferred figure is Nero fiddling while Rome burns, the discovery that emperor has no clothes, or the sovereign pomp and circumstance of the world population conference, the underlying message is the same—a refusal by governments to face the prime challenges of our world in realistic terms. Therefore, I would argue that the future of world order is too important to leave to the wisdom and action of governments.

At the same time, the process of global reform is a moral and political one, an awakening of consciousness and mobilization of effective energies. In this respect that anonymous African woman at Bucharest is correct to deplore the tendency of Westerners to over-intellectualize their proposals, exhibiting the biggest fallacy of the Enlightenment. Any person's particular situation in space and time represents a provincial perspective, whatever the rhetoric, and is incapable of providing an ideal solution for the whole.

My own experience suggests that the most positive development at the moment is that a global multilogue of these issues of the future of world order is beginning to take place. No undertaking seems more worthwhile at present than the exchange of views with creative non-official representatives of the main cultural and political traditions of our world, not for the sake of discussion, but to build the foundation for a social movement dedicated to the creation of a peaceful and just system of world order. I have devoted most of my professional time over the past several years to an exercise of this kind, known as the World Order Models Project.[37] It is itself a non-trivial social fact that such an undertaking is conceived and carried forward at this historical moment. The impact of such consciousness-raising is disappointing on the level of action. There is no immediate authentic response to the sort of question posed by Bernard Malamud—that is, what should I do if I don't want to live in a world of malnourished and starving children.

At the most, by evolving a globalist paradigm we can interpret more fully and accurately what is happening and what we can do about it than is possible by relying on the internationalist paradigm.[38]

In my view, a different set of historical forces are at work and underlie the deepening international crisis. These forces are inclining the world system toward the emergence of a form of central guidance or scheme of global integration that is superseding the state system. This integrative momentum is undergirded by the scale and administrative capacities of business enterprise, especially the multinational corporation. While the sun may occasionally have set on the Union Jack even during the apogee of the British Empire, the same may not be said of the Hertz banner or the Pepsi billboard.[39] The interaction of territorial sovereign states is increasingly at variance with the *functional logic* of planning, guidance, and budgeting that are needed for a planet that has less and less surplus capacity and is more often faced with the realities of scarcity.[40] Put in different terms, to achieve stable solutions for the future, if possible at all, presupposes *a new system of world order* including as an essential structural element *a system of non territorial central guidance*. By emphasizing non-territoriality we are ruling out a territorial world state (even on a federal or confederal model) as a world order solution that is either desirable or necessary. I believe there are several plausible variants of non-territorial central guidance, the most

37. For an account of the World Order Models Project see General Introduction by Professor Saul H. Mendlovitz, its primary architect, in *id.* at *xvii*.

38. This is the main theme of lectures given at Yale Law School in March 1974. Falk, "A New Paradigm for International Legal Studies: Prospects and Proposals," 84 *Yale L.J.* 969 (1975).

39. Point borrowed from Barnet & Müller, *supra* note 23.

40. See Ophuls, "The Scarcity Society," *Harpers,* April 1974, at 47.

plausible of which would be highly regressive and unpleasant even as compared to the inadequacies of the present international order. For purposes of abbreviation and clarity I shall refer to the state system as S_1 and to the prospect of a new superseding system as S_2. I will also distinguish between positive or desirable world order systems by putting a plus (+) sign before the S, to negative or undesirable systems by putting a minus (-) sign before the S, and to mixed results by combining signs (±). Thus, Professor Bull's solution is an instance of $+S_1$, Kissinger's an instance of $-S_2$, and of my own proposals an instance of $+S_2$.[41] Part of my argument is that the future belongs to S_2, although the variant of S_2 that will prevail is far from clear.

Let me evolve this perspective a step further. I identify the present moment in history as situated relatively late in the life of S_1 and identify it as S_0, in the following schematic terms: In such a context I place emphasis on the options available in the interval of uncertain duration that separates S_0 from S_2. (see Table 1). It is this interval that I identify as the period of Transition (i.e., $S_0 \rightarrow S_2 = T$) which in turn is subdivided into three parts: $T1, T2, T3 = T = S_0 \rightarrow S_2$.[42] My own view of Transition to $+S_2$ is based on three sets of developments correlated with the three stages of Transition: (see Table 2)

T1 = Consciousness-Raising in National Arenas
T2 = Mobilization in Transnational Arenas
T3 = Transformation in Global Arenas and Construction of Non-Territorial Central Guidance Mechanism.

The gist of my argument is that S_1 is doomed by the need to manage interdependencies, amid scarcity, although the energies of nationalism remain dominant, and if anything, are leading to further patterns of assertion at the present time.[43] As a result the immediate prospect is for a highly coercive and reactionary S_1 arrangement, a $-S_1$ that seeks to stem the tide of disintegration by manipulation, if possible, by brute force to the extent necessary. My overall conclusion can be formulated as a hypothesis consisting of three principal parts:

(1) There is no way to sustain a contractual relationship between the people and the government at the state level without protracted

41. There are an array of positive (+)S_2 models possible. Some are depicted in Chapter III of my book. *A Study of Future Worlds* (1975) and others are more fully and adequately depicted in the various perspectives embodied in the World Order Models Project. See *On Creating a Just World Order* (S.H. Mendlovitz ed. 1975).

42. In $+S_1$ conceptions of global reform, the changes are by definition of an intrasystemic character. For one compelling analysis along these lines see S. Brown, *New Forces in World Politics* 185-215 especially (1974).

43. These patterns of assertion are associated with the resource diplomacy of the industrial countries and the redistributive strategies of the Third World.

reliance on repressive force so long as S_1 persists;
(2) To achieve a social contract on the state level based on some notion of consensual rule it will be simultaneously necessary to reach a social contract on a global level;
(3) A global social contract presupposes a successful process of transition to a condition of $+S_2$ which is organized around the emergence of non-territorial central guidance capabilities as well as drastic redistribution of power, wealth, and influence.

Given such an interpretation of world order prospects, two questions seem paramount:

Can this favorable outcome be brought about?

What is the most beneficial way for individuals and groups to work toward this result?

These questions bear on the politics of transition, and we lack traditions of speculation that might offer guidance. In essence, the quest is for the sort of outlook that one associates with Wolfgang Friedmann's work, an outlook that is visionary without being utopian. It is *visionary* in the crucial sense of transcending the constraints of present arrangements of power. But it is *anti-utopian* in the equally crucial sense of providing a politics of transition to link the present with a preferred future.[44]

44. A very thoughtful book on these issues is B. Moore, Jr., *Reflections on the Causes of Human Misery* (1972).

Table 1: System Change and Historical Process

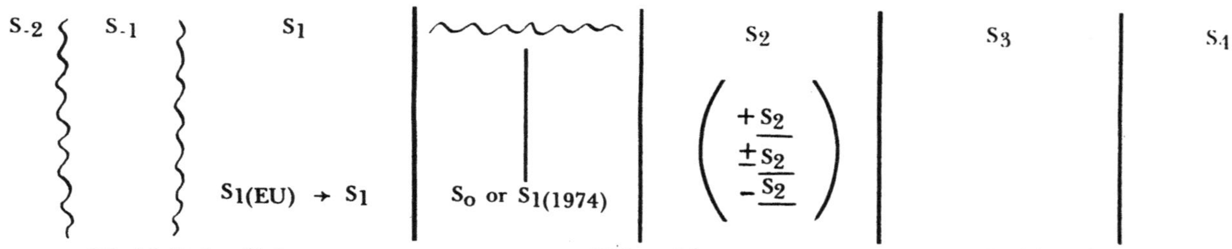

World Order Values

V_1 = Peacefulness
V_2 = Economic well-being
V_3 = Social and political justice
V_4 = Ecological quality

$S_1(EU)$ = European regional state system
$S_1(EU) \rightarrow S_1$ = transition from a regional to a global state system

T(t)ransition

$T = S_o \rightarrow S_2$
T1 = Consciousness
T2 = Mobilization
T3 = Transformation
$t = So \rightarrow S_1$ (next phase, e.g., 1815, 1918, 1945)

Positive Futures

$+S_2$ = Survival
$+S_3$ = Development
$+S_4$ = Transcendence

Negative Futures

$-S_2$ = Repression
$-S_3$ = Dehumanization
$-S_4$ = Subhumanization

Table 2: Transition Path to $+S_2$

T1 = Domestic Arenas change in Consciousness; preeminence of V_1, V_2, V_3, V_4 as basis for response to S_1 world order crisis and adoption of $+S_2$ as desirable outcome.

T2 = Transnational Arenas dominate process of mobilization to implement changes of consciousness achieved in T1.

T3 = Global Arenas dominate process of transformation to actualize in authority structures a new constitutional order (non-territorial central guidance) and a new social contract based on the postulates of $+S_2$.

THE WORLD BANK'S IMPACT ON INTERNATIONAL LAW A CASE-STUDY IN THE INTERNATIONAL LAW OF COOPERATION*

A. A. FATOUROS

By his concern with and emphasis on an emerging "international law of cooperation" Wolfgang Friedmann greatly contributed to our perception and understanding of the current state of the international legal process.[1] In contrast to the traditional "international law of coexistence," which he saw as consisting mainly of rules of abstention concerned with the delimitation of national sovereignty, the law of cooperation is "concerned with the organization and implementation of

A.A. FATOUROS is Professor Law, Indiana University (Bloomington).

*This essay is based in part on research conducted in connection with a project on the impact of international organizations on the legal system of member states, jointly sponsored by the Carnegie Endowment for International Peace and the International Legal Center. Wolfgang Friedmann was senior adviser to the project and had seen early drafts of some of the studies. A companion paper, entitled "The World Bank: A Study of the Institution's Impact on Its Borrowers," [hereinafter cited as "World Bank Study"], will appear in the volume collecting the project's findings. A few sections in the present essay (namely, those on the legal character of loan agreements and on the World Bank's role in aid coordination and development guidance) summarize discussions in that paper.

1. The earliest formulation is found in Friedmann, "Some Impacts of Social Organization on International Law," 50 *Am. J. Int'l L.* 475, 507 (1956); *cf.* W. Friedmann, *Law in a Changing Society* 460 (1960). Clearer and progressively better elaborated discussions appear in his later writings: "The Changing Dimensions of International Law," 62 *Colum. L. Rev.* 1147, 1154, 1162-65 (1962); *The Changing Structure of International Law* 67-70 (1964); "The Relevance of International Law to the Processes of Economic and Social Development," in 2 *The Future of the International Legal Order* 3 (R. Falk & C. Black eds. 1970) [hereinafter cited as Friedmann, "The Relevance"]; "Droit de coexistence et droit de coopération. Quelques observations sur la structure changeante du droit international," 6 *Revue Belge de droit international* I (1970) [hereinafter cited as Friedmann. "Droit de coexistence"]; "General Course in Public International Law," 127 Académie de Droit International, *Recueil des Cours* 91 (1969) [hereinafter cited as Friedmann, "General Course"]; "Human Welfare and International Law – A Reordering of Priorities," in *Transnational Law in a Changing Society. Essays in Honor of Philip C. Jessup* 113 (W. Friedmann, L. Henkin, & O. Lissitzyn eds. 1972). The brief discussion in this paragraph is based on these later formulations.

Friedmann's "two-tiered approach" was forcefully criticized in McDougal & Reisman, "The Changing Structure of International Law? Unchanging Theory for Inquiry," 65 *Colum. L. Rev.* 810 (1965). For a brief response see Friedmann, "The Relevance," *supra*, at 9 n. 14.

joint endeavors on a binational, regional, or multinational level directed to human welfare."[2] This law has an affirmative thrust; it deals with substantive, rather than jurisdictional, issues, thus reaching deep into the internal life of nations. Its consequent sensitivity to differences in "political, economic and social structure and principles," makes it depend for its existence and operation on the perception of common interests by the parties involved. As a result, it has grown mainly on a regional basis; on the universal or quasi-universal level, it is found chiefly in two types of areas: first, technically oriented fields, where the advantages from cooperation are immediate and easily perceivable (*e.g.*, communications and transport); second, areas immediately affecting human welfare, in particular those relating to assistance for the development of less developed countries.

The International Bank for Reconstruction and Development (IBRD, the World Bank) has played a significant role in this area. Wolfgang Friedmann frequently acknowledged it expressly,[3] more important, he devoted much of his later work to research into its role.[4] The present essay attempts to examine the interaction between the developing law of cooperation in this domain and international law as a whole. Its primary focus is not on "World Bank law" as such, that is to say, the law that has grown out of and around the Bank's relations with member states, in their capacity as lenders or borrowers; it focusses instead on the impact of the Bank's activities (and of "World Bank law") upon the international legal process.

Like all international organizations, the World Bank is at the same time an international actor and a stage upon which other international actors (primarily its members) are performing. Fully to understand its role in either guise it is necessary to study its structure and its internal decision-making processes. This task will not be undertaken here.[5] Making virtue out of the necessity of brevity, we shall deal only with four aspects of the Bank's activity, aspects which largely determine and delimit its influence upon the structures and processes of the international legal order. We shall examine, in sequence, the Bank in its

2. Friedmann, "The Relevance," *supra* note 1, at 10.

3. See, *e.g.*, *id.* at 5, 12-14; Friedmann, "General Course," *supra* note 1, at 112, 116-18; Friedmann, "Droit de coexistence," *supra* note 1, at 6-7.

4. See in particular, W. Friedmann, G. Kalmanoff, & R. Meagher, *International Financial Aid* (1966). And note the importance attributed to the World Bank in W. Friedmann & G. Kalmanoff, *Joint International Business Ventures* (1961); W. Friedmann & J.P. Beguin, *Joint International Business Ventures in Developing Countries* (1971).

5. For a brief attempt at such a study see the first part of the "World Bank Study," *supra* note (*). A comprehensive study of the problem which, however, does not deal specifically with the World Bank, is R. W. Cox, H.K. Jacobson *et al.*, *The Anatomy of Influence* (1973).

formal capacity as a subject of international law, acting within established legal structures; the Bank's explicit lawmaking activities; its indirect, though deliberate, efforts at influencing certain substantive international law principles; and finally, other lawmaking effects of World Bank action, the intended or unintended impact on international law of some of its other policies and activities.

I. THE BANK AS SUBJECT OF INTERNATIONAL LAW

Personality and Immunities

It is generally accepted that the World Bank has the legal capacity necessary for carrying out its functions.[6] The Articles of Agreement provide expressly for the Bank's "full jurisdictional capacity," but this relates to domestic (municipal) law only. International personality is based on inference alone. In the Articles of Agreement as well as in the Bank's actual practice, the "Bank" is an entity distinct from its members; indeed a complex network of rights and duties exists between it and them. International personality being a matter of degree, several "international law subjects" of differing kinds coexist in today's international society; mere ascription of international personality does not by itself answer the concrete questions of the extent and even the quality of their rights and duties. The Bank's personality is legally defined and therefore delimited and constrained by its function; institutional actions which go beyond functional requirements may be denied international legal validity. Definition of function thus becomes determination of validity.

The Bank's privileges and immunities are governed by Article VII of the Articles of Agreement.[7] This "little code" of immunity[8] presents one major peculiarity. The Bank is given jurisdictional immunity only against claims by, or deriving from member states. It is not immune as far as action by private persons are concerned, even when the actions

6. For an excellent succinct discussion of the issues see Broches, "International Legal Aspects of the Operations of the World Bank," 98 Académie de Droit International, *Recueil des Cours* 297, 323 ff. (1959) [hereinafter cited as Broches].

7. Articles of Agreement of the International Bank for Reconstruction and Development, *opened for signature* Dec. 27, 1945, art. VII, 2 U.N.T.S. 134 [hereinafter cited as IBRD Articles].

8. The apposite description is J.F. Lalive's, "L'immunité de juridiction des Etats et des organisations internationales," 84 Académie de Droit International, *Recueil des Cours* 205, 365 (1953).

are not related to the Bank's borrowing activities.[9] A significant distinction is thus established between the rights of member countries, in their dealings with the Bank as borrowers or guarantors, and those of private persons as lenders or otherwise.

The rationale for restricting the immunity of financial agencies in their capacity as borrowers is said to have "a functional basis,"[10] namely, the need to reassure the international financial community, the institution's potential lenders. C.W. Jenks has argued that such differential treatment may be attributed to a distinction similar to the one between public and private acts (acts *de iure imperii* and *de iure gestionis*) in the so-called restrictive theory of sovereign immunity in domestic law.[11] The point may have validity as to the relationships of members *inter se* or with the Bank in their capacity as "shareholders"; it is questionable when applied to a member in its capacity as borrower or prospective borrower. In the latter case it would not seem that its objective relationship to the Bank is any more or any less *de iure imperii* than that of a Bank lender. It is true, however, that member states have rights and presumably remedies which are not available to private parties, precisely because they are the Bank's shareholders.[12]

Whatever the exact qualifications, the practical significance of these

9. Art. VII, sec. 3. The relevant sentence provides:

> Actions may be brought against the Bank only in a court of competent jurisdiction in the territories of a member in which the Bank has an office, has appointed an agent for the purpose of accepting service or notice of process, or has issued or guaranteed securities.

Identical provisions are found in the charters of the other members of the World Bank Group (IFC and IDA), as well as of the Inter-American Development Bank. It is interesting to note, however, that the related provision (art. 50(1)) in the Articles of Agreement of the (much more recently established) Asian Development Bank limits the Bank's vulnerability to private actions not arising out of its financial activities.

> The Bank shall enjoy immunity from every form of legal process, except in cases arising out of or in connection with the exercise of its powers to borrow money, to guarantee obligations, or to buy and sell or underwrite the sale of securities, in which cases actions may be brought against the Bank in a court of competent jurisdiction in the territory of a country in which the Bank has its principal or a branch office, or has appointed an agent for the purpose of accepting service or notice of process, or has issued or guaranteed securities.

A similar, but more succinct, formulation is found in the Articles of Agreement of the African Development Bank (Art. 52).

The Inter-American Development Bank has had experience in such litigation. See, in particular, Lutcher Celulose e Papel v. Inter-American Development Bank, 382 F.2d 454 (D.C. Cir. 1967). For an earlier (1954) unpublished case involving the World Bank, in which the Bank apparently did not plead immunity, see 13 M. Whiteman, *Digest of International Law* 50-51 (1968).

10. Broches, supra note 6, at 309.

11. C.W. Jenks, *International Immunities* 152 (1961).

12. Once again, the Asian Development Bank's Articles of Agreement (Art. 50, sec. 2) spell out more clearly the legal situation:

> Notwithstanding the provisions of paragraph 1 of this article, no action shall be

provisions is difficult to determine. The importance of the distinction may be greatest on a symbolic plane: the Bank's dual status, as business enterprise (bank) and international public body (development agency), makes it vulnerable to private creditors but immune to public borrowers.

Legal Character of Loan Agreements

An inquiry into the legal character of a legal instrument can be an exercise in doctrinal irrelevancy but it may also be used to raise (although not necessarily answer) important real problems. Determination of the legal character of the Bank's loan agreements may affect such practical issues as the proper procedures for the instruments' entry into force and the determination of the applicable law. Yet, as in so many other instances, it is the actual practice of the Bank, rather than doctrinal debate, that provides answers to these questions.

The Bank itself has not asserted expressly any doctrinal position, but its practices are consistent with the views advanced by its legal officers. Their argument may be summarized as follows: [13] The World Bank possesses international personality; in its transactions with governments, it acts under international law. Its agreements with them, therefore, concerning loans granted to a government or guarantees for loans granted to independent agencies, come themselves under international law; they are public international agreements. The view is reinforced by invocation of a standard clause in the Bank's General Conditions according to which the legal situation of the parties to these instruments is not affected by national laws. [14] Furthermore, acceptance by the UN Secretary-General of the Bank's loan and guarantee

> brought against the Bank by any member, or by any agency or instrumentality of a member, or by any entity or person directly or indirectly acting for or deriving claims from a member or from any agency or instrumentality of a member. Members shall have recourse to such special procedures for the settlement of controversies between the Bank and its members as may be prescribed . . . in contracts entered into with the Bank.

A similar provision is also found in the Inter-American Development Bank Articles of Agreement (Art. XI, sec. 3(2)), which otherwise follow the World Bank pattern.

13. The summary is based on Broches, *supra* note 6, at 339-73. See also Broches & Boskey, "Theory and Practice of Treaty Registration with Particular Reference to Agreements of the International Bank," 4 *Nederlands Tijdschrift Voor International Recht* 159 ff., 277 ff. (1957); G. Delaume, *Legal Aspects of International Lending and Economic Development Financing* 81-85 (1967); R. Lavalle, *La Banque Mondiale et ses filiales: Aspects juridiques et fonctionnement* 166-79, 226-31 (1972) [hereinafter cited as Lavalle].

14. "9.01. The rights and obligations of the Bank, the Borrower and the Guarantor

agreements for registration under article 102 of the UN Charter leads to an inference that they are admitted as international legal instruments.[15] Concerning loan agreements where the borrower is not a state, a different argument is advanced. These are not formally governed by international law, since the borrower is not a subject of international law. Yet each loan agreement is part of a complex transaction, a most significant element in which is the guarantee agreement with the government of the state in whose territory the project is located; the government becomes a "joint co-debtor" and guarantees the loan unconditionally "as a primary obligor, and not as surety merely." It follows that the loan agreement itself "partakes of the international character" of the other dealings between Bank and member state. At the very least, this process results in "the internationalization of the loan agreement to the extent of insulating it from the effect of municipal law."[16]

This line of argument is attractive but not wholly persuasive. The basic point at issue is the attempted overclarification of the status of the Bank's instruments. All agreements of international "persons" are not necessarily treaties. That the UN Secretariat has accepted to register loan and guarantee agreements is surely not enough to indicate acquiescence by the international community. No serious problem has ever arisen involving this practice, the point was at issue in no dispute, there has been no obvious reliance on such registration by the Bank or its co-contractors. As to inferences from that single clause in the General Conditions, these are at best uncertain, since the clause might be understood as merely asserting the overriding applicability of the contract, as "law for the parties."[17] The international legal order is moving in the direction of recognizing more than one kind of international agreements. Instruments not wholly subject to any national legal system may be subject to international law without becoming thereby identical with international treaties. The World Bank's loan

> under the Loan Agreement, the Guarantee Agreement and the Bonds shall be valid and enforceable in accordance with their terms notwithstanding the law of any state, or political subdivision there, to the contrary."

IBRD, *General Conditions Applicable to Loan and Guarantee Agreements* (Jan. 31, 1969) [hereinafter cited as IBRD, *General Conditions*]. The provision's language has been carried over from earlier loan regulations.

15. It is interesting to note that the Bank was initially quite reluctant to register its agreements and it was the UN Secretariat that kept insisting that it should. See E. Mason & R. Asher, *The World Bank Since Bretton Woods* 562-63 (1973) [hereinafter cited as Mason & Asher].

16. Broches, *supra* note 6, at 352.

17. As C.W. Jenks has put it, "this suggests that the rights and obligations arising under these instruments constitute an autonomous body of law." C.W. Jenks, *The Proper Law of International Organizations* 179 (1962).

and guarantee agreements may be considered as international agreements of a new type, partly similar to but also partly differing from classical diplomatic agreements.[18] Such an approach underlines existing ambiguities and difficulties; it does not attempt to resolve, by doctrinal fiat, the very real problems of the manner in which such "peculiar" instruments function.

The actual practice of the World Bank is compatible with this position. If loan and guarantee agreements are to be treated as formal public international law instruments, it would seem to follow that, within each borrowing state, the treaty-making procedure prescribed by constitutional and other rules should be used. This is indeed the practice in several states but many governments do not treat Bank agreements in this manner. The World Bank has coped, on the whole successfully, with this problem by requiring, in its General Conditions, that as a precondition of the instrument's effectiveness, "evidence satisfactory to the Bank" must be furnished to the effect that the agreement is "duly authorized" and "constitutes a valid and binding obligation."[19] The Bank thus makes sure that the borrowing (or guaranteeing) government will be legally bound, but avoids specifying the precise legal form to be used. The government is free to follow the treaty-making route or any other route as long as it reaches similar results. Practice has varied somewhat over the years. References to treaty-making procedures or to legislative action have been on occasion inserted in agreements. In recent years the Bank has strongly encouraged borrowing states to enact broad provisions authorizing government departments to conclude loans or to guarantee loans to independent agencies.

The Bank's formal avoidance of an express doctrinal stand on this point is of a piece with its failure expressly to provide that international law is applicable. As a complex institution of long standing, it avoids taking doctrinal legal positions when it does not have to. It prefers to deal with particular legal problems, leaving it to scholarly commentators to draw their own doctrinal conclusions. Its demand for evidence satisfactory to it on the internal validity and binding force of loan and guarantee agreements has been defended on the ground that the lender has a significant interest in assuring itself of the validity of the borrower's commitment in the borrower's own law.[20] The point is

18. Such a view, in differing formulations, has been advanced by several legal scholars. See Adam, "Les accords de prêt de la Banque Internationale pour la Reconstruction et le Développement," 55 *Rev. Générale Droit International Public* 41 (1951); J. Salmon. *Le rôle des organisations internationales en matière de prêts et d'emprunts. Problèmes juridiques* 223-32 (1958); Lavalle, *supra* note 13, at 166-79.

19. IBRD, General Conditions, *supra* note 14, Tss. 1.01, 11.02.

20. Broches, *supra* note 6, at 403.

well taken. From yet another angle, the demand for evidence satisfactory to the Bank follows from the lack of insistence on formal criteria of commitment (such as a general undertaking to utilize treaty-making procedures); it is a functional equivalent of rigid formal requirements. It may even be argued that the flexibility the Bank allows itself on this point supports the position advanced earlier concerning the non-traditional legal character of its agreements more than it does the attribution to them of a strict treaty character.

International Law Constraints on World Bank Activities

As a subject of international law, the World Bank operates within a framework of legal constraints established by international law. Some are found in the Bank's Articles of Agreement; others may be drawn from principles of customary law and other sources of the law of nations. One can only raise the question of the existence and identity of such constraints and briefly explore a few issues in illustration.

A most important area in which World Bank activities touch upon international law principles, and are presumably limited, or at least shaped, by them, is the extent of the Bank's involvement in the domestic affairs of borrowing countries. The international law principles concerning respect for the sovereignty and independence of nations are *prima facie* presumed to be binding on international organizations as well as states. Proper study is only possible in concrete context. What constitutes permissible or impermissible interference, on the part of a particular international organization, depends on the organizztion's functions, the subject matter of its action, etc. As already noted, it is a principal feature of the international law of cooperation that it allows, indeed promotes, much greater "vertical" penetration than traditional international law would permit. Still, certain limits must exist; not all kinds or degrees of penetration are equally lawful or legally proper. Certain tests and conditions must be met. It is submitted that no single criterion is sufficient freely to permit any and all penetration (or "interference.")

In the case of the World Bank, the issue of interference in the domestic affairs of borrowing countries is usually met by three sets of arguments: First, the Bank is a "cooperative institution"; its aims coincide with those of its borrowers, there is no opposition or conflict in their interests. Joint action by the Bank and the borrowing nation is a manifestation of such cooperation, not an interference by the former into the affairs of the latter. Secondly, the Bank's concerns are predominantly technical; they relate to the better use of scarce resources, determined in an objective manner. They are not political in that they do not involve questions of policy as to which reasonable (competent) people may differ. Thirdly, everything the Bank does in a state it does with the consent of that state; that consent suffices to remove any taint of improper intervention.

The last of these arguments is the most difficult to rebut. International law has traditionally been perceived as consisting of rules of *ius dispositivum,* from which states could depart at will. No action, by a state or any other entity, could be deemed unlawful, if the state affected had consented to it. Recently, however, demands for the recognition of certain fundamental principles of *ius cogens* have been forcefully expressed and have found wide acceptance. At the same time, various kinds of "pressure," short of the use of force, have been denounced as impermissible coercion, whose presence vitiates any expression of consent. Such considerations are surely relevant to the case at hand.[21] The other arguments raise issues of fact as well as law. The Bank is not outside international politics. Its policies and decisions reflect in part, in varying degrees, the interests and perceptions of the Bank's "major shareholders." Even to the extent that the Bank plays the role of an impartial technical advisor, problems remain. Technical advice is not necessarily nonpolitical, in its implications and impact. In matters affecting vital national decisions, the lack of imperialistic design does not suffice as a defense against charges of interference. It is not only the intent behind external involvement that counts. Independence, individual or collective, does not mean freedom from "bad" domination alone; it means capacity freely to decide on vital issues, free of all coercive dictation by external forces.

A second area in which international law principles are important is that of the relations between international organizations. The Bank's relations with the United Nations and the various affiliated agencies[22] have been predictably marked by a competition for primacy, which in the aid field goes under the name of "responsibility for coordination." In spite of this, however, and of the institutions' reluctance to define more clearly their legal relations, there has been considerable actual cooperation, with several United Nations agencies providing their expertise in areas where the Bank has been relatively weak or inexperienced and vice-versa. A similar pattern of cooperation and competition has prevailed in the Bank's dealings with the OECD and its Development Assistance Committee and with the several regional development banks.

A clearcut case of conflict with the United Nations arose over the

21. And *cf.* the "World Bank Study," note (*) *supra.*

22. The topic is covered in detail in Mason & Asher, *supra* note 15, at 559-94 (chapter 17).

Bank's granting of loans to the Union of South Africa and Portugal, in the face of United Nations resolutions condemning them for their racial and colonial policies. The incident is too well-known to merit detailed discussion here.[23] It illustrates vividly the Bank's perception of its role and its relationship to the United Nations. The final outcome—even though, as in all compromise solutions, both sides came out victorious—shows clearly the actual freedom of movement the Bank possesses within its largely self-imposed constraints. It is significant, moreover, that the incident was dealt with throughout in terms of legal relations between international institutions, not as a case of breach of norms that had already hardened into custom.

Another related question is that of the World Bank's dealings with *de facto* or otherwise irregular governments. The Bank's General Counsel and an associate have touched on this problem in a joint paper,[24] stressing that, in this as in other matters, the Bank "has always been solely concerned with the establishment of a proper legal framework for its loans." The authors acknowledge that dealings with *de facto* governments involve additional risks; "purely legal considerations" are not sufficient. "A practical judgment must ultimately be made" balancing possibilities and risks and considering a number of factors: recognition by other countries and international organizations, transitional or not character of the government, "the past record of the country concerned" (especially with respect to political stability), the nature of the project and its controversial or not character, etc. The authors further note that "it is the Bank's policy to allow a certain period of time to pass" to determine the government's stability and attitude.

A study of the Bank's record in this area would be of great interest but detailed information is lacking. One relatively well documented case is that of Greece.[25] Because of its failure to settle prewar public foreign debts, Greece did not for a long time receive any World Bank loans. In the early 'sixties debt settlement negotiations reached relative completion. After signature of several settlement agreements, the Bank

23. For the relevant documents see *UN Juridical Y.B. 1967,* at 108-32; 6 *Int'l Legal Mat'ls* 150-87 (1967); and 8 *id.* 444, 1339 (1969). And *cf.* Bleicher, "UN v. IBRD: A Dilemma of Functionalism," 24 *Int'l Organization* 31 (1970); Lavalle, *supra* note 13, at 139-47; Broches, discussion, in *Foreign Development Lending: Legal Aspects* 296 (S. Rubin ed. 1971) [hereinafter cited as *Development Lending*].

24. A. Broches & P. Sella, "International Bank for Reconstruction and Development," in *Development Lending, supra* note 23, at 79, 82-84.

25. Information is publicly available because a U.S. Congressional subcommittee conducted a hearing on the matter, where competent American officials provided details. See House Committee on Banking and Currency, Subcommittee on International Finance, *Proposed World Bank Loan to NIBID of Greece. Hearing of March 14, 1968* (1968). On another aspect of the Greek case see text accompanying notes 50-51 *infra.*

began, in 1966, negotiations with a potential borrower, a development bank. Approval of the loan was held up until signature of the last debt settlement, which was effected on December 22, 1967. By that time, however, Greece was under a military regime which had overthrown the constitutional government of the country. The Bank was apparently prepared to grant the loan yet decided to delay further because of a then recent unsuccessful counter-coup (December 13, 1967). By early March 1968, the Bank had presumably assured itself concerning the attitudes and stability of the Greek military regime and it proceeded to grant the loan. Most likely, it had also noted its continuing recognition by other governments, which had been in some doubt at the end of December. Later political and economic developments in Greece appear not to have troubled the Bank's perception of the regime's stability and the country's creditworthiness. In the next six years, six more loans were made to that country, the latest one in early 1974, after considerable domestic disturbances and in rapidly worsening economic conditions, in particular, heavy foreign indebtedness and high inflation, both directly attributable to the military regime's economic policies.

II. EXPLICIT LAWMAKING ACTIVITY OF THE WORLD BANK

Like other international actors, the World Bank contributes directly to the development of international law through the proposal and drafting of, and participation in, international conventions, especially conventions establishing international institutions. The creation of the International Finance Corporation and the International Development Association has received enough attention to make further discussion here unnecessary.[26] The Bank's involvement may be seen as expressing its decision to shape its own institutional goals, methods, and limits: the World Bank Group must be seen more accurately as a single multifaceted institution rather than as several discrete entities.[27] More recent explicit lawmaking has led to the conclusion of the Convention

26. *Cf.* B.E. Matecki, *Establishment of the International Finance Corporation and United States Policy* (1957); D. Baldwin, *Economic Development and American Foreign Policy, 1943-62* (1966) [hereinafter cited as Baldwin]; J.P. Sewell, *Functionalism and World Politics* (1966) [hereinafter cited as Sewell]; Mason & Asher, *supra* note 15, at 79-82.

27. As Jean Touscoz has astutely noted, creation of affiliated institutions was, in the nineteen-fifties, the Bank's principal response to Third World criticism. Touscoz, "Le groupe de la Banque Mondiale face aux exigences du développement," 6 *Revue Belge de Droit International* 10 (1970).

on the Settlement of Investment Disputes Between States and Nationals of Other States and the establishment of the related Center. Certain suggestions for the establishment of a multilateral investment insurance agency are still at the stage of, rather hopeless, proposals. Finally, in considering the Bank's lawmaking activities it is useful briefly to refer to some issues in which, by contrast, the Bank has avoided becoming involved.

Convention and Center for the Settlement of Investment Disputes

The Convention for the Settlement of Investment Disputes Between States and Nationals of Other States has its origins in proposals for an international code for the protection of private foreign investment that surfaced in the mid-fifties.[28] After study of these proposals, the United Nations Secretariat as well as the Bank's General Counsel concluded that such a project faced insuperable doctrinal and practical obstacles; they both favored instead the conclusion of a procedurally-oriented convention instituting a system of conciliation and arbitration.[29] A draft was prepared by the World Bank staff, discussed extensively with member governments and, in its final form, approved by the executive Directors on March 18, 1965. The convention entered into force on October 14, 1966, after deposit of twenty ratifications. It has by now been ratified by sixty-five states.[30]

The Convention establishes an International Center for Settlement of Investment Disputes (ICSID), composed of representatives of each contracting state, and administered by a Secretary-General. Its task is to facilitate conciliation and arbitration of disputes between a member state and a foreign investor national of another member state. Consent of all parties concerned is required; it may be given generally and in advance and cannot be unilaterally withdrawn. Once consent has been

28. For a review of early proposals see Fatouros, "An International Code to Protect Private Investment—Proposals and Perspectives," 14 *U. Toronto L.J.* 77 (1961); Fatouros, "The Quest for Legal Security of Foreign Investments—Latest Developments," 17 *Rutgers L. Rev.* 257, 275-84, 293-301 (1963) [hereinafter cited as Fatouros, "The Quest"].

29. United Nations, "The Promotion of the International Flow of Private Capital. Progress Report by the Secretary-General," February 26, 1960, U.N. Doc. E/3325, paras. 191-208; "Further Report," May 18, 1961, U.N. Doc. E/3492, paras. 259 ff; Note by A. Broches, IBRD General Counsel, Aug. 28, 1961, repr. in 1 *History of the Convention on the Settlement of Investment Disputes between States and Nationals of Other States* pt. 1, at 1 (1968).

30. For a brief history, detailed analysis, and exhaustive bibliography of the convention see Broches, "The Convention on the Settlement of Investment Disputes between States and Nationals of Other States," 136 Académie de Droit International, *Recueil des Cours* 331 (1972) [hereinafter cited as Broches, "The Convention"].

given, the Center is in a position to neutralize any attempt by a party to prevent proceedings through non-cooperation or abstention. Arbitral awards issuing from such proceedings are binding on all contracting parties.

The origins of the Convention lie in the same concern for improving the private foreign investment "climate" that has affected other aspects of the World Bank's work. The Convention's basic purpose is to provide protection to foreign investments - in order to create confidence among prospective investors and thus encourage investment in less developed countries.[31] Although concern for host country interests is not wholly absent, their protection is not one of its primary objectives, host states being presumed capable of defending their own interests through domestic law measures.

The establishment of systematic, clear and flexible procedures for the settlement of investment disputes is no doubt a valuable contribution. The drafters of the Convention have attempted to balance the benefits and sacrifices that developed countries and foreign investors on the one side and less developed countries on the other are being asked to make. Yet, the system established leads to a new legal equilibrium which ultimately favors foreign investors. In the absence of institutional procedures or substantive principles which assure an effective process of legal change promoting the development of less developed countries, the establishment of a stable system of quasi-judicial adjudication of legal disputes is objectively in support of the economic (and political) *status quo*.

The very structure of the Convention illustrates the basic problem. Three categories of parties are directly involved: the host countries, the countries of origin of the investment, and the private firms - nowadays mainly multinational enterprises—with their headquarters in the latter and their investments in the former. But only the two first categories are contracting parties to the Convention; and only members of the first and third categories may be parties to a dispute to be settled on the basis of the Convention. There is a critical gap here. The states party to the

31. The IBRD General Counsel places differing emphasis on each of the elements of the assertion made in the text. He writes:

> The Convention has sometimes been regarded as an instrument for the protection of private foreign investment. This characterization is one-sided and too narrow. The purpose of the Convention is to promote private foreign investment by improving the investment climate for investors and host States alike.

Id. at 348. He proceeds to cite the "balanced" character of the convention and the ability of host states to enforce arbitral awards abroad. Yet, he states one paragraph later:

> From the legal point of view the most striking feature of the Convention is that it firmly establishes the capacity of a private individual or a corporation to proceed directly against a State in an international forum. . . .

Id. at 349.

Convention may limit their own future freedom of action, but the investors' freedom is left unaffected, save to the extent to which it is limited by enforcement of arbitration awards against private parties. The imaginative structure of possible partial, limited and successive consent built by the Convention, an important juridical achievement in itself, may still be inadequate, for the parties' legal freedom of consent is only part of the picture. The very existence of the Convention, the fact that a host state may now bind itself in a definite and fairly effective manner toward investors, changes the previously existing bargaining position of investors and host countries.

A final important trait of the IBRD Convention is its being administered by the World Bank. A recent study pointed out that "the Bank has the necessary competence and authority in capital importing as well as capital exporting countries to assure the efficient operation of a regulatory system."[32] The operative word is "authority." The Bank appears prepared to exercise its "authority" to bring about compliance with the Convention. In a discussion of the problem, the Bank's General Counsel observed:

> As to sanctions, it has been stressed by several speakers that these could come into existence through the intervention of the World Bank . . . We try to be very discreet and not to exercise even moral pressures on potential signatory countries or in order to obtain the effective application of the convention by the signatories. But it is possible that if a state violates a very clear obligation expressed in the Convention, the organs of the Bank and of other affiliated institutions and perhaps the financial and foreign assistance community will be seriously reticent to receive favorably requests for assistance on the part of that state . . . In the presence of the Convention, if a state consents to the competence of the Center, if there is an award rendered against that state and it does not execute that award, we have a very clear and very definite situation and problems of conscience will not be present in the same manner as they would otherwise be or will not be present at all.[33]

Use of the Bank as the executive organ of the international financial community raises most acutely the question of its proper role. It is not self-evident that policing host state infractions in this area is necessarily part of the Bank's assigned task.

32. M. Amadio, *Le contentieux international de l'investissement privé et la Convention de la Banque Mondiale du 18 Mars 1965* 60 (1967).

33. A Broches, discussion, in *Investissements etrangers et arbitrage entre Etats et personnes privées—La Convention BIRD du 18 mars 1965* 129-130 (1969) [translated from the French].

Multinational Investment Insurance Agency

This project, too, had its origins in the failure of investment code proposals in the 'fifties, combined with the continuing operation of national investment insurance programs, first by the United States and then by other capital-exporting countries. Once again, the OECD has been active in focussing attention on possible multilateral arrangements. The World Bank's first response to these proposals was a thoughtful staff study,[34] analyzing in some detail possibilities and problems and taking on the whole a less than enthusiastic position. Insistent formal pressures by OECD and; somewhat paradoxically, by UNCTAD[35] brought the matter back into the Bank's hands. On the basis of a draft agreement submitted by the OECD in June 1965,[36] the IBRD staff prepared and communicated to governments in November 1966 a draft of Articles of Agreement for an International Investment Insurance Agency. A new amended draft was circulated in August 1968. After years of seemingly rather desultory discussions, the projected agreement did not materialize. In 1972, the Bank prepared a last draft, which was circulated with a memo in the spring of 1973 suggesting to Member governments that further initiatives would have to be taken by them, rather than the Bank.[37] The chances of revival and general adoption of the project appear at this time minimal.

There are significant differences among the several draft proposals, as far as one can tell under the limitations imposed by the Bank's selective secrecy policy. An autonomous agency is generally envisaged, affiliated with the World Bank, in which both developed and less developed—or in the terms more appropriate to the topic, capital-exporting and capital-importing—countries would participate. The exact manner and extent of participation in the financing and

34. IBRD, *Multilateral Investment Insurance. A Staff Report* (1962). For some early discussions see Brewer, "The Proposal for Investment Guarantees by an International Agency," 58 *Am. J. Int'l L.* 62 (1964); Fatouros, "The Quest," *supra* note 28, at 284-93; Broches, "International Investment Guaranties: Possibilities and Problems," 56 *Proc. Am. Soc'y Int'l L.* 81 (1962).

35. *Cf.* UNCTAD-I, Recommendation A. IV. 12, para. 7 (1964); UNCTAD-II, Resol. 33 (II) (1968).

36. Its text was printed and discussed in Martin, "Multilateral Investment Insurance: The OECD Proposal," 8 *Harv. Int'l L. J.* 280 (1967). For a perceptive analysis of the problems of such proposals see G. Schwarzenberger, *Foreign Investments and International Law* 170-81 (1969) [hereinafter cited as Schwarzenberger].

37. *Cf. IBRD/IDA Annual Report* 69 (1973). Successive drafts have been kept on a restricted circulation basis, being made available to governments with no injunction of secrecy but provided to independent scholars at the discretion of Bank officials. However the 1972 draft and the accompanying Staff Memorandum have been reprinted in a U.S. Congressional document, *The Overseas Private Investment Corporation: A Critical Analysis*, prepared for the House Committee on Foreign Affairs (Sept. 4, 1973), at 130 and in T. Meron, *Investment Insurance in International Law* 259 (1976).

governance of the agency[38] by the capital-importing countries is one of the matters in the debate. Other controversial issues concern the agency's subrogation rights and dispute settlement. It is on these issues and on several of their immediate consequences, that the project seems to have found its principal difficulties.[39] For present purposes, at any rate, the Bank's involvement, even if somewhat unenthusiastic, illustrates its concern for the protection of private foreign investment as a condition for a desirable world economic order.

Areas of Inaction

The World Bank's initiatives in support of private foreign investment are rationalized, in formal and informal argument, in terms of the necessity to establish and uphold certain principles of public policy. These principles do not represent merely special interests of the developed countries or of the international financial community, but work, in the long run, in the common interest of both developed and developing countries. When private investors feel secure, foreign investment in less developed countries on fair and proper terms is encouraged—so the argument goes.

The argument is cogent, once certain assumptions are made as to the possible role of private foreign investment in development. While several less developed countries are no longer willing to accept these assumptions,[40] it may be argued that they are built into the very

38. The 1972 draft provided for limited participation by capital-importing countries in the financing of working capital and administrative expenses; only "sponsoring" (*i.e.*, investing) countries would share in the payment of claims for losses. The complicated formulas for election and voting power of Directors in that draft resulted in an equal number of Directors from capital-importing countries and capital-exporting countries, but with 65% of the votes in the hands of the Directors of the latter; on certain "sensitive" issues a qualified majority was required.

39. The underlying problems are the lack of a common perception of the proper role of private foreign investment, on the part of capital-importing countries, and the differing, indeed competitive, perceptions of national interests in this area, on the part of the capital-exporting. National insurance programs can resolve such fundamental questions by political fiat, although recent congressional concern in the United States over the underlying assumptions and ultimate effects of the investment guarantee program show that serious questions arise even in that relatively simpler context. International arrangements need a more definite consensus. A homogeneity in the perceptions of national interest among developed countries far greater than that which obtains in fact would seem to be needed before a multilateral scheme can seriously advance. The same objection, *mutatis mutandis,* may be raised concerning the scheme proposed by Georg Schwarzenberger, *supra* note 36, at 180-81, which envisages a program established and operated solely by capital-importing countries. There is even less homogeneity of perception among these countries than there is among the capital-exporting.

40. Critical descriptions of the role of foreign investment and the possible benefits to be derived from it are increasingly found in the literature on development. Obviously, in so complex an area no simple either/or proposition can be valid. For some valuable moderate discussions see G. Myrdal, *The Challenge of World Poverty* 325-35 (1970); K. Griffin, *Underdevelopment in Spanish America* 117-48 (1969).

existence and structure of the World Bank by the Articles of Agreement; they constitute part of its ideological premises and are binding on its officers who are not free to question them. The argument is not wholly persuasive, given the broad actual margin of freedom in setting policies that the Bank enjoys. Be that as it may, other issues may also be raised. First, it may be questioned whether a particular measure or policy is necessary or appropriate to bring about the intended effects. Second, and more important, the public record may be read to show reluctance on the part of the Bank to undertake to strengthen, establish or enforce principles of public policy which would impose constraints on the freedom of action of foreign investors and thus better insure the fairness of the terms on which investments are made. Two examples of such reluctance will be mentioned; the many possible modalities of Bank action and inaction in this respect cannot be exhaustively rehearsed.

One area is that relating to restrictive business practices on the part of foreign investors. The Bank does not treat such considerations as pertinent to its work.[41] From what we know, it has never sought to study and analyze the problem in order to evolve any principles of policy—whether to be incorporated in a treaty, to be administered by a special institution, or to be part of the Bank's general policies. No doubt, national policies and interests in this area are by no means easy to reconcile; there is no easily perceived single set of international principles of conduct. Nonetheless, as recent studies by and for the UNCTAD Secretariat[42] indicate, the question is not totally intractable and it is possible to formulate a number of propositions, of a fair degree of certainty and general applicability, concerning clearly noxious restrictive practices.

A second area, related to the preceding, is that of the growth and activities of the multinational enterprise. Its peculiar characteristics, namely, the amount of resources at its disposal, its flexibility, its ability to move on many levels, in many directions and in several countries, have given it a significant ability to evade national regulation in developed countries, but especially in less developed ones.[43] The relevance of such problems to development is obvious and the area

41. *Cf., e.g.,* L. Nurick, discussion, in *The Effectiveness of International Decisions* 459 (S.M. Schwebel ed. 1971) [hereinafter cited as *The Effectiveness*].

42. See, among the most recent, UNCTAD* *Restrictive Business Practices, interim Report* (1971); R. Vernon, *Restrictive Business Practices* (1972); *Restrictive Business Practices in Relation to the Trade and Development of Developing Countries: Report by the Ad Hoc Group of Experts* (1974). For efforts in a related and partly overlapping area, *cf.* UNCTAD, "The Possibility and Feasibility of an International Code of Conduct on Transfer of Technology," June 6, 1974, U.N. Doc. TD/B/AC.11/22.

43. For further elaboration on this issue, see Fatouros, "The Computer and the Mudhut: Notes on Multinational Enterprise in Developing Countries," 10 *Colum. J. Transn'l L.* 325 (1971); Fatouros, "Problèmes et méthodes d'une réglementation des entreprises multinationales," 101, *J. Droit Int'l* 495 (1974).

seems particularly suitable for the World Bank's talents. Yet, the Bank has not addressed itself to the question.

The Banks's reluctance to act in such areas must be attributed to a number of factors: the management's perception of the institution's proper role; its assessment of the actions and policies likely to be approved or objected to by member states, especially the Bank's "major shareholders," and the international financial community; and, its perception of the principal areas where international action is needed. The Bank appears to proceed on the assumption that host governments possess both the legal competence and the actual capacity to impose conditions relating to public policy on foreign investors. In reality, however, the capacity to initiate, elaborate and implement such policies and decisions is sorely missing in most less developed countries. The same lack of skills and institutional structures which makes it necessary for the Bank to provide "development guidance" often makes developing countries unable to control and regulate effectively the foreign companies seeking to invest, or that are already established, in them. The technical expertise and familiarity with the methods, opinions, and actors in the international financial community which make the World Bank effective in its other work could be usefully employed to assist in the establishment of principles and institutions imposing effective constraints on foreign investors in deference to the interests of developing countries and to common world interests.

III. INDIRECT LAWMAKING: STRATEGIC NONLENDING

The World Bank's use of the "negative sanction" of refusing to lend in order to promote certain favored principles and policies has received by now considerable attention and study.[44] In the present context, one particular set of principles is of immediate concern, both because it directly relates to a controversial and rapidly changing area of international law and because it is a topic on which the Bank's policy has been relatively clearly stated and firmly adhered to. At issue is the Bank's well-established practice of refusing to lend to states that have not settled their public foreign debts, or that have expropriated foreign-owned property or cancelled concessions or other contracts held by foreign investors without "appropriate" compensation.

External Debt

Emphasis on the need for settlement of external debts by borrowing countries is found very early in the World Bank's history. Its Second Annual Report (Sept. 1947) points out:

44. *Cf.* Baldwin, *supra* note 26, at 37. See also references cited note 3 *supra*.

> There exist today a number of deterrents to the free flow of private capital . . . to the underdeveloped nations. If the Bank, by use of its resources, its influence and the technical specialists on its staff, can help to remove some of these deterrents, it will have achieved an important task in the development field.
>
> The first step is the improvement of the credit position of many of the countries concerned. There are several things which those underdeveloped nations with a poor credit standing can do to improve their position. Perhaps the most effective would be for them to clear up their external debt records. It is not suggested that every underdeveloped country with outstanding foreign bonds in default should or could resume payment on its bonds in accordance with their original terms . . . On the other hand, it is important for the countries concerned to give clear evidence of their desire to do their utmost to reach fair and equitable agreements with their creditors.

After mentioning the possibility of setting up "an impartial body of technical experts" to recommend "just settlements" of such debts the Report further qualified its suggestions:

> [T]here is no suggestion that all remedial measures which may appear necessary in the case of any given country must be completed before that country may qualify for a loan from the Bank . . . But while the Bank is willing to consider making a loan concurrently with the adoption by the borrowing country of whatever program for financial and monetary stability and the reestablishment of credit may appear necessary in the particular case, the Bank cannot assist a country which neither has such stability or credit nor a willingness to take action to achieve them. Such lending would be neither prudent nor productive. Furthermore, it would cause the Bank to lose the confidence of the investment community, and with it, the very source of the major portion of its loanable funds.[45]

This first statement is quite typical. First, the question of external debt settlement is placed in the context of "improvement of credit standing;" it thus becomes a factor in the Bank's judgment of a country's creditworthiness.[46] Subsequent references to the problem are

44. IBRD, *Second Annual Report* 13 (1947). For an important restatement of the argumentation see also IBRD, *Fifth Annual Report* 13 (1950).

46. But *cf.* D.E. Lilienthal, *The Journals of David E. Lilienthal The Harvest Years 1959-1963,* at 481 (1971):

> "Credit-worthy," said George [Woods] scornfully; "that's the word they use. That means saying *No.*"

The entry, dated June 20, 1963, reports a discussion with Mr. Woods upon his becoming President of the World Bank.

often couched in such more general terms as "re-establishment of credit" or action "to rehabilitate its credit standing." Secondly, borrowing countries are not asked immediately to resume payment but only to make clearly evident their willingness to reach agreement concerning payment. Yet, it is not at all obvious how such willingness can be made manifest otherwise than through actual conclusion of debt payment settlements. Bank press releases and statements celebrate conclusion of settlement agreements, not mere willingness to settle.[47] Thirdly, the requirement is attributed in part to the necessity, for the Bank, to retain the confidence of the international financial community. Finally, the non-absolute character of the requirement is stressed: it is not a condition for granting loans, but only an element in the Bank's over-all judgment. Similar assertions, stressing one or more of these elements, are found in many subsequent Bank statements and reports. In later years, the "success" of this policy is also noted - with becoming modesty rather than triumph.[48]

A review of the Bank's practice further illustrates the importance attributed to this requirement. The very first loan to a less developed country, the 1948 loan to Chile, was long delayed because of discussions on the settlement of defaulted external debts. The day after agreement between foreign bondholders and Chile was reached, two loans to the country were announced.[49] Another prime illustration is the case of Greece, which was refused, on this ground, any loan from the World Bank for twenty years. Efforts to settle matters were made at several points but they seem to have petered out.[50] Negotiations with the foreign debt bondholders proceeded at a glacial pace; the first agreements, concerning some of the several series of debts, were concluded in the early 1960's, the last one being signed in December 1967. A $12.5 million loan which had been held in suspense over two years to await the settlement of the prewar debts was immediately granted.[51]

By the late 'sixties, most outstanding prewar public debts had been

47. See text accompanying notes 49-51 *infra*.

48.

> This position appears in various cases to have had considerable influence on the policies of its member countries. Whatever the degree of influence, it is an observable fact, for example, that nearly all those member countries which had defaulted external debts outstanding at the end of the war have begun – and in most cases successfully concluded – negotiations for settlement.

IBRD, *Tenth Annual Report* 35 (1955). And *cf.* IBRD, *Twelfth Annual Report* 5 (1957); IBRD, *Policies and Operations* 41 (1963).

49. See Mason & Asher, *supra* note 15, at 155-57. *Cf.* IBRD, *Fourth Annual Report* 20 (1949).

50. For brief discussions, see the sections on external debt and its problems in the successive World Bank annual reports.

51. See Mason and Asher, *supra* note 15, at 221-226. For much useful information and analysis, see, P.B. deFontenay, *Multilateral Debt Renogotiations: 1956-1958* (IBRD-IDA, Economics Dept., Report No. EC-170, 1969).

settled. In the meantime, new problems appeared, and the Bank's interest shifted to another direction. By this time, it had become obvious, and increasingly so in the early seventies, that many developing countries were burdened with far too heavy external debt service obligations. These debt obligations arose in the main out of direct public and private loans to governments and public authorities, rather than the flotation of bonds, as in the prewar period. Along with other international institutions, in particular the OECD, the World Bank has assisted in negotiations leading to rescheduling of various countries' debts. The Bank has been most reluctant to agree to rescheduling of debts to itself, although its continued lending at a steady, or increased, rate to countries with debt service difficulties might be construed as being, whether explicitly or not, a form of debt rescheduling.[52]

Nationalizations

The Bank's policy on expropriations of foreign-owned property, or cancellations of agreements with foreign investors, without appropriate compensation has followed the same line as its debt settlement policy. Although there was no explicit mention of this problem in the 1963 edition of the *Policies and Operations* handbook, related statements of Bank officials were reported in the press in the late 'fifties. The current formulation is quite comprehensive:[53]

> The Bank, charged under its Articles to encourage international investment and itself a creditor, has a direct interest in the creation and maintenance of satisfactory relations between its members and their foreign creditors. Where the Bank is contemplating lending to a member country whose credit is impaired by the existence of a dispute over a default on its foreign debt or over compensation for foreign-owned property which has been expropriated, it must first be satisfied that the government is making serious efforts to reach a fair and equitable settlement and that there are good prospects that the matter will be cleared up satisfactorily.[54]

The policy is more precisely expressed in a 1971 "Operational Policy Memorandum," recently allowed to be made public:

52. For related details, see *id.* at 35-37.

53. IBRD/IDA, *Policies and Operations* 44-45 (1974 ed.).

54. The language in the previous edition of this handbook (1971) was slightly, but significantly, different. It spoke of "serious efforts to reach a fair and equitable settlement" and required in addition that the Bank be satisfied "that there are good prospects that the matter will be cleared up satisfactorily." For criticism of that language, see Escott Reid, *Strengthening the World Bank* 62-63 (1973).

> The Bank will not lend for projects in a country if it considers that the position taken by that country with respect to alien owners of expropriated property is substantially affecting its international credit standing. Nor will it appraise projects in such a country unless it has good grounds for believing that the obstacles to lending will soon be removed.

The memorandum further provides that reasons for not proceeding with lending operations include:

> (1) A denial of liability for compensation coupled with a refusal to submit the dispute to judicial or quasi-judicial determination.
>
> (2) An admission of liability for compensation in general terms coupled with either an offer of compensation obviously inadequate in amount or terms of payment and not subject to negotiation, or else a failure to negotiate in good faith over such matters or to submit them to judicial or quasi-judicial determination.
>
> (3) A failure, in the Bank's judgment, to make reasonable efforts to arrive at settlement.
>
> (4) A failure to pay and, if required, to transfer abroad compensation in accordance with the terms of an agreed settlement, a judicial decree or an arbitral award.[55]

A review of recent informal discussions shows remarkable lack of clarity on the subject. The confusion is partly due to the Bank officials' insistence on the qualifying words rather than the basic policy. As the Bank's General Counsel put it, "we have not been advocates of the dispossessed, but advocates of amicable settlement . . . "[56] The Deputy General Counsel, on his part, described this policy as essentially similar to the "Hickenlooper Amendment"[57] in U.S. law.[58] Yet, when in another discussion an eminent United States lawyer (not a Bank official) described Bank policy in these terms,[59] an Executive Director of the

55. Repr. in Mason & Asher, *supra* note 15, at 747 n. 11. An earlier version was referred to and paraphrased in T. Hayter, *Aid As Imperialism* 15, 31 n. 7 (1971) [hereinafter cited as Hayter]; her mention of the document was criticized by Bank officials as a breach of confidence (*cf. id.* at 202), although it is hard to see how reference to a document setting out a publicly acknowledged policy is objectionable, unless the language or tone of the document does not wholly correspond to those of public statements—which does not appear to be the case, at least for the 1971 version.

56. Broches, discussion, in *Development Lending, supra* note 23, at 298.

57. 22 U.S.C. Sec. 2370(e) (Supp. IV, 1974).

58. Nurick, discussion, in *The Effectiveness, supra* note 41, at 462.

59. Monroe Leigh, discussion, in *Foreign Investment in Latin America: Past Policies and Future Trends* 71 (J. Lacey ed. 1970).

Bank denied the existence of any such policy.[60] A member of the Bank's legal staff proceeded then to explain it, noting among other things that:

> How much effort is required is, from the World Bank's point of view, largely an objective question, not a subjective one . . . The Bank asks whether the potential borrower has done enough to reassure the international investment community that it is not irresponsible or hostile. If the international investment community actually responds to these efforts, or if the World Bank considers it ought to respond to the gestures that have been made, that suffices for the Bank.[61]

There is even more confusion and uncertainty concerning the actual instances in which this policy has been invoked, partly, no doubt, because rarely if ever is this issue the sole operative factor. The Bank's General Counsel admits that the policy was an important factor in refusing loans to the U.A.R. but has denied that it was applied in the case of Tanzania.[62] Others have mentioned, in addition, Algeria, Burma, Ceylon, Iraq, Zaire, Indonesia, Brazil, Costa Rica, and Guatemala as countries against which the policy has been applied.[63] In the early 'seventies, the issue arose with particular intensity, after takings of property of U.S.-based multinational firms in Western Hemisphere countries.[64] At the 1972 Annual Meeting of the Board of Governors, the Chilean delegate attacked the World Bank management for refusing loans to Chile because of its nationalization of U.S. copper companies.[65]

The precise degree of flexibility and sophistication the Bank brings to the application of its policy concerning nationalization is a much

60. A. Ramirez-Eva, discussion, in *id.* at 78; and *cf. id.* at 79-80.

61. P. Szasz, discussion, in *id.* at 109. For a simpler formulation of the policy, by yet another World Bank official see Raphaeli, "IMF, the World Bank Group, and the Developing Countries," in *Multinational Cooperation: Economic, Social and Scientific Development* 151, 168 (R.S. Jordan ed., 1972):

> A country is considered uncreditworthy when it has behaved in a manner which defies the accepted canons of international financial morality by defaulting on debt obligations or expropriating foreign assets without entering serious negotiations concerning compensation.

62. Broches, discussion, in *Development Lending, supra* note 23, at 298-99.

63. Hayter, *supra* note 55, at 31 n. 7; Mason & Asher, *supra* note 15, at 747.

64. See Mason & Asher, *supra* note 15, at 338. And *cf.* M. Hudson, *Super Imperialism. The Economic Strategy of American Empire* 164-65 (1972) [hereinafter cited as Hudson].

65. IBRD-IFC-IDA, 1972 Annual Meetings of the Boards of Governors, *Summary Proceedings* 53-59 (1972). And see Sigmund, "The 'Invisible Blockade' and the Overthrow of Allende," 52 *Foreign Affairs* 322, 327-29 (1974); Letter from A. Lowenthal to the Editor, 52 *id.* 644; Collins, "Tightening the Financial Knot," in IDOC (Int'l N. American ed.) No. 58, 70, at 73-74 (1973).

debated question. The Bank insists that its policy is no rough and ready rule of thumb and that its decisions are made with great concern and care. The impression of a number of students of Bank practice does not fully uphold this view.[66] Be that as it may, the problem remains that the policy itself is open to question. The fundamental issue is whether it is part of the World Bank's task, as an international institution of near-universal membership, to police the behavior of borrowing countries toward foreign investors and foreign bondholders, in compliance with an intangible and indeed nonexistent code of conduct of the "international financial community." Justifications in terms of pragmatic considerations, such as the pressures of creditor countries and the "objective" effect on a country's credit standing, do not suffice.

There is no doubt that the Bank's "major shareholders" are concerned by the threat of nationalization of their nationals' assets by host states. The United States, in particular, has long put special emphasis on the issue and has recently asserted that such considerations will determine the votes of its representatives in the governing boards of international financial agencies.[67] Yet, while some responsiveness to creditor nations' pressures is realistically to be expected from an international organization, there are limits to be observed. The Bank cannot refuse to carry out its purposes merely because this is desired by one or more influential creditor countries. Not every desire of the Bank's "major shareholders" is equally legitimate. A policy must be justified on its own terms. This is where the second pragmatic argument, creditworthiness, comes in. There is, no doubt, a connection between a country's outstanding default on external debts or an uncompensated expropriation and its credit standing abroad. But this connection is neither simple nor certain. Ever since the nineteenth century, the external debts of poor countries have been notorious for excessive burdens, often murky origins, and widespread speculation before and after default. Foreign investors have been aware of these problems and have reacted accordingly. Expropriations, too, have often affected property whose legal status was at best dubious or whose origins were linked to colonial conquest or gunboat diplomacy. While such complexities may be absent in some cases, or may not suffice to justify

66. See, Mason & Asher, *supra* note 15, at 745-49; Reid, *supra* note 54, at 62-63; Ohman, "Comment: A Social Radicalism," in *The World Bank Group, Multilateral Aid, and the 1970's* 27, 29 (J.P. Lewis & I. Kapur eds. 1973). And *cf.* Hudson, *supra* note 64, at 164-65.

67. *Cf.* President Nixon's Jan. 19, 1972 Statement on Economic Assistance and Investment Security in Developing Nations, 66 *Dept. State Bull.* 152, esp. at 154 (1972); and the so-called "Gonzalez Amendments" to the International Development Association Act (22 U.S.C. Sec. 284j (1970), *as amended,* Supp. II, 1973) and the Inter-American Development Bank Act (22 U.S.C. Sec. 283r (1970), *as amended,* Supp. II, 1973). And *cf.* Letter from A.C. Weed to the Editors, *Foreign Policy* No. 8, at 161 (Fall 1972).

the host government's action, yet, the whole problem cries out for sympathetic inquiry and specific decisions in concrete contexts, rather than "rules of thumb," however labelled. The potential harshness of private commercial action in this connection is tempered, in some cases and to some extent, by the operation of the very profit motive which moves it. In their pursuit of gain, the members of the international financial community are often willing to forgive a lot of infractions of formal "rules," especially when the victims are their competitors. Paradoxically, the World Bank, being both a bank and a development institution, is likely to end up being harsher and more rigid than private commercial entities in its policies against borrowing countries.

The relevance of such questions to international law is self-evident. The legal treatment of foreign property is a highly controversial and, at best, still undecided issue in current international law.[68] The legal debate over external public debt defaults has now subsided considerably, not because doctrinal differences have disappeared but because the importance of external public loans in the international market has radically diminished as far as less developed countries are concerned. The controversy over expropriation of foreign property, which started in earnest in the nineteen 'twenties, continues unabated and is far from being resolved. Yet, international law does not appear to have moved in the direction favored by the Bank. Successful or not, however, the World Bank's strenuous efforts to strengthen the traditional rules concerning the treatment of foreign investment raise serious questions concerning the propriety of such activity on the part of a near-universal international agency whose principal mission is to foster development.[69]

IV. LAWMAKING EFFECTS OF BANK ACTIVITY: EXPANDING THE AREA OF INTERNATIONAL CONCERN

To discuss comprehensively the indirect, and sometimes not intended, lawmaking effects of World Bank activities would require a

68. It is, of course, often asserted that the matter is well-settled and beyond reasonable dispute; *cf.* Haight, "United Nations Affairs," 2 *Int'l Law.* 162, 163-64 (1967): "It is a gross perversion of the facts to refer to 'a vanishing consensus' on the basic principles of international law governing the protection of foreign private investments." Such assertions must be seen as what they are, namely, a well-known method of arguing in favor of a particular legal position.

69. The type of policy-making involved in this instance differs significantly from that found when governing bodies of international organizations pass formal resolutions which reflect the views of a majority of members and not those of opposing members. In such cases, it is the institution's political organs that are acting, not international civil servants; moreover, the decisions in question usually lack any coercive character, directly or indirectly.

much longer study. In its role as lender the Bank is faced with a variety of incidental legal problems, for instance, where projects are constructed on territory disputed by two nations or relate to the use of international rivers. Although the manner in which the Bank deals with these issues affects international law, these cases will not be discussed here. The study will focus instead on three main areas, some of them only indirectly connected with the Bank's lending activities. A first area is that of mediation in international disputes; the second concerns the role of the Bank as leader of consortia and "consultative groups;" and the third is that of "development guidance" or technical assistance.

A fourth important area of impact is that of the legal system and the legal institutional structure of borrowing countries. This topic is studied in some detail in a companion study[70] and will not be dealt with here, except to point out that, to the extent that the Bank exerts its influence over the choice of development projects, in borrowing countries and over their institutional structure, organization and eventual operation, the established allocation of jurisdiction in the international legal process—that is to say, in oversimple terms, the distinction between a nation's external and internal affairs—is radically revised. Eventual effects on international law are far reaching.

International Mediation

The World Bank—more accurately, its top management—has, on occasion, played the role of mediator in international disputes. In a recent book, the three following major instances were studied in some detail: [71] the Bank attempted unsuccessfully to help settle the dispute over the nationalization of the oil industry in Iran; it brought about an agreement between Pakistan and India concerning the utilization of the waters of the Indus river; and it tried to arrange for the financing of the Aswan High Dam in Egypt by the Western powers. It lent subsequently its "good offices" to Egypt and the Suez Canal Co. for the settlement of the latter's claims arising from the canal's nationalization. The President of the Bank also assisted in the settlement of a dispute between the City of Tokyo and French bondholders of a 1912 loan. A more recent and far more complicated case is the involvement of the World Bank Group at the early stages of the Pakistan-Bangladesh conflict, at a time when this was not yet an international dispute. The Bank's ap-

70. See "World Bank Study," *supra* note (*).

71. Mason & Asher, *supra* note 15, at 595-643. There is considerable literature by now on each of these incidents, although most of it (except in the case of the Indus River) does not focus on the Bank's role. But see D. Snow, "The World Bank as an Actor in International Politics," (unpublished Ph.D. dissertation, Indiana University, 1969) [hereinafter cited as Snow].

parent effort to inquire into the situation in East Pakistan and to back its findings with suspension of economic aid to Pakistan by itself as well as by the members of the Bank-led consortium represents an important positive involvement of the Bank in international political affairs.[72]

In terms of the impact on the international legal process, not much can be derived from these incidents. They are too few and depend too much on their particular facts. The most important aspect is the very presence of the Bank, its availability as an institution and as a source of trustworthy officials to be utilized as mediators in disputes which, in addition to their political importance, have significant economic and financial aspects. The Bank would appear to be more successful in this role when it attempts to influence less developed countries than when it deals with developed ones, but the evidence is too disparate to allow generalizations. Even the use of the Bank's resources as a lender, which must be held to account in major part for its success in the Indus case, by no means assures success. Finally, the Bank's acting, in several of these cases, essentially as a mediator between a nation and the "international financial community" provides another important glimpse of the Bank's position.

Aid Coordination

The Bank's role is more susceptible of definition with respect to its activities in coordinating aid to developing countries. In the consortia and consultative groups it has sponsored it is by no means a mere participant, nor is it, as the usual term would have it, a simple "coordinator." As John White has pointed out "[w]hen the bilateral aid-givers associate themselves with an operation of the World Bank, they are not just agreeing to work together. They are implicitly promoting a particular institution to a position of leadership."[73]

The formal legal aspects of consortia and of consultative groups are limited. In the case of the former, participating (donor) countries are supposed to commit themselves in advance as to the amount of aid they will provide; consultative groups involve no binding pledges of this sort. Over the years, however, the real difference between the two has considerably diminished. Their terms of reference are vague. "They leave plenty of room for manoeuvre, which makes sense so long as there is someone in a position of responsibility with a clear idea of how that

72. For a first brief discussion see Reid, *supra* note 54, at 167-69.

73. J. White, *Pledged to Development* 26 (1967) [hereinafter cited as White]. This section relies extensively on this excellent study. And see also Snow, *supra* note 71, at 176-216; Mason & Asher, *supra* note 15, at 510-28.

room for manoeuvre can best be exploited."[74] That someone, by necessity perhaps as much as by deliberate choice, is the World Bank.

The Bank has nearly full control of the establishment and operation of aid coordination groups. Its favorable attitude, if not its sponsorship, is generally indispensable for a group's creation. The conditions the Bank has established for sponsoring such groups[75] reflect certain objective, operational, reasons but also serve to ensure a dominant role for the Bank. After the group's creation as well, the Bank retains a key procedural role as its formal convenor. It can apply pressure on the recipient country or, for that matter, on the donors, by threatening to call a meeting or by refusing to call one. It plays, moreover, an all-important substantive role. It provides an analysis and evaluation of the recipient's economy and of its needs, problems and proposals. The periodic review of the country's "performance" by the group is chiefly based on the Bank's studies and judgments. While in theory its role is advisory and technical, in reality the Bank comes very close to making most judgments and evaluations on behalf of the donors. At the same time, it works closely with the recipient in formulating a development plan and in preparing the submissions to the aid coordination group.[76]

The World Bank's involvement in aid coordination significantly enhances the Bank's influence over the policies of recipient countries. By pooling its own financial, managerial and technical resources with those of donor countries and institutions, the Bank gives up very little of

74. White, *supra* note 73, at 174-75.

75.

(1) the country is receiving substantial external aid from several sources and there is *prima facie* need for coordination;

(2) both the recipient government and the aid-givers representing the bulk of external financing to the country agree that the Bank should organize some sort of coordinating machinery;

(3) there are reasonable prospects that the Bank/IDA will itself be in a position to provide financing for the country's development;

(4) a sufficient volume of projects can be expected to be forthcoming (with the help of technical assistance in project preparation if necessary) to provide an adequate vehicle for external assistance; and

(5) the existence of governmental machinery which offers reasonable prospects that coordination can have constructive results.

IBRD & IDA, *Policies and Operations* 42-43 (1971). In the 1969 edition of the booklet, the last condition was formulated somewhat differently: "Governmental stability and attitudes in the recipient country must be such as to offer reasonable prospects that the coordination effort will have constructive results." *Id.* at 54 (1969). One wonders whether the new formulation represents a change in policy or is merely designed to give an inoccuous appearance to the same policy line.

76. In his valuable study of the World Bank "as an actor in international politics," Donald Snow, *supra* note 71, distinguishes between the Bank's "internal" (within states) and "external" (between states) role. He acknowledges, however, that the distinction breaks down when considering the Bank's aid coordination activities, because their internal and external aspects and functions are intimately related.

its own independence of action and acquires at the same time the ability largely to dispose of, or at the very least strongly to influence the disposition of, the other donors' resources, even though the donors' ability to eventually resist the Bank's proposals cannot be denied.

The Bank could try to have a more important impact on the donor countries' policies. Aid coordinating groups could assume additional responsibilities such as: greater emphasis on fund-raising, better allocation of the aid burden, and a more systematic distribution of functions among donors. The World Bank seems to have resisted such an expansion of responsibilities. The final result is:

> First, in its bilateral relations with the recipient country, the World Bank is prepared in principle to accept an almost unlimited degree of operational involvement. Secondly, in its relations with the bilateral donors, and in the recipient's relations with them also, the World Bank puts its faith in an appeal: "Come, let us reason together."[77]

We may recognize in this description the same pattern we found in other aspects of the Bank's work; that is, the institution is willing, if not eager, to participate in the recipients' domestic decision-making processes, while carefully respecting the donor countries' autonomy of decision-making.[78]

Development Guidance

The World Bank's activities, related and unrelated to lending, which may be brought under this broad heading present one common feature of major importance for international law, namely, the Bank's extensive involvement, and indeed active participation in the recipient countries' domestic decision-making processes, as economic analyst, adviser, creditor and supervisor. This marks a novel and certainly significant development.[79]

77. White, *supra* note 73, at 179-80.

78. This attitude may no doubt reflect the Bank's (*i.e.*, the Bank management's) judgment as to its inability significantly to influence the major donor countries' policies. Experience in the early 1970s, when, in trying to implement the Pearson Commission's recommendations, World Bank President McNamara sought unsuccessfully to increase the number and enhance the work of aid coordination groups, may indicate that this assessment is nothing if not realistic. See Mason & Asher, *supra* note 15, at 526-28; Reid, *supra* note 55, at 146-48. But is realism enough?

79. The nearest precedent in international legal practice might be the institution of "international financial controls," imposed on debtor countries in Latin America and Eastern Europe around the turn of the century. See Andréadès, "Les Contrôles financiers internationaux," 5 Académie de Droit International, *Recueil des Cours* 1 (1924); Strupp, "L'intervention en matière financière," 8 *id.* 1 (1925). Despite the similarities, however, there are signficiant differences in the current world environment and the character, methods and objectives of the principal actors.

A large part of the Bank's development guidance function[80] is discharged in connection with lending such as, for instance: assistance in identifying and formulating projects, prior to actual negotiations with the Bank or during and by means of discussions concerning a loan application; and, assistance in the execution of projects or after their completion, for example, advice to development finance companies and to family planning projects. The Bank also undertakes pre-investment surveys and sectoral studies, either on its own or as agent for the UN Development Program. Finally, the Bank's resident representatives in various regions are charged, along with the general supervision of the projects financed by the Bank Group, with providing assistance and advice to borrowing countries.

Development guidance is not always tied to lending. From the earliest year of its operation, the Bank has, on request, sent special missions to study and report the conditions of a member's economy and the prospects for economic development. The Bank prepares, usually on a confidential basis, annual reviews of the economy of borrowing countries.[81] Finally, the Bank's economic research staff prepares, and increasingly publishes, a great number of studies. The World Bank also provides a considerable amount of training to officials and individuals from less developed countries.

The Bank's development guidance activities assume a multiplicity of forms; increased emphasis is now laid on them in Bank literature. This role of the Bank was initially seen as necessary because of the lack of projects prepared in accordance with the Bank's views and methods.[82] Over the years, however, development guidance has acquired near-autonomous status as a Bank function, although it retains intimate links to lending. That the Bank's advice can be backed by the express or implied promise of loans and credits is one reason for its effectiveness. However, the simultaneous discharge of two discrete functions - lending and advising — cannot help but affect the manner in which each of them is discharged. While the Bank stresses the harmonious relationship between its two roles, it is not difficult to imagine situations where a development guide's advice may have to be at variance with the policies and positions of a lending agency.[83] True, the World Bank has been

80. For a good summary, from a legal standpoint, of the Bank's "technical assistance" activities see Lavalle, *supra* note 13, at 240-47. And *cf.* IBRD & IDA, *Policies and Operations* 47-52, 55-56 (1971); IBRD & IDA, *Annual Report* 61-67 (1972); *Annual Report* 63 ff. (1973).

81. The Bank's findings may be "confidential" even *vis à vis* the state concerned. See Sella, Discussion, in *Development Lending, supra* note 23, at 213: "Our appraisal reports containing all the assumptions we have made and the reasons eventually trickle back to the borrower indirectly. We do not give them directly and I think this is unfortunate."

82. *Cf.* Sewell, *supra* note 26, at 284.

83. Service, or settlement, of old debts is an obvious case where the Bank's advice is affected by its being a lender, as well. Clearly, the Bank *qua* development guide is in no position to recommend debt repudiation or similar measures. The Bank's aversion to nationalization of foreign firms may be another similar constraint.

able increasingly to escape from the confines of the financial community's established truth; it still remains a bank and its approach is necessarily influenced by its character as such. But the development process is far too complex and raises too many novel problems and implications to be dealt with adequately on the basis of bankers' wisdom.

V. SOME TENTATIVE CONCLUSIONS

This essay offers too summary a review of a quarter century of complex and continuing activity on the part of the World Bank to allow anything but the most tentative conclusions - questions and hypotheses rather than actual findings. Yet, established learning concerning the possibilities of international action to promote development is so limited that even such uncertain lights may be of some help.

The first modality of World Bank impact on the international legal process derives from its own existence and action. In a society composed of a hundred and fifty or so full members (*i.e.* states), the addition of one more member, especially one that is both active and powerful, is of significance. Picking up again Wolfgang Friedmann's categories, we might note that the World Bank has been reasonably active in the creation of yet another kind of "international law of coexistence," the law governing the relations among international organizations. In its relations with the United Nations and with OECD's DAC, the Bank has tried to establish legal rules of delimitation and allocation of jurisdiction among equal, or at least equally autonomous, organizations.

A second modality of impact involves the Bank's more or less explicit lawmaking activity, direct as well as indirect, namely, its creation of ICSID and its impact on the international law concerning external public debt and nationalization of foreign property. The effectiveness or success of its work is open to debate. What is important for present purposes is that the Bank's efforts in these areas can only have serious impact on the policies and legal positions of borrowing (*i.e.,* developing) countries. They affect minimally, if at all, the legal position of developed countries.

A similar configuration of stance and attitudes obtains as to the third modality of impact, that arising out of the bank's activities as aid coordinator and development guide. This area might be considered the paradigm of the international law of cooperation: joint activities directed at a common goal, international development; participation of an international agency in the domestic decision-making processes of (borrowing) countries; disregard of traditional rules and limits of international allocation of Jurisdiction. Our study, however, makes evident one important feature of the law of cooperation in this area—it is one-sided, it moves in a single direction. "Cooperation" in disregard of traditional jurisdictional restraints involves primarily, almost exclusively, the borrowing (developing) countries; it hardly exists with respect to the developed countries, whether in their capacity as creditors and major shareholders of the Bank or in that of donor members of consortia. The World Bank's functional, relatively non-political character (in the sense of a lack of immediate involvement in everyday world politics) may give it a certain moral authority, when dealing with developed countries But it is a major factor of strength as against the developing countries. For, in dealing with donor states, or with more politically oriented groups, these countries, individually or as a group, can at least attempt to bargain by trading off political concessions against economic aid (or relative autonomy in handling such aid). They have no equivalent bargaining counters when dealing with the World Bank.

The causes of the lopsided character of the international law of cooperation have been clearly and accurately noted by Wolfgang Friedmann; the long-range as well as the short-run interests of developed and developing countries are quite different. While both pursue their perceptions of national interest, in this as in other areas of international law, and while foreign aid undoubtedly serves certain immediate as well as long-term interests of the donors.

> In any meaningful sense, . . . there is no reciprocity between the interest of the United States or Britain or France in assisting, bilaterally and through multilateral institutions, the development of Tanzania or India or Colombia and the interest of these countries in receiving such assistance.[84]

This also applies to sanctions, which depend upon shorter-run interests. To the extent that the law of cooperation is enforced by means of the granting or withholding of rewards, the borrowing countries are the only ones to be immediately affected. As Friedmann put it:

> By virtue of the expertise of its staff, and with a gradually strengthened financial autonomy, the World Bank has acquired a status where exclusion from eligibility for a loan - or from participation in an international consortium, or availability of advice, would be a severe penalty for the great majority of its members, who are potential borrowers. This of course does not affect the minority of members—the principal

84. Friedmann, "The Relevance," *supra* note 1, at 13.

> capital subscribers—who do not need World Bank loans or technical assistance. To this extent, it must be admitted that there are two classes of members. This is perhaps an inevitable aspect of the world's division into rich and poor nations.[85]

We are dealing here with existing structures of power and influence within the international community. The role of World Bank officials is important but not determinative. No doubt, within the interstices of their constraints, there are things they could have done or can do, directions in which they can move, risks they can take without incurring too strong a reaction from their creditors and major shareholders. Most important, they can be more candid, to themselves as well as to the world outside the Bank; they can more openly recognize the extent to which political realities shape technical and expert choices. Yet, the fundamental problem remains that, as an international institution in a radically unequal world, the World Bank is bound to conform in some manner and to some extent to prevailing power patterns. It can escape from such constraints only at the risk of total ineffectuality.

These constraints may affect quite radically the quality of the international law of cooperation; the lopsided character of the process cannot help but affect the substance of the law. The radical inequalities prevalent in today's world community are thus likely to be reflected in the evolving legal principles and rules, which may tend to impose more limitations upon the weaker members of the international society and allow greater freedom from legal constraints to the more powerful ones. The findings in the present study appear to suggest such a pattern in the legal and institutional relations between the World Bank and its developing and developed members, If equality among nations is to be more than a formal principle and if respect for national autonomy is to be given pride of place among international legal principles, in a manner similar to that in which individual freedoms are protected in democratic constitutional orders, then a fundamental objective of the international legal order should be that the developing

85. Friedmann, "General Course," *supra* note 1, at 117. He noted further that "the increasing influence of the developing countries in the United Nations creates a countervailing factor which greatly reduces the danger of undue pressure." *Id.* This last point may be far more debatable.

It should be noted, moreover, that the granting or withholding of tangible rewards (*e.g.*, loans) is not the only manner in which cooperation is assured. Cross-cultural influences, especially through the presence of a transnational financial (and technocratic) elite, may in many cases play an equally important role. Institutions such as the International Labor Organization may thus influence at least some of their members nearly as much as the World Bank. This is a major conclusion of the collective study mentioned in note (*) *supra*. Evidence of the role of the "international financial community" is found, of course, in all serious studies of the World Bank.

international law of cooperation must make these principles effective. No body of law automatically growing out of functional imperatives can be certain to conform to preferred political and moral values. While the development of an international law of cooperation is a definite advance in the international legal process, great effort is needed to shape it so that it will better serve the interests of the entire world community.

SOME LEGAL ASPECTS OF THE ANDEAN ECONOMIC INTEGRATION

F.V. GARCÍA-AMADOR

I. THE OBJECTIVES AND MECHANISMS OF THE SUBREGIONAL AGREEMENT

The legal aspects of Andean economic integration can best be approached by a brief look at the history of the Cartagena Agreement[1] and at the objectives and mechanisms of economic integration it establishes. This undoubtedly will contribute to better understanding of the legal and institutional framework of this new Latin American integration process.

F.V. GARCIA-AMADOR is Director of the Department of Legal Affairs of the General Secretariat of the Organization of American States. The observations and opinions expressed in this article are attributable only to the author.

Postscriptum. After this paper was prepared and sent for printing, a number of most relevant developments have taken place with regard to the legal validity of the acts of the Andean institutions and the reception given to these acts in national legal systems. On the one hand, there is the special legislation (first in Colombia and afterwards in Venezuela), stating that the Decisions of the Commission of the Cartagena Agreement, which deal with or modify matters that fall within the power of the legislature, have to be submitted for its approval for their entry into force in the country.

In this connection it is worthwhile to mention the 1975 Decisions of the Colombian Supreme Court of Justice, where the unconstitutionality of Colombian Law No. 8 is declared and where the validity *erga omnes* of the Commission of the Andean Agreement is upheld on the basis of the supranational character of some of the powers granted to such a Commission.

In view of the impossibility of adding to this paper a thorough presentation of these developments, the author refers the reader to his book *El Ordenamiento Jurídico Andino, Un Nuevo Derecho Comunitario* (Edicionas De Palma, Buenos Aires). An English version is to be published.

1. Agreement on Andean Integration, *done* May 26, 1969 [hereinafter cited as Catagena Agreement]. An English version of the Cartagena Agreement may be found in 8 *Int'l Legal Mat'ls* 910 (1969). The original Spanish text is available in Instituto para la Integración de América Latina, *Boletín de la Integración*, June 1969. By decision No. 1 of the Commission created by the Agreement on Andean Subregional Integration the latter was designated as the Cartagena Agreement (*Acuerdo de Cartagena*). Though it was signed in Bogotá, the subregional instrument was negotiated and finally agreed upon in that Colombian city. Although not officially so titled, the Agreement also is frequently called the "Andean Pact" (*Pacto Andino*).

Brief history of the Agreement

The origin of the subregional agreement lies in the Bogotá Declaration, signed by the Presidents of Colombia, Chile and Venezuela and the personal representatives of the Presidents of Ecuador and Peru, in the Colombian capital on August 16, 1966. In that Declaration the Presidents stated that:[2]

> 2. Consequently, we have decided to promote joint action to obtain with LAFTA the approval of specific measures which will fulfill the goals contained in this declaration and, especially to promote joint action for the adoption of practical formulas that will provide an adequate treatment in accordance with the conditions of our countries, which are characteristic of those with relatively less developed economies, or of insufficient market. These are the indispensable means to attain a harmonious and balanced development of the region within the spirit of the Montevideo Treaty.[3]

In conformity with the aims expressed in the foregoing paragraph, the authors of the Declaration made a number of specific recommendations, one of which was the adoption of a system of programmed lowering of duties that would take into consideration the different levels of development by countries and by sectors, and the elimination of all barriers that impede the trade of articles originating in the region. In addition, an immediate program of action was agreed upon, which included some concrete commitments and a mechanism for their prompt and effective fulfillment.

A second and most important step toward Andean subregional integration was the one taken by the Heads of the American States at the meeting held in Punta del Este, Uruguay, April 12-14, 1967. In their Declaration[4] the Presidents of America decided, in connection with LAFTA, *inter alia,*

> To promote the conclusion of temporary subregional agreements, with provision for reducing tariffs within the subregions and harmonizing treatments toward third nations more rapidly than in the general agreements, in keeping with the objectives of regional integration. Subregional tariff

2. An English version of the Bogotá Declaration was published in OEA/Serie A/X-IV/CIAP/54, at 9 (1966) [hereinafter cited as Bogotá Declaration].

3. *Id.*

4. Declaration of the Presidents of America, April 14, 1967, in Inter-American Institute of International Legal Studies, *Instruments Relating to the Economic Integration of Latin America* 395 (1968).

> reductions will not be extended to countries that are not parties to the subregional agreement, nor will they create special obligations for them.[5]

This first definition of the so-called "subregional agreements" was complemented by another passage of the Declaration which declared that "[t]he countries of relatively less economic development will have the right to participate and to obtain preferential conditions in the subregional agreements in which they have an interest."[6] Thus agreement was reached at the highest political level to promote the conclusion of the subregional agreements conceived of in the Bogota Declaration, and in this way to promote, within the framework of LAFTA,[7] economic integration processes capable of ensuring more harmonious and balanced development in the region through the more accelerated, dynamic integration of a group of countries with insufficient markets and relatively less developed economies.

To implement the Punta del Este decisions the LAFTA organs took several steps. First, the Council of Ministers met in Asunción, Paraguay, in August and September, 1967, and adopted two resolutions: a) Resolution 202, requesting the Conference of the Contracting Parties of the Montevideo Treaty to approve the regulations to which subregional agreement should be subject, and b) Resolution 203, by which the bases of the subregional agreement that had been submitted by Colombia, Chile, Ecuador, Peru and Venezuela were approved. That same resolution delegated to LAFTA's Permanent Executive Committee the authority to verify the compatibility of the subregional agreement that was to be subscribed to with the bases referred to above, and with principles enumerated in the second article of Resolution 202. The Conference was requested to examine during its regular session the progress of the agreement and its adequacy for achieving the principal objectives of the Montevideo Treaty.[8] Next, the Conference of the Contracting Parties met in December of the same year and approved, by its Resolution 222 (VII), the "Regulations to be applicable to the subregional agreements."[9] As will be seen in the following section, this

5. *Id.* art. II, *para.* 2, subpara. d.

6. *Id.*

7. In regard to this aspect the Declaration explicitly says that "all the provisions set forth in this section fall within or are based upon the Treaty of Montevideo."

8. Treaty Establishing a Free Trade Area and Instituting the Latin American Free Trade Association, *done* Feb. 18, 1960, in Inter-American Institute of International Legal Studies, *Instruments Relating to the Economic Integration of Latin America* 207 (1968) [hereinafter cited as Montevideo Treaty]. The Spanish text of Resolutions 202 and 203 may be found in Instituto para la Integración de América Latina, 2 *Derecho de la Integración* 161, 162 (1968).

9. *Id.* at 165. An English version of the resolution may be found in 7 *Int'l Legal Mat'ls* 851 (1968).

resolution contains the rules as well as the fundamental principles governing the legal and institutional relationships between LAFTA and the Andean Group.[10]

Negotiations for the conclusion of the subregional agreement itself still took some time and the agreement was not signed until May 26, 1969. In accordance with Resolution 203, as well as Article 110 of the Cartagena Agreement, it was submitted to the LAFTA Permanent Executive Committee which, on July 9th of the same year, declared it compatible with the Montevideo Treaty. The Agreement entered into force on October 16, 1969, the date on which the third "act of approval" (*acto de aprobación*) was communicated to the LAFTA Executive Secretariat, as provided for in Article 10. The Agreement was signed by only five of the six current Member Countries (Bolivia, Colombia, Chile, Ecuador and Peru). Venezuela did not sign it until February 13, 1973, and therefore had to follow the somewhat elaborate procedure of adherence provided for in Article 109.[11]

Objectives and mechanisms

The essential purposes and aims of the subregional agreements are evident from the Declarations of Bogota and of the Presidents of America as well as from the resolutions of LAFTA organs. Obviously, these purposes and aims appear much more elaborate when viewed in the light of the objectives and mechanisms of the Cartagena Agreement. To facilitate the brief description that follows, the text of Chapter I of the Agreement[12] is set forth below:

Chapter I

OBJECTIVES AND MECHANISMS

> *Article 1.* The present Agreement has as its goals: to promote a balanced and harmonious development of the Member States, to accelerate this development through economic integration, to expedite their participation in the integration processes as stipulated in the Montevideo Treaty, and to create a climate favorable to the conversion of LAFTA into a common market, all of these designed to secure the

10. "Andean Group" (*Grupo Andino*) is another expression which, though not officially sanctioned, is frequently used to designate this subregional economic integration process.
11. See section II(a) *infra*.
12. Cartagena Agreement, *supra* note 1.

progressive improvement of the living standards of the peoples of the Subregion.

Article 2. A balanced and harmonious development must be conducive to an equitable distribution of the benefits resulting from integration of the Member States by effecting a reduction of the existing discriminations that aggravate them. The achievements of the process should be periodically assessed, taking into account, among other factors, its effect on the expansion of global exports of each State, the conduct of its trade balance with respect to the Subregion, the development of its gross territorial product, the generation of new employment, and its capital formation.

Article 3. To achieve the goals set by the present Agreement, the enumerated operations and measures shall be employed, *inter alia*:

(a) Coordination of economic and social policies, and unification of domestic law in pertinent fields;

(b) Joint programming, intensified subregional industrialization processes, and execution of Sectorial Programs of Industrial Development;

(c) Greater acceleration in the trade liberalization program than that adopted generally within the LAFTA framework;

(d) A common external tariff, attained by progressive stages through a minimum common external tariff;

(e) Programs directed toward stimulation of development in the agricultural and livestock sector;

(f) Channelling of resources from inside and outside the Subregion to provide investment financing necessary to the Integration Process;

(g) Physical integration; and

(h) Preferential treatment to be accorded to Bolivia and Ecuador.

Article 4. For the better achievement of the present Agreement, the Member States shall undertake the necessary efforts to seek adequate solutions for the problems arising from the land encirclement of Bolivia.

Articles 1 and 2 of the Agreement are explicit. Essentially the idea is to promote a balanced and harmonious development of the Member Countries, to accelerate this development through economic integration and to create a climate favorable to the conversion of LAFTA into a common market. These broad objectives would be achieved by the mechanisms and measures enumerated in Article 3.

Chapter III of the Agreement provides for the "coordination of economic polity and development planning," the first of the mechanisms enumerated in Article 3. It was under one of the provisions of this chapter that the well-known Decision 24 was adopted, that is, the common system for treatment of foreign capital and trademarks, patents, licenses and royalties, or so-called "Andean Foreign Investment Code."[13] Two other important decisions have been adopted by the Commission under provisions of Chapter III: Decision 46, on the uniform system to govern multinational enterprises,[14] and Decision 49, on directives to serve as a guide for the unification of legislation on industrial incentives in the Member Countries.[15] Also worthy of mention is Decision 22, on permanent procedures and machinery necessary to achieve the harmonization of policies and the coordination of the development planning of Member Countries.[16]

The next chapter of the Cartagena Agreement deals with another mechanism: "industrial programming." In order to achieve the goals set forth in Article 32, the Commission approves Sectorial Programs of Industrial Development, to be jointly implemented by member countries. So far only one sectorial program has been approved, that on the metal mechanic sector, despite the efforts of the Commission and the Board to prepare and approve another on the petrochemical industry.[17]

The "liberalization program" of the Agreement is governed by the elaborate provisions of Chapter V. This mechanism "has as its goal the elimination of charges and restraints of all kinds encumbering the importation of goods originating in the territory of the Member Countries."[18] "The Liberalization Program," states Article 45, "shall be automatic and irrevocable, and shall include all products, in order to attain total liberalization not later than 31 December 1980," and "[r]estraints of all kinds shall be eliminated not later than 31 December 1970," according to Article 46.

Some of the articles that follow set forth the functions of the subregional organs in connection with the products that are to be reserved for Sectorial Programs of Industrial Development. A number of decisions have been taken in the performance of such functions.[19] Other provisions empower those organs to prepare a schedule of goods not being produced within any of the subregional countries, nor

13. An English version of Decision 24 may be found in 11 *Int'l Legal Mat'ls* 126 (1972).

14. An English version of Decision 46 may be found in *id.* at 357.

15. Decision 49 was approved in December 1971. Except for one or two, the decisions of the Commission and the resolutions of the Board have been published in Spanish only in document form with no other reference than the date of the session on which they were approved.

16. Decision 22 was approved in December 1970.

17. Decisions 57 and 57a were approved in July-August and September 1972, respectively.

18. Cartagena Agreement, *supra* note 1, art. 41.

19. Decisions 25 and 26, approved in December 1970, and 59 and 60, approved in December 1972.

reserved for any sectorial programs, and to select those to be reserved for production in Bolivia or Ecuador.[20]

Chapter VI of the Agreement contemplates both a common external tariff, to be fully operative by December 31, 1980, and a minimum common external tariff to be approved by the Commission prior to December 31, 1975.[21] The first step taken to implement these provisions was the approval by the Commission of the minimum common external tariff for the goods that are included in the first stage of the Common Schedule described in Article 4 of the Montevideo Treaty. This particular tariff, which is contemplated in Article 49 of the Cartagena Agreement, was to be applied by Colombia, Chile and Peru as of April 14, 1970.[22] The next step was the approval of the minimum tariff itself, that is, the tariff contemplated in Articles 63 and 64 of the Agreement.[23] Certain special provisions should be mentioned; for instance, the rules on the common external tariff established by Sectorial Programs governs with respect to those products subject to the Programs.[24] Article 66 authorizes the Commission to modify the levels of common tariffs in the measure and at the times considered desirable for the reasons specified in the Agreement.[25]

The other mechanisms of Andean economic integration are no less noteworthy than those mentioned. As regards the "measures on agriculture and livestock,"[26] the Member Countries are to coordinate their national policies and their plans for agro-livestock development, taking into consideration the objectives prescribed in the Agreement.[27] Insofar as "competitive commercial practices"[28] are concerned, the Commission has already adopted the "rules indispensable to forestall or to remedy any practices which might constitute unfair competition within the Subregion, such as 'dumping' undue price manipulation, . . . "[29] As to the "safeguard clauses,"[30] the Agreement contemplates, first, the case of a Member Country that finds itself in one of the situations, covered in Chapter VI of the Montevideo Treaty, caused by factors alien to the liberalization program of the Agreement; in such a

20. Resolution 7 of the Board, in force since September 1972 and Decisions 27, 51 and 61 of the Commission, approved in December 1970 and March 1972, respectively.

21. Cartagena Agreement, *supra* note 1, arts. 61, 63, 64.

22. Decision 12,. approved in April 1970.

23. Decision 30, supplemented by Decision 33, approved in December 1970 and March 1971, respectively.

24. Cartagena Agreement, *supra* note 1, art. 65.

25. This power was exercised through Decision 30, approved in December 1970, with respect to minimum tariff levels established by Decision 12.

26. Cartagena Agreement, *supra* note 1, ch. VII.

27. *Id.* art. 69.

28. *Id.* ch. VIII.

29. *Id.* art. 75. See Decision 45, approved in December 1971.

30. Cartagena Agreement, *supra* note 1, ch. IX.

case the country may invoke the safeguards consonant with the provisions of that Chapter and of pertinent resolutions.[31] A second case occurs when, as the result of the imposition of the liberalization program of the Agreement, serious disadvantages are caused for the economy of a Member Country, or a significant sector of its economic activity; in such a case the country may, with advance authorization of the Board, apply corrective measures of an emergency nature and in a non-discriminatory manner.[32]

Another mechanism of the Cartagena Agreement deals with the origin of goods.[33] The provisions of this chapter are not substantive and merely entrust the subregional organs with functions relating to the adoption of measures necessary to classify the origin of goods[34] and to establish specific requirements of origin for certain products.[35] Acting under the latter provision the Board has adopted two resolutions.[36] "Physical integration"[37] is a mechanism designed to solve infrastructural problems that unfavorably affect the process of economic integration of the subregion; such action may be exercised principally in the fields of energy, transportation and communications.[38] On the basis of this and other provisions of Chapter XI the Commission has adopted two decisions.[39] Under Chapter XII (Financial Matters) the Member Countries coordinate their national policies in matters of finance and payments to the extent necessary to expedite achievement of the goals of the Agreement.[40]

The last mechanism enumerated in Article 3 is thoroughly regulated in Chapter XIII of the Agreement (Special Regime for Bolivia and Ecuador). The special regime is defined as follows: "In the progressive elimination of the differences presently existing in the development of the Subregion, Bolivia and Ecuador shall enjoy special treatment to permit them to achieve a more accelerated rate of economic

31. *Id.* art. 78. Chapter VI of the Montevideo Treaty, *supra* note 8, contains elaborate provisions on the subject especially with respect to the situation and conditions in which a Contracting Party is authorized to adopt safeguard clauses.

32. Cartagena Agreement, *supra* note 1, art. 79. By its Resolution 20, approved on February 13, 1973, the Board declared unwarranted a request of Peru for authorization to apply corrective measures under Article 79. A third case is contemplated in the Agreement: when a monetary devaluation effected by one Member Country alters the normal competitive conditions (Art. 80).

33. Cartagena Agreement, *supra* note 1, ch. X.

34. *Id.* art. 82.

35. *Id.* art. 83.

36. Resolutions 1 and 18, approved on April 26, 1971 and January 7, 1974, respectively.

37. Cartagena Agreement, *supra* note 1, ch. XI.

38. *Id.* art. 86.

39. Decisions 56 (International Transportation by Road) and 71 (Creation of a Physical Integration Council), approved in March 1972 and May-June 1973.

40. Cartagena Agreement, *supra* note 1, art. 89.

development, through effective and immediate participation in the advantages of area industrialization and liberalization of trade."[41] The same article provides that, to achieve this aim, the subregional organs shall propose and adopt the necessary measures, in conformity with its rules. Then, in sections corresponding to the various mechanisms, the Agreement stipulates special treatment for the respective fields (*e.g.*, industrial policy, commercial policy, common external tariff). Both the Board and the Commission have already adopted numerous measures to discharge their responsibility in the achievement of the objectives of the special regime.[42]

II. RELATIONSHIP WITH THE LAFTA LEGAL ORDER

In the preceding section we observed the important links and relationships that exist between the process of subregional integration and LAFTA. Their juridical and institutional aspects are of fundamental interest in the study of Andean law.

The question of compatibility

The first of these aspects involves the "compatibility" of the Cartagena Agreement with the basic treaty of LAFTA (the Montevideo Treaty), and, as is stated in Resolution 222 (IV), with "its protocols and other instruments that constitute the legal structure of the Association." Although the compatibility of subregional agreements has been formally accepted, in principle, by virtue of the Declaration of the Presidents of America and of subsequent resolutions of the LAFTA organs, it is interesting to know the reasons the question of compatibility was raised and the criteria contributed to its solution. Furthermore, the declaration of compatibility of the Agreement with LAFTA by the LAFTA Permanent Executive Committee resolved the question only in regard to the original basic instrument of Andean integration. As we will see, the question of compatibility can just as easily be posed in regard to other subregional agreements to be signed in the future, and to certain aspects of the Cartagena Agreement or of the "secondary law" that it generates.

As has been indicated in a thorough study that was made of the

41. *Id.* art. 91.

42. For instance, Decisions 29, 34 and 65, approved in December 1970, March 1971 and September 1972, respectively.

question of compatability of the Agreement with LAFTA, from the juridical point of view it is a matter of "knowing how to avoid the infringement of the commitments assumed by a group of countries signing an agreement of subregional integration upon the commitments assumed by those same countries participating with an entirety of states in the process of global integration."[43] Among the second group of commitments, the most-favored-nation clause stipulated in Article 18 of the Montevideo Treaty is stressed in particular.[44] How is it possible to overcome the evident, or at least apparent, incompatibility between this commitment, agreed upon by all Contracting Parties in the Treaty, and, for example, the commitment of a group of them to a special lowering of duties that does not extend to the remaining Contracting Parties?

Cárdenas and Peña describe different formulas that were tested, particularly in LAFTA itself, such as "unanimous renunciation" by the Contracting Parties of the exercise of the rights emanating from the most-favored-nation clause, implementation of this renunciation by a protocol of amendments to the Treaty in accordance with Article 60, and a "functional" interpretation of Article 18.[45] The latter approach, to which the two authors lean, seems to rest on a solid foundation in light of the Montevideo Treaty. First of all, the most-favored-nation clause is not applicable absolutely in the context of the Treaty; the Treaty authorizes exceptions in those cases that concern facilitation of frontier trade and in cases of non-extensive concessions in favor of relatively less developed countries.[46] In addition to other arguments, such as the one related to the trade liberalization program of the Treaty, an analogy exists between the question of compatibility of subregional agreements and the question already presented in connection with the mutual industrial agreements contemplated in Article 16(b), which emphasizes the goal of "complementary economics."[47] Despite the Treaty provisions the Conference of the Contracting Parties through Resolution 99 (IV), expressly agreed that those not par-

43. Cárdenas & Peña, "Los Acuerdos Subregionales y el Tratado de Montevideo," in Instituto para la Integración de América Latina, 2 *Derecho de la Integración* 10 (1968) [hereinafter cited as Cárdenas & Peña].

44. Article 18 of the Montevideo Treaty, *supra* note 8, reads as follows: "Any advantage, benefit, franchise, immunity, or privilege applied by a contracting Party in respect of a product originating in or intended for consignment to any other country shall be immediately and unconditionally extended to the similar product originating in or intended for consignment to the territory of the other contracting Parties."

45. Cárdenas & Peña, *supra* note 43, at 15-16.

46. See articles 19 and 32(a), respectively.

47. Article 16(b) reads as follows: "With a view to expediting the process of integration and complementary economies referred to in Article 15, the contracting Parties: . . . b) May negotiate mutual agreements on complementary economies by industrial sectors."

ticipating in such an agreement would only benefit from the resulting advantages of the agreement through appropriate compensation or by means of due assurance of the reciprocity principle. Hence the correctness of the conclusion that identical reasoning is possible in regard to the applicability of the most-favored-nation clause to the subregional agreements, inasmuch as these agreements are related to the trade liberalization program and implement the minimal program contemplated in the Montevideo Treaty.

The considerations set forth above and others made it possible to override the difficulties and doubts that arose at the beginning and to accept a thesis favorable to compatibility. This does not mean, however, that the problem is over once a subregional agreement is declared compatible by the competent LAFTA organ. Of course, the legal order, *i.e.,* the secondary law, that Andean integration generates through the acts of subregional institutions must be compatible with the Montevideo Treaty and with the other pertinent LAFTA instruments. Amendments to the Cartagena Agreement will also be subject to the requirement of compatibility as will adherence to the Agreement.[48] Thus, compatibility is not automatic and unconditional but rather is subject to both substantive and procedural rules.

Normative dependency and hierarchical relationships

As to other aspects of the relationship between the Cartagena Agreement and the LAFTA legal order, one can observe that the Agreement is not self-sufficient. For instance, in accordance with Article 44 of the Agreement, "[t]he provisions of Article 21 of the Montevideo Treaty shall be applicable in cases involving matters of tax, assessment or other internal liens." Article 108 has a different scope since it purports to fill gaps only in regard to the special regime for Bolivia and Ecuador; it states: "Wherever no provision is made in this Agreement as to special treatment for Bolivia and Ecuador, the principles and provisions of the Montevideo Treaty, as well as the LAFTA Resolutions favoring the Relatively Less Economically Developed Countries, shall be considered as incorporated therein." Another such general provision is found in Article 114 of the Agreement according to which the Montevideo Treaty and the LAFTA Resolutions "shall be applied in supplementary manner." As may be observed from

48. The adherence by Venezuela had to meet the specific requirements set forth in Resolution 165 of the LAFTA Permanent Executive Committee. In this connection see the instruments reproduced in 12 *Int'l Legal Mat'ls* 344 (1973).

this provision, the application of the LAFTA legal order as a whole is authorized whenever there is no applicable suregional rule. Thus, the role assigned to LAFTA of complementing the Andean legal order is reinforced.

This relationship of normative dependency of the subregional legal order with respect to the LAFTA legal order necessarily affects the hierarchical relationship between the two. First of all, the provision relative to the supplementary nature of the LAFTA legal order quoted above seems to indicate that it is a *special* legal order since the Andean legal order prevails with respect to the subregion, over the general LAFTA legal order.[49] In other words, the LAFTA legal order will be applicable only when the subregional order is silent or when its application is expressly provided for in specific situations. Were the second exception omitted, the thesis of the primacy of the subregional order would be inconsistent with the general, basic rule explicitly established in the Cartagena Agreement. In effect, Article 114 begins by stating that "[t]he provisions of this Agreement shall not affect the rights and obligations derived from the Montevideo Treaty and the LAFTA Resolutions . . . . " This clause seems quite logical in the light of the fundamental requirement of compatibility: how could a subregional agreement be considered compatible with the LAFTA legal order if there were provisions in the agreement that affected the rights and obligations derived from that legal order?

In addition to the general clause just mentioned, the Agreement contains others applicable to specific matters or situations. Thus, in accordance with Article 60, "[t]he commitments adopted under the Montevideo Treaty in compliance with the LAFTA Liberalization Program shall prevail over the provisions of the present chapter [Chapter V] to the extent that the former may be more advanced than the latter." Here, again, the exception is fully comprehensible; how could provisions of the subregional liberalization program continue to prevail over commitments adopted under the LAFTA program when such commitments were more advanced than the subregional ones? After all, one of the fundamental purposes of the subregional Agreement is precisely that of "reducing tariffs within the subregions and harmonizing treatments toward third nations more rapidly than in the general agreements . . . . "[50]

A second specific situation and another equally understandable exception is contemplated in Article 72 by which trade in agro-livestock products is "fully subject" to Article 28 of the Montevideo Treaty and

49. See Instituto Interamericano de Estudios Jurídicos Internacionales, *Derecho de la Integración Latinoamericana, Ensayo de Sistematización* 1048 (1969) [hereinafter cited as Instituto Interamericano].

50. See text accompanying note 5 *supra* for the full text of this quotation from the Declaration of the Presidents of America.

the Resolutions that complement it. Still another exception is found in Article 113 of the Agreement, which reiterates a principle already formulated in Declaration of the Presidents, *i.e.,* "The advantages pledged under this Agreement shall not be extended to non-member Countries, nor create for them any obligation based thereon." Given its *special* character, the Agreement is autonomous within the subregion with regard to tariff reductions and other advantages that are agreed upon, but this autonomy does not authorize the creation of any special obligation for the other Contracting Parties of LAFTA.

There are further aspects of the relationship between the subregional and LAFTA legal orders that could be considered, if space permitted. However, before turning to the next subject emphasis should be placed on the essential characteristic of the relationship, namely, the *derivative character* of the Cartagena Agreement and of the subregional legal order as a whole, which "derives from the general legal order of LAFTA, as a particular application to the subregion."[51] The question of *compatibility* is hardly the first aspect of the relationship between the two legal orders with respect to which the *derivative* character of the subregional legal order can be clearly observed. The transitory nature of the Cartagena Agreement itself further illustrates the point. Under Article 110 the Agreement "shall remain in effect as long as the goals achieved within the general framework of the Montevideo Treaty do not surpass those established therein."[52] The adherence clause of the Agreement is a further expression of its *derivative* character; under Article 109 the Agreement shall remain open to adherence only by the other Contracting Parties to the Montevideo Treaty. Nevertheless, none of these links and relationships between the two legal orders amount to a situation of absolute dependence and subordination. A thorough analysis of the subregional legal order, both from the viewpoint of the Agreement itself and of the *secondary law* that it is generating, would reveal a *sui generis* legal order, characterized by a high degree of autonomy and self-sufficiency.[53]

51. Instituto Interamericano, *supra* note 49, at 1047.

52. The "transitory" nature of the Agreement must be understood within the framework in which it was conceived. In the discussions of the Committee of Experts that prepared the draft agreement it was understood that the "transitory" nature of the instrument applied only to the trade liberalization program and the common external tariff, and not to certain permanent objectives of the Agreement, such as joint programming, coordination of national development plans, and sectorial programs of industrial development. See "Memorañdum del Comité de Expertos & la Sexta Reunión de la Commisión Mixta," quoted in *id.* at 1049, 1077-78.

53. The Roundtable that was held at the Central University of Venezuela, Caracas, under the auspices of the Inter-American Institute of International Legal Studies, May 11-15, 1970 on the legal and institutional problems of the Andean Subregional Agreement, concluded on this point that "in spite of the derivative character of the Agreement, it enjoys the necessary autonomy . . . ." Orrego Vicuña, "Análisis de la Práctica chilena," in Instituto para la Integración de América Latina, *Boletín de la Integración,* Oct. 1970, at 42, 52 [hereinafter cited as Orrego Vicuñ].

III. THE ACTS OF THE ANDEAN INSTITUTIONS

The law of Andean economic integration becomes most interesting when approached from the viewpoint of the acts of the subregional organs.[54] These acts result from the exercise of the vast competence *ratione materiae* and powers attributed to such organs. In this section we will attempt to define the nature and validity of those acts in the light both of the Cartagena Agreement and of practice.

Competence "ratione materiae" and powers of the institutions

Each basic instrument of an international organization has a system for the distribution of competence *ratione materiae* and powers between the organs of the international organization and the member states. The Cartagena Agreement has its own such system, which can best be described by distinguishing among three categories of matters. The first category has to do with those matters on which one specific action is assigned to the organs, *i.e.*, the Commission and the Board, and another action, that of implementation, is assigned to the Member Countries. Articles 27 and 28 of the Agreement fall under this category. The Commission, upon the proposal of the Board, was to "approve and present for consideration of the Member Countries," prior to December 31, 1970, a "common system for treatment of foreign capital and likewise, systems for . . . ," and "[t]he Member Countries pledge themselves to adopt the measures necessary to implement such systems

54. The "principal organs" of the Cartagena Agreement are the Commission and the Board (Art. 5). The former "is the supreme organ of the Agreement, constituted by one plenipotentiary representative from each of the Member Countries' Governments" (Art. 6). The latter "is the technical organ of this Agreement, consisting of three members, and it may act only in the concerted interest of the Subregion as a unit" (Art. 13). As to the nature of these two organs the following passages from the report of the Committee of Experts that was in charge of the drafting of the Agreement are worth quoting. "By reason of their distinct structure and competence, these organs ensure a system of institutional equilibrium which responds satisfactorily to the objectives of the Agreement. It would be useless to adopt advanced goals of subregional programming and harmonious development without the establishment of the legislative authority and the technicocommunity authority, each with the hierarchy, strength and ability to function for the continuing solution of the problems inherent to such a vast, complex and difficult undertaking." "On the other hand, noteworthy security is provided for the subregion and its countries by the equilibrium between governmental strength and community strength, between the political approach of the former and the technical approach of the latter." *Informe del Comité de Expertos a la Quinta Reunión de la Comisión Mixta*, at 4, anexo 5, Doc. De. Bo./Co./Mx/V/dt.1.

within the six months following approval by the Commission."[55] Thus, the competence established by the Agreement over this category of matters is not exclusive either from the point of view of the subregional organs or the Member Countries. In other words, the act of such organs does not become fully valid until the Member Countries take action to implement it.[56]

The second category involves those matters with respect to which a type of *exclusive* competence is attributed to the subregional organs. Actually, the Agreement does not explicitly contemplate the type of measures by the Member Countries to implement the acts that it provides for in articles such as Article 27. Unless the Agreement specifies or implies that an action should be taken in specific cases, it is reasonable to assume that the exercise of this competence or power results in acts which are fully valid for and in the Member Countries. This assumption becomes most relevant when one observes that the majority of the matters covered by the Cartagena Agreement fall within this second category. By way of illustration in regard to the Liberalization Program,[57] the Commission, upon the proposal of the Board, "shall prescribe what products are to be reserved for the Sectorial Programs of Industrial Development."[58] A second example is provided by another important mechanism of the Agreement, namely, the power of the Commission to approve, on the proposal of the Board, a minimum common external tariff.[59]

The third and last of these categories comprises those matters with respect to which the Agreement attributes to the subregional organs the power to authorize the Member Countries to perform certain acts or omissions specifically mentioned therein. Obviously, it is not a question here of whether the act of the organ requires implementation at the national level in the same sense as in the two previous categories since, by its very nature, this power cannot be shared with the Member Countries. The power is attributed to various fields or mechanisms of the Agreement, especially with regard to competitive commercial practices[60] and saving clauses.[61] It has been exercised by the competent organ several times, both to authorize and to refuse authorization to the requesting state.[62]

55. Cartagena Agreement, *supra* note 1, art. 27.

56. In compliance with the provisions of Article 27 the Commission approved Decision N° 24 and the Member Countries adopted their respective measures to implement it.

57. Cartagena Agreement, *supra* note 1, ch. V.

58. *Id.* art. 47. See Decisions mentioned note 19 *supra*.

59. See Decisions mentioned notes 22-23, 25 *supra*.

60. Cartagena Agreement, *supra* note 1, ch. VIII.

61. *Id.* ch. IX.

62. In this connection see, for instance, Resolution 20 of the Board, of February 13, 1974, declaring unwarranted the request by Peru for authorization to apply corrective measures under Article 79 of the Agreement.

Legal validity of the acts of the Andean institutions

There is one aspect of the competence *ratione materiae* and powers of the Andean institutions that deserves further comment, namely, the legal effects or validity of those acts, which the Agreement attributes to the exclusive competence of the subregional organs. In subsection C below we will examine this same aspect from the viewpoint of the reception given such acts in the domestic legal order of the Member Countries, but it is important here to refer in greater detail to what seems to be the intrinsic *erga omnes* validity of these acts.

The Cartagena Agreement lacks provisions like those, for instance, of Article 189 of the Rome Treaty[63] creating the European Economic Community, wherein the form and effect of the acts of the EEC Council and Commission are defined; the article states that Regulations "shall have a general application. They shall be binding in every respect and directly applicable in each Member State."[64] The subregional Agreement mentions the acts of its organs only once. Article 6 states that "[t]he Commission shall express its will in the form of 'Decisions.' " However, even in this case the Agreement does not define those acts or determine their validity as far as the domestic legal order of the Member Countries is concerned.

An effort to improve this situation has been made through the Regulations of the Commission by distinguishing between the Decisions which "involve obligations for the Member Countires or for the organs of the Agreement" and those that contain no binding provisions. Article 11 of the Board's Regulations refers to Resolutions as the form that it will adopt in the exercise of "its own decision-making powers." However, these provisions are of little help in filling the gaps that concern us here.[65] In a sense the explicit statement of the Board that the Decisions of the Commission "are binding for the States from the very moment at which they are approved lends more weight to the submission that the acts of the subregional organs have objective validity."[66] Likewise, the statement by the Commission that the

63. Treaty Establishing the European Economic Community, *done* March 25, 1957, 298 U.N.T.S. 11 (unofficial English version).

64. See text of the full articles and other references in E. Stein & P. Hay, *Law and Institutions in the Atlantic Area* 85-86 (1963).

65. In effect, the first distinction was made having in view the date of entry into force of the two types of Decisions, and the second with a view to giving a name to the acts of the Board other than the proposals that this organ must present to the Commission in the exercise of the competence that the Agreement attributes to both organs. The Regulations of the Commission and of the Board were approved by Decisions (N° 6 and 9, respectively) of the Commission.

66. *Informe de la Junta sobre el cumplimiento del Acuerdo y las Decisiones,* July 14, 1973, at 2, Doc. COM/XII/dic. 3.

"adherence of Venezuela to the Cartagena Agreement signifies its acceptance of the Decisions approved by the Commission until this date . . . ," and the identical one *vis-a-vis* the Resolutions of the Board,[67] seem to be an indirect but unequivocal assertion of the *erga omnes* validity of the acts of the two subregional organs.[68]

From the standpoint of legal theory, there seems to be no doubt of the correctness of the assertion of the *erge omnes* validity of the acts of the Commission and Board. Both the spirit and the letter of the provisions of the Agreement dealing with the competences and powers of the subregional organs clearly reveal the binding character of the acts to which we are referring. In the institutional system of the European Community this is explicitly stated; however, the absence of an explicit statement to this effect does not preclude other systems from attributing to the acts of their organs the same legal validity. What matters is the intention of the States parties to the basic instrument, and on this point there is no room for doubt in the legislative history of the Andean Pact.

Reception given to the acts of the Andean institutions in national legal systems

State practice in the subregion is not always in conformity with what seems to be the correct interpretation of the Cartagena Agreement with regard to the validity of the acts of the subregional organs. To begin with, the process of domestic approval of the Agreement itself showed from the outset that not all legal minds in the Member Countries were prepared to accept the rather far-reaching *community law* elements of the Agreement. The case brought to the Colombian Supreme Court was simply the occasion on which the conflict of legal opinions became more dramatically evident.[69] The same Court in a subsequent case on the constitutionality of the decree implementing Decision 24 (the "Andean Foreign Investment Code") in accordance with Article 27 of the Agreement adopted a traditional, rigid, approach and considered that the executive should have submitted that subregional act to the consideration and action of the legislature.[70] Despite the express and clear

67. See Decision 70, art. 37, reproduced in 12 *Int'l Legal Mat'ls* 356 (1973).

68. The Venezuelan law referred to below in note 71 *infra,* approved, in addition to the Cartagena Agreement, only a specified number of Decisions, not all.

69. For a detailed analysis of the case see Orrego Vicuña, "La incorporacioń del ordenamiento juridíco subregional al derecho interno, Analisis de la practica y jurisprudencia de Colombia," in Instituto para la Integración de América Latina *Boletín de la Integración,* Oct. 1972, at 39 [hereinafter cited as Orrego Vicuña, *Análisis de Colombia*]. For Chilean practice see Orrego Vicuña, *supra* note 53.

70. See selected passages of the Court Decision in Orrego Vicuña, *Analisis de Colombia, supra* note 69, at 51-54. An English version of the Decision may be found in 11 *Int'l Legal Mat'ls* 574 (1972).

provisions of Article 27, the Court treated Decision 24 in the same way it treated the Cartagena Agreement, that is, virtually as if it were a treaty.

These developments, though negative enough from the point of the juridical principles involved, have not thwarted the entry into force of the instruments in question in each Member Country. The real threat to the normal and effective functioning of the subregional legal order are the laws approving the Cartagena Agreement that were passed in Colombia and Venezuela. Each contains a clause to the effect that subregional acts that modify national legislation or deal with matters subject to the jurisdiction of the legislature require approval by the latter.[71] Such a clause virtually amounts to a reservation since "it purports to exclude or to modify the legal effect of certain provisions" of the Agreement "in their application" to those Member Countries.[72] In fact, from the point of view of international law, clauses of this kind do not constitute a reservation, particularly in view of the fact that the Cartagena Agreement itself expressly prohibits reservations.[73] However, since those clauses have domestic legal effects they might affect *de facto* the very essence of the subregional legal order created by the Andean Pact, for they make potentially inoperative the institutional system for the distribution of competence *ratione materiae* and powers established by the Pact.

Despite the foregoing the subregional legal order has been functioning reasonably well so far as its reception in the domestic legal systems is concerned. The Board has verified that a number of Decisions of the Commission "have not been put into force in the territory of one or several countries and, as said before, sometimes in none."[74] But this does not seem to be the real question to be raised. The question that should concern us is not whether countries do not "put into force" the acts of the subregional organs in due time but rather how they do it. In other words, the real question is whether the idea that all subregional acts require a sort of formal *transformation* or *incorporation* still

71. See Colombia Law Nº 8 of April 4, 1973, the full text of which is reproduced in Instituto para la Integracion de América Latina, *Boletín de la Integración*, July 1973, at 226; Venezualan Law of Sept. 26, 1973, in *Gaceta Oficial,* Nov. 1, 1973, Nº 1620 *Extraordinario.*

72. A "reservation" to a treaty or any other conventional instrument, according to the Vienna Convention on Treaties, "means a unilateral statement, however phrased or named, made by a State, when signing, ratifying, accepting, approving or acceding to a treaty, whereby it purports to exclude or to modify the legal effect of certain provisions of the treaty in their application to that State." Vienna Convention on the Law of Treaties, *open for signature* May 23, 1969, art. 2, para. 1(d), United Nations Conference on the Law of Treaties, *Official Records* 289, U.N. Doc. A/CONF. 39/27 (1971).

73. Cartagena Agreement, *supra* note 1, art. 109.

74. See reference cited note 66 *supra,* at 4.

prevails; apparently it does.[75] This idea seems to be shared by one of the subregional organs. In a report, prepared for a different purpose, the Board thought that a solution might be found if provisions such as the following were included in the treaty that it proposed:

> *Article 2.* The Decisions of the Commission *are binding* upon Member Countries *from the moment of their approval.*
> They shall be *directly applicable in the territory of the Member Countries* from the date specified in their text or, in the absence thereof, eight days after their publication in the official Journal of the Agreement. However, when a Decision shall so require, a national legal act shall be necessary for it to enter it into force in the territory of the Member Countries.
> *Article 3.* The Member Countries are obligated to adopt the measures of a general or special nature that may be necessary to ensure the application, compliance and execution of the norms that belong to the juridical structure of the Cartagena Agreement.
> They are also committed not to apply nor to adopt any measure that would be contrary to those norms or interfere with their application in any way.[76]

Provisions like the foregoing in an additional instrument to the Cartagena Agreement would bring the latter closer to the European treaties and would, undoubtedly, help to improve the present situation. It should still be stressed that each one of those provisions is implied—and some even explicitly stated—in the Agreement. Therefore, what would be most helpful would be for competent national authorities to accept, when appropriate, that acts of the subregional organs are valid by the sole fact of their having been adopted, that the source of their validity lies in their having been approved by competent organs, and that the

75. This explains why even the same type of domestic instrument and the common expression "to put into effect" are used in connection with Decisions approved under Articles 27 and 28 of the Agreement, on the one hand, and with Decisions approved under articles where measures by the Member Countries to implement them are not contemplated, either explicitly or implicitly, on the other hand. Compare, for instance, two Ecuadorian decrees, one relating to Decision 24 and one relating to Decisions 57 and 57-a (Sectorial Program of Industrial Development of the Metal-mechanic Sector), in which this same expression is used: "Declarase en vigencia en el territorio nacional. . . ." See text of the decrees in *Registros Oficiales* of August 19, 1971 and of April 4, 1973, respectively.

76. *Informe de la Junta sobre el establecimiento de un órgano jurisdiccional del Acuerdo de Cartagena,* Dec. 12, 1972, at 29, Doc. COM/X-E/di 5 (emphasis added). Before this report was adopted the Board had invited experts from the Member Countries, European and other Latin American countries (*Primera Reunión de Expertos—Organo Jurisdiccional,* June 26-28, 1972), to discuss, *inter alia,* the particular problem that we are referring to. For a brief presentation of the views of the experts from Member Countries see *Resumen Comparativo de las Respuestas de los Consultores Nacionales al Cuestionario de la Junta,* June 23, 1972, Doc. JUN/ROJ/di 10.

actions or measures by Member Countries required to implement the acts constitute merely a mechanical element of the whole subregional lawmaking process.[77]

77. A number of national decrees in some of the Member Countries seem to reflect this conception. See documents cited note 76 *supra* and *Decretos Nacionales que Ponen en Aplicación Decisiones Adoptadas por la Comisión,* Nov. 29, 1973, Doc. J/RI.AT/12/Rev. 2 for a list of decrees passed up to the date of the document. Indeed this type of national instrument, though it constitutes the exception rather than the general rule, gives a further support to the cónception of the subregional law-making process advocated in this paper.

THE INTERNATIONAL MONETARY SYSTEM AND CHANGE: RELATIONS BETWEEN THE MODE OF NEGOTIATION AND LEGAL TECHNIQUE

JOSEPH GOLD

I. INTRODUCTION

The Bretton Woods Conference of July 1944 agreed to create an international monetary system governed by a multilateral treaty and administered by the International Monetary Fund. The Articles of Agreement as drafted at the Conference by the representatives of 44 governments established rights and obligations for member countries in relation to monetary matters, and created a pool of resources to assist members to observe their obligations. The new function of ensuring the adequacy of global monetary reserves by allocating to members, or cancelling, a new reserve asset called the special drawing right (SDR), was conferred on the Fund by the first amendment of its Articles, which became effective in July 1969. The Articles, which on June 1, 1977 had been accepted by 130 countries, remain the major legal instrument of the system.[1]

The creation of the system is a leading example of the modern international law of cooperation, about which Wolfgang Friedmann wrote with insight. Circumstances have required the adaptation, and now the reform, of the system. From time to time, there have been fears that general cooperation might be jeopardized by the tendency of a limited number of members to negotiate developments in the system among themselves. This practice has troubled other members because they have wanted to be represented in negotiations that affected the system as a whole. Professor Friedmann also noted "the sanction of non-participation" by which the benefits of cooperation are withdrawn from

JOSEPH GOLD is General Counsel and Director of the Legal Department of the International Monetary Fund, Washington, D.C. The views expressed in this article are the personal views of the author and not necessarily those of the Fund.

1. In the rest of this article, the international monetary system is usually referred to as "the system;" the Articles of Agreement of the Fund as "the Articles;" member countries of the Fund as "members;" monetary reserves as "reserves;" and special drawing rights as "SDRs." The "Executive Directors" of the Fund refers to the organ composed of 20 "executive directors."

countries that neglect the obligations they have undertaken in connection with cooperation. Exclusion from negotiations, although not a sanction, is likely to be regarded with equal displeasure by those affected.

This article deals with the interplay between negotiation in small groups of members and the reaction of other members, and with the influence of the mode of negotiation on the legal technique employed to give effect to the results. Four episodes since Bretton Woods are discussed: the "two-tier" arrangements for gold, the Fund's General Arrangements to Borrow (the GAB), the emergence of SDRs, and the effort to reform the system.

II. THE "TWO-TIER" ARRANGEMENTS FOR GOLD

Gold was a fundamental element in the system created at Bretton Woods, but the proposed second amendment of the Articles has as one of its objectives a gradual reduction in the role of gold. Under the original Articles, which in this respect were not affected by the first amendment, the par values of currencies are expressed, directly or indirectly, in terms of gold as a common denominator, and par values determine the parity relationship between any two currencies. The Articles bind each member to take measures to keep the rates in exchange transactions in its territory within narrow margins around the parity between its own currency and the currency for which it is exchanged. The system developed in such a way that many members performed this obligation by intervening in the exchange markets to buy and sell their own currency for U.S. dollars; other members intervened with the currency of a member that intervened with U.S. dollars; and the United States stood ready to buy and sell gold for U.S. dollars in transactions with all other members. The reserves of members were composed, therefore, of gold and U.S. dollars or currencies convertible into U.S. dollars, but the proportions and amounts in which these assets were held by individual members varied, with some holding little or no gold.

From early days the system was under stress because gold was not only a reserve asset but also a commodity held by private parties. Moreover, some monetary authorities were willing to change the composition of their reserves by transactions in gold in which the prices were not compatible with par values. The Articles proscribe transactions in gold between members at the price inconsistent with the par value of the currency exchanged for gold, but a member may sell gold at a premium or buy it at a discount provided that the other party is not a member. The Articles do not proscribe transactions of any kind between private parties, with the result that markets were validly established in which private parties (or non-member countries) are able to deal at prices unrelated to par values, and in which even members may engage in some transactions. The prices that developed in these markets were often thought to be evidence that par values were unsound and likely to be changed. These expectations promoted the purchase of gold because in terms of a currency the value of gold increases if the currency is devalued. The expectations intensified the uncertainties that bred them, so that the behavior of the private markets was both symptom and contagion.

At one time, the Fund recommended that members should refrain from engaging in external transactions at a premium and should prevent their residents from entering into them, but the effort failed. A different policy was introduced by a few members in late 1961 when their central banks agreed to form a Gold Pool through which to sell, and later to buy, gold in the London market and maintain prices close to par in that market. The partners in this "informal"[2] consortium were the central banks of six European members (Belgium, France, Germany, Italy, the Netherlands, and the United Kingdom) and one non-member (Switzerland), together with the Federal Reserve authorities of the United States. The seven European central banks were described as the "BIS group of central banks."[3] France became an inactive partner in June 1967. The arrangements were negotiated outside the Fund but were in conformity with its Articles. At the prices maintained by the action of the Pool, members were able to purchase gold in the market without violating their obligations.

Prior to 1966, the Pool was a net purchaser of gold, but in 1967 large amounts of gold were drained from the reserves of the consortium as a consequence of political crisis, the size of the deficit in the U.S. balance of payments, and the devaluation of sterling. By March 1968, the losses became intolerable, and the London market was closed temporarily. The Secretary of the U.S. Treasury and the Chairman of the Federal Reserve Board announced on March 14 that they had invited the governors of the central banks of the other six active partners in the Pool to consult on coordinated measures to ensure orderly conditions in the exchange markets on the basis of the fixed official price for gold.

The governors and their advisers, together with officials from some treasuries, gathered in Washington, D.C., on March 16 and 17, at a

2. U.S. Dep't Treasury, *Annual Report of the Secretary of the Treasury on the State of the Finances for the Fiscal Year Ended June 30, 1964,* at 337, 339 (1965) [the Treasury reports will be cited hereinafter as *Annual Report of the Secretary of the Treasury, 19*].

3. *Id.* at 337. They were among the eight European central banks represented on the Board of Directors of the Bank for International Settlements (BIS).

meeting that was attended also by the Managing Director of the Fund and the General Manager of the BIS. The governors issued a communique on March 17, in which they recorded their agreement to end the Pool and to institute what was known as the two-tier gold system. The heart of the communique was the following paragraph:

> The Governors agreed to cooperate fully to maintain the existing parities as well as orderly conditions in their exchange markets in accordance with their obligations under the Articles of Agreement of the International Monetary Fund. The Governors believe that henceforth officially held gold should be used only to effect transfers among monetary authorities and, therefore, they decided no longer to supply gold to the London gold market or any other gold market. Moreover, as the existing stock of monetary gold is sufficient in view of the prospective establishment of the facility for Special Drawing Rights, they no longer feel it necessary to buy gold from the market. Finally, they agreed that henceforth they will not sell gold to monetary authorities to replace gold sold in private markets.

This agreement was designed to conserve the total official stock of gold but not increase it if all members refrained from purchasing gold in the market in accordance with the view that purchases were no longer necessary. The official and the private markets would be insulated from each other, and it was hoped, therefore, that the private demand for gold would cease to endanger the system. Gold would continue to be used as a reserve asset, but with diminishing importance. Increases in global reserves that were necessary for the prosperity of the system would be provided not by gold, the historic "ultimate" reserve asset, but by the new asset, the SDR.

The two-tier system was created by what purported to be an agreement among the governors of seven central banks, and ministers were not mentioned. The agreement may have taken this form because the central banks had the legal authority to engage in gold transactions, and because an agreement among them avoided whatever complications would have arisen had they decided to propose an agreement among governments.[4] It is obvious that an agreement of such importance could not have been made without the involvement and

4. *Report on the Bretton Woods Agreements Act,* H.R. Rep. No. 1484 (to accompany H.R. 10162), 87th Cong., 2d Sess. 7-8 (1962).

approval or even direction of governmental authorities.[5] Although the communique was issued by the governors, the Secretary of the U.S. Treasury was one of the two sponsors of the meeting, and the governors referred to "their obligations" under the Articles, under which the obligations are binding on "countries" or on "governments".

In their communique the governors invited the cooperation of other central banks in the new policies. The Federal Reserve Board brought the communique to the attention of other central banks, and U.S. ambassadors were instructed to explain it to finance ministries and central banks,[6] but they were not invited to adhere formally to the agreement. By April 12, 1968, 59 other countries had given "a general assurance" of their intention to cooperate and another 11 had "made comments to U.S. representatives which appear to be sympathetic to the objectives of the communique but which did not comprise a clear statement of intent to adhere to the policies of the communique".[7] The United States was active not only in soliciting declarations of support for, but also in promoting observance of, the policies of the communique.[8]

The Pool did not provoke concern even though it was created by a small band of central banks. Calling them the "BIS group" may have been intended to justify their restricted number, but this justification may have been less responsible for the equanimity of non-participants than the contribution to the Pool imposed by participation. Acceptance of the Pool by non-participants made it difficult for them to object to its termination, but the more important reason for the widespread, although not universal,[9] approbation of the two-tier arrangements was the assumption that the system had been improved. When, however, on November 13, 1973 the participants terminated their agreement, there was some reaction, partly because of the absence of advance notice to those whose support had been solicited, and partly because of un-

5. See, for example, *Economic Report of the President: Transmitted to the Congress January 1969 Together With the Annual Report of the Council of Economic Advisers* 134-35 (1969).

6. *Hearings on the International Monetary Fund's Special Drawing Rights Proposal and the Current International Financial Situation Before the Subcommittee on International Finance of the House Committee on Banking and Currency,* 90th Cong., 2d Sess., at 6 (1968).

7. *Id.* at 8. In addition, South Africa and France made their positions clear and one country simply acknowledged receipt of the communique.

8. *Hearings on the Proposed IMF Quota Increase and its Implications for the Two-Tier Gold Market Before the Subcommittee on International Exchange and Payments of the Joint Economic Committee,* 91st Cong., 1st Sess., at 58 (1970), reproduced in *Annual Report of the Secretary of the Treasury,* 1970, at 441.

9. See note 7 *supra.*

certainty about the further intentions of the participants, but mainly because a step that had implications for the future of gold had been taken by a few countries at a time when the subject of gold was being discussed in the Committee of Twenty.

The legal classification of the agreement that created the two-tier arrangements can be debated. It has been pointed out that agreements among central banks are not treaties or international agreements.[10] This view rests on formal considerations and not on the importance of the agreements or on the absence of governmental involvement or interest. Recent cases on the immunity of central banks from suit have distinguished between their governmental or public and non-governmental or private functions.[11] The agreement on the two-tier system was promoted or subsequently endorsed by governments even though in form it was an agreement among a few central banks. Governmental authorities made it clear that the policies of the communique would apply to their gold reserves,[12] and some governments changed their regulations or practices in order to give effect to the communique. Central banks settle their problems by consent, but if it had become necessary to determine what law governed the agreement, it is difficult to see what alternative there would have been to international law.

III. THE GENERAL ARRANGEMENTS TO BORROW

In 1958, many members made their currencies convertible for non-residents, and in early 1961 they went further and undertook to perform the obligations of convertibility under the Articles. It became evident that the Fund would need further resources to support the relaxation of restrictions by members. The need would be for more of the currencies of members in a strong balance of payments and reserve position, because these were the currencies that would be suitable for assisting members in difficulties in their balances of payments. It was impracticable to augment the Fund's holdings of currencies by selective increases in quotas and subscriptions. On February 10, 1961, the Managing Director proposed to the Executive Directors that the Fund should make contingent arrangements under its power to borrow. A few days earlier, President Kennedy had sent a message to Congress in which he had stated that although the United States had never used the

10. See Myers, "The Names & Scope of Treaties," 51 *Am. J. Int'l L.* 574, 601 & n. 129 (1957).

11. See *Trendtex Trading Corporation v. Central Bank of Nigeria* (1977) 1 All E.R. 881, and Ph. Kahn, Note, *Journal du Droit International,* No. 3 (July 1976), pp. 687-91.

12. See, for example, *Canadian Statements on Gold Pool Decisions,* released by Information Office of Canadian Embassy, Washington, D.C., March 18, 1968.

Fund's resources, it would exercise its rights when this was appropriate. In addition, he had supported the Fund's efforts to promote the use in its transactions of the currencies of other industrialized countries so as to reduce the burden on the U.S. dollar. The Fund might not have been able to provide these other currencies in the necessary amounts, however, if the United States had been disposed to exercise its massive rights to financial assistance under the Articles.

In April 1961, the staff presented a study in which it suggested that certain industrial members should enter into individual commitments to lend their currencies to the Fund at its request. The study pointed out that a collective agreement among potential lenders was unnecessary. The criteria employed for the selection of lenders showed that they should be eleven in number (United States, United Kingdom, France, Germany, Canada, Japan, Belgium, Netherlands, Italy, Austria, and Sweden).

Later studies by the staff mentioned three possible legal techniques: a general decision of the Fund to which members would adhere, a multilateral agreement of the Fund and members, and bilateral agreements between the Fund and individual members on basically uniform terms with minor variations required by a member's special circumstances.

Negotiations were conducted in Paris in November 1961[13] by the Managing Director and staff with representatives of the treasuries and central banks of the members originally suggested by the staff except Japan and Austria.[14] A Franco-American plan was advanced according to which a decision of the Fund would have provided for a symbiotic fund to which a participant would have been able to resort on its own initiative. The Managing Director rejected the plan because this and other features of it were incompatible with the Articles. The staff then drafted an arrangement that took account of the views expressed in the negotiations and was consistent with the Articles. This draft was discussed by the Executive Directors, and in December 1961 it was accepted, with minor amendments, by the representatives of ten members (the nine that had attended in November and Japan). The final version was adopted by the Executive Directors on January 5, 1962 as a decision entitled the General Arrangements to Borrow, which became effective on October 24, 1962. Only a majority of the votes cast was necessary for adoption of the decision. The ten participating members had much more than a majority of the total voting power.

13. Representatives of the ten potential lenders convened as a group for the first time, at the invitation of the Secretary of the United States Treasury, during the Annual Meeting of the Board of Governors of the Fund in September 1961.

14. Austria was never involved in the negotiations.

The preamble of the GAB declares that each of the ten participants[15] stands ready to lend, on the terms of the decision, supplementary resources up to a stated amount in its currency in order "to forestall or cope with an impairment" of the system. The participants undertake to consider, but not necessarily comply with, requests by the Managing Director for loans. Although the decision attempts to give some appearance of bilateral loans, the participants made a separate arrangement among themselves, without involving the Fund, by which they agreed to decide collectively whether individual participants will comply with calls to make loans. For this collective procedure outside the Fund, the participants adopted rules of their own on voting power and its exercise, which had the effect of moderating what the voting strength of the United States and the United Kingdom would have been had the provisions of the Articles been followed. The procedure also gave participants the opportunity they had wanted to form an opinion of their own on the policies of a participant if it sought assistance from the Fund in support of those policies.

The GAB, it has been said, resembles a statute in form, and indeed in early drafts was entitled an "Act". This title was abandoned because of some national sensibilities about "international legislation". The GAB is clearly subject to international law as a decision of the Fund, but a full analysis of its legal character raises certain questions that are not pursued here because they have been discussed elsewhere.[16] One question is whether the GAB is not only a decision of the Fund but also an international agreement[17] between the Fund and the participants even though two of them are central banks and even though the participants are not bound to lend. If the GAB is an international agreement, another question that arises is whether it is a single agreement of the Fund with the participants jointly or ten bilateral agreements.

The GAB was criticized from the outset, and not solely by developing members, on the ground that it might reduce the Fund's authority. The participants might agree positions among themselves on issues of importance for the Fund, and their voting power would enable them to make their views prevail in the Fund. Some critics objected to the exclusiveness of the GAB not only because the participants were limited in

15. Two of them are the Deutsche Bundesbank and the Sveriges Riksbank instead of Germany and Sweden because of considerations related to domestic law.

16. See Gold, "On the Difficulties of Defining International Agreements: Some Illustrations from the Experience of the International Monetary Fund," in *Economic and Social Development: Essays in Honour of Dr. C.D. Deshmukh* 27 (S.L.N. Simha ed. 1972).

17. At times during the drafting of the GAB it was entitled "A General Agreement" or "Agreement" but these titles were abandoned so as to give participants maximum flexibility in deciding what legal measures were necessary to enable them to adhere.

number but also because they would lend to the Fund solely for financing their own transactions with it. The critics were not pacified by the argument that supplementary resources for the transactions of participants would make more of the Fund's ordinary resources available for the rest of the membership.

The GAB provides that other members may adhere to it if the Fund agrees and no participant objects. There have been no further adherents. The original participants might have felt that participation could not be limited once any new adherent was accepted. They might also have thought that it would be less efficient to discuss issues of international monetary policy in a larger group.

The GAB is notable for a number of reasons. For example, certain of its provisions contributed to concepts connected with SDRs and the transactions of the Fund that were included in the amendment of the Articles in 1969.[18] Again, the GAB is the instrument that gave rise to the Group of Ten and that remains its only "charter", for which reason on occasion some critics have opposed its prolongation. The Ten consist, at ministerial level, of the finance minister and central bank governor of each of the ten countries, and, at the lower level, of their deputies. The Managing Director of the Fund participates at the ministerial level and members of the staff, as his representatives, at the level of the deputies. Others have been invited to attend, including representatives of Switzerland, a non-member of the Fund.

The Ten began to meet at once at the time of the Annual Meeting of the Fund's Board of Governors and has met on many other occasions. ministerial representatives have given mandates to their deputies on issues that have not been confined to the GAB but have affected general features of the Fund and the system. On some occasions, the Ten have gone beyond discussion and have reached agreement on the positions they would support in the Fund. The Group quickly developed an identity and regarded itself almost as a *de facto* international organization. These developments created increasing concern among non-participants. Many of them have held the view that the participation of the Managing Director and his representatives was not, and should not be, a substitute for the direct involvement of other members in discussions and negotiations of interest to all members. The critics were not mollified by parallel discussions in the Fund of issues that were being discussed by the Ten. It was obvious that the executive directors appointed or elected by the Ten were affected by the conduct of negotiations elsewhere by senior representatives of their countries.

18. Note the concepts of currency convertible in fact, reserve position in the Fund, and readily repayable indebtedness of the Fund under a loan agreement.

IV. SPECIAL DRAWING RIGHTS

In the early sixties it became apparent that the system might face problems of international liquidity. On the one hand, it was necessary to ensure that there would be adequate liquidity. On the other hand, the conviction grew that the system should not have to rely on continued deficits in the balance of payments of the United States, because the uncontrolled expansion of official holdings of dollars would destabilize the system. The problem of international liquidity was examined in the Annual Reports of the Executive Directors of 1963 and later years and in studies of the staff. Studies and discussion were undertaken by the Ten as well,[19] but this activity sharpened discontent among other members because they felt that an issue of great importance for the system was being negotiated within a restricted company.

By mid-1965, it began to appear that some mode of negotiation would have to be found in which all members could join. On July 10 the Secretary of the U.S. Treasury suggested that a committee could be established at the next Annual Meeting of the Board of Governors that would prepare for an international conference. On September 28, 1965, the Ten issued a communique in which they recognized the usefulness of procedures that would coordinate the efforts of their deputies and the Executive Directors.[20] As a result, in 1966 and 1967

19. See paragraph 5 of the Communique of the Group of Ten issued on October 2, 1963 by Douglas Dillon, Secretary of the Treasury of the United States, on behalf of the Group of Ten:

"The Ministers and Governors have noted with approval the statement by the Managing Director that the International Monetary Fund will develop and intensify its studies of these long-run questions. They, for their part, have now instructed their Deputies to examine these questions, and to report to them on the progress of their studies and discussions over the course of the coming year. They requested the Deputies in carrying out these studies to maintain close working relations with the International Monetary Fund and with other international bodies concerned with monetary matters. Any specific suggestions resulting from the studies by the Deputies will be submitted to the Ministers and Governors for consideration."

20. See paragraph 9 of this communique:

"The Ministers and Governors recognize that, as soon as a basis for agreement on essential points has been reached, it will be necessary to proceed from this first phase to a broader consideration of the questions that affect the world economy as a whole. They have agreed that it would be very useful to seek ways by which the efforts of the Executive Board of the Fund and those of the Deputies of the Group of Ten can be directed toward a consensus as to desirable lines of action, and they have instructed their Deputies to work out during the coming year, in close consultation with the Managing Director of the Fund, procedures to achieve this aim, with a view to preparing for the final enactment of any new arrangements at an appropriate forum for international discussions."

there were four meetings, of several days in duration, of the executive directors and their alternates with the deputies of the Ten. The executive directors and alternates attended *ex officio* but, in order to avoid certain legal and other difficulties, they did not sit as an organ of the Fund. The Managing Director and the chairman of the deputies acted as joint chairmen, with the former presiding in the meetings in Washington and the latter in the meetings elsewhere. The problems of arranging the joint meetings were not simply logistical, and one executive director never did attend.

The meetings, which after a time concentrated on versions of a plan for the creation of reserves drafted by the staff of the Fund, did much to bring about agreement on the final text of the *Outline of a Facility Based on Special Drawing Rights in the Fund*. The Outline was endorsed by the Ten in August 1967 and by the Executive Directors in September. The Board of Governors approved it at Rio de Janeiro later in September and instructed the Executive Directors to prepare the necessary amendment of the Articles, a task which they completed on April 16, 1968 after 74 meetings. The amendment took effect on July 28, 1969, in accordance with the provision that a proposed amendment becomes effective after it has been accepted by three-fifths of the membership and members exercising four-fifths of the total voting power.

The nine executive directors of developing members had disliked certain provisions in the proposed amendment, and the Managing Director had presented their objections at a meeting of the Ten in Stockholm in March 1968, but the objections did not prevail. That experience made an impression on developing members that affected their position at a later date in connection with reform. Developing members nevertheless proceeded to accept the proposed amendment, which could not have become effective without acceptance by a large proportion of them, because it was incontestable that the amendment as a whole was beneficial for the system.

During much of the lengthy period that preceded the amendment there was support within the Ten for a facility that would confine the allocation of a new reserve asset to a select number of members, including but not necessarily confined to the Ten. According to this view, the needs of other members for reserves would be met in different ways, such as the grant of the new reserve asset to them by the Ten or by the creation of new rights to make unconditional use of the Fund's resources. The distinction between the limited group and other members was defended with the arguments that the former were "major countries with a key role in the functioning of the international monetary system", that they would have a special responsibility for the success of any scheme, and that they would have the resources to back a new asset.[21]

It became increasingly difficult to maintain this distinction in the face of insistence, particularly by the Managing Director, that there was no rational basis for distinguishing among members, that all needed reserves, and therefore that reserves should be allocated to all. For a group of wealthy countries to confine the allocation of a new reserve asset to themselves would have been too embarrassing.[22] The affront to other members might have been too costly in political consequences for some of the countries that could expect to be in a limited group, and also in demands on them for compensatory benefits. Moreover, allocations to all members of a new asset on the basis of quotas in the Fund, the key for distribution that was finally agreed, meant that the probable members of any conceivable limited scheme would receive a major proportion of all allocations made through a general scheme. The political difficulties of insisting on the distinction between two classes of members was responsible in part for the joint meetings, but once they were held the difficulties became insurmountable.

The course of negotiation helped to resolve not only the problem of participation but also the problem of the legal technique by which the scheme should be put into effect. Four techniques had been considered: a change in the Fund's policies on the use of its resources without amending the Articles; and agreement between the Fund and a limited group of members under which the Fund would manage a scheme on their behalf; the creation of a new organization as an affiliate of the Fund; and amendment of the Articles. The first of these techniques did not offer enough scope for the new function that was contemplated. The second technique was eliminated once it was agreed that all members would be able to share in allocations. The reasons for the choice of amendment instead of an affiliate have been examined in an earlier article,[23] but it may be recalled that the eligibility of all members to participate was an argument against an affiliate also.

V. REFORM OF THE SYSTEM

On August 15, 1971 the United States announced that, with minor

21. See Communique of the Ministerial Meeting of the Group of Ten on July 25 and 26, 1966 in The Hague, paragraphs 5 and 6B. See also Report to the Ministers and Governors by the Group of Deputies, transmitted on July 8, 1966, paragraphs 56, 67, and 83.

22. The Group of Ten, *Report of the Study Group on the Creation of Reserve Assets: Report to the Deputies of the Group of Ten,* May 31, 1965, para. 121.

23. See Gold, "Legal Technique in the Creation of a New International Reserve Asset: Special Drawing Rights and the Amendment of the Articles of Agreement of the International Monetary Fund," 1 *Case Western Reserve J. Int'l L.* 105, 115-23 (1969).

exceptions, it would not convert U.S. dollars held by the monetary authorities of other countries into gold or other reserve assets. Grave disturbances in the exchange markets followed this action. The Ten held a number of meetings in order to work out a realignment of exchange rates that would eliminate disequilibrium. These meetings culminated in the "Smithsonian Agreement" of December 18, 1971 and a decision of the Fund of the same date with respect to exchange rates.

Disquiet was provoked among members by the mode of negotiating the Smithsonian Agreement, and it was not allayed by the argument that the realignment was confined to the currencies of the Ten. The realignment affected most members, but in addition it appeared to be a portent of the way in which negotiations might be conducted on the reform of the system following its breakdown. Indeed, the Ten had instructed their deputies as early as September 1971 to formulate the issues involved in reform. The Board of Governors adopted a resolution of its own on October 1, 1971 requesting the Executive Directors to report on reform. A fifth joint meeting of the executive directors and the deputies of the Ten was held on December 16, 1971 as the result of an initiative by the 9 directors of developing members.

The choice of a body in which to negotiate reform was discussed in the joint meeting and became the subject of much subsequent bargaining. There was widespread support, even among some members of the Ten, for the Executive Directors as the appropriate body, because they were an expert and representative body, were in continuous session, and had the assistance of an expert staff. But there was also some opposition to the idea. Some of the reasons for opposition were these: a reform would call for political decisions, which could be negotiated most effectively by officials with political responsibility; decisions might be required on economic questions outside the province of the Fund; radical departures from the Bretton Woods system might be necessary; the restructuring of the Fund as an organization could be contemplated. The choice of the Ten was impracticable because its exclusiveness had become a serious political disadvantage. Furthermore, the negotiation of the Smithsonian Agreement may have convinced some who took part that there was an imbalance in the composition of the Ten. The United States was one among ten but the EEC had multiple representation. It was always clear that the *elan vital* of the Ten depended on the willingness of the United States to participate.

The reluctance to choose existing bodies led to informal suggestions that a body might be formed of a small number of negotiators, each of whom would represent five or six members or blocs of members with common interests. Even when negotiations are proceeding in an established body, there is a tendency for a smaller number of participants to consult informally among themselves, particularly when progress is slow, notwithstanding the concern that this consultation creates among the other participants. The idea that a small group should be given formal recognition did not prosper because members do not regard their interests as so close that they can be represented satisfactorily by a few negotiators. The experience of the Fund shows that members prefer direct involvement, or at least representation related to small and homogeneous groups, in the process by which decisions are taken.

The direct involvement of all members was impracticable, and the alternative had to be a smaller body, but one that the membership at large would consider representative. The composition of such a body had to correspond, therefore, to some accepted model. The influence of an existing model was illustrated in 1966 when a negotiating body broader than the Ten was being considered in connection with international liquidity and it was suggested that the body should be an advisory committee of the Board of Governors consisting of the ministers of finance and governors of the central banks of the Ten and of ten other members chosen according to a formula based on five geographical groupings. The proposal was resisted in the Ten, in which one opinion was that the committee would be too large and might diminish the authority of both the Executive Directors and the deputies. In the Fund, the proposal was criticized because the executive directors of developing countries felt that their expert knowledge should be employed and that deputies from their countries who had not participated in the discussions of the Executive Directors or the Ten might be at a disadvantage in negotiating with the deputies of the Ten. But another and major objection was that the proposal had no relation to the structure of the Fund. The Committee would seem therefore to be arbitrary in its composition, and members at large would not have the sense that they were represented.

In November 1968 the Ten had assembled in Bonn, hastily and with a sense of crisis, to consider the exchange relationship between the French franc and the deutsche mark. In 1969, when the Executive Directors were studying flexibility in exchange rates, it was suggested that a more orderly and representative procedure for dealing with such crises was desirable. A proposal for an Advisory Committee of the Board of Governors was discussed in April 1969, and although the idea received much support, it petered out because some executive directors believed that ministers, unlike executive directors, would not be willing to take instructions from other ministers of the constituency appointing them, and because the Committee might undermine the authority of the Executive Directors. The staff was asked to study the idea and in May submitted a plan for a committee based on the structure of the

Executive Directors, but the plan was not discussed by the Executive Directors.

The plan was circulated again, together with a more detailed project based on it, in January 1972. These and subsequent memoranda along the same lines were discussed intensively for almost six months, and they led to a decision by the Executive Directors on June 28, 1972 to recommend to the Board of Governors the adoption of a proposed resolution for the establishment of an ad hoc Committee of the Board of Governors on International Monetary Reform and Related Issues. The resolution was adopted with effect from July 26, 1972.

The Committee was established within the framework of the Fund and followed the system of the twenty "constituencies" of members that appoint or elect executive directors under current practice. The idea of the Committee had broad support and met the wishes of most developing members, even though at the meeting of the Board of Governors in Nairobi one governor described the Committee as composed of lions lying down with lambs. The Committee consisted of one person, who was expected to be a governor of the Fund, minister, or someone of comparable rank, appointed by each constituency by whatever procedure it chose. Each person on the Committee could appoint not more than two associates and four advisors. Provision was made for associates in order to permit trade or other non-financial ministers to attend when issues not directly related to monetary matters were on the agenda, but in practice the larger constituencies saw the positions of associates and advisors as opportunities to appoint monetary officials from numerous members within the constituency. The Committee elected its own chairman, and chose the governor of the Fund for Indonesia. The Managing Director was entitled to participate in all meetings.

The resolution also created the Deputies, who prepared the work of the Committee. Each member of the Committee was able to appoint not more than two deputies, who could have not more than four advisors or not more than five if the constituency exceeded 10 members. Once again, these arrangements permitted the attendance of officials from many countries within a single constituency. The executive directors, alternate executive directors, and members of the staff as representatives of the Managing Director also attended. The Deputies established a Bureau, composed of a British national as Chairman and Vice-Chairmen of American, Brazilian, Ghanaian, and Japanese nationality, for the purpose of advancing the work of the Deputies.

The Managing Director and the Chairman of the Deputies collaborated in order to coordinate the work of the Executive Directors and of the Deputies on reform. The Ten did not take up the subject of reform, but developing members resolved at Lima in November 1971 to create a group of representatives in order to ensure the full participation of developing countries in the negotiation of reform and the protection of their interests. This action was taken at a time when developing countries expected the Ten to be active in connection with reform. The group consisted of 24 ministers or senior officials, appointed in equal numbers by the African, Asian, and Latin American members. The Deputies of this body consisted of the deputies of the Group of 24 and the executive directors of developing members. In order to avoid the charge of exclusiveness, the representatives of any developing members not appointed to the Group were allowed to participate in any meeting at either level. The Group was active in attempting to agree positions on the issues of reform, particularly in connection with the special interests of developing members.

The task of the Committee was to report to the Board of Governors on all aspects of the reform of the system. In view of the structure of the Committee, it was natural that the question would be raised of the legality of applying the Fund's system of weighted voting power. It has been settled that weighted voting power applies only to the organs of the Fund. The Committee was instructed to report the views of all members, with their names, if it did not arrive at unanimous opinions.

The resolution establishing the Committee contemplated that the reform would be made effective by whatever amendments of the Articles were necessary to give effect to the Committee's recommendations. At one stage it was suggested that a new treaty might be preferable to amendment, probably because it was foreseen that a radical rewriting of the Articles would be necessary. The suggestion might have been made in order to avoid the necessity for the acceptance of proposed amendments by a large proportion of members. Agreement on the technique of a new treaty could have been coupled with the understanding that a new treaty should become effective on acceptance by a smaller number of members than is required for amendment. Support for a new treaty quickly receded because of the numerous legal and financial problems that it would have created and also because of the realization that the technique of amendment was available however sweeping the revision of the Articles might be.

On June 14, 1974 the Committee of Twenty produced an *Outline of Reform,* but reported to the Board of Governors that supervening events had made impracticable reform of the kind foreseen at an earlier date. Reform would have to be an evolutionary process, but meanwhile immediate steps, including certain amendments, might be undertaken. The process of negotiating and drafting amendments was concluded when the Board of Governors approved the proposed second amendment on April 30, 1976. It is now before members for their acceptance. The proposal represents a massive amendment of the Articles that in substance falls between the immediate steps considered by the Committee of Twenty and the full plan that had been their original objective.

VI. CONCLUSIONS

The four episodes of monetary history discussed in this paper illustrate a number of features of the negotiation of change in the international monetary system:

(i) Members of the Fund are numerous and their economies and interests diverse. These are among the reasons why members have formed groups based on some principle of identity that they perceive. A powerful group may achieve changes in the system by its own action. The agreement it reaches for this purpose may be difficult to classify according to established concepts of international law. The various agreements of members of the Gold Pool are examples of these phenomena.

(ii) The parties to an agreement reached in such a group may seek a wider endorsement of their action. Once again, the agreement of the active members of the Gold Pool to establish the two-tier arrangements for gold is an example of this tendency. The understandings reached with other countries were probably all of the variety attributed to gentlemen. The GAB is an example of endorsement by means of decision taken in the Fund, in which the group has preponderant voting power. The GAB has novel features as both a decision of the Fund and an agreement between the Fund and the participants.

(iii) The actions of a powerful group may provoke sentiments on the part of other countries that range from quiet displeasure to vociferous criticism. The GAB has inspired the latter reaction because it illustrates the propensity of a powerful group to reach and give effect to agreements beneficial to itself.

(iv) The Group of Ten emerged as a result of the GAB, and exercised great influence on monetary affairs in the sixties. For a time it seemed that the result of its main activity, the discussion of the deliberate creation of reserve assets to satisfy the need for reserves, would be a scheme of special benefit to the Ten. A number of legal techniques seemed possible for giving effect to such a scheme. Political realities, however, required a broadening of the discussion. The procedure by which other members of the Fund became involved was joint meetings of the executive directors of the Fund and the deputies of the Group of Ten. Thereafter, it was no longer realistic to assume that the legal technique for giving effect to an eventual scheme would be anything but amendment of the Articles for the benefit of all members.

(v) Political experience made most members of the Group of Ten unwilling to support the negotiation of reform of the system outside the Fund. Before the decision was taken to conduct the negotiation within a new body in the Fund, the Committee of Twenty, developing members, recalling the earlier role of the Group of Ten, formed their own Group of 24 to promote their interests. Notwithstanding the compromises that had to be made in order to have the negotiation conducted within an advisory body of the Board of Governors, that solution ensured that agreement on reform would be made effective by amendment of the Articles. At one time, however, a few members were coquettish about the idea of a new treaty, perhaps in the hope that it could require acceptance by fewer members than is necessary for amendment.

(vi) There is, of course, another conclusion that can be drawn. It is that in monetary affairs the modern international law of cooperation is affected by centrifugal as well as centripetal forces.

NON-IDENTIFICATION OF THE MAJORITY AND MINORITY IN THE PRACTICE OF THE INTERNATIONAL COURT OF JUSTICE

ROSALYN HIGGINS

I

On 9 May 1973 separate applications were filed by Australia and New Zealand, instituting proceedings against France in respect of the holding of atmospheric nuclear tests by France in the Pacific Ocean. The Court was asked to declare such testing contrary to international law and to prohibit any further tests. Australia on 9 May 1973 and New Zealand on 14 May 1973 asked the Court, pending a final decision, to grant interim measures of protection. These would require France to desist from any further atmospheric nuclear tests pending the judgment of the Court. On 16 May 1973 France informed the Registrar by letter that the Court was manifestly not competent and that the French government could not accept its jurisdiction. Nor would it appoint an agent in the case. It is not our purpose here to examine the claims, in so far as they are related to the competence of the Court to indicate provisional measures, of Australia, New Zealand or France; [1] or the response of the Court. Rather, we note that the Court, by a vote of 8-6, indicated certain measures including an instruction to France to avoid nuclear tests causing the deposit of radioactive fall out on Australia, New Zealand or its dependencies. The Court also decided that in the next phase written proceedings should first be addressed to the questions of the jurisdiction of the Court to entertain the dispute, and of the admissibility of the applications. Dissenting opinions were attached by Judges Forster, Gros, Petren and Ignacio Pinto. These judges were four in number, whereas the interim awards record a vote of six dissenting judges. The Orders of the Court were, as is customary, collegiate and anonymous. Declarations were attached by Judges Jiménez de Aréchaga, Waldock, and Singh, and by Judge *ad hoc* Sir Garfield Barwick. It will readily be noted that it is not possible to see from Orders of 22 June 1973, granting interim measures, the full

.ROSALYN HIGGINS is Visiting Fellow, Center for International Studies London School of Economics; and, member of the Board of Editors of the American Journal of International Law, International Organization, and the British Yearbook of International Law.

1. See Higgins, "French Tests and the International Court," 29 *The World Today* 277 (1973).

composition of the majority and minority in the Court.

This essay looks at the topic of non-identification of the votes in the International Court of Justice.

II

It is not obligatory for a judge either to make his vote public or to give his reasons for the view he takes. Article 57 of the Statute provides "If the judgment does not represent in whole or in part the unanimous opinion of the judges, any judge shall be entitled to deliver a separate opinion." The 1946 Rules of the Court provided, in Article 74, that the judgment shall contain, *inter alia,* the number of judges constituting the majority. Paragraph 2 of Article 74 goes on to say "Any judge may, if he so desires, attach his individual opinion to the judgment, whether he dissents from the majority or not, or a bare statement of his dissent." These provisions remain untouched in the amendments to the Rules of 10 May 1972, appearing now as Article 79. In this, the Court has followed a long standing practice of the Permanent Court of International Justice. Article 57 of the Statute of the Permanent Court had provided that "dissenting judges are entitled to deliver a separate opinion" and Article 74 of the 1936 Rules had stipulated that dissenting judges may attach to the judgment "either an exposition of their individual opinion or a statement of their dissent."

A study of the *travaux préparatoires* leading to the permissive but not obligatory terminology of the relevant articles in the Statutes and successive Rules, is instructive.[2] Much of the initial debate centered on the preliminary central issue of whether there should be any right at all of public dissent. The Commission of Neutral States (Denmark, the Netherlands, Norway, Sweden and Switzerland) had reported in February 1920 that in the case of non-unanimity, the sense of dissenting opinions should be mentioned in the decision - that is to say, anonymously.[3] The Council of the League of Nations then set up the Advisory Commission of Jurists, a ten-nation body. The rule which they adopted in their draft was to allow dissenting judges to have their dissents recorded, but without any statement of reasons. The League organs then debated this draft, with opinion being sharply divided over the issue of publicity for dissenting views. Article 57 of the Court's Statute was the outcome - containing the provision, which still holds good, that if a judgment is not unanimous, those dissenting have the right to attach an individual opinion.

It will thus be seen that a right, but not a duty, was granted. Indeed,

2. The best commentary is to be found in the chapter on "Publicity or Secrecy of the Deliberations in the Permanent Court of International Justice," in 1 J. Verzijl, *The Jurisprudence of the World Court* 405, 408 (1965) [hereinafter cited as Verzijl].

3. *Id.* at 410. It seems that the delegates of Norway and Sweden would have preferred the publication of the dissenting opinions.

all the debate had been in terms of whether dissenting judges could secure a right to be identified as dissenting and perhaps also to give their reasons. Yet the final wording clearly allows of a situation where silence is permissible—though the debates were not directed to the desirability of allowing silence by some within a system where published dissents by others are permisslbe. One has therefore to extrapolate from the reasons given in the *travaux* for the existence and publication of dissents, reasons relevant to an option to remain silent notwithstanding.

It may be noted that Article 57 of the Permanent Court's Statute did not itself require the publication of the division of votes. Only in 1926, when the first Rules were amended, was it provided that the decision should record the number of Judges forming the majority. Up to that time, the correct number in favour of the Permanent Court's findings remained unknown. Moreover, by its first Rules of Court of 24 March 1922 the Court effectively interpreted Article 57 of the Statute so as to allow the mere statement of dissent, as well as an exposition.[4] In the earlier years—until the Rules of 1926 made it impossible—dissenting opinions were sometimes attached to the private meeting at which the final vote was taken, with the public record of the dissent being subsequently made.[5] Article 57 of the Permanent Court's Statute also referred only to contentious proceedings, and not to Advisory Opinions. The first Rules of the Court allowed, in Article 71, a statement or exposition of dissent for Advisory Opinions;[6] and again, it was the amended Rules of 1926 which (Article 71 (1)) provided for the recording of the number of judges forming the majority in an Advisory Opinion. The debates and the decisions taken focused, as before, on the rights of dissenters to make their position—and perhaps also their views—public. It did not centre on any duty to do so.

Since 1926 there has therefore grown up the practice of attaching dissenting opinions in both contentious cases and advisory opinions. The wording of the relevant provisions of the Statutes of both the Permanent and International Court, and the successive Rules of each, has also allowed the occurence of the occasional practice of not identifying certain votes at all.[7]

There have been several cases before the International Court where it

4. See *Id.* at 411; M. Hudson, *The Permanent Court of International Justice, 1920-1942,* at 588 (1943).

5. 3 *P.C.I.J. Annual Report* (ser. E) 216-17 (1927).

6. The practice grew up that dissents could be attached to Orders. See, *e.g.*, Advisory Opinion on the Customs Régime Between Germany and Austria, [1931] P.C.I.J. serv. A/B, No. 41 at 91.

7. For example, while only four judges voted against the adoption of the opinion, only three of the dissenting judges were named in the *Advisory Opinion on the Free City of Danzig and International Labour Organization,* [1930] P.C.I.J. ser. B, No. 18.

has not been possible to identify all the votes. In the *Fisheries Case*[8] judgment of 18 December 1951 the Court was composed of Judges Basdevant, Guerrero, Alvarez, Hackworth, Winiarski, Zorîcíc, De Visscher, McNair, Klaestad, Badawi, Read and Hsu Mo. By 10 votes to 2 the Court decided that the method employed for the delimitation of the fisheries zone by the Royal Norwegian Decree of July 12, 1935 was not contrary to international law; and by 8-4 it found that the base lines fixed by the said decree in application of this method were not contrary to international law. Judge Hackworth appended a brief statement indicating his agreement with the Court's conclusions, but basing this outcome on a finding of proven historic title by Norway. Judges Alvarez and Hsu Mo wrote separate opinions. And Judges McNair and Read appended a joint dissent. It is thus not clear who the two additional dissenting judges were on the second part of the Court's findings. Interestingly, Sir Arnold McNair, though of the nationality of one of the parties before the Court, had no hesitation in openly voting against the position of his country, or in giving his reasons in a learned dissent.

In the *Anglo-Iranian Oil Case*[9] (preliminary objection) of 22 July 1952, the Court was composed of Judges Guerrero, McNair, Alvarez, Basdevant, Hackworth, Winiarski, Zorîcíc, Klaestad, Badawi, Read, Hsu Mo, Levi Carneiro, Armand-Ugon and Judge *ad hoc* Sandjabi. It found, by nine votes to five, that it had no jurisdiction. McNair attached an individual opinion, and there were four named dissents - Judgrs Alvarez, Hackworth, Read, and Carneiro. One may speculate that the fifth vote came from the *ad hoc* judge. In any event, the other judge who was a national of one of the parties - Sir Arnold McNair - once again spoke out in forthright fashion.

In *The Right of Passage over Indian Territory Case* (Preliminary Objections),[10] November 26, 1957, the Court was dealing with no fewer than six preliminary objections. The Bench in this case was Judges Hackworth, Badawi, Guerrero, Basdevant, Winiarski, Zorîcíc, Klaestad, Read, Armand-Ugon, Kojevnikov, Zafrullah Khan, Lauterpacht, Quintana, Cordova, Wellington Koo, and *ad hoc* judges Chagla and Fernandes. The first and second preliminary objections advanced by India were rejected by fourteen votes to three. The third was rejected by sixteen votes to one, and the fourth by 15 votes to 2. The Court decided by 13 votes to 4 to join the fifth preliminary objection to the merits, and by 15 votes to 2 to join the sixth preliminary objection to the merits. In this case it is possible to identify a sufficient number of dissenters for the maximum of four dissenting votes. Klaestad and

8. [1951] *ICJ Reports* 116.
9. (Jurisdiction), [1952] *ICJ Reports* 93.
10. Case concerning the Right of Passage over Indian Territory (Preliminary Objections), [1957) ICJ Reports 125.

Fernandes both agreed that the fifth preliminary objection should have been rejected. Chagla joined the other *ad hoc* judge in dissent - an uncommon occurrence - but on the grounds that all the preliminary objections should have been accepted. Badawi issued a dissent, and Kojevnikov wrote a short statement saying that he was unable to agree with the Court as it should declare itself without jurisdiction at this stage. But what still is not clear is which of the judges that have been named voted which way on each of the six preliminary objections.

In the merits phase of the *Rights of Passage*[11] case, 12 April 1960, the Court was composed as for the preliminary phase, save that Judges Guerrero, Zorîcíc, Read and Lauterpacht were not sitting, while Judges Spender and Spiropoulos were. The Bench totalled fifteen in number for this case. By 13 votes to 2 the Court (1) rejected the fifth preliminary objection; and by 11 votes to 4 (2) rejected the sixth preliminary objection. By 11 votes to 4 it (3) found that Portugal had in 1954 a right of passage between the Enclaves of Dadra and Nagar-Aveli, and the coastal district of Daman and between these enclaves, to the extent necessary for the exercise of Portuguese sovereignty over the enclaves and subject to the regulation and control of India in respect of private persons, civil officials and goods in general. By 8 votes to 7 the Court held (4) that Portugal did not in 1954 have such a right in respect of armed forces, armed police, arms and ammunition; and by 9 votes to 6 that (5) India had not acted contrary to its obligations resulting from Portugal's right of passage. Declarations were made by Judges Klaestad, Basdevant, Badawi, Kojevnikov, and Spiropoulos. Judge Kojevnikov reiterated his position of the earlier phase—that Portugal failed by virtue of the remaining preliminary objections. He agreed only with the Court's fifth finding. Judge Willington Koo wrote a separate opinion. Dissents were appended by Judges Winiarski, Badawi, Armand-Ugon, Quintana, Spender, and Judges *ad hoc* Chagla and Fernandes (for their different reasons). One imagines that the maximum dissenting figure of seven (in regard to the Court's fourth finding) came when these judges joined with Judge Kojevnikov.

So far only contentious cases have been addressed. However, in the Advisory Opinion given by the Court in respect of *The Maritime Safety Committee of the Inter-governmental Maritime Consultative Organization*[12] (8 June 1960) the full voting was again not apparent. The Court was here composed of Judges Klaestad, Zafrullah Khan, Basdevant, Hackworth, Winiarski, Badawi, Armand-Ugon, Kojevnikov, Quintana, Cordova, Wellington Koo, Spiropoulos, Spender and

11. Case concerning the Right of Passage over Indian Territory, [1960] *ICJ Reports* 6.

12. Advisory Opinion on the Constitution of the Maritime Safety Committee of the Inter-governmental Maritime Consultative Organization, [1960] *ICJ Reports* 150.

Alfaro. By nine votes to five the Court found that the Maritime Safety Committee of IMCO, which was elected on 15 January 1959, was not constituted in accordance with the Convention for the Establishment of the Organization. Judges Klaestad and Quintana each appended dissents; but who were the other three who voted against the Court's finding?

In 1964, in the *Barcelona Traction*[13] (preliminary objections) case a comparable situation arose. Here Armand-Ugon sat as an *ad hoc* judge, along with Ganshoff van der Meersch. The rest of the Court consisted of Judges Spender, Wellington Koo, Winiarski, Badawi, Spiropoulos, Fitzmaurice, Koretsky, Tanaka, Bustamante, Jessup, Morelli, Padilla Nervo, Forster and Gros. The Court (1) by 12 votes to 4 rejected the first preliminary objection (2) by 10 votes to 6 rejected the second preliminary objection.

In the *Nuclear Tests Case,*[14] to which we referred above, there was a vote of 8-6 in favour of the interim measures. Four judges dissented (Forster, Gros, Petrén, Ignacio-Pinto), and four others (Jiménez de Aréchaga, Waldock, Singh and Barwick) appended declarations, in terms that made it clear they formed part of the overall majority. The Court was on this occasion composed of the above listed judges (Sir Garfield Barwick being Judge *ad hoc*) and Judges Ammoun, Bengzon, Onyeama, de Castro, Morozov, and Ruda. It is not possible to see from the records which two of these last named judges voted along with the dissenting judges to make a total of six, and which four joined the majority to make the total of eight. In other words, the votes of Judges Ammoun, Bengzon, Onyeama, de Castro, Morozov and Ruda remain secret.

Certain brief comments should be made here. First, in so far as there is an argument that secrecy protects the judges who are nationals of an interested party to act free from any pressures, we may note that the judges with nationalities most closely involved—Gros of France, Forster of Senegal and Ignacio-Pinto of Dahomey—all voted openly, choosing to append dissents. One must look elsewhere for the reasons underlying the decision of these judges who exercised their right to remain silent and unidentified. Second, the Court decided not only to grant interim measures of protection, but that written proceedings should be directed to the question of the jurisdiction of the Court to entertain the dispute and of the admissibility of the Application. Non-admissibility is usually raised in relation to claims by the respondent.[15] As a directive to counsel this was unclear; and was made the more so by

13. Case concerning the Barcelona Traction, Light and Power Company, Ltd. (Preliminary Objections), [1964] *ICJ Reports* 6.

14. (New Zealand v. France) (Interim Protection), [1973] *ICJ Reports* 135.

15. *Id.* at 142.

the silence of six members of the Court. Further, the Court stated,[16] as it has done many times before,[17] that it could not exercise its power to indicate interim measures of protection unless the rights claimed in the Application, *prima facie,* appeared to fall within the purview of the Court's jurisdiction. In dealing with this, the Court merely listed the substantive claims of the Applicants and stated that "it cannot be assumed *a priori* that such claims fall completely outside the purview of the Court's jurisdiction, or that [the Applicants] may not be able to establish a legal interest in respect of these claims entitling the Court to admit the Application."[18] The Court here put the substantive claims and the question of admissibility in close proximity. It listed the jurisdictional claims and counterclaims, in very brief summary, earlier in its Orders, and summarized:

> the material submitted to the Court leads it to the conclusion, at the present stage of the proceedings, that the provisions invoked by the Applicant appear, prima facie, to afford a basis on which the jurisdiction of the Court might be founded; and . . . the Court will accordingly proceed to examine the Applicant's request for the indication of interim measures of protection.[19]

There was no more detailed examination of any of the jurisdictional issues, nor of the substantive issues in so far as they related to admissibility.[20] Both the dissenting judgments and the declarations revealed a concern with points relating to the next phase which counsel would have to address. They were hindered by not knowing any of the views - either in dissent or in separate declarations - of the six silent members of the Bench.

In the *Nuclear Tests* case there had appeared some speculation, ahead of the Order for Interim Measures, about the probably decision by the Court. Statements appeared in the Australian press which were later the subject of an investigation by the Court, through its Registrar. The Court subsequently, on 26 March 1974, adopted a resolution in which it "expresse[d] its strong disapproval of the making, circulation or publication of all statements anticipating or purporting to anticipate

16. *Id.* at 139.

17. Fisheries Jurisdiction Case (Federal Republic of Germany v. Iceland) (Interim Protection), [1972] *ICJ Reports* 30 at 33. For a good resume see I. Shihata, *The Power of the International Court to Determine Its Own Jurisdiction* 170-80 (1965).

18. Nuclear Tests Case (New Zealand v. France) (Interim Protection), [1973] *ICJ Reports* 135 at 140; Nuclear Tests Case (Australia v. France) (Interim Protection), [1973] *ICJ Reports* 99 at 103.

19. Nuclear Tests Case (New Zealand v. France) (Interim Protection), [1973] *ICJ Reports* 135 at 138.

20. See *id.* at 142.

or forecast the manner in which judges of the Court will cast their votes in a pending case . . . "[21] Similar speculation can only be encouraged by judges not identifying their votes. Finally, it would require a lack of a sense of humour to fail to note that the Court "adopted the above resolution by eleven votes to three" - not unanimously, and with the votes not identified!

On 13 July 1973 the Court issued another order concerned with interim measures of protection - this time in the case concerning trial of Pakistani prisoners of War (Pakistan - India). On 11 May 1973 Pakistan had instituted proceedings against India in respect of a dispute concerning charges of genocide made against 195 Pakistani nationals who were in Indian custody. Pakistan further asked that, as an interim measure of protection, the Court should direct that charges of genocide should not interrupt repatriation of prisoners of war and civilian-internees; and that even individuals who were in the custody of India and charged with genocide should not be transferred to Bangladesh for trial until the Court had ruled on Pakistan's claims concerning jurisdiction. The Court was composed of Judges Lachs, Forster, Gros, Bengzon, Petrén, Onyeama, Ignacio-Pinto, Morozov, Jiménez de Aréchaga, Waldock, Singh and Ruda. Negotiations proceeded on the diplomatic level and Pakistan asked the Court to postpone consideration of its request for interim measures. The Court found that as urgency was of the essence for interim measures, it was not called upon to pronounce on the original request. By 8 votes to 4 the Court decided that written proceedings should be addressed to the jurisdiction of the Court to entertain the dispute, and fixed time limits.[22] Judge Najendra Singh appended a separate opinion and Judge Petrén a dissent. The classification of Judge Petrén's opinion as a dissent seems correct, though there is some confusion. Under the order itself, and initialled by the President and the Registrar, there appears the announcement that Judge Singh appended a separate opinion and Judge Petrén a dissenting opinion.[23] Judge Petrén's opinion is headed "Dissenting Opinions" (*opinions dissidentes*); although in the French text the running page heading remains "op. diss.," in the English text it becomes "sep. op."[24] He states in his opinion—the contents of which are beyond the scope of this essay—

> I was in a position to assent to the operative paragraph of the Order, the terms of which concern solely the organization of the

21. International Court of Justice, Communiqué No. 74/2, March 26, 1974.

22. The case was ultimately withdrawn from the lists, but remained of interest in the context of the topic here under discussion.

23. Case concerning Trial of Pakistani Prisoners of War (Interim Protection), [1973] *ICJ Reports* 328 at 331. The French text speaks of "*son opinion dissidente.*"

24. *Id.* at 335.

> further proceedings on the question of the Court's jurisdiction.
> If I have nevertheless voted against the Order, it is essentially on account of paragraphs 13 and 14.[25]

For present purposes we may merely note that, while the vote is recorded as 9 to 4, the position of only two judges is identifiable. Had the case proceeded to its next phase, this could have been significant for counsel in their preparations.

In attempting to comment on this practice of the nonidentification of all the votes, which is more common than has perhaps been generally supposed, it is necessary to return to the reasons advanced for or against a system of secrecy.

Two major sets of reasons have been advanced in support of the Statute provision whereby judges are not bound publicly to record their votes or to state their reasons. Indeed, these arguments were also initially advanced, in the years preparatory to the establishment of the Permanent Court, to urge that dissents should not be permissible at all. The first argument is that dissents and separate opinions are damaging to the authority of the Court. It was argued that the great moral and intellectual quality of a decision of the Court would be weakened if it did not appear to be unanimous. That this view must be examined seriously is clear; in the Court the bench is customarily composed of large numbers - much larger than in a national Court—and where there is a narrow majority, and the minority opinions are lengthy and are published, minority opinions can detract from the authority of the Court's decision.[26] In the final analysis one comes back to the reality that what determines authoritativeness is not unanimity, or the length of opinions, but quality: "[It] is not the division of votes, but the force of the arguments of majority and minority which determines the moral authority of the decision."[27] Lauterpacht wisely summarises the issue thus:

> no formal authority can in the long run shield a defective decision from the impact, in proportion to its merits, of a dissent. Mere dissent cannot weaken the authority of the decision. The merits of the dissent may have that effect. On the other hand, if the dissent is one-sided or extravagant, it will add

25. *Id.* at 335-36.

26. The *South West Africa Cases* ([1950] *ICJ Reports* 128, [1962] *ICJ Reports* 319, [1966] *ICJ Reports* 6) are examples; both the jurisdictional and merits cases being decided by small majorities, with lengthy and important dissents. And even in cases with larger—and indeed very large—marjorities (such as *Barcelona Traction*) the dissents and separate opinions can seem disproportionate in size to the Court's decision.

27. Verzijl, *supra* note 2, at 416.

emphasis to the balance and the restraint of the decision of the Court.[28]

Thus it can be argued that published dissents are a stimulus to the production of the best possible majority decision - as well as, in the celebrated words of a Chief Justice of the Supreme Court, "an appeal to the brooding spirit of the law, to the intelligence of a future day."[29] We conclude that it is the calibre of the majority opinion, and not its unanimity, which will provide the authority that the Court has traditionally and correctly sought; and that, paradoxically, the publication of thoughtful separate opinions and dissents may play a useful role in bringing this about by defining the majority view.

Historically, a related cautionary note was advanced, namely, that the Permanent Court was meant to be a final court, without appeal, and that this could only be guaranteed by not permitting alternative views to emanate from the bench, which would provide, as it were, grounds for appeal. Further, there was and is a widespread variation in domestic practice on the question of publication of dissents. This was reflected in the deep divisions on this question expressed both at the drafting stage of the Statute of the Permanent Court, and in the discussions of the Permanent Court in 1926 when it considered possible revisions of the Rules.[30] The Court itself was divided on the right to append dissenting opinions. Secret voting was fairly usual among the continental legal systems, with a strong Anglo-Saxon tradition to the contrary. The discussion ran partly, though not entirely, along national lines: Anzilotti was strongly in favour of open votes though secret voting in Court is the normal practice in Italy. M. Politis, three years later,[31] thought that this building up of an international jurisprudence was best served by following English-speaking practice in arbitral matters. The

28. H. Lauterpacht, *The Development of International Law by the International Court* 67 (1958) [hereinafter cited as Lauterpacht].

29. C. Hughes, *The Supreme Court of the United States* 68 (1928).

30. For an interesting and informative account see Hambro, "Dissenting and Individual Opinions in the ICJ," in 16 *Zeitschrift für Ausländisches Offentliches Recht und Völkerrecht* 229 (1956) [hereinafter cited as Hambro]. He points out, among such interesting information, that the award in the *Ambatielos Case* ([1953] *ICJ Reports* 10) did not even mention the votes.

31. The matter was dicsussed in the 1929 Committee for the Revision of the statute, in view of the possibility of United States adherence to the Statute.

publication of dissents had been influential in the development of international law.

Certainly in the United Kingdom it has been the custom for Courts to publish the decision and reasons (however brief) of all the judges. This has been the procedure followed in the Court of Appeal and the House of Lords, and has not been considered to damage the authority of the majority view. The Privy Council, for reasons relating to its singular position within the British Commonwealth,[32] has until recently been an obvious and important exception. It has been suggested by a well-informed commentator that

> obscurities in the reasons of occasional opinions of the Privy Council merely cover the fact that the judges have not been as one in their approach and that the opinion has been modified to take account of their differences.[33]

In the United States Supreme Court, of course, the majority opinion is identified as being written by one named Justice, with the views of any concurring or dissenting judges being made known. Jefferson had rejected the idea of an opinion being arrived at "with the silent acquiescence of lazy or timid associates,"[34] and delivered as if unanimous. He thought that it should be obligatory for each judge to state his own position publicly in each case - whether he supported the majority or minority. But the volume of Supreme Court work did not make such a solution possible. The American and Anglo-Saxon practice have contrasted sharply with the continental legal system.

The second major reason advanced for silence by dissenting judges was not so much a matter of cultural traditions as of political assessment. It was urged that a rule whereby dissents were not publicly permitted would protect national judges and *ad hoc* judges from undesirable pressures. Edvard Hambro, though he is in favour of published dissents, puts a related point: the existence of the right to attach a dissent means that a national judge feels under a pressure to write a dissent even though he would have been happier and less embarrassed if it had not been incumbent upon him to do so.[35] But, although the *ad hoc* judges customarily reacted in this way, from time

32. For an excellent analysis see McWhinney, "Judicial Concurrences and Dissents: A Comparative View of Opinion-writing in Final Appellate Tribunals," 31 *Can. B. Rev.* 595 (1953).

33. *Id.* at 601.

34. Letter from Thomas Jefferson to Thomas Ritchie, Dec. 25, 1820, in 12 *The Works of Thomas Jefferson* 178 (P. Ford ed. 1904).

35. Hambro, *supra* note 30, at 233-34.

to time national judges[36] have shown their willingness to explain in detail why they disagree with some or all of the legal views of their governments.[37] Their freedom to do so publicly is a guarantee of the independence of the Court, available for all to see. A system whereby dissent was not allowed would encourage the view that national judges invariably and blindly support their governments' views.

It should be noted that, whether they are published or not, the views of dissenting judges must necessarily continue to play a significant part in the work of the Court. Although the formulation of the Court's judgement or opinion is necessarily a private procedure, certain authentic accounts exist. Edvard Hambro, writing from his personal experience as Registrar of the Court gave[38] a clear picture of how a collective view was arrived at. Lauterpacht, writing in 1958 stated that the resolution adopted by the Court in 1931 and revised in 1936, still represented the procedure followed by the Court.[39] This resolution, though not formally part of the Rules of the Court, was adopted by the International Court in 1946 and annexed as a footnote to Article 30 of the Rules. On 5 July 1968 the Court adopted a new Resolution concerning the International Judicial Practice of the Court.[40] Article 33 of the Revised[41] Rules of the Court carries reference to this Resolution in a footnote. The new Resolution is more detailed than the old one, spelling out with great precision the sequence by which all judges have the opportunity to identify the problems as they see them, and to make their views known. For our purposes here - limited to identifying the vote of dissenting opinions and the publication thereof - we will merely note that in the 1936 Resolution, after the conclusion of both written and oral hearings, and an initial deliberation held under the direction of the President to bring out the questions to be solved, "3 . . . The President ensures . . . that each judge has made known his impressions

36. The Advisory Commission of Jurists, meeting in July 1920, recommended that the fact of opposition be reported, with no reasons being allowed. The De Lapradelle Report explains that the Commission had not been prepared to permit the statement of reasons because it wished to avoid lengthy arguments on the part of the "national" judges against an unfavourable decision, but that in that case it could hardly confer on the other judges the right to set forth their dissenting opinions. Apparently the idea was also advanced that "national" judges might be forbidden to disclose their views, in order to ease their position, but this was abandoned. Verzijl, *supra* note 2, at 411.

37. *E.g.*, Anzilotti in the Case of the S.S. "Wimbledon," [1923] P.C.I.J. serv. A, No. 1; the Polish judge in the Advisory Opinion on Railway Traffic Between Lithuania and Poland, [1931] P.C.I.J. ser. A/B, No. 42; the Belgian and British judges in the Oscar Chinn Case, [1934] P.C.I.J. serv. A/B, No. 63; and Lord McNair in the Fisheries Case, [1951] *ICJ Reports* 116.

38. 7 *Current Legal Problems* 218 (1954).

39. Lauterpacht, *supra* note 28, at 63-65. See also the more racy account given by Judge Dillard in 67 *Proc. Am. Soc'y Int'l L.* 296 (1973).

40. [*1967-1968*] *ICJ Yearbook* 88 [hereinafter cited as 1968 Rules).

41. Amendments adopted on 10 May 1972, [1971-1972] *ICJ Yearbook* 3.

in regard to them. 4. At a suitable interval of time after this deliberation, each judge expresses his personal view in writing in the form of a note, without committing himself to a definite opinion."[42] After the President has, on the basis of these notes, prepared a plan of discussion, and after further deliberations, "6. At a subsequent and final deliberation each question is discussed, put to the vote by the President and decided."[43] Under the 1968 Resolution - where the function of identifying the problems is more rigorously separated from the function of offering preliminary views therein - all judges are again required to submit a written note. The Resolution indicates in some detail what is expected:

> 4. (i) At a suitable interval of time after this deliberation, each judge prepares a written note which is distributed to the other judges.
> (ii) the written note contains the judge's views on the questions which have been called to notice by indicating:
> (a) whether any questions would be eliminated from further consideration or should not, or need not, be decided by the Court;
> (b) the precise formulation of the questions which should be answered by the Court;
> (c) the judge's tentative opinion as to the answers to be given to the questions in (b) and his reasons therefor;
> (d) his tentative conclusion as to the correct disposal of the case.[44]

Moreover, after further examination of this written note, "all judges . . . must declare their views."[45]

No resolution can, of course, ensure that all judges participate with equal vigour; some judges will always be more prominent in the work of the Court than others. Nor is that prominence to be equated with the number of separate or dissenting opinions that appear under the name of a particular judge. Up to this stage, therefore, both before and after the 1968 Resolution, the judge who ultimately forms part of the minority will play an active role, explaining his views on the issues collectively identified. To his colleagues, even if not to the public,[46] he is required to make clear both his position and his reasons.

42. *I.C.J.* ser. D, No. 1 at 63. See also Lauterpacht, *supra* note 28, at 64.

43. References cited note 42 *supra*.

44. 1968 Rules, *supra* note 40.

45. *Id.*

46. As for those judges who wish to deliver a separate or dissenting opinion, they are required to circulate their drafts after the first reading of the decision of the Court "and before the draft of the decision as prepared for the second reading has been circulated" (references cited note 42 *supra*, art. 8), "with a time limit fixed by the Court" (1968 Rules, *supra* note 40, art. 7, para. ii).

The discussion above leads to three conclusions.

III. CONCLUSIONS

I. *First Conclusion*

It seems that, notwithstanding the requirement under the Resolution on the internal practice of the Court whereby all judges must indicate their views on all questions before the Court, it is generally undesirable that they should remain silent as to which way they voted, and the reasons therefor. The judicial function is a public, as well as a private one. The strengthening and development of international law require not only private participation in reaching a judicial decision, but the full elucidation, explanation and criticism of such decisions. At its broadest, the issue may be stated thus: international law, being a decentralized legal system, relies heavily on the full and overt participation of the judges of the International Court. It has been persuasively suggested that it is not the number of votes, but the force of the arguments, which impresses the experts and finally also public opinion. These arguments should therefore be disclosed.

> There must be the widest possible opportunity to become acquainted with them, to support them, and also, if necessary, to criticise them. The whole trend of the development of international adjudication, and thus also of international justice itself, depends upon it.[47]

Any national or political considerations—even the belief that it is easier to avoid becoming involved in political matters by remaining silent in certain circumstances—are surely outweighed by basic beliefs in the nature of the judicial function. It is surely right that[48] juridical convictions must be openly declared, because ultimately it will not be the secrecy of the deliberations, but on the contrary their publicity, which will guarantee international confidence in the decisions of the Court. Equally, who can doubt that the contribution by the Court to international law and the settlement of disputes rests to a large degree upon the completeness and thoroughness of its exposition? It depends on the exposition and formulation of "the law behind the cases."[49] A related point[50] is that the Statute of the Court requires that the representation of the principal legal systems of the world should be assured. It would be ironic and unsatisfactory if that diversity of ap-

47. Verzijl, *supra* note 2, at 416-17.
48. *Id.* at 417.
49. A point made—a phrase used—by Lauterpacht. Lauterpacht, *supra* note 28, at 71.
50. Also convincingly advanced by Lauterpacht. *Id.* at 69.

proach could only find expression in the private deliberations of the Court or in the common denominator of the collective decision. The logic of these arguments is to suggest that, while it is undesirable for the votes of some judges go unidentified, it is hardly more satisfactory to have the vote recorded, without reasons being given. In other words, dissenting votes should be recorded, and the reasons for them given. This is because: "a bare dissent, unaccompanied by reasons, is of no greater value than a decision without reasons; it presumes to substitute the authority of the individual Judge for the strength of the argument underlying the dissent."[51]

A system which prefers dissents to be public, with reasons given, is a

> safeguard of the individual responsibility of the Judges as well as of the integrity of the Court as an instritution. In a tribunal which, by reason of the circumstances encompassing its activity, is exposed to imputations of influence of extraneous considerations, . . . [such a system] constitutes a powerful safeguard. It precludes any charge of reliance on mere alignment of voting and lifts the pronouncements of the Court to the level of the inherent power of legal reason and reasoning.[52]

We have already indicated that the practice of the Court does *not* in fact show that it is national judges who rely on the right for their votes to be unidentified, their views unspoken. Indeed, some judges, mindful of the political milieu in which the Court exists, have insisted that their position is best protected by overtness. Speaking of the possibility of publishing a dissenting opinion, a former President of the Court said

> the possibility of publication [of dissenting opinions] was a guarantee against any subconscious intrusion of political considerations, and . . . judgments were more likely to be given in accordance with the real force of arguments submitted.[53]

The same arguments obtain *a fortiori* in respect of our preferment of a moral duty to publish the fact of and reasons for a dissent.

If the judicial contribution to international law is to be made to its fullest, if the political considerations do not in fact militate in favour of silence, then equally the authority of the Court is not impaired by the attachment of dissents. This too we have sought to contend in the preceding pages. The findings of the Informal Inter-Allied Committee on the Future of the Permanent Court of Justice[54] in 1944 are still

51. *Id.* at 67-68.

52. *Id.* at 68-69.

53. Huber, "Ko-existenz und Gemeinschaft," 1956 *Züricher Student* No. 3, at 52.

54. Informal Inter-Allied Committee on the Future of the Permanent Court of International Justice, "Report," 39 *Am. J. Int'l L. Doc. Supp.* 1 (1945).

persuasive today. The Committee noted that matters which came before the Court are necessarily difficult, and an appearance of unanimity produced by the absence of dissenting judgments would be misleading. If those judges who dissented were not identified, there would be speculation, continued the Report with commendable foresight: "In these circumstances, we think it far better that those who dissent should say so in open court and give their reasons."[55] The Committee went on to observe that there was a psychological advantage in letting the losing side see—through dissenting opinions—that its arguments had been fully taken into account. After identifying the contribution that dissents can make to the development of international law, the Committee went on:

> For these reasons we would not only preserve the system of dissenting judgments, but go further than the relevant provision of the existing Statute, which only confers a right on dissenting Judges to deliver a separate opinion. In our view it should be obligatory on any Judge who dissents from the majority to state his reasons for so doing.[56]

II. *Second Conclusion*

So far as contentious cases are concerned, it is particularly desirable that the voting should be identifiable, with reasons given, in phases relating to preliminary objections or to interim measures. From a functional point of view it is a hindrance to counsel not to know, to the fullest extent possible, the views that judges have on the prima facie grounds for jurisdiction before the granting of interim measures and proceeding to a full examination of jurisdiction, or on the jurisdictional issues before proceeding to the merits. This is particularly so if the majority of the Court votes for the joinder of certain preliminary objections to the merits—or if, as in the *Nuclear Tests Case,* the jurisdictional issues still lie ahead—and indeed, are complicated by questions of admissibility.

III. *Third Conclusion*

Still less does there appear to be any justification for silence as to vote and reasons in so far as advisory opinions are concerned. The Court is the judicial organ of the United Nations, and although there is a discretionary element in the exercise of its advisory jurisdiction,[57] it will

55. *Id.* para. 81, subpara. *b.*
56. *Id.* para. 82.
57. Statute of the International Court of Justice annexed to the Charter of the United Nations, *done* June 26, 1945, art. 65, 59 Stat. 1055 (1945), T.S. No. 993.

not easily refuse to provide legal advice for the authorized United Nations organs. The requests come from United Nations organs and not from States—though in most cases[58] States members of the United Nations have an interest in the outcome. It had long been thought that there are, *stricto sensu,* no "national" judges in an advisory opinion.[59] Certainly judges cannot reasonably feel that their judicial independence and freedom from political pressures commends non-identification and silence in a request for legal advice from a United Nations organ or authorised agency. Yet as we have shown, in the *IMCO Case* the votes are not fully identifiable. The other side of the coin is that the duty of all the judges—and not just those forming the majority—to contribute to the development of international law is arguably even greater in the area of advisory jurisdiction. We do not find persuasive—for reasons that have been advanced above—the view that a divided opinion would be of little help for the organ requesting it. It is to be hoped that the practice of not divulging the votes of all the judges, or their reasons for dissent—which had occurred more often than is generally realized—will not grow. Indeed, there are good arguments for hoping that, even though the recent amendments to the Rules of the Court have not touched the point, this practice will fall into disuse.

58. With administrative tribunal questions being the main exception.

59. South Africa unsuccessfully sought, in the 1971 *Advisory Opinion on the Legal consequences for States of the Continued Presence of South Africa in Namibia (South West Africa) notwithstanding Security Council Resolution 276* (1970), [1971] *ICJ Reports* 16, to secure a judge *ad hoc* on the grounds that she had no national on the bench, while nationals of other countries hostile to her position were on the bench, and her legal rights were at issue. In the *Western Sahara* Case [1971] *ICJ Reports,* a judge *ad hoc* was allowed in a case on which an advisory opinion was sought. Mauritania and Morocco had both requested a judge *ad hoc*. The Court by order of 22 May 1975 found that Morocco was entitled under Articles 31 and 68 of the Statute of the Court and Article 89 of the Rules of the Court to choose a person to sit. The Court found that there appeared to be a legal dispute between Morocco and Spain regarding the territory of Western Sahara and that it was being asked to give an advisory opinion upon a legal question actually pending between two or more states, [1975] *ICJ Reports* 6. The condition for the application of Article 89 of the Rules was thus satisfied in the case of Morocco whereas it was not in the case of Mauritania there being, in the view of the Court, no legal dispute pending between Mauritania and Spain.

THE GENERAL WELFARE AS A LEGAL INTEREST

C. WILFRED JENKS

I. THE SOUTH WEST AFRICA CASES

The *South West Africa Cases*,[1] in which the International Court of Justice decided in 1966 by the casting vote of its President that Ethiopia and Liberia had not established any legal right or interest appertaining to them in the subject of the claim, raised issues fundamental for the future of international law which will continue to be much debated for a generation to come. The *Namibia* Case[2] in which (in an advisory opinion given to the General Assembly in 1971) the Court subsequently held on the basis of resolutions of the General Assembly and the Security Council that the continued presence of South Africa in Namibia is illegal has not set these questions at rest.

The largest of these questions was how far, in a changing world, the Court may give legal recognition to "values or interests which had previously been excluded from the sphere of law"[3] or must take the law as it finds it.[4] This is no new question and will always be with us. Within this large question a more specific issue which constitutes an aspect of it was brought into sharp focus. How far is the general welfare a legal interest which can be invoked by parties whose interest in the subject matter of the claim is the general welfare and not "individual prejudice or individual substantive interest"?

The contrasted views appear clearly in the opinions.

The majority of the Court held that the claimants had not established a legal interest entitling them to a decision in their favour. They held that the decision in a previous phase of the case that the parties were

The late C. WILFRED JENKS was Director General of the International Labour Organization; Honorary Fellow of Gonville and Caius College, Cambridge; Member of the Institute of International Law; and a member of the International Academy of Comparative Law.

1. [1966] *ICJ Reports* 6.
2. Advisory Opinion on Namibia, [1971] *ICJ Reports* 16.
3. South West Africa Cases, [1966] *ICJ Reports* 51, 252 (dissenting opinion).
4. *Id.* at 48.

entitled to invoke its jurisdiction was "not the same thing as finding the existence of a legal right or interest relative to the merits of the claim."[5] Jurisdictional clauses, they considered, "do not determine whether parties have substantive rights, but only whether, if they have them, they can vindicate them by recourse to a tribunal."[6] States in their individual capacity "can appear before the Court only as litigants in a dispute with another State, even if their object in so doing is only to obtain a declaratory judgment" and the moment they so appear "it is necessary for them, even for that limited purpose, to establish, in relation to the defendant party in the case, the existence of a legal right or interest in the subject-matter of their claim, such as to entitle them to the declarations or pronouncements that they seek: or in other words that they are parties to whom the defendant State is answerable under the relevant instrument or rule of law."[7] The terms of the mandates, unlike those of the minorities treaties, did not give Members of the League a right enforceable by legal process to exact compliance, outside the procedure of the Council of the League, with the provisions of the mandates relating to the general conduct of the mandatory as distinguished from those provisions protecting the special interests of particular Members of the League.[8] Ethiopia and Liberia were therefore, not entitled, as former members of the League, to claim from the Court compliance by South Africa with the provisions relating to its general conduct as a mandatory. From this reasoning the majority concluded that:

> the argument amounts to a plea that the Court should allow the equivalent of an "*actio popularis,*" or right resident in any member of a community to take legal action in vindication of a public interest. But although a right of this kind may be known to certain municipal systems of law, it is not known to international law as it stands at present: nor is the Court able to regard it as imported by the "general principles of law" referred to in Article 38, paragraph (1)(c), of its Statute.[9]

The other view was most fully and clearly stated in the dissenting opinion of Judge Jessup who, reaffirming views which he had expressed in the jurisdictional phase of the *South West Africa Cases* in 1962,[10] emphasized the degree of legal recognition of general interest in the motivation and operation of certain of the peace settlements of 1919-

5. *Id.* at 37.
6. *Id.* at 39.
7. *Id.* at 34.
8. See *id.* at 36-47.
9. *Id.* at 47.
10. [1962] *ICJ Reports* 319, 425.

1920.[11] "[G]reat charters of human liberties," he said, "were signed and ratified and became binding on States."[12] Provision was made for recourse to the Permanent Court of International Justice in matters relating to their application:

> To be sure, each area of general interest in the Peace Settlements had its own system and the role of the Court was different as suited the needs of each case. But the point which stands out is the recognition of the right of States *in the general interest,* and without needing to assert direct injury suffered by them or their nationals, to resort to the Court for an authoritative interpretation of the meaning of the obligations which States had assumed in order that labour, and minorities and dependent peoples might enjoy international protection. . . . [I]n the era of the Paris Peace Treaties, States could invoke the Court in the general international interest when their own particular interests were not involved.[13]

This historical background, described at length in the opinion,[14] gave the parties standing to submit the matter to the Court:

> I agree that there is no generally established *actio popularis* in international law. But international law has accepted and established situations in which States are given a right of action without any showing of individual prejudice or individual substantive interest as distinguished from the general interest.[15]

The issue is clearly drawn.

Where and how should the development of the law proceed from this point on? On this question the issue may be much less sharply drawn.

It is of quite special interest in this connection that Sir Gerald Fitzmaurice, one of the judges who in the *South West Africa Cases* was among the majority who held that "the equivalent of an "*actio popularis*" is "not known to international law as it stands at present" and could not be regarded as "imported" into international law by the "general principles of law"[16] referred to in the Statute, has more recently, in his Special Report for the Centenary of the Institute of International Law on *The Future of Public International Law and of the International Legal System in the Circumstances of Today,*[17]

11. [1966] *ICJ Reports* at 371 (dissenting opinion).
12. *Id.* at 373 (dissenting opinion).
13. *Id.* at 374 (dissenting opinion).
14. *Id.* at 374-87 (dissenting opinion).
15. *Id.* at 387-88 (dissenting opinion).
16. *Id.* at 47.
17. G. Fitzmaurice, *The Future of Public International Law and of the International Legal System in the Circumstances of Today* para. 113(b).

argued *de lege ferenda* that the creation of "a direct right to initiate action solely on the basis not merely of a personal interest but of the general interest" would "tend to open many at present fast-closed doors, by no means confined to one part of the world" and would in so doing realise the aspiration which I have expressed elsewhere that "the law should become the law of a true community, nourished by and giving nourishment to each successive stage in the development of the community" in which the general welfare is "a legal interest enforceable by and for all."

II. "ACTIO POPULARIS" FOR THE FUTURE

The time may, therefore, have come for a fresh look at the whole subject with the emphasis on the future.

Three different questions call for examination: 1. How desirable is it that international law should recognise an *actio popularis* and in what types of case? 2. How far should we regard the *South West Africa Cases* as the last word on the present state of the law? 3. What kind of steps can we envisage, *de lege ferenda,* to create an *actio popularis* in appropriate types of case?

How desirable or important it is that international law should recognise an *actio popularis* depends on the view taken of the scope and province of the law. On the view that international law consists essentially of rules demarcating the jurisdiction of states and defining their rights against and obligations towards each other, an *actio popularis* is at best an anomaly, justified, if at all, only in highly exceptional cases in which two conditions are fulfilled: firstly, that the beneficiary of the substantive rights and interests in issue is not in a position to act effectively on his own behalf; and secondly, that this possibility was so clearly foreseen that specific and unequivocal provision was made for it. These conditions will be regarded as less rigorous on the view that "a legal right or interest need not necessarily relate to anything material or 'tangible,' and can be infringed even though no prejudice of a material kind has been suffered,"[18] and that there is "nothing extraordinary in a State having a legal right to vindicate a purely altruistic interest"[19] because the whole tendency of the contemporary development of the law has been to give a larger place to general interests of the community which are not, and cannot be, measured by the material or "tangible" interests of particular members. The conditions may not wholly disappear but inaction by the direct beneficiary, rather than proof of a total impossibility of action, may

18. South West Africa Cases, [1966] *ICJ Reports* 6, 32.
19. *Id.* at 33.

justify the *actio popularis* and less specific and unequivocal provision for the *actio popularis* may be required; it becomes more legitimate to recognise such a right in a case arising in changed circumstances not foreseen in advance.

There are three broad areas in which the contemporary development of the law makes an *actio popularis* increasingly desirable: human rights; economic stability and growth; and scientific and technological development. Human rights is an area in which inhibitions upon effective action by the immediate beneficiaries may be particularly serious, but this is by no means the only reason for which an *actio popularis* may be both justifiable and desirable. In all these areas the rights and interests of particular parties merge into broader rights and interests and prejudice thereto are a matter of general concern in a wider community. The broad community interest in respect for human rights, the promotion of the general welfare, and the social discipline of scientific and technological development far transcends the interest of particular parties in particular transgressions of the developing law on these subjects. Such a community interest may also be less invidious to invoke and enforce in the always complex context of general interests, specific interests, and wholly disparate elements in bilateral relations which are, and have to be, continuously weighed against each other.

It may facilitate progress in the matter if we succeed in disentangling one from the other the separate and successive questions which need consideration in order to determine whether an *actio popularis* is appropriate in a particular type of case and what redress should be available through such an action. May it not be desirable to distinguish three questions, namely:

(a) whether the particular party is entitled to invoke the jurisdiction of the Court, tribunal or other appropriate body to which the matter has been submitted?
(b) whether the particular party is entitled to a declaration or other appropriate finding on the subject of the claim?
(c) whether the particular party is entitled to damages or any other specific redress in respect of the subject of the claim?

The Court itself, in the *South West Africa Cases,* distinguished between jurisdiction and standing. It upheld its jurisdiction in 1962 and denied the standing of the claimants in 1966. The judgment is very clear on the point, as it had to be to deny standing after upholding jurisdiction. A sufficient interest to invoke a jurisdictional clause did not, the Court held, establish "a sufficient interest in the subject-matter of their claim"[20] These were different matters. "The faculty of invoking

20. *Id.* at 37.

a jurisdictional clause depends on what tests or conditions of the right to do so are laid down by the clause itself. To hold that the parties in any given case belong to the category of State specified in the clause, that the dispute has the specified character, and that the forum is the one specified, is not the same thing as finding the existence of a legal right or interest relative to the merits of the claim."[21]

The same reasoning is equally applicable to the distinction between standing to obtain a declaration of rights and duties on a matter involving the general welfare, and rights and duties on a matter involving the general welfare, and entitlement to damages or some other specific redress in respect of individual substantive interest. Standing to obtain a declaration of rights and duties may well be broader than entitlement to specific redress, though the latter should not be too narrowly construed where a broad general interest and a multiplicity of specific applications of the general interest merge almost imperceptibly into each other.

If on these grounds we take the view that there may be cases, and perhaps an increasing number of cases, in which it is desirable that there should be an *actio popularis,* it continues to be of interest to consider how far the *South West Africa Cases* foreclose the matter as a statement of the present law, even for those who do not question their authority as wrongly decided. The judgment in the *South West Africa Cases* does not deny that "States may have a legal interest in vindicating a principle of international law, even though they have, in the given case, suffered no material prejudice, or ask only for token damages."[22] On the contrary, it indicates that "The Court simply holds that such rights or interests, in order to exist, must be clearly vested in those who claim them, by some text or instrument, or rule of law; —and that in the present case, none were ever vested in individual members of the League under any of the relevant instruments, or as a constituent part of the mandates system as a whole, or otherwise."[23] The decision must therefore be regarded as limited to the highly special circumstances of the particular cases. To distinguish a future case we do not, by the terms of the decision itself, need even a text or instrument clearly providing for an *actio popularis* if we can invoke a "rule of law" which justifies it. Such a rule may be one which has long been well established, but it may equally well be some contemporary development of the law.

While the possibility of progress towards the recognised acceptance of an *actio popularis* by the further progress of custom or by an evaluation of "general principles of law" different from that adopted by the Court in 1966 is by no means barred, such progress will remain uncertain and

21. *Id.*
22. *Id.* at 32.
23. *Id.* at 32-33.

precarious for much too long a period of time unless provision for an *actio popularis* in appropriate cases is made in some more systematic way and on some formal basis. It may be useful to envisage three possible successive stages in a process of giving the *actio popularis* a recognised status in the law of nations.

The first stage would be a much fuller study of the subject. Such a study would be very much in the tradition of Wolfgang Friedmann's many pioneer contributions to the exhaustive examination of topics calling for new departures in international and comparative law. On the occasion of the Centenary of the International Law Association, this author suggested that the I.L.A. should devote special attention to the question of the collective stake in civil liberties and means of making it procedurally effective, nationally and internationally, by such methods as the recognition of an *actio communis* or *actio popularis*. A broader study might encompass all aspects of the general welfare as a legal interest including in particular the collective stake in the full spectrum of human rights, the collective stake in economic stability and growth, and the collective stake in the impact on the ecosphere and society of scientific and technological development. It might devote special emphasis to the procedural means whereby the collective stake in the general welfare can be effectively invoked and enforced as a legal interest.

The second stage could be the approval in declaratory form, by the General Assembly of the United Nations or in some other appropriate way, of principles and procedural suggestions concerning the general welfare as a legal interest which are found, on responsible examination of such a study, to command a sufficiently wide measure of agreement to be acceptable to a sufficient number of governments. This does mean that it would be necessary to await virtual unanimity in the matter; but action would be premature until it was assured of solid and widespread support.

The third stage might consist of parallel measures and series of measures. One such measure might consist of the conversion of the provisions of the proposed declaration into formal international objectives expressed in treaty form. The treaty would contain a comprehensive formulation of the general welfare as a legal interest, with special reference to human rights, economic stability and growth, and the impact of scientific and technological development. Or course, this would involve problems, notably among them that of determining the point at which the general interest becomes sufficiently assessable and measureable to be legally enforceable, and that of whether there is a point at which proceedings must be regarded as vexatious or otherwise unreasonable rather than a legitimate assertion of the general interest.

Given these difficulties it may be wise to explore whether there is any possibility of making more immediate progress by providing specifically for an *actio popularis* in defined circumstances in general agreements dealing with particular aspects of human rights, economic co-operation, or the impact of scientific and technological development. The possibility of so doing should be considered systematically when such agreements are under discussion, but it must be admitted that the present position as regards the inclusion of any jurisdictional clause in such agreements is most discouraging.

All this will take a long time; but it is certainly not too soon to consider a long-term strategy in the matter. In a matter so important, but so difficult, it would be folly to disregard any of the alternative possibilities of progress; prudence suggests the wisdom of pursuing all of them as opportunities occur.

TREATIES AS "LEGISLATION"

ROBERT Y. JENNINGS

The Judgment of the International Court of Justice in the *Fisheries Jurisdiction Case*[1] carries an intriguing paragraph which, after referring to the Third Conference on the Law of the Sea, continues:

> The very fact of convening the third Conference on the Law of the Sea evidences a manifest desire on the part of all States to proceed to the codification of that law on a universal basis, including the question of fisheries and conservation of the living resources of the sea. Such a general desire is understandable since the rules of international maritime law have been the product of mutual accommodation, reasonableness and cooperation. So it was in the past, and so it necessarily is today. In the circumstances, the Court, as a court of law, cannot render judgment *sub specie legis ferendae,* or anticipate the law before the legislator has laid it down.

Insofar as the Court is saying that it can only apply existing law and is not itself a legislator the paragraph is little more than a truism. But it is the phrase "before the legislator has laid it down" (*"avant que le législateur l'ait édicté"*) that gives pause. It may well be that the Court here is merely speaking metaphorically and calling upon the obvious municipal law analogy. But if it is referring to the Third Conference on the Law of the Sea, the question occurs whether the conference can be regarded in any but a fanciful sense as a legislator; and what exactly is meant by the "codification of that law on a universal basis"?

First it must be said that this is different from the question posed to the International Court of Justice in the *Reparation for Injuries Suffered Case,* when it said that "the Court's opinion is that fifty States, representing the vast majority of the members of the international community, had the power, in conformity with international law, to bring into being an entity possessing objective international personality, and not merely personality recognized by them alone, together with

ROBERT Y. JENNINGS QC. is Whewell Professor of International Law in the University of Cambridge, Fellow of Jesus College.

1. [1974] *I.C.J. Reports* 3 at 23.

capacity to bring international claims".[2]

There is no suggestion of any truly legislative element here. It is an essential part of the function of every system of law to enable persons to do a number of things, such as creating corporate or non-corporate bodies, disposing of property, making various dispositions, and so on. Thus, it is elementary that States can, provided they do it "in conformity with international law," create an entity which has objective existence in that law, and the existence of which third States must respect, just as in domestic law a plurality of persons can make a club, or a company or other corporation "in conformity" with the law, the existence and personality of which company other persons must respect, whether they approve of its existence or not. As to the personality of the United Nations, the only question is whether it was really necessary to involve "the vast majority of members of the international community" in order to create an entity having objective international personality. Perhaps the Court was merely indicating an *a fortiori* case. In any event this was hardly a question of legislation.

In a like manner it must be said that the making of any lawful treaty must affect third States in that, though not bound by the terms of the treaty, they must nevertheless respect it as an instrument binding upon the parties, and should not interfere with its operation between the parties. As W.E. Hall put it, in what is still one of the best written general text books on international law in the English language: "In a secondary manner the due conclusion of an international contract also affects third parties. A state of things has come into existence which, having been legally created in pursuance of the fundamental rights of states, other countries are bound to respect . . . . So long therefore as a contract is in accordance with law, or consistent with the safety of states not parties to it, the latter must not prevent or hinder the contracting parties from carrying it out."[3] But this obligation of third States stems from the general law, not from the terms of the treaty. And the duty of third States to respect a treaty does not mean that a treaty can impose obligations or even rights upon them without their consent, nor of course can a treaty purport to encroach upon rights which third States enjoy under the general law, or indeed under their own treaties.

The question whether treaties can by their terms bind or benefit third States is dealt with in articles 34-38 of the Vienna Treaty on the Law of Treaties.[4] Article 34 states the general principle that: "A treaty does not create either obligations or rights for a third State without its consent." Articles 35, 36 and 37 deal with the case where a treaty is

2. [1949] *I.C.J. Reports* 174 at 185.

3. W. Hall, *A Treatise on International Law* 402 (8th ed. 1924).

4. *Open for signature* May 23, 1969, United Nations Conference on the Law of Treaties, *Official Records* 289, U.N. Doc. A/CONF. 39/27 (1971) [hereinafter cited as Vienna Convention on the Law of Treaties].

intended by the parties to create rights or obligations for particular third States and provides that it is only possible to create obligations for third States if "the third State expressly accepts that obligation in writing." The distinction between right and obligation is not always as clear cut as these articles seem to assume; but the governing principle must be that whenever there is an element of obligation, consent in writing is required, and consent in some form is required in any event. There is here therefore no trace of an exception to the *pacta tertiis* rule, which, as a recent authority has put it, "is supported both by general legal principle and by common sense."[5]

Article 38 of the Vienna Treaty, however, provides:

> Nothing in articles 34 to 37 precludes a rule set forth in a treaty from becoming binding upon a third State as a customary rule of international law, recognized as such.

This provision does not contemplate in any way that a treaty may as such become binding upon third parties. It is merely a proviso inserted out of abundant caution lest it be supposed that the *pacta tertiis* rule could inhibit the development of customary law which coincides with, and perhaps was inspired by, rules already expressed in a multilateral treaty. The words "recognized as such" make it clear that any general obligation can only proceed from custom and cannot proceed from the treaty. Indeed the criticism of article 38 heard at the Vienna Conference was that the question how treaty rules might be transformed into custom was purely a question of customary law and had nothing to do with the law of treaties.[6]

This, however, would be too formal an approach. Wide participation in a treaty may clearly be cogent evidence in an inquiry whether the requirements for the establishment of a new custom has been satisfied. This is especially so when it falls to an international tribunal to decide whether a new custom has or has not come into being. For judicial decision itself often has a decisive part to play in the final crystallization of new custom.[7] The position has been put so well by Professor Baxter that it will be best to adopt his words:

5. I. Sinclair, *The Vienna Convention on the Law of Treaties* 76 (1973).

6. Vienna Convention on the Law of Treaties, *supra* note 4, art. 38.

7. For example, the pronouncements of the International Court of Justice in the *Nottebohm Case,* on the Hague Convention of 1930 on Certain Questions relating to the Conflict of Nationality Laws. See the Nottebohm Case, [1955] *I.C.J. Reports* 4. *See also* Baxter, "Multilateral Treaties as Evidence of Customary International Law," 41 *The Brit. Y.B. Int'l L. 1965-66* 275 at 295 (1968) [hereinafter cited as Baxter], where he says: "Prior to 1930, and indeed until the decision in *Nottebohm,* the propositions asserted in Article 5 had not been free from doubt."

Professor Baxter's article should be consulted as a major study of this whole question, to which the present writer does not purport to do more than to add a note referring to new materials which have appeared since Professor Baxter wrote his article.

> In principle he who maintains that the law created by a treaty has passed into customary international law has the burden of demonstrating that the norms of the treaty have been accepted and applied in the relations of States. He must thus adduce evidence of the practice of States from the time of the adoption of the text of the convention, when it presumably began to exercise its influence, until the critical date of the litigation, dispute, or other occasion for the application of the law. This burden may be discharged in either of two ways: The first is to demonstrate that the treaty or a particular article thereof has been accepted by non-parties by express reference to the treaty or article—that is, through a sort of incorporation by reference into customary law. The other is to show the state of customary international law independently of the treaty and then that the rule of customary law is the same as that of the treaty. Even in the latter case, the proof of the law is somewhat simpler than in the absence of the treaty, for once the ground has been laid, one is entitled to rely on the black letter of the treaty. Even though the foundation may not be simple to lay, a structure of treaty law is more persuasive and authoritative than a structure constructed of the diverse and jumbled materials of State practice.[8]

This whole question has recently been illuminated by the careful analysis to be found in the Judgment of the International Court of Justice in the *North Sea Continental Shelf Cases.*[9] It will be remembered that it had been contended for Denmark and the Netherlands that even if article 6 of the 1958 Geneva Convention on the Continental Shelf (with its equidistance principle for establishing boundaries between neighbouring States) was not itself binding upon Germany since Germany had not ratified the treaty, nevertheless, as the Court summarized the argument, "through positive law processes, the equidistance principle has come to be regarded as a rule of customary international law, so that it would be obligatory for the Federal Republic in that way, even though Article 6 of the Geneva Convention is not, as such opposable to it."[10]

This involved three distinct inquiries. First there was the question whether Article 6 was a codification of a customary rule already established as such when the treaty was adopted. Secondly, there was the question whether the adoption of the rule in the treaty was itself the culmination of a process of development into established custom; the coping stone to complete and stabilize the edifice. Thirdly, there was

8. Baxter, *supra* note 7, at 296.
9. [1969] *I.C.J. Reports* 3.
10. *Id.* at 37.

the question whether the treaty provision had inspired, or generated, or assisted, the development, subsequent to the date of the treaty, of a new rule of custom. To put the three lines of inquiry differently, did a customary rule, similar to the rule of the treaty, exist *before* the adoption of the treaty, or *simultaneously* with the adoption of the treaty, or come into being at some moment *subsequent* to the date of the treaty?[11] Or again, in the words of the Judgment in the *North Sea* cases, whether it was "necessary to examine the status of the principle as it stood when the Convention was drawn up, as it resulted from the effect of the Convention, and in the light of State practice subsequent to the Convention."[12]

Denmark and the Netherlands had, in the course of the oral hearing, conceded that they had not contended that Article 6 "embodies already received rules of customary law in the sense that the Convention was merely declaratory of existing rules."[13] The first of the questions stated above therefore did not arise. The Court was free to address itself to the second question, namely the contention of Denmark and the Netherlands that, although prior to the 1958 Conference the law of the continental shelf was only in the formative state, yet "the process of the definition and consolidation of the emerging customary law took place through the work of the International Law Commission, the reaction of governments to that work and the proceedings of the Geneva Conference." This emerging customary law became "crystallized in the adoption of the Continental Shelf Convention by the Conference."[14] In short, the argument was made that the process of the creation of a customary rule culminated and was completed by the adoption of the treaty.

The Court found the answer to this question relatively easy. It was after all essentially a matter of consulting the preparatory work of the treaty to find out what the situation actually had been. Article 6 had been adopted almost unchanged from the draft of the International Law Commission. And it appeared from the records of the Commission that the principle of equidistance as it figured in Article 6 "was proposed by the Commission with considerable hesitation, somewhat on an experimental basis, at most *de lege ferenda,* and not at all *de lege lata* or as an emerging rule of customary international law. This is

11. It would be possible to analyse the inquiry in other and more elaborate ways: but this classification, depending upon the time of the development of a customary rule in relation to the time of a treaty, seems to be the most useful for practical purposes.

12. [1969] *I.C.J. Reports* at 37. The Court also inquired at length whether the equidistance rule had an *a priori* validity independent of the treaty (see *id.* at 20-37) but this aspect is not relevant to the present inquiry.

13. *Id.* at 38.

14. *Id.*

clearly not the sort of foundation on which Article 6 of the Convention could be said to have reflected or crystallized such a rule."[15]

The Court then proceeded to consider what inferences might be drawn from the fact that Article 6 was not amongst those articles of the Convention in respect of which the faculty of making reservations was excluded; and it drew the inference that Article 6 was "not regarded as declaratory of previously existing or emergent rules of law."[16] Denmark and the Netherlands having said that they did not contend that the equidistance principle was previously existing law, this examination of the effect of the reservation clause was presumably addressed only, or at least mainly, to the question whether Article 6 had represented "emergent rules of law." This is certainly a very nice distinction in any actual case. Some care is required in construing the observations of the Court in regard to a faculty of reservation. For it does not seem that the presence or absence of a faculty of reservation actually *requires* any inference either way. It is lawful for parties to a treaty, amongst themselves, to contract out of an existing rule of law that is not *jus cogens*; and there seems no logical reason why this should not be made facultative by a power of reservation.[17] On the other hand it might frequently be considered that certain stipulations in question are *not* required by existing general law. It must be concluded, therefore, as indeed the careful language used by the Court indicates, that the particular inference drawn in this case was in regard to the circumstances of that case and does not in any way attempt to lay down a general presumption.

The Court then turned to the question whether a rule of customary law, equivalent to the equidistance principle of Article 6, had come into being subsequent to the Convention, "partly because of its own impact, partly on the basis of subsequent State practice."[18] This was a conclusion which, as the Court pointed out, "involves treating the Article as a norm-creating provision which has constituted the foundation of, or has generated a rule which, while only conventional or contractual in origin, has since passed into the general *corpus* of international law, and is now accepted as such by the *opinio juris,* so as to have become binding for countries which have never, and do not, become parties to

15. *Id.*

16. *Id.* at 39.

17. It is true that the Court said "no reservation could release the reserving party from obligations of general maritime law existing outside and independently of the Convention, and especially obligations formalized in Article 2 of the contemporaneous Convention on the High Seas, expressed by its preamble to be declaratory of established principles of international law." *Id.* at 40. But this must refer to obligations to third parties.

18. *Id.* at 41.

the Convention."[19] Such a result, though it did occur from time to time, was "not lightly to be regarded as having been attained."[20]

The Court described the conditions that would have to be fulfilled before it could be persuaded that such a position had indeed been attained.

The first requirement enunciated by the Court was that the provision in question must, "at all events potentially, be of a fundamentally norm-creating character such as could be regarded as forming the basis of a general rule of law." The Court had little hesitation in deciding that the equidistance principle as it was embodied in Article 6 of the Convention did not fulfil this requirement. In that article the equidistance method was put second to an obligation to effect delimitation by agreement: "an unusual preface to what is claimed to be a potential general rule of law." Further, the equidistance principle was qualified also by the somewhat imprecise notion of "special circumstances." Finally, the faculty of making reservations did "add considerably to the difficulty" of regarding Article 6 as having generated a rule of general law.[21]

These are all reasons directly related to the particular case before the Court. The question remains how far it is possible to formulate any general criteria for this quality of a "fundamentally norm-creating" character. Professor D'Amato, who has made a major contribution to our understanding of the nature of customary law, says: "Certainly not all provisions within a particular treaty are generalizable as customary norms. As easy example of a non-generalizable provision found in nearly every treaty is the clause, usually at its end, providing for the specific means of ratification."[22] Of course, to speak of a "specific" means is rather to beg the question at issue. But is it really the case that a ratification clause, requiring for instance a certain proportion of ratification by signatories to bring the treaty into force, is inherently incapable of becoming a general norm? Surely not; it may be obvious that such a clause does not in fact represent general law, but we know this not by looking at the "character" of the clause but by looking at it in the light of the general law of treaties. Nor need a "fundamentally norm-creating character" be limited to potentially universal norms; a provision that is apposite only to a particular region might still be the stuff of regional customary law.

Perhaps in the end it comes down to something very like the old learning about the distinction between the *traité*-contrat and the *traité-loi*. In any event it would seem that this criterion is probably best ap-

19. *Id.*
20. *Id.*
21. *Id.* at 42.
22. A.D'Amato, *The Concept of Custom in International Law* 109 (1971).

plied in conjunction with the acid "participation" test which the Court next turns to in its consideration of the matter. In short, the ultimate test of a norm-creating character may be found in the subsequent history of wide participation and acceptance of the rule or in the lack of it.

The Court goes on to describe this further requirement for the development of custom out of treaty in the following terms: "With respect to the other elements usually regarded as necessary before a conventional rule can be considered to have become a general rule of international law, it might be that, even without the passage of any considerable period of time, a very widespread and representative participation in the convention might suffice of itself, provided it included that of States whose interests were specially affected."[23] This requirement then has two elements: passage of time, and widespread representative participation. Evidently the latter is the more important because the implication of what the Court says is that sufficiently wide participation may enable "any considerable" period of time to be dispensed with; clearly the converse would not be true. The passage of time in itself is of no moment; it is merely the element necessary in some degree at least to enable establishment and appreciation of the required participation. A customary rule of law does not, like a good wine, actually require passage of time as such. In this respect the situation is different from the acquisition of a title: as for instance in the *Fisheries Case*[24] where the passage of time, coupled with acquiescence, was substantive in constituting title. Thus, says the Court in the *North Sea cases*:

> Although the passage of only a short period of time is not necessarily, or of itself, a bar to the formation of a new rule of customary international law on the basis of what was originally a purely conventional rule, an indispensable requirement would be that within the period in question, short though it might be, State practice, including that of States whose interests are specially affected, should have been both extensive and virtually uniform in the sense of the provision invoked; — and should moreover have occurred in such a way as to show a general recognition that a rule of law or legal obligation is involved.[25]

In the light of these requirements the Court tested the situation in the case before it by reference both to participation in the Convention and to State practice generally. The tally of ratification it found "though respectable, hardly sufficient"[26] The answer, it is submitted, might have

23. [1969] *I.C.J. Reports* at 42.
24. [1951] *I.C.J. Reports* 116.
25. [1969] *I.C.J. Reports* at 43.
26. *Id.* at 42.

been different had the Convention, like the one on the High Seas, purported to be declaratory of already received rules or principles of customary law. Such a codifying treaty which has not been widely ratified may still carry great weight as evidence of custom by reason of its intrinsic merit as a statement of established law.[27] However, when the question is whether the treaty has itself generated new law, it would be obtuse to suggest that this could have happened though the treaty itself has been sparsely ratified.

The participation requirement, however, refers ultimately to participation in the acceptance and practice of the rule rather than of the treaty which inspired the rule. The very question at issue is the legal position of third States which have not elected to become parties to the treaty; there is no problem with those who have become parties. The requirement therefore must include widespread acceptance of the rule amongst representative third States, including those whose interests are specially affected. Moreover, this participation must be on the basis of legal obligation as evidence of the *opinio juris*; and this the Court made very clear indeed. "The States concerned must therefore feel that they are conforming to what amounts to a legal obligation. The frequency, or even habitual character of the acts is not in itself enough."[28]

Obviously the more widespread and representative the participation in the actual treaty, the easier becomes the burden of proving a new custom. However, the relevance of the number of actual ratifications can hardly be put higher than that. It would be contrary to all principle to hold that a regime established by an essentially contractual instrument could be opposable as such against representative and specially interested States which had elected not to accept the treaty. The very existence of ratification and acceptance clauses in multilateral treaties negatives the notion that such a treaty could of itself and without the evidences of custom become legislative for concerned States which do not ratify or accept.[29]

There is another important aspect of this matter of third States and

27. As indeed in the case of the Vienna Convention on the Law of Treaties, *supra* note 4. This has not yet had sufficient ratifications to bring it into force, but it is frequently cited as evidence of the general international law of treaties.

28. [1969] *I.C.J. Reports* at 44.

29. A treaty may certainly be one of the distinctly rare kind which are, in the words of the late Sir Hersch Lauterpacht, of a "so-called legislative character" and which "having regard to the number of their signatories, approach universality (1 H. Lauterpacht, *International Law, Being the Collected Papers of Hersch Lauterpacht* 116 (E. Lauterpacht ed. 1970)); *viz.*, one of "certain treaties of a general character, approaching or described as international legislation, which, while in strict law binding only upon the parties thereto and while subject to denunciation, are so widely accepted that, for some purposes, they may be considered to constitute universal international law." *Id.* at 115. But if participation in the treaty actually itself approaches universality, then *res ipsa loquitur.* There is no problem.

the reach of treaties of a norm-creating character. It must be remembered that third non-party States may include not only those States which were in being at the time the treaty was concluded but also States that have become members of the international community since that time. It is well known that new States have tended to be somewhat suspicious of the proposition that they are bound by existing rules of custom, in the shaping of which they had no part. And for that reason also they have tended to favour treaty law on the ground that it is law to which they must have given their consent. It would be a curious turn of events if it were now to be suggested that treaties might have a legislative effect in circumstances any less stringent than those required for the recognition of customary law.[30]

The careful restatement by the International Court of Justice in the *North Sea Continental Shelf Cases* of the strict limits of the treaty as an instrument of legislation was very opportune. For there has been a tendency, not least in relation to the law of the sea, to assume that a new treaty could in some way legislate for States generally, without their co-operation. But there are no short cuts. The ultimate test is always that of effectiveness. Not complete effectiveness, but sufficient effectiveness. The tests laid down by the International Court are in reality tests of effectiveness. It would do no good at all to international law if treaties were written in terms apparently generally binding if the effective result were an empty political gesture rather than law.

30. It is apposite here to mention the reasons given by Venezuela at the Vienna Conference on the Law of Treaties for opposing the draft Article 38, which was said to be incompatible with the sovereignty of States. Except for *jus cogens,* continued the representative of Venezuela, that country "would not assume obligations it had not formally accepted, still less obligations it had expressly rejected." United Nations Conference on the Law of Treaties, *Summary Records* 444, U.N. Doc. A/CONF.39/11 (1971).

THE JURISPRUDENCE OF CONTRACTS

HARRY W. JONES

If I had my way about it, Jurisprudence would not be a third year elective, as it is at most of our law schools, but a first semester, first year course. "Just as the twig is bent the tree's inclined," the poet[1] tells us, and an inclination towards the philosophy of law is a set of mind readily observable in many men and women who have achieved distinction or, what is even more important, personal fulfillment in law as a vocation. This, then, is a kind of invitation to jurisprudence, addressed principally to law students, most of all to first year law students, and drawing for illustrations on materials students encounter quite early in the first law school year.

Law as a cultural form,[2] and that is surely one illuminating and professionally rewarding way to look at law, differs from art and literature in its approach to reality and value. Art, at its best, invests ordinary objects and ideas with heightened excitement and intensity: Cezanne's apples, Wordsworth's daffodils, Vermeer's milk jugs, Kafka's waiting rooms. Law, by contrast, tends to play down the dramatic quality of the great ideas and culturally complex institutions with which law deals and to diffuse their excitement into rules, procedures, and carefully-wrought principles. That, on balance, is just as well. Law is something that pertains to reason, as Thomas Aquinas told us centuries ago, and the life of reason is quieter and less manic than the life of emotional expression. We would not want our judges to be poets unless, like Holmes, they could be major poets, and major poets usually have more urgent things to do than spend three years studying law.

Yet we need a reminder, once in a while, that the values, ideas and social realities that are forever at work in law are not as neutral, not as cut-and-dried, as they seem to be when perceived only through a glass

HARRY W. JONES is Cardozo Professor of Jurisprudence at Columbia University School of Law.

This paper was delivered on October 4, 1973 at the School of Law of the University of Cincinnati as the first lecture in the School of Law's new Visiting Scholars Program.

1. A. Pope, *Epistles to Several Persons* (*Moral Essays*], *Epistle I,* line 150 (1734).

2. *An Essay on Man* (1944) by Ernst Cassirer analyzes language, myth, art, religion, history and science as cultural or "symbolic" forms. One wishes that Cassirer had brought the same analysis to bear on law. His last book, *The Myth of the State* (1946), suggests the rich possibilities but does not quite reach them.

of lawyer terminology and lawyer doctrine. I suggest, for example, that an anthropologist who wants to reconstruct the risks and strains and interpersonal frictions that characterize American life in the second half of the twentieth century might do better to start with a good first year casebook in Torts than with anything else available in print. A political philosopher or an historian might do equally well to begin with Civil Procedure, because the strategies, thrusts and parries embodied in, say, the Federal Rules of Civil Procedure reveal - when seen in imaginative perspective - such progress as we have made in seven hundred years of the common law tradition towards putting remedial justice on sound procedural grounds. Much the same thing could be said about almost every other course in the law school curriculum, and certainly not least about the course in Contracts.

It is not just what you and I, as students of the law, are taking for the moment as the objects of our study; it is how we are *looking* at these objects. Hand, Cardozo and Karl Llewellyn found excitement, intellectual and aethetic challenge, in problems and social phenomena that would have bored lesser men to death. That, today anyway, is how I want you to look at the law of contracts, not just at a body of doctrines - rules, precedents, statutes, restatements - but at what the discerning eye will see underlying it all: the deeply ingrained power that the idea of contract has had, throughout recorded history, on the minds of men and women; the centrality of contract as a basic institution of contemporary society; and the significance of freedom of contract as one of the great "constitutional" devices for the dispersion of power in a society fearful, as ours has always and rightly been, of the concentration of too much power in too few hands.

I. ON CONTRACT AS IDEA AND SOCIAL INSTITUTION

Have I overstated my thesis? Consider, then, the emotive and symbolic power of the idea of contract and the moral conceptions that cluster about it. To most people, at all stages of history, there is a certain self-evident rightness about *pacta sunt servanda,* the moral imperative that obligations freely agreed to are to be honored and performed. Its oldest expression in our Western tradition is perhaps in the Hebrew conception of religious duty as stemming from a covenant between Jehovah and his people, a solemn contract, renewed each generation, by which the parties - both parties, mind you - are forever bound. When the people of Israel in the wilderness worshipped at the feet of the golden calf, they were guilty of sin, but even worse - as my beloved friend and master, Edwin Patterson, would have said - they were guilty of material breach of contract discharging Jehovah from performance of his side of the holy bargain.

The notion of political obligation as contractual in nature, that is, of an historical or hypothetical social contract as the basis of government by consent, appears at least as early as Plato's *Crito,* in which Socrates, rejecting an offered opportunity to escape from his death cell and the hemlock, speaks eloquently of the covenant between the citizen of Athens and the *polis,* the civil community of the city. Socrates, having enjoyed the benefits of that civil contract for a long lifetime, is now obliged to accept the correlative burden, even though it be an unjust conviction. Hugo Grotius, the revered "father of international law," saw *pacta sunt servanda* as the basis, the only basis, of international law. Three centuries later, Hans Kelsen, certainly the most influential legal philosopher of our own time, had recourse to the same old idea - *pacta sunt servanda,* agreements are to be honored - as the indispensable first-stage norm of the international legal order.[3]

In our political tradition, the one we share with England, the idea of political obligation as duty stemming from contract emerges with the Renaissance, never to disappear from philosophy or practical politics. Thomas Hobbes, the philosopher of "law and order," and John Locke, the philosopher of individualism and civil liberties, differed on almost everything else but agreed on two basic propositions: *First,* that medieval notions of the Divine Right of Kings had no place in an enlightened age; and *Second,* that the only satisfying replacement for Divine Right was the conception of a social contract - real historically or hypothesized as a rational necessity; they are never one hundred percent clear on this - as the origin, source and basis of civil society. To be sure, Hobbes's social contract was very different from Locke's; in Hobbe's conception, individual rights were not reserved when the heretofore ungoverned people came together to agree on how they were to be ruled thereafter, and the Sovereign, king or whoever, was not a party to the contract. In other words, as a careful student in Contracts-B might put the politico-legal situation, the Sovereign was a third party beneficiary with rights against every subject and duties to no one. So it is not surprising that Jefferson, Madison and the other draftsmen of the documents of American liberty wrote the Locke version of the social contract, not the Hobbes version, into our constitutional philosophy. It is government by consent, but the Sovereign, too, is bound to perform his side of the bargain, and material breach discharges contractual obligation in government as in private transactions. So Jefferson would have said and, indeed, virtually did say in the Declaration of In-

3. H. Kelsen, *General Theory of Law and State* 369-70 (1945).

dependence.[4]

We use the phrase "government by consent" so often and so easily that we tend to forget its origin in the classic analogy of political obligation to contractual duty. Perhaps this is because the idea, the analogy, has been over here for a long time. Some day, if you find yourself wearied by the *minutiae* of offer and acceptance, look at the Mayflower Compact of 1620. It records an historical moment of peril and high drama, but it reads like a formal contract of sale:

> IN THE NAME OF GOD, AMEN. We, whose names are underwritten . . . [d]o by the Presents, solemnly and mutually, in the Presence of God and one another, covenant and combine ourselves together into a civil Body Politick, for our better Ordering and Preservation . . . And by Virtue hereof do enact, constitute, and frame, such just and equal Laws . . . as shall be thought most meet and convenient for the general Good of the Colony, *unto which we promise all due Obedience.* IN WITNESS whereof we have hereunto subscribed our names at Cape Cod the eleventh of November . . . Anno Domini, 1620.[5]

When an idea, here the idea of contractual assent and consequent contractual duty, has such symbolic power as to cause hard-headed men to use it to express their deepest aspirations, it is not an idea to be brushed off as technical or purely rhetorical. So it should not surprise us that the best book on political philosophy written in this decade, Professor John Rawls's massive study, *A Theory of Justice,* rejects all other ways of beginning and proceeds by postulating a kind of social contract as the basic norm of any just society.[6] nor was it at all surprising, when we were having our great debates over civil disobedience a few years ago, that all sides in the controversy, however located along the spectrum of views from the philosophical right to the philosophical

4. "The history of the present King of Great Britain is a history of repeated injuries and usurpations, all having, in direct object, the establishment of an absolute tyranny over these states. . . . We, therefore, . . . declare . . . that these united colonies are . . . absolved from all allegiance to the British Crown. . . ." *Declaration of Independence,* in Congress, July 4, 1776. The factual allegations might be controverted, but the contract theory is sound enough.

5. *Sources of Our Liberties* 60 (J. Cooper & R. Perry eds. 1959) (emphasis added).

6. "My aim is to present a conception of justice which generalizes and carries to a higher level of abstraction the familiar theory of the social contract as found, say, in Locke, Rousseau, and Kant. . . . [T]he guiding idea is that the principles of justice for the basic structure of society are the object of the original agreement. They are the principles that free and rational persons concerned to further their own interests would accept in an initial position of equality as defining the fundamental terms of their association." J. Rawls, *A Theory of Justice* 11 (1971).

left, rediscovered the social contract theory and cast their varying arguments in its terms. "There is no right of civil disobedience in a society of consent," said those to the right. "The citizen can take part in the processes of public decision-making and so is under obligation to obey the laws so arrived at, both those he approves and those he opposes."[7] Off to the far left, at the other ideological extreme, an argument was heard that sounded more like Rousseau's version of the social contract than Locke's, but was social contract theory just the same: "Yes, one is bound by laws that he himself has participated in making - participated personally, that is, and not just through a representative - but otherwise there is no contractual duty." And those in the hapless liberal middle, where prisoners of rationality like me are wont to dwell, had our versions of social contract theory, too, stressing, as we usually did, the Lockean point that the State, too, is a party to the social contract or insisting that legal obligation, if based on essentially contractual assent, has limited or no application to any social or racial group that is excluded from electoral and other democratic processes.[8]

The point I have been making, however, is not that there were different variations on the social contract theme but that the symbolism was shared. Everybody seems to become a social contract theorist sooner or later, when the chips are down, however remote the analogy from commercial bargain to civil society may be in formal analysis - as, indeed, it seems remote to me. Contract, somehow, is a compelling and durable idea in the mind, perhaps even in the subconscious, of mankind. One only fools himself if he underrates the idea's persuasive power. This can have mundane and very practical consequences. Suppose, for example, that you are counsel for the defendant in a contract case some day, ten or twenty years from now. Do not be too astonished, and try to hold your rage in proper professional check, if a high appellate court dismisses your most ingenious and technically unassailable defensive argument and decides against you in an opinion that really says nothing more than: "well, there was a *contract*, wasn't there, and a man ought to do what he has promised to do."

Let us change our focus now from contract as moral and philosophical idea to contract as a basic social institution, one comparable in importance to such other pervading social institutions as property, the family, even the institution of representative government. In a society like ours, people live not by birds in the hand but by promises: for example, anyone's job is an exchange of promises, by him

7. For a trenchant statement of essentially this position see Rostow, "The Rightful Limits of Freedom in a Liberal Democratic State," in *Is Law Dead?* 39 (E. Rostow ed. 1971).

8. As in my 1968 Rosenthal Lectures, "And Lastly, of Civil Disobedience," in H. Jones, *The Efficacy of Law* 92, 98 (1969).

to work and by his employer to pay agreed or understood wages. Investments are essentially promises by corporate power-holders to manage a business in proper ways and to pay dividends as earned. A bank account is a promise to hold and return money deposited; even money is a promise, though rather less reliable than in earlier days, by government to pay something on due presentation. A few years ago, there was a lively musical comdey called "Promises, Promises!", and that is largely what our material society amounts to. J.K. Galbraith may or may not have been right to characterize our national community as *The Affluent Society;* he would have said something unquestionably true, and perhaps of even greater economic significance, if he had called us the *promissory* society. And a promissory society, by definition, is one energized and bound together by the institution of contract. That may seem a very remote consideration when you are reading an ordinary contract case, but it is a perspective not to be forgotten altogether when you are trying to arrange the details of contract law into a form that makes practical working sense.

The philosophers and historians of law have not, perhaps, spoken in quite these terms, but they have certainly not been unaware of what we are calling today "the *jurisprudence* of contracts." Thus Jeremy Bentham, when he set out to formulate the ends or values of a legal order, put "security of expectations" in the very first place.[9] Law and government exist, said Bentham, to insure the security, that is, the practical realization, of the reasonable expectations of the men and women who constitute a given civil society. An enforceable bill of rights, considered in Benthamite terms, insures my *expectation* that my freedoms of movement and expression will not be interfered with arbitrarily and without sufficient cause. The criminal law, when effective, serves to secure my expectation that my liberty to go about my own business will not be impaired by the violence or overreaching of *non*-governmental wrongdoers. The law of property secures my expectation that I may continue to enjoy what is mine unless I have freely parted with it. The law of contract - and "law of contract" here includes what we elsewhere break up into such seegments as commercial transactions, partnerships, corporations, labor law and many more - has as its ultimate purpose the security of those reasonable expectations that arise from agreement between seller and buyer, borrower and depositor, stockholder and corporation, employer and organized employees. This essentially is Bentham's analysis, and it has never been improved on.

The best known statement of all this is, I suppose, the conclusion expressed by Sir Henry Maine, late in the Nineteenth Century, in his renowned study, *Ancient Law*. After surveying most of what was then

9. 1 *Bentham's Theory of Legislation* 126 (C. Atkinson ed. 1913).

known about the primitive and early legal systems of the Eastern and Western worlds, Maine recorded this judgment: —"The movement of the progressive societies had hitherto been a movement *from Status to Contract.*"[10] What Maine is saying here is that in primitive communities and others that have kept the character of "static" societies, what a man or woman is or does depend above all on his status, that is, on the fixed legal and social condition into which he was born or into which he, willy-nilly, has been moved. Thus to know what X's legal rights and duties are, the important question to ask is whether X be wife, child, slave, serf, feudal retainer, Brahmin, untouchable, master, servant or whatever. In "progressive" societies, as Maine characterizes them, one's legal rights and duties depend far less on caste or fixed social condition and far more on expectations created and obligations assumed by his own contracts.

Maine's aphorism that historical progress has been a movement from status to contract reflects, of course, the great social value attributed to freedom of contract in the Nineteenth Century liberal tradition of the English Whigs and their American counterparts. But freedom of contract is far from an absolute value, as my colleague, the late Wolfgang Friedmann, has made clear in his perceptive books, *Legal Theory* and *Law in a Changing Society.*[11] We have learned since Maine and Justice Field that outer limits have to be put on freedom of contract in a less individualistic, more highly industrialized society like our own, and there are countless legal interventions in freedom of contract even in "capitalist" countries: minimum wage acts, workmen's compensation, required social security contributions, prescribed contract forms for insurance policies, to name only a few. Looking at Maine's aphorism another way, the legal rights and duties that exist between today's industrial worker and his employer are created not by private contract between them but by a collective bargain negotiated between the employer and the union to which the employee belongs. X's take-home pay from General Motors and his other working conditions depend not on a contract between X and General Motors but on X's status as a union member and General Motors employee. Indeed, the development towards collective and standarized bargains has gone so far in our day that many analysts of our society see Maine's movement as cyclical, that is, a movement, even and particularly in the "progressive" societies, from status to contract and now back to status.

Viewers with alarm are forever proclaiming and lamenting the death of freedom of contract, but this, I suggest, is a simplistic and in-

10. H. Maine, *Ancient Law* 141 (New Universal Library Edition 1905). The italics and capitalization are Maine's.

11. W. Friedmann, *Legal Theory* 400-91 (5th ed. 1967); W. Friedmann, *Law in a Changing Society* 119-38 (Penguin 2d ed. 1971).

complete analysis. Consider these examples. A statute barring the forfeiture of premiums paid on a lapsed life insurance policy diminishes freedom of contract only in the doctrinaire sense that insurers no longer can impose forfeiture clauses on a "take it or leave it" basis. Because of the inequality of bargaining power, such clauses were never the subject of realistic negotiation between insurer and insurance applicant. Similarly, it is wildly unrealistic to see a minimum wage law only as an interference with the individual employee's freedom to contract for less than subsistence wages. What has happened in these and like instances is that areas of decision formerly subject to the rule of superior economic power have been brought within the reach of law.[12] The incidence of genuine contractual bargaining has not necessarily been reduced; indeed, government interventions designed to establish equality of bargaining power may conceivably make contract a more vigorous institution in our day than in Sir Henry Maine's.

The government interventions we have just been considering do not, in any event, extend across the board of possible contractual action. The employment relation may have become a relationship of status for the typical industrial worker, but practically every other relationship of his life is arrived at and regulated by the contracts he enters into with landlords, grocers, physicians, car dealers, banks and others. Even his church contribution is not a prescribed tithe, as when church membership was an imposed status, but a contractual pledge. So I suspect that old Sir Henry Maine is nearer to the truth, even in contemporary conditions, than most of his critics. From status to contract is a long historical movement, and we have not really reversed the trend, however much we may have compromised it or set new ground rules for negotiation.

II. PRIVATE CONTRACT AND THE DISPERSION OF POWER

So far, I have offered two hypotheses, two perspectives, that seem to me to go to the heart of "the jurisprudence of contracts": first, that the idea of contract has been and is an idea of remarkable moral and symbolic power, and second, that contract has had and retains a central position as one of the basic institutions of our society. These two hypotheses, taken together, suggest a third, one strangely neglected in Anglo-American scholarly literature, except in the writings of Willard Hurst.[13] Let me state my hypothesis as broadly and boldly as I can, and

12. I have developed the argument at some length in "The Rule of Law and the Welfare State," 58 *Colum. L. Rev.* 143 (1958).

13. A superb analysis of the significance of private contract as an institution of policy-making runs through W. Hurst, *Law and Economic Growth: The Legal History of the Lumber Industry in Wisconsin* (1964). See particularly the section on "The Law and Legal Process as Part of the Situation." *Id.* at 52-61.

then try to justify it. Contract - that is, the reasonably limited but prevailing liberty of individuals and groups to enter into agreements with each other as to their future behavior - is, in one aspect, a profoundly constitutional phenomenon. By "constitutional," I mean that private contract is a device, fully as important as the Constitution's division of political functions into legislative, executive and judicial, for the dispersion and wider sharing of power. We are accustomed to examining institutions like federalism and separation of power in these terms. Where does it take us if we use the same perspective in appraising the theory and, even more important, the consequences of the institution of contract?

Our political tradition has always been fearful of the concentration of too much power over things and events in too few hands. Countless decisions have to be made in society, some of them "legal," some "social," some "economic." Many, perhaps most, of today's important decisions have all three aspects: decisions concerning the quality of life, the settlement of disputes, the use of inevitably limited public resources. We are apprehensive, most of us, when it seems that all of these decisions, or too many of them, are in the hands of the same man or even the same department of government. The dispersion of decision-making power into as many hands as possible is, in democratic theory, almost an end in itself, one to be pursued wherever manageable, even at the cost of duplication and inefficiency. Accordingly, we have doctrines like the separation of governmental powers, and intricate checks and balances that make it difficult for any one of the political departments to do everything it wants to do.

Private contract operates in a subtler but equally significant way. So long as, and to the extend that, freedom of contract exists in a society, there are decisions, often of great social importance, that are made not by government or any department of government but by private individuals and organizations. This sharing of power by government and private citizens may usually work to the overall social advantage, as the freedom of contract liberals of the Nineteenth Century thought it almost always did. Or it may work often or even usually to the overall social disadvantage, as many contemporary critics believe. On either appraisal, the fact remains that decision-making power has been dispersed. Government and all its ministers have far fewer decision-making opportunities in a society characterized by liberty of contract than in one in which all or most economic and social decisions are made by public power-holders.

Unless one bears in mind this power-dispersing attribute and effect of the institution of private contract, it is impossible to understand or interpret the course of American economic and social development. A look at one hundred years of federal and state statute books will not tell you very much about the ways and means of American industrialization and economic growth from 1820 to 1920. So long as virtually unrestrained freedom of contract remained in the ideological saddle, Congress and the state legislatures set only the outer bounds on what might be done by private initiative and agreement. Private contract and private contractual procedures were dominant across the board in matters involving the utilization of resources, the directions of the public transportation system, and the patterns of funding and security for industrial, import and consumer financing. The private lawyers who drafted the contracts and devised the standard contract forms may have been doing more significant work, even in terms of the public weal or woe, than the lawyers who drafted the statutes and executive orders.

Would it have been better, during the formative periods of American economic development, if these crucial decisions had been made by public authority rather than by private negotiation and agreement? It often seems to us now, looking at economic and social inequalities and at a continent plundered of its resources, that public power-holders—legislatures, governors, Congresses, Presidents, and administrators—might have made wiser and fairer decisions. Yet when we think of such blunders and corruptions of public power as occurred in relation to the Credit Mobilier of 1869-72, the leasing of Teapot Dome in the Harding Administration - and perhaps such more recent transactions as those involving Mr. Vesco or the I.T.T. - we become rather less certain that national growth would have been greater, or would today be on sounder foundations, if less power had been left to private contract and more given to the elected and appointed holders of public authority.

In any event, that is not the way it was, nor is it today, in the areas of economic decision-making. Perhaps we need a kind of double-entry bookkeeping on the private ordering of economic affairs. On the *debit* side, one will have to list all the socially important instances in which private freedom of contract was exercised in a selfish, nearsighted or oppressive way. The list will be long, painfully so. But there will be entries, too, on the *credit* side: private initiatives, effected through the institution of contract, that were bolder, certainly wiser - if only for reasons of enlightened self-interest - and farther looking than comparable government decisions would have been. "What is good for General Motors" may not be "good for the country," but the manufacture of cars by General Motors may have been better for the country than to have had all our automobiles manufactured by a government bureau with headquarters in the Commerce Department or the Pentagon. Perhaps the best achievable solution, the one to which we are surely moving, is a kind of mixed government of economic affairs, with scope left for private contractual initiative subject to the veto power of public authority.

When private contract is seen in this perspective, as a device for the diffusion of power, one begins to grasp the full significance of Hans Kelsen's lifetime insistence that the making of a private contract is a law-creating act.[14] What Kelsen is saying, as I understand him, is that in any society where freedom of contract exists the state delegates to its citizens a part of government's law-making power. Nor is this thesis of Kelsen's as outlandish as it may seem on first impression. After all, when X and Y, by contract, have promised to act in a specified way, that action is as "binding" on each of them as if it were prescribed by an act of the state legislature if - and here is the big analytical *if* - the agreement is one that the state will enforce through its courts and other legal processes. It is this element of potential state enforcement that makes the private contract *law* for the parties, even though one of them now wants to renege on what he has promised to do.

Jurisprudential theory can be put to work to clarify issues of contract law far more often than is usually recognized. Consider how the Kelsen analysis of contract-making as a *law*-creating act clears the way for realistic appraisal of the complex and often inconsistent decisions in which courts, on one theory or another, have denied enforcement to so-called "illegal bargains"[15] or, as the older terminology called them, "agreements against public policy." Recent "illegal bargain" decisions have, as you doubtless know, taken a stricter view than formerly and denied enforcement to what once would have been considered essentially private and lawful arrangements. Occasionally one hears criticism of this greater judicial severity. Is not a court unduly interfering with freedom of contract when it denies enforcement to what it considers an "unconscionable" bargain or to an agreement in which the parties have promised to act in a way the court considers socially disadvantageous? Not at all, I am inclined to say, and I think the great Kelsen would be with me. What the court is doing, in the case put, is refusing to exert the power of the state in support of what it considers to be an unfair or socially disadvantageous private ordering of affairs. And to one who has read his Kelsen, the theory seems plain enough. Such an attempted exercise of private law-making power in an oppressive or socially

14. H. Kelsen, *General Theory of Law and State* 137 (1945).

15. See, for examples, the cases brought together in Chapter 4, "Illegal Bargains," in E. Farnsworth, H. Jones & W. Young, *Cases and Materials on Contracts* (1965). An illustration of the increasing severity of the judicial approach is McConnell v. Commonwealth Pictures Corp., 7 N.Y.2d 465, 166 N.E.2d 494, 199 N.Y.S.2d 483 (1960). The much discussed "unconscionable contracts" provision of the Uniform Commercial Code (*UCC* sec. 2-302) is influencing many courts toward closer scrutiny of the fairness of bargains. But Karl Llewellyn, the Code's principal draftsman, always insisted, rightly I think, that *UCC* sec. 2-302 is not a drastic policy innovation but an effort to state a principle clearly justifying results that courts were already reaching in oppressive bargain situations—but justifying on other and less candid grounds.

disadvantageous way is beyond the law-making authority delegated to private citizens by the institution of freedom of contract.

We have now gone close to full circle, so perhaps the third of my hypotheses should be retraced. To the extent that it retains vitality in a society, the institution of private contract operates to diffuse power, to divide decision-making opportunities between government, on the one hand, and private power-holders on the other. Contract-making is a law-making process, because the requirements of a valid contract are law for the parties, something they must do just as surely as they must obey state statutes, except that the promised behavior can be compelled only by civil and not by criminal sanctions. But there is always a potential state veto in the background, the most important form of which is the traditional authority of the courts, however sparingly they may have used it in the past, to deny enforcement to oppressive or socially injurious private engagements. It is that veto which serves, or can be made to serve, to resolve the conflicts that arise often and inevitably between freedom of contract as a political value and social interest and, on the other side, the public interest in commercial fairness and socially advantageous economic arrangements. The "illegal bargain" cases are, I think, the most thought-provoking cases to be found in a Contracts casebook and are, to my mind, as interesting as any a student will ever study in law school. If horrifies me now to remember that during most of my twenty-five years as a teacher of Contracts I used to brush them off with a few comments or - *mea maxima culpa* - tag them for mere outside reading. But then, on Kelsen's showing and mine, perhaps the "illegal bargain" cases should not be taught in Contracts at all, but rather in Constitutional Law as the inseparable first cousins of the cases on federalism and delegation of legislative power.

In the law of contracts, as elsewhere in life, deeper currents flow under the surface than are visible at first glance. There is an old Talmudic saying: "Search the Torah, and search it again, for there is everything in it." Hugo Black would, I am sure, have said the same thing about the Constitution of the United States. Perhaps, after a quarter-century of teaching it, I have come to feel that there is everything in Contracts.

FORCE MAJEURE ET CONTRATS INTERNATIONAUX DE LONGUE DURÉE

PHILIPPE KAHN

La détermination de l'étendue de l'engagement réel des parties a toujours joué un rôle important dans la négociation et la rédaction des contrats internationaux. En partaiculier depuis que la nouvelle typologie distingue mieux les opérations d'échange, les opérations de production et les opérations d'approvisionnement[1] un soin tout spécial est apporté dans les contrats de production et d'approvisionnement aux garanties qu'accepte de fournir le vendeur ou l'investisseur, aux clauses d'exonération de responsabilité. Le dispositif est centré sur l'exécution du contrat et tend à en assurer l'effectivité. Les systèmes législatifs nationaux ont souvent des préoccupations analogues: ainsi le système français dans son interprétation jurisprudentielle contient-il des définitions de qualité pour suppléer un éventuel silence des parties et est-il sévère pour les fournisseurs professionnels, leur rendant difficile la limitation de responsabilité par des clauses de garantie trop étroites. De même a-t-il une conception des clauses d'exonération très restrictive. Mais ces systèmes nationaux, tournés vers l'exécution et élaborés à l'occasion des contrats d'échange du commerce international qui ont été jusqu'à ces dernières années les principaux contrats utilisés et restent les mieux connus, n'ont pu résister aux données concrètes des nouveaux contrats internationaux, les contrats de production et d'approvisionnement.

En effet, il existe une donnée essentielle qui oppose les contrats d'échange aux contrats de production et d'approvisionnement et permet de rapprocher les deux dernières catégories, c'est l'incidence du temps. Les contrats de production et d'approvisionnement sont conclus pour une longue période. Leur durée est rarement inférieure à deux ans (vente d'usine clés en main) et avoisinent souvent quinze ou vingt ans (exploitation de matières premières, contrats d'approvisionnement

PHILIPPE KAHN est Directeur de Recherche au Centre national de la recherche scientifique (Centre de recherche sur le droit des marchés et des investissements internationaux de Dijon).

1. Kahn, "Lex mercatoria et pratique des contrats internationaux: l'expérience française," dans *Le contrat économique international* 171 (Travaux des VII's journées juridiques Jean Dabin 1975).

en gaz) sans même mentionner les vieux contrats de concession dont la durée s'étalait entre soixante et quatre-vingt-dix-neuf ans. Or une chose est certaine, c'est que le temps va modifier considérablement les conditions d'exécution du contrat par rapport à celles qui sont envisagées au moment de sa conclusion. Et ce n'est sans doute pas un des moindres paradoxes que l'on rencontre dans ces opérations que le contrat qui est destiné à stabiliser les relations entre les parties par la maîtrise du temps soit condamné d'emblée à ne pouvoir remplir son rôle. Aussi dans des contrats de plus en plus nombreux, des techniques de révision des contrats sont-elles utilisées. Elles sont destinées à permettre aux parties d'adapter leur contrat aux données nouvelles et au changement de circonstances et finalement d'aboutir à son exécution.

On rencontre d'abord des clauses de révsion générale. Les unes sont vagues et abstraites. Elles font simplement obligation aux parties de se rencontrer à des périodes déterminées pour discuter les difficultés d'exécution et tenter de trouver une solution. Sur ce canevas général, elles comportent de nombreuses variantes. Les autres sont beaucoup plus précises. Ce sont celles connues aussi sous le nom de "*hardship clause.*"[2] Elles interviennent quand les circonstances entraînent sur l'exécution du contrat des effets fondamentalement différents de ceux qui avaient été envisagés lors de sa conclusion. Les conditions de la révision, sa procédure, ses effets sont minutieusement réglés. D'autres clauses sont des clauses de révision partielle. Les plus connues et les plus fréquentes sont les clauses de révision de prix. Toutes ces clauses sont des clauses de révision expresses. Ce que nous voudrions démontrer ici c'est que les parties utilisent également des techniques qui normalement ont un tout autre rôle pour introduire des clauses de révision implicites et partielles qui constituent un moyen nouveau d'adapter le contrat aux évolutions conjoncturelles et aux révolutions technologiques sans avoir à mettre en oeuvre ni à discuter des clauses de révision *stricto sensu* toujours complexes et contentieuses en soi. L'exemple le plus frappant est celui des clauses de force majeure, telles que la pratique la plus récente les élabore.

Traditionellement, la force majeure constitue une excuse à la non exécution de ses obligations par l'une des parties. Elle entraîne d'une part l'absence de responsabilité du débiteur défaillant et d'autre part—s'agissant d'une obligation essentielle du contrat—l'interruption de celui-ci, sa résolution. La Cour de cassation française interprétant le code civil a une conception très stricte de la force majeure qui l'a conduite à ne retenir que des événements étrangers au débiteur, im-

2. *Cf.* Oppetit, "L'adaptation des contrats internationaux aux changements de circonstances: la clause de '*hardship*,' " 101. *J. Droit Int'l* 794 (1974).

prévisibles et irrésistibles.[3] Cette tendance à la sévérité est confirmée par le refus de la Cour de cassation de tenir compte des changements de circonstances (refus de la théorie de l'imprévision). En effet, la notion de contrat implique la stabilité, la certitude et la sécurité des relations entre les parties qui ne peuvent être atteintes que dans des circonstances tout à fait exceptionnelles. Des remarques analogues peuvent être faites pour le droit anglais ou pour le droit américain même si des assouplissements importants ont été apportés par rapport à la position française (*cf. Uniform Commercial Code*). Mais il s'agit alors de règles applicables au domaine commercial.[4]

La pratique actuelle des contrats internationaux de production et d'approvisionnement par une extension de la notion de force majeure et une modification de ses effets par rapport à l'institution traditionnelle sans rejeter l'aspect exonératoire de la force majeure en fait une notion tout à fait nouvelle qui sert à adapter, au moins partiellement, le contrat aux circonstances nouvelles. C'est du moins le schéma qui nous est apparu après examen d'une cinquantaine de clauses de force majeure et c'est ce que nous allons essayer de démontrer en étudiant successivement la définition puis les conséquences de la force majeure dans les contrats internationaux de longue durée.[5]

I. LA DÉFINITION DE LA FORCE MAJEURE

Comme toujours dans le domaine du droit international économique, les évolutions ne sont pas linéaires et un nombre encore très important de clauses sont construites sur le modèle des lois nationales des pays les plus influents dans le commerce international, modèle anglo-saxon ou modèle continental. C'est ainsi qu'encore maintenant certains contrats se contentent d'indiquer qu'il n'y aura pas de responsabilité en cas d'inexécution à la suite de la force majeure sans autre précision sur la notion

3. 2 H. , L. , & J. Mazeaud, *Traité théorique et pratique de la responsabilité civile* no. 1540 (6th ed. 1965); M. Alter, *L'obligation de délivrance dans la vente de meubles corporels* 300 (1972); B. Starck, *Droit Civil, Obligations* no. 21, p. 99 *et seq*. (1972); G. Farjat, *Droit privé et l'économie, théorie des obligations* 343 (1975).

4. La Convention de La Haye du 1 juillet 1964, texte de grande importance doctrinale en l'absence d'un nombre suffisant de ratifications permettant l'entrée en vigueur, conserve la rigueur traditionnelle en ce qui concerne la définition de la force majeure si elle est plus large pour ses effets.

5. Pour une approche de la même idée, Delaume, "Excuse for Non-Performance and Force Majeure in Economic Development Agreements" 10 *Column, J. Transnat'l L.* 242 (1971); Adde un peu en retrait G. Delaume, *Transnational Contracts* ch. V, sec. II, nos. 5.07-.12 (1975). Nous avons essayé de ne pas reproduire l'abondante documentation citée par Delaume à laquelle il faut se référer. Pour une approche traditionelle et à la lumière du droit comparé, *Some Problems of Non-performance and Force Majeure in International Contracts of Sale* (1961).

et sur les effets. Mais généralement on rencontre une formulation plus élaborée que l'on peut ramener à une classification à trois branches: soit la clause donne une définition de la force majeure dans un concept abstrait, soit la clause contient une énumération de cas, limitative ou non, soit la clause comporte une énumération de cas complétée par une définition. Cette dernière formulation tend à devenir la plus fréquente.

Dans les définitions les plus simples, souvent inspirées du droit continental, on rencontre l'idée que la force majeure doit être étrangère aux parties, imprévisible, irrésistible. De même, les énumérations les plus simples contiennent des cas qui touchent à la météorologie, à la guerre, à la politique. Ces clauses varient peu d'un contrat à l'autre. Les cas cités se rapprochent à la fois des listes administratives que l'on peut tirer des risques couverts par l'assurance du commerce extérieur (risque politique, risque catastrophique) et des listes que l'on pourrait dresser à partir des casuistiques jurisprudentielles étatiques. Nous sommes encore en présence du fond commun des causes d'exonération en matière contractuelle. Elles sont bien connues et une simple citation de rappel suffira:

> Par cas de force majeure ou par cas fortuit, il faut entendre tout événement qui, indépendamment de toute faute ou de tout fait de la partie, et de façon imprévisible pour elle, rend absolument impossible l'exécution des obligations contractuelles, à l'exclusion des événements qui rendent cette exécution plus difficile ou plus onéreuse (Contrat belgo-africain portant sur des biens d'équipement minier).

Ou, pour citer une énumération de cas très poussée:

> *For the purposes of this Agreement, force majeure shall mean was (whether declared or not and including existing wars) revolution, invasion, insurrection, riot, civil commotion, bad violence, sabotage, blockade, military or usurped power, lightning, serious destruction, explosion, fire, storm, wind, shortage of water, drought, flood, earthquake, epidemic, quarantine, boycott by foreign government of aluminium exporter by Valco, and strikes or as regards Valco acts of the Government of Ghana or other Governmental authority in Ghana which affect the operation of the Volta development or the Smelter or other facilities upon which such operation is completely dependent and acts of any foreign government affecting the importation of equipment or materials by Valco including refusal of export or import licenses and restrictions embargo allotment allocation or other limitation. (Agreement between Volta River Authority and Volta Aluminium Company).*

Dans le cadre de l'énumération, on trouve dans les contrats les plus récents une évolution très intéressante en ce sens qu'elle tient le plus grand compte de l'intervention de l'Etat dans la vie économique moderne et des difficultés qu'il y a quelquefois à distinguer l'Etat agent politique et l'Etat agent économique. Il en résulte qu'aux interventions traditionnelles sont ajoutées la limitation à la liberté d'exécuter un contrat que pourrait apporter la participation de l'Etat à l'activité de l'entreprise, qu'elle soit obligatoire ou volontaire, la limitation de production ou l'exportation, le paiement de redevances en nature qui peut diminuer les quantités de produits dont dispose le vendeur sans compter les interventions plus brutales et plus traditionnelles comme la nationalisation ou la révocation d'une concession (vente d'hydrocarbures méditerranéens par une société américaine à un acheteur européen). On pourrait penser que pour ce dernier point par exemple, l'énumération traditionnelle visant l'Etat devrait suffire. En réalité, et c'est ce qui fait l'intérêt de la mention à notre point de vue, s'agissant dans le cas précipité de contrat de livraison de pétrole par une société d'un groupe multinational, des difficultés dans un pays d'approvisionnement ne conduisent pas forcément à une impossibilité totale de livraison car les sources d'approvisionnement du groupe sont variées. On n'est plus en présence d'un cas de force majeure dans l'optique traditionnelle, mais de l'adaptation du contrat à une situation politique qui a des répercussions importantes sur son exécution mais qui ne conduirait pas à une impossibilité d'exécution totale. Cette clause n'est pas isolée, on la rencontre avec des variantes en fonction de la nature du produit objet du contrat et de la nature de l'intervention de l'Etat dans bien d'autres contrats. Ainsi dans un contrat portant sur la vente d'une usine destinée à fabriquer des fibres synthétiques (vendeur européen, acheteur coréen), nous extrayons d'une longue énumération qui a déjà visé l'intervention de l'Etat, la mention suivante: . . .

> *rules or regulations of governmental authorities, declaration of national emergencies by executive order or legislation, mobilization of industry whereby essential materials or labor required for completion of the work hereunder are allocated and controlled by executive order or legislation, controls of prices of materials and stabilization of wages and salaries at levels higher than those prevailing prior to the effective date of the Agreement . . .*

De même, dans le cadre traditionnel, on peut noter d'autres tentatives d'élargissement de la notion par une vision plus sociale des rapports contractuels: ainsi en est-il lorsque la grève dans les établissements du débiteur est prise en considération. L'élargissement est encore plus grand lorsque la liste est indicative et non pas limitative. En effet, si la clause donne le droit par analogie ou par déduction d'étendre les cas expressement cités et que ces cas sont eux-mêmes nombreux et semblant relever d'une philosophie assez laxiste, on en arrive vite à une véritable remise en cause du contrat à la première difficulté sérieuse. On peut dire que la notion de force majeure telle qu'elle apparaît dans des formules encore traditionnelles, forme transition avec celle qui est utilisée dans des contrats internationaux de plus en plus nombreux et dont on peut penser qu'elle va se généraliser.

Dans l'optique actuelle, constitue un cas de force majeure, tout événement qui affecte suffisamment les parties pour que l'exécution du contrat ne puisse se faire à la date contractuelle pourvu que l'événement échappe à leur contrôle. Mais cette directive générale doit être affinée considérablement en fonction de la nature des contrats, des personnes parties au contrat, et des qualificatifs que reçoit le contrôle lui-même qui est une notion susceptible de plus et de moins.

A) Pour les contrats d'approvisionnement, nous prendrons l'exemple du gaz car les ventes internationales de gaz n'ont pas encore d'histoire et elles sont conclues pour des durées très longues (autour de vingt ans), elles sont donc très significatives de l'évolution.[6]

Au-delà des énumérations et des formules précitées qui forment le standard minimum de la force majeure internationale, on trouve une appréhension très concrète des problèmes spécifiques de l'industrie gazière. En l'état présent des techniques et des structures du marché, l'exploitation internationale du gaz repose sur des installations industrielles onéreuses et compliquées, sur un moyen de transport nouveau, le méthanier, et sur un moyen de transport mieux connu mais complexe, le gazoduc. Aussi dans certains contrats comme celui conclu entre la société algérienne Sonatrach et la société américaine El Paso (Contrat El Paso No. 1),[7] sont visés spécialement les incidents sérieux affectant la production, le transport, le traitement, le stockage et le chargement du gaz du côté du vendeur, le transport, le déchargement, le stockage, la regazéification et la distribution vers les principaux clients du côté de l'acheteur. Il s'agit en résumé des incidents (*serious accidental damage*) liés à la technologie du gaz et à ses contraintes.

Deux éléments paraissent particulièrement intéressants à souligner, c'est d'abord la vision globale de l'exploitation du gaz qui est reçue et non pas simplement les rapports liés à l'échange puisque les événements qui pourront agir sur l'exécution du contrat sont envisagés dès les puits de production jusqu'à l'arrivée du gaz chez les principaux clients de l'acheteur. Dans le contrat El Paso, le principal client est celui qui achète 10% au moins des quantités annuelles livrées par le vendeur à

6. Pour une étude plus complète des ventes de gaz dans leur spécificaté de contrat d'approvisionnement, V. Kahn et autres, "La vente internationale de gaz," dans *Les Hydrocarbures gazeux et le développement des pays producteurs* 235 (1974).

7. Dans le même sens, Contrat Sonatrach—Panhandle du 17 août 1973, art. XIII.

l'acheteur; dans d'autres contrats qui retiennent également la défaillance des sous-acquéreurs de gaz pour cause de force majeure la notion de client principal n'est pas définie mais la défaillance des sous-acquéreurs (si les autres conditions sont réunies) ne devient une excuse que si elle porte sur certaines quantités, 20% des quantités journalières de gaz achetées. Dans ce dernier contrat, la force majeure chez le client doit s'entendre comme celle qui a été définie dans le contrat principal; dans le contrat Sonatrach-El Paso, le vendeur reçoit le droit de participer à la négociation des clauses de force majeure avec les sous-acheteurs. On rapprochera ces pratiques de celle des contrats internationaux de sous-traitance où généralement la clause de force majeure reproduit celle du contrat principal et où le vendeur peut invoquer à l'égard de l'acheteur la force majeure survenant chez son sous-traitant. Le but poursuivi est au premier chef d'harmoniser des contrats qui doivent aboutir à la réalisation du contrat principal mais la conséquence, peut-être non toujours voulue, d'une harmonisation des complexes contractuels est de préparer l'unification internationale des clauses de force majeure.

Dans les contrats de production du type vente d'usine clés en main et de ses dérivés, on rencontre encore de nombreuses clauses de force majeure dans l'acceptation traditionnelle et même quelquefois aggravées par des exclusions précises alors que l'événement aurait peut-être pu entrer dans la conception classique. Ainsi, dans une vente de biens d'équipement, une clause énumérative brève complétée par "autres événements" reconnus par l'arbitrage comme cas de force majeure, exclut expressément les manques de main-d'oeuvre, de matériel et les retards des fournisseurs du vendeur dont on aurait pu penser que moyennant certaines conditions ils auraient été admis. Et la clause n'est pas isolée; ce retour en arrière s'explique assez bien dans la mesure où les ventes d'usines clés en main font la charnière entre opérations d'échange et opérations de production, ce qui se marque entre autre par la brèveté relative de la durée d'exécution des contrats, qui est souvent de deux ou trois ans. Dès que la durée devient plus longue, on retrouve des systèmes analogues à ceux des autres contrats. En revanche pour les contrats d'investissement, la pratique moins sophistiquée que pour les contrats d'approvisionnement, car les engagements sont moins précis, aboutit au même résultat. En effet, ici on a moins à insister sur les données très concrètes d'un processus de fabrication ou de production qui met face à face un vendeur et un acheteur qu'envisager dans les rapports entre un investisseur étranger et un Etat d'accueil les raisons qui justifieraient soit les retards de l'investisseur dans l'accomplissement de son investissement mais dont il est déjé le premier sanctionné puisque c'est la source de son profit, soit les refus de l'Etat de maintenir certaines garanties ou certaines incitations.

L'évolution en dents de scie de la notion de force majeure selon les types de contrat relève sans doute de plusieurs explications. Mais il faut remarquer qu'elle est d'autant plus souple que la structure du contrat oblige les parties à une plus grande coopération pour son exécution. Les accords de coopération industrielle qui, soit à titre de contrat autonome, soit comme élément d'un contrat complexe se multiplient à l'heure actuelle exigeant une participation des deux parties et non plus simplement un *do ut facias* ou un *facio ut facias* qui caractérisent les contrats un peu anciens. C'est pourquoi après avoir stipulé des clauses rigoureuses de force majeure, puis des clauses descriptives de l'environement social à prendre en considération pour admettre l'existence d'un cas de force majeure, la pratique peut s'orienter vers des formules synthétiques et générales. La première formule utilisée a été celle de "cause (événement) en dehors du contrôle des parties" et elle est maintenant substituée par "en dehors du contrôle raisonable des parties," "*beyond the reasonable control of the party affected by*" . . . Nous reviendrons sur cette notion qui constitue la définition la plus riche de portée. Mais auparavant, il paraît dans la rédaction de certaines clauses que l'on trouve d'ailleurs aussi bien dans les contrats de production que dans ceux d'approvisionnement.

L'incertitude naît du fait que certaines clauses, soit comme ajout à une énumération de cas, soit à titre de définition, font référence à la force majeure telle qu'elle est "*internationally regarded as force majeure*" ou dans le cas de force majeure reconnu par l'arbitrage ou dans le cas de force majeure tels qu'ils sont définis par la Chambre de Commerce Internationale. Il s'agit d'une technique bien connue dans les contrats internationaux, qui consiste à délocaliser le contrat en faisant appel à des formules du genre de celles qui viennent d'être citées. Ces formules sont pour principal object d'exclure l'application d'un droit national et d'y substituer le droit international, le droit transnational, le droit international économique, la nouvelle lex mercatoria suivant les auteurs et une terminologie encore peu fixée. Ce qui est remarquable ici est que la délocalisation est indépendante de la loi applicable au contrat dans son ensemble qui est différent. C'est déjà la preuve de l'importance attachée par les parties à la clause de force majeure. Mais c'est aussi la preuve d'une recherche d'une conception plus large que celle retenue par la loi applicable au contrat. Ainsi dans des contrats où il y avait une clause de force majeure C.C.I., la loi applicable était le droit suisse qui se rattache aux conceptions continentales en la matière même si théoriquement certaines circonstances pouvaient conduire à la révision du contrat. Certes, l'efficacité de ces clauses est discutable. En particulier pour ceux qui nient la réalité d'un droit international économique élaboré en dehors du système étatique, le droit international de la force majeure n'existe pas. Même pour ceux qui admettent l'existence d'un système international a-étatique, l'existence de règles précises relevant d'un droit matériel international et concernant la force majeure est peut-être douteuse. Pour notre part, et c'est à quoi tend cette étude, nous pensons qu'il existe une convergence suffisante dans les solutions retenues dans les contrats de production et d'approvisionnement pour que des arbitres et même des tribunaux judiciaires saisis puissent opérer un règlement du différent sur la base du droit international économique.

B) Le problème lié à la personalité de l'état et qui surgit surtout à l'occasion de l'exécution des contrats d'investissement porte sur les raisons que l'Etat peut invoquer pour se libérer de ses obligations contractuelles. Plus exactement y a-t-il une notion de force majeure qui soit propre à l'Etat. Il est évident qu'il n'y a aucune difficulté lorsque l'Etat n'a pu construire une route dans les délais prévus avec l'investisseur en raison d'inondations catastrophiques. C'est le cas classique. Le véritable problème est de savoir dans quelle mesure des troubles politiques, économiques, sociaux, survenant en cours d'exécution du contrat doivent être pris en considération et si oui à partir de quel degré d'intensité. Il ne s'agit pas vraiment de la théorie des changements de circonstances qui conduit à la révision du contrat parce que la situation à un moment de l'exécution est foncièrement différente de celle existant au moment de la conclusion du contrat et de façon définitive (ou du moins prolongée) mais de mesurer les conséquences sur l'exécution d'un contrat où l'Etat est partie de circonstances—conjoncturelles—qui entraînent la prise de mesures par l'Etat qui sans viser forcément le contrat ont des répercussions sur lui. Le problème est encore mal saisi par la pratique. Nous avons déjà cité des clauses où l'intervention de l'Etat dans l'exécution du contrat était décrite avec un soin particulier. Mais il s'agissait de l'intervention de l'Etat en tant que tiers conduisant à l'exoneration d'un des contractants. Il semble qu'une démarche analogue devrait être entreprise lorsque l'Etat est partie au contrat. On trouve déjà quelques indications dans cette direction quand, par exemple, l'Etat annonce son intention de ne pas nationaliser l'investissement étranger mais se réserve le droit d'y procéder si les circonstances l'exigent ou quand les parties considèrent comme non contraires à leurs engagements réciproques une réduction d'activité résultant de l'évolution de la conjoncture économique. Nous n'avons pas rencontré de clauses plus précises sur une force majeure spécialement adaptée à l'Etat co-contractant mais notre échantillon est modeste. Une tentative a été faite cependant par *l'International Law Association* dans son modèle de contrat-type pour les investissements étrangers dans les pays en voie de développement adopté lors de la cinquante-sixième conférence tenue à New Delhi (28 déc. 1974—4 janv. 1975) pour cerner le problème. En effet, aux termes de l'article 17 du contrat-type, après une définition générale de la force majeure intermédiaire entre la conception traditionnelle et la conception la plus novatrice,[8] il est précisé qu'on prendra en considération pour apprécier l'existence d'un cas de force majeure la responsabilité de l'Etat vis-à-vis de ses nationaux et de la Communauté internationale, en particulier en cas de difficultés économiques ou de troubles politiques, etc. . . Il y a donc bien une appréciation différenciée du comportement de l'Etat par rapport à celui de son co-contractant parce qu'il est l'Etat pour l'établissement de cas de force majeure en introduisant des aspects de la conjoncture interne ou internationale qu'on ne retiendrait pas dans une perspective traditionnelle.

Là encore, bien que les termes ne soient pas utilisés, c'est l'événement en dehors du contrôle raisonnable de l'Etat qui sert de directive. Mais comme nous l'avons déjà indiqué, l'expression est de plus en plus formellement insérée dans les contrats internationaux de longue durée, qu'il s'agisse de contrats de production ou de contrats d'approvisionnement.

C) La formule "en dehors du contrôle raisonnable des parties," comme toute formule qualitative caractérisant un comportement, est difficile à définir sur le plan juridique.

Tout d'abord l'idée implique que les comportements à comparer soient ceux de personnes comparables. Ainsi la convention de La Haye du 1er Juillet 1964 sur la vente internationale d'objets mobiliers corporels établit-elle la comparaison entre des personnes de même qualité placées dans une situation identique (article 74: Exonération). Il est utile de le préciser car les droits nationaux ont tendance à construire un modèle abstrait de comportement qui n'a aucun lien avec le milieu où il est censé agir. C'est pourquoi d'ailleurs de nombreux contrats replacent bien l'étude du comportement dans le milieu concret où il agit. C'est ainsi que dans un contrat de fourniture de pétrole nous avons noté que la clause de force majeure exonère les contractants de leur responsabilité si l'événement empêche, diminue, retarde la production, le transport, la vente, la livraison ou la réception du pétrole "*in the customary manner,*" c'est-à-dire "*in accordance with the general practices of the petroleum industry.*" Cette référence implique en tout cas un examen très concret de la situation en cause et une attitude relativement indulgente: une communauté d'entrepreneurs n'est pas une société de héros. Et cette référence aux usages de la profession est fréquente quand le contrat est conclu dans un milieu professionel assez homogène. Une formule un peu plus développée se trouve dans l'expression événement "*beyond the control of a party acting in accordance with the standards*

8. La force majeure est définie comme toute situation échappant au contrôle des parties qui rend l'exécution du contrat très difficile ou impossible.

of a reasonable and prudent operator" où se trouvent bien mis en relief les comportements que doivent avoir des entrepreneurs agissant dans un milieu professionnel déterminé.

Dans d'autres contrats, l'approche de la notion est encore plus précise puisqu'il est écrit dans la clause de force majeure que l'événement ne doit pas pouvoir être surmonté si ce n'est pas l'usage de moyens raisonnables à des coûts raisonnables. Le contrôle ici est donc divisé puisque les contractants distinguent d'une part les moyens à mettre en oeuvre et d'autre part leur coût. La distinction n'est peut-être pas aussi réelle qu'elle le paraît car il y a une étroite corrélation entre les moyens et le coût. Plus les moyens mis en oeuvre sont importants et sophistiqués et plus ils coûtent cher. Mais il y a malgré tout une certaine indépendance de facteurs car surmonter la force majeure pourrait exiger la mise en oeuvre de moyens peu onéreux mais immobilisant des hommes et du matériel pour une durée trop longue, par exemple par rapport aux résultats escomptés sans que le coût soit excessif. Au-dela de cette difficulté, l'intérêt principal est de bien marquer que presque tous les événements peuvent être surmontés si on y met les moyens et l'argent nécessaires, mais que dans un contexte économique qui est celui du fonctionnement d'entreprise, on n'utilise pas n'importe quel moyen à n'importe quel coût. Ceux-ci doivent être supportables et ne pas conduire le débiteur défaillant à trop compromettre le fonctionnement de son entreprise.

On a ainsi une idée assez claire de ce que représente un contrôle raisonnable sur l'événement même si cas par cas la discussion reste largement ouverte. Mais cette conception conduit à faire intervenir des facteurs qui relèvent de la vie économique et sociale et qui n'ont plus rien à voir avec la fatalité ancienne qui frappait les contractants, rendait l'exécution du contrat impossible et exonérait le débiteur. Il s'agit donc bien pour les parties au moment où elles contractent de se ménager les moyens de réviser leur accord dans des cas déterminés. On remarquera que les clauses de révision générale et plus spécialement les clauses de *hardship*, clauses nouvelles, empruntent beaucoup à la conception de la force majeure telle que nous venons de la décrir.[9] On y retrouve en particulier les mêmes références à la conduite d'un contractant prudent et raisonnable. Les autres conditions et les conséquences sont sans doute différentes mais la fonction de clause de révision partielle que remplit actuellement la clause de force majeure explique l'existence de stipulations analogues.

L'étendue des cas de force majeure dans l'évolution actuelle est légèrement corrigée par un formalisme rigoureux.

9. Oppetit, *supra* note 2, p. 801.

En effet, dans presque tous les contrats, le droit d'invoquer la force majeure est soumis à un formalisme dont le non-respect aboutit dans la plupart des cas à sa déchéance (si la partie concernée ne remplit pas ses obligations—en l'espèce d'information—elle ne pourra invoquer le cas de force majeure). Ce formalisme s'il est rigoureux est assez simple. Il repose sur l'idée d'information. Le débiteur défaillant doit immédiatement avertir son cocontractant de la survenance du cas de force majeure et de sa durée probable. L'avertissement se fait par une voie rapide (télécommunication) complété et confirmé ultérieurement par une lettre recommandée ou non, avec des éléments de preuve sur la réalité de l'événement et sur son incidence sur l'exécution du contrat.

Deux exemples suffiront à éclairer le propos:

Vente de biens d'équipement:

> Dans la mesure où la livraison serait empêchée partiellement ou entièrement par un cas de force majeure le vendeur sera tenu à en informer l'acheteur par télégramme. Le vendeur est tenu également à informer l'acheteur du retour à l'état normal.
>
> Cet avis doit être confirmé—au plus tard cinq jours après—par une lettre recommandée.
>
> Le vendeur est tenu à prouver le cas de force majeure par des documents dignes de foi.
>
> . . . . . .

Vente de gaz:

> *A party claiming relief on account of force majeure shall:*
>
> a) *as soon as practicable give notice to the other party of the happening said to constitute force majeure such notice including information about the circumstances and a statement of the steps and time necessary to remedy failure and afford facilities for examining such circumstances including facilities for a site inspection if desired at the expense and risk of the party making the examination . . .*

Une telle rigueur dont on a des germes dans le système classique de la force majeure est justifiée. La multiplication des causes d'exonération augmente le nombre des inexécutions, leur complexité et leur souplesse entraînent des divergences d'interprétation. Or, la présomption est quand même dans le sens que les obligations contractuelles doivent être exécutées. Celui qui veut renverser la présomption doit au moins prévenir du trouble et apporter les preuves du bien-fondé de son action.

En résumé, par rapport aux droits nationaux, on peut constater qu'il y a une progression de la notion de force majeure dans les contrats internationaux qui fait de cette dernière non pas l'expression et l'incidence de la fatalité sur l'exécution du contrat, mais une règle de comportement dans certaines circonstances particulièrement graves. Déjà à ce stade par l'admission de cas de plus en plus nombreux et d'une définition de plus en plus laxiste, on est vraiment en présence de clauses de révision partielle. Il reste à faire la même vérification pour les effets de la force majeure.

II. LES CONSÉQUENCES DE LA FORCE MAJEURE

L'examen des conséquences de la force majeure confirme l'évolution de l'institution, faire un système de révision partielle d'un système prévu pour attribuer les risques du contrat.

Dans le droit commun traditionnel, l'événement de force majeure entraîne généralement deux conséquences: la première est la rupture du contrat, la seconde est l'absence de responsabilité du débiteur défaillant, donc la charge d'inexécution pour le créancier. La force majeure est bien un procédé d'attribution de la fatalité.

A. —*La non-responsabilité du débiteur.*

Dans les contrats internationaux de production et d'approvisionnement, la non-responsabilité du débiteur est reconnue selon les formules suivantes:

Vente d'une brasserie en Roumanie:

> Pour les retards ou la non-exécution des obligations dues à la force majeure, aucune des parties ne peut réclamer à l'autre des pénalités des intérêts ou tout autre dédommagement ou participation au préjudice souffert par elle à cause de la force majeure.

Vente d'une usine de fibres synthétiques en Corée:

> *Any loss or damage or delays in, or failure of performance of either party hereto shall not constitute default hereunder or give rise to any claims for damages if and to the extent that such loss, damage, delay or failure is caused by Force Majeure.*

Vente d'un complexe chimique en Colombie:

> Les retards ou les manquements à cet avenant encourus par l'une ou l'autre des parties ne constitueront pas des cas de non-accomplissement et ne donneront pas lieu à réclamation, indemnité ou amende lorsque ces retards ou manquements seront dus . . .

Vente de petrole Moyen-Orient-Europe:

> *No failure or omission to carry out or observe any of the provisions or conditions of this Agreement shall give rise to any claim against either party or be deemed a breach of this Agreement if such failure or omission arises from any cause reasonably beyond the control of either party.*

Il n'y a donc pas, semble-t-il, de différence avec les règles légales et jurisprudentielles de droits nationaux. Pourtant déjà l'esprit du système s'éloigne du système étatique. En effet, la partie défaillante ne doit pas rester passive devant l'événement, elle a à sa charge de faire tous ses efforts pour revenir à une situation normale. C'est du moins ce qui est spécifié dans d'assez nombreux contrats. Cette obligation étant complétée par celle d'informer le créancier sur la suite des événements. On peut citer comme clause significative de cette obligation la clause suivante, empruntée à une vente clés en main d'une usine de produits chimiques au Brésil, le vendeur étant européen:

> *The contracting parties have to act both during the force majeure event and with respect to its consequences in compliance with the principle of "Bona fides" in view of realizing the economical aim defined in Chapter I, so as to remedy the loss of time caused by the force majeure as soon as possible and to get the contractual obligations performed within the shortest possible time.*

Là encore, on notera que la Convention de La Haye du 1er Juillet 1964 qui est le texte international le plus récent sur ce type de problème fait également obligation au débiteur défaillant et excusé d'essayer de limiter le dommage causé au créancier. Cette obligation pour le débiteur de faire preuve d'une diligence particulière pour remédier aux dommages causés par la force majeure est tout à fait dans la logique du système qui étend les cas de force majeure à des situations économiques et techniques. Cependant la sanction d'une telle obligation est rarement prévue. On peut se demander si la déchéance que l'on trouve pour l'information du créancier au moment où la force majeure vient empêcher l'exécution du contrat n'est pas ici une sanction trop forte, et s'il ne suffirait pas d'accorder simplement une réparation pour le préjudice qu'aurait pu empêcher le débiteur.

B.—*Le sort du contrat.*

En revanche, en ce qui concerne la rupture du contrat, la différence est essentielle avec les conceptions de la plupart des droits nationaux. En effet, dans les contrats internationaux, le contrat en principe n'est pas rompu sauf s'il est évident qu'il ne pourra jamais s'exécuter un jour. Or, les parties ont généralement intérêt à suspendre l'exécution du contrat plutôt qu'à rompre leurs relations et de chercher chacune pour soi un nouveau partenaire et ceci pour plusieurs raisons.

Tout d'abord, les négociations portant sur la conclusion d'un contrat de production ou d'approvisionnement sont longues. Il n'est donc pas certain que chercher un nouveau partenaire pour le créancier lui fasse gagner du temps par rapport à la date de remise en vigueur de l'exécution suspendue. Ensuite comme nous l'avons montré, les événements constitutifs de la force majeure sont de plus en plus souvent liés à la vie politique, économique, technologique et de moins en moins à la géophysique. Il en résulte que dans de nombreux cas la force majeure agira dans les mêmes conditions sur tous les contrats relevant d'un mêmeobjet dans une même zone géographique. Enfin, pour une partie des contrats, dans l'état de concurrence oligopolitique qui caractérise le marché international, le choix des partenaires est réduit et les contractants sont souvent des contractants obligés. En tout état de cause le maintien des relations contractuelles malgré la survenance d'un événement interruptif d'exécution répond à la philosophie générale des contrats internationaux pour lesquels l'exécution en nature malgré les difficultés est le but recherché par les parties qui n'interrompent leurs rapports que dans des circonstances exceptionnelles même dans le cadre de la responsabilité pour faute. Ici, aussi, le caractère "raisonnable" de la suspension est inscrit en filigrance si la notion n'est pas aussi franchement utilisée que pour la définition de la force majeure.

L'absence de rupture s'exprime selon des clauses du type suivant qui tendent toutes à prendre en considération la durée de l'effet de la force majeure sur l'exécution du contrat.

Vente d'équipement de chauffage en U.R.S.S.:

> En cas de force majeure . . . , le délai de livraison ou de la remise de la documentation technique se prolongera en proportion de la durée des cas de force majeure.

Installation d'une raffinerie:

> *The time of delivery shall be extended by the number of proved working days which the builder has lost due to such circumstances as set out above, even if the cause of the delay occurred after the date of delivery stated in this contract.*

Installation de raffinerie d'huiles alimentaires en Roumanie:

> En cas de force majeure . . . Les obligations des deux parties se prolongent automatiquement de la durée du retard dû et justifié par la force majeure.

Vente et installation de matériels téléphoniques au Pérou:

> *Toda programmación de entregas e instalacion serà pospuesta por un periodo, por lo menos, equivalente a aquèl durante el cual las causas indicadas tuvieron existencia.*

Ces données doivent être interprétées et precisées. En raison de la durée contractuelle d'exécution des contrats de production et d'approvisionnement, l'exécution finale à la suite de la suspension due à la force majeure peut suivant les cas se comprimer dans le délai restant à courir ou déborder la date contractuelle. Par exemple, dans le premier cas, s'agissant d'une vente d'une usine clés en main, il peut y avoir simplement retard dans le démarrage de certains ateliers, de certaines productions mais respect final de la date prévue ou au contraire non-respect de la date prévue. Dans les contrats d'approvisionnement, après la période de suspension, les quantités non livrées peuvent être livrées dans la période restant à courir, après cette période, ou ne jamais être livrées, seules l'étant les qualités normalement livrables entre la reprise du contrat et sa date d'achèvement. Chaque clause devrait donc indiquer nettement comment joue exactement le maintien du contrat. Souvent dans les contrats de production, il y a prolongation au-delà de la date contractuelle. Pour les contrats d'approvisionnement, les quantités qui auraient dû être livrées pendant la durée de la force majeure sont annulées dans de nombreux cas mais toutes les solutions et toutes les nuances sont possibles. Le contrat est véritablement réadapté aux besoins des parties.

Mais si le principe de la suspension de l'exécution du contrat et de sa reprise après la disparition de l'effet de la force majeure est accepté sous une forme identique dans la plupart des contrats les divergences apparaissent lorsqu'il faut tirer les conséquences de la prolongation de la force majeure au-delà d'un certain délai. En effet, la suspension ne peut être que temporaire. Si la force majeure poursuit son effet trop longtemps, les parties ne restent plus dans la neutralité passive que constitue l'attente. Et la plupart des clauses prévoient qu'au bout d'un certain délai variable suivant les contrats mais le plus souvent de six mois ou un an, le contrat est remis en question selon des modalités très différentes puisqu'elles conduisent soit à la rupture immédiate, soit à la renégociation de l'accord.

Dans quelques clauses, le créancier ou le débiteur ou les deux parties (l'alternative repose sur des raisons techniques ou des rapports de force selon les cas) reçoivent le droit de rompre le contrat qui de suspendu est définitivement interrompu sans responsabilité du débiteur. Ainsi peut-on citer la clause suivante qui est très représentative de ce courant: "Si ces événements durent plus de six mois, chaque partie a le droit de renoncer à l'exécution des obligations contractuelles." Il s'agit d'un retour au droit commun des droits étatiques après une tentative de maintien du lien contractuel.

La déviation est donc légère et ne constitue qu'une adaptation à des contrats de type particulier de la règle normale. On ne peut donc pas parler véritablement de révision. Mais il ne semble pas que ce soit la clause la plus généralement utilisée. A travers le matériel statistique dont nous disposons, c'est la renégociation étant elle-même enferméedans un cadre plus ou moins large et susceptible d'aboutir à des résultats plus ou moins importants.

Dans un premier type de clause, on rencontre une formule que l'on peut qualifier d'intermédiaire entre les clauses de résiliation après suspension et les clauses de renégociation. Elle s'exprime par la stipulation suivante:

> Si un cas de force majeure provoque un retard de plus de dix mois, les parties se concerteront sur les mesures à prendre. Si un accord n'intervient pas, l'une ou l'autre des parties pourra demander la résiliation du contrat par voie d'arbitrage.

La résiliation n'est donc pas automatique dès la fin du délai de suspension. Les parties doivent entrer en rapport et négocier sur les suites à donner à la force majeure. C'est donc bien une clause de renégociation mais elles n'ont aucunement l'obligation d'arriver à un résultat. La résiliation sera la suite judiciaire (juridiction arbitrale) du désaccord des parties sur les mesures à prendre: prolongation de la suspension, résiliation, modification du contrat. On remarquera qu'en cas de désaccord, les solutions possibles se résolvent en une alternative: prolongation de la suspension qui est l'état de fait ou demande de résiliation adressée aux arbitres aussi bien par le débiteur que par le créancier. On peut s'étonner de ce détour par la voie arbitrale, onéreuse et longue, alors qu'il aurait été plus simple d'envisager une résiliation automatique dès lors que le désaccord est établi. Mais sans doute la notion de désaccord n'est pas une notion simple et il peut être utile de le faire enregistrer de façon certaine; de plus, l'organisation de la rupture d'un contrat de production ou d'approvisionnement est souvent assez complexe car le contrat n'est pas ou exécuté ou inexécuté. Il est partiellement exécuté et il y a des actes qu'il faut conduire à leur fin y compris des actes de maintenance. Les arbitres sont l'instance neutre qui prend les mesures de liquidation du contrat. La clause est cependant ambiguë en ce qui concerne les pouvoirs réels des arbitres. Sont-ils obligés de prononcer la résiliation dès lors que la force majeure a suspendu l'exécution du contrat pendant le temps prévu et que les parties ne se sont pas mises d'accord sur une solution ou peuvent-ils sinon modifier le contrat pour tenir compte des incidences de la force majeure du moins prolonger la suspension en prenant ou non des mesures d'attente. Nous pencherions plutôt pour l'obligation des arbitres de prononcer la résiliation, leur rôle étant de vérifier que les conditions de la résiliation sont bien réunies et de liquider éventuellement les rapports entre les parties. On retrouve là les pouvoirs du juge étatique français quand il doit prononcer la résolution d'un contrat et c'est en cela que la clause est une clause intermédiaire.

Mais dans les cas les plus nombreux après l'écoulement du délai de suspension ou dès l'origine de l'événement de force majeure, s'il s'avère qu'il fera sentir son effet au-delà du délai de suspension, on entre sans erreur possible dans une véritable procédure de réadaptation du contrat, de révision au sens propre. En effet, les parties doivent se rencontrer et examiner les incidences de la force majeure sur l'exécution du contrat et sur les modalités des différentes prestations.

On peut citer deux clauses à titre d'illustration:

1re clause:

> Si par suite de cas de force majeure, le Maître de l'oeuvre ou le constructeur ne pouvaient exécuter leurs prestations telles que prévues au contrat pendant une période de six mois, les parties se rencontreront dans les plus brefs délais pour examiner les incidences contractuelles des dits événements en particulier sur les prix et les délais de la poursuite des presentations respectives . . .

2e clause:

> *If the force majeure lasts longer than six (6) months, buyer and seller shall without delay meet to consult each other and try to find an appropriate remedy to the situation and to reach agreement thereon.*
>
> *When considering the measure to be taken, buyer and seller shall give due and serious attention to the difficulties caused by the above mentioned circumstances and make serious attempt at finding a fair solution . . .*

A la lettre, les parties ne peuvent discuter que des effets de la force majeure sur l'exécution du contrat. Mais comment ne pas tenir compte de la conjoncture économique dans laquelle se déroule la nouvelle négotiation. Si un contrat doit être prolongé d'une anné ou deux et qu'au moment de la nouvelle négociation certains prix de revient ont considérablement changé à la suite d'une crise de l'énergie par exemple, c'est tout l'équilibre du contrat qui est remis en cause.

Le contenu des contrats à moyens et à long terme repose partiellement sur les prévisions des parties quant à l'évolution de la conjoncture économique, technologique et politique. Tout contrat à long terme est un contrat aléatoire en ce sens que les prévisions sont soumises à trop d'événements incertains pour être exactes. Les clauses d'indexation de prix sont la prolongation des prévisions primitives des parties. En revanche, les clauses qui font appel à des mécanismes de révision non quantifiables mécaniquement ouvrent en réalité même dans les cas de révision partielle et implicite comme dans les clauses de force majeure une négociation sur l'ensemble du contrat. Chaque partie a connaissance de ce qui s'est passé entre le moment de la conclusion du contrat et celui de sa suspension, donc elle a une vision nouvelle de l'économie du contrat. La tentation est grande pour les parties ou pour l'une des parties d'essayer de profiter de la discussion ouverte sur la seule détermination des conséquences de la force majeure sur l'exécution du contrat pour l'étendre à la révision de l'ensemble du contrat. Le problème est bien perçu par certains contractants qui tentent de distinguer accord sur l'exécution ultérieure du contrat et examen de l'opportunité de poursuivre l'exécution du contrat en tenant compte des circonstances nouvelles. Mais si la distinction est théoriquement pertinente, sur le plan pratique, elle est difficile à mettre en oeuvre et de l'examen de l'opportunité à la révision, la frontière est vite franchie. Quoi qu'il en soit, plus ou moins étendu selon la bonne foi ou la volonté des parties, le système retenu est bien un système d'adaptation et non pas de liquidation du contrat selon la théorie des droits étatiques.

Le système butte sur un obstacle de taille, c'est que laissées à leur seule initiative les parties courent le risque de ne jamais se mettre d'accord. C'est un écueil auquel on se heurte également dans les clauses de révision en dehors de tout événement précis comme la force majeure. Les parties qui prévoient une discussion sur les conséquences de la force majeure sur le contrat prévoient également l'intervention du tribunal arbitral. Ainsi les deux clauses précitées contiennent-elles respectivement les deux stipulations suivantes:

> Au cas où les parties ne pourraient se mettre d'accord dans les plus brefs délais, les conséquences relatives à ces événements seront portées à l'appréciation de l'arbitrage tel que prévu à l'article . . .

et "*If the fair solution is not reached within three months, it shall be solved by arbitration.*" C'est une mission excessivement lourde qui est confiée aux arbitres et inhabituelle car normalement ils ne se prononcent que sur des prétentions juridiques opposant les parties.[10] Les parties sont certainement sensibles à la mission exceptionelle confiée aux arbitres car elle ne résulte pas de la clause d'arbitrage générale que l'on rencontre dans la plupart des contrats internationaux, mais d'une clause spéciale insérée dans la clause de force majeure qui confère aux arbitres un pouvoir spécial. Cette insertion accentue encore le particularisme et l'importance de la force majeure dans les contrats de longue durée. Mais elle ne constitue finalement qu'un des moyens mis à la disposition des parties pour élaborer les règles de droit dont elles ont besoin. Et puisque l'arbitrage repose avant tout sur la volonté des parties, il paraît normal que celles-ci confient aux arbitres les différents caractéristiques d'une société en plein bouleversement même si les termes de référence de leur mission dépassent ceux habituellement établis dans des arbitrages que trop de rigorisme figerait. La notion de force majeure dans sa construction actuelle permet aux parties une adaptation prudente de leurs relations à certains aspects de la conjoncture et ici comme ailleurs la soumission des différents à l'arbitrage vient couronner une construction qui autrement resterait branlante.

Pour conclure cette brève étude, il nous semble que l'élaboration de la notion de force majeure dans les contrats internationaux de production et d'approvisionnement dans une présentation schématique et volontairement excessive est pourtant un bon témoignage de l'existence d'une lex mercatoria ou d'un droit transnational économique. Dans un domaine très technique, celui d'une institution exonératrice de la responsabilité du débiteur, les contractants ont su utiliser et déformer une construction des droits étatiques rigide pour en faire un instrument finalement assez élaboré et apte à satisfaire un besoin de plus en plus pressant: dans une conjoncture en continuelle évolution, adapter leur contrat sans le bouleverser dans les circonstances assez graves. Une fois de plus le rôle de l'arbitrage dans cette construction de la pratique apparaît comme primordial. Nous ignorons si des sentences ont été rendues réajustant un contrat à la suite de la survenance d'un cas de force majeure et du désaccord des parties sur la suite à donner, mais l'arbitrabilité d'un tel différend oblige les parties à chercher à s'entendre et constitue un ultime recours. Il y a bien ici un système complet puisque la règle de droit matériel est posée, de même quelquefois la règle de conflit spécifique et qu'enfin la juridiction arbitrale est choisie pour sanctionner la construction des praticiens et ce système n'est pas arbitraire.

Il marque ce qu'on pourrait appeller le dynamisme contractuel des parties pour essayer d'appréhender efficacement le temps dans des relations économiques internationales de plus en plus instables et complexes et que le droit n'arrive plus à enfermer dans des formules uniques et permanents.

10. *Id.* p. 808-09.

STRIKES AND THE LAW — SOME RECENT DEVELOPMENTS IN WESTERN EUROPE

OTTO KAHN-FREUND

More than forty years ago Wolfgang Friedman and I were colleagues in the Berlin Labour Court, and throughout the many years of our close friendship we shared an interest in the law governing labour relations. Friedmann saw it, as he saw everything, in the context of a far reaching and penetrating analysis of the relation between law and its social environment, as one element in the adjustment of corporate and of governmental power and of both to the interests of the individual.[1] It was one of the manifestations of the impact which social change has upon the law—that impact whose masterly description and analysis is perhaps the most significant of the many outstanding contributions he made to legal scholarship and learning. It may be apposite to dedicate to his memory this modest tribute which is concerned with a subject close to his interest—the attitude of the law to industrial conflict, and the influence which varying ideologies and types of social organisation have had upon that attitude.

I

No one surveying the problem of industrial conflict in Western civilization can fail to perceive that the so-called right to strike has two distinguishable ideological roots. These two ideologies or methods of justifying the right to strike are not of course neatly separated from each other like legal concepts—they are types of attitudes which overlap and penetrate one another. One is to the effect that the strike and the lockout are institutions complementary to collective bargaining. They are in this view—to paraphrase Clausewitz—the continuation of collective negotiations with other means, and this purpose both justifies stoppages of work and determines the limits of their legality. There is another way of looking at the strike as a social phenomenon; one can see in it the exercise of a fundamental freedom of the individual,

SIR OTTO KAHN-FREUND Q.C. is Professor Emeritus. University of Oxford; Fellow of the British Academy; formerly Professor of Law, University of London; and, Arthur Goodhart Visiting Professor of Legal Science, University of Cambridge.

1. W. Friedmann, *Law in a Changing Society* 347 ff. (2d ed. 1972).

comparable to the freedom of association or the freedom of expression: the right to stop work in association with one's fellows in order to demonstrate one's opinion, to use political pressure, and also to influence one's own or other people's conditions of employment. The first of these attitudes is traditional in the countries of Northern and North Western Europe—in Britain, in Germany, in Scandinavia and also in the United States, in Canada and in Australia—whilst the second has traditionally predominated in France and in Italy and has had a decisive impact on the law in those countries.

II

The two different sets of political ideas are crystallised in the law in two different concepts of the right to strike. This term, "*the right to strike,*" is loosely employed in political and also often in legal argument. It is capable of bearing at least two quite distinct meanings. The word right may be, and often is, used in a non-Hohfeldian sense, and may denote no more than a freedom from legal constraint, from prohibitions enforced through penal or civil sanctions. In this sense those enjoying the so-called (or miscalled) right to strike can stop work collectively or organise or finance such stoppage without being exposed to orders for damages, injunctions, or prosecutions—provided always that in doing so they do not infringe someone else's contractual rights. In terms of Hohfeld's jurisprudential analysis[2] this right is a privilege or liberty or freedom—an exemption, *e.g.,* from a person's right (in the strict sense) to claim damages for, say, civil conspiracy or interference with a contract; —and it may be an immunity—an exemption from another person's power, *e.g.,* to terminate a contract, or, more important, to obtain a conviction in a criminal court. But, whether *privilege* or immunity, it may be defined objectively or subjectively, in terms of the nature of the act done or in terms of the person doing it, *e.g.,* in terms of the act being done "in contemplation or furtherance of an industrial dispute" or in terms of the act being done by or on behalf of a trade union.[3] We shall, therefore, distinguish objective and subjective privileges and immunities. Both are, as a matter of legislative policy, linked with the approach to the strike as an institution complementary to collective bargaining.

The right to strike may, however, be and is in some legal systems a

2. W.N. Hohfeld, *Fundamental Legal Conceptions* 35 ff. (Paperback ed. W.W. Cook 1966).

3. For examples of the "objective" definition see: Conspiracy, and Protection of Property Act, 1875, 38 & 39 Vict., c. 86, section 3; Trade Union and Labour Relations Act, 1974, c. 52 section 13 (Great Britain); Norris-LaGuardia Act sections 4-5, 29 U.S.C. sections 103-04 (1970) (United States) (1932 Statute). For example of the "subjective" definition see: Trade Disputes Act, 1906, 6 Edw. 7, c. 47 section 4 (now repealed); Trade Union and Labour Relations Act, 1974, c. 52, section 14 (Great Britain).

true Hohfeldian right; that is, it may give to its holder a claim against others to act or not to act in a certain way, *e.g.*, against the employer to pay wages in certain circumstances. More than that, this right to strike may be guaranteed by a Constitution, and thus be protected against encroachment by legislation, including, where—as, *e.g.*, in Italy—unconstitutional statutes can be annulled, encroachment by legislation. Such constitutional protection could, of course, be given to a mere privilege or immunity, but in fact we find that an express constitutional guarantee coincides with the conferment of a true right. As a matter of legislative policy the true *right* to strike expresses the principle that, in resorting with others to a concerted stoppage, the individual exercises a fundamental civil liberty.

In 1941 Lord Wright said in the leading case of *Crofter Hand Woven Harris Tweed Co. v. Veitch*[4] that "[t]he right of workmen to strike is an essential element in the principle of collective bargaining," but this was intended as a reference to the freedom from liability for civil conspiracy whose limitations were contested in the case. The word "right" was not here used in the strict sense any more than in section 13 of the United States Labor-Management Relations Act, 1935-1947, by which nothing in the Act, except as specifically provided for therein, is to be construed so as to "interfere with or impede or diminish in any way the right to strike" or to affect its limitations or qualifications. Neither the United States nor the United Kingdom has ever known a right to strike as Hohfeld would have defined the term.

Contrast with this the Preamble to the Constitution of the Fourth French Republic of 1946 which, in 1958, was incorporated in the present Constitution, that of the Fifth Republic—"*Le droit de grève s'exerce dans le cadre des lois qui le réglementent*"—, or article 40 of the Italian Constitution of 1948 in which the same words appear, translated in Italian. This constitutional formulation establishes a right in the true sense, *un droit de grève* and not merely *une liberté*;[5] this is a distinction that is identical with that made by Hohfeld between right and privilege or immunity. Indeed in 1952,[6] in an article which has become a classic, the famous Italian constitutionalist Calamandrei distinguished between three possible attitudes of the law towards the strike: (1) it can suppress it, as Italian law sought to do under Fascism; (2) it can tolerate it, by exempting those involved from certain penal or civil sanctions; and, (3) it can create a right to use it. This was done, he says, when Italy enacted

4. [1942] A.C. 435, 463.

5. P. Durand & A. Vitu, 3 *Traité de Droit du Travail* No. 253, at 713 ff. (1956) [hereinafter cited as Durand & Vitu]; H. Sinay, "La Grève" 6 *Traité de Droit du Travail* 97 ff. (G.H. Camerlynck ed. 1966) [*hereinafter cited as Sinay*].

6. Calamandrei, "Significato costituzionale del diritto dello sciopero," 1 *Rivista Giuridica del Lavoro* 22 (1952).

article 40 of its present Constitution. In France and in Italy the individual and the relative collective entity are entitled to resort to strike and the exercise of this right overrides private rights of others.

These two attitudes towards the legal nature of the right result from differences in the significance of that right in the history of political ideas to which I have referred. This is their ideological background. Let us now look at their practical consequences, and especially at three of these: the relation between the strike and the contract of employment; the legality of the wildcat strike; and, the right to strike in the public sector.

III

What is the effect of a strike on the contracts of employment of those who participate in it? To this question the law can give three answers: (a) the strike may terminate the contract, with the result that on resumption of work it is for the employer to decide whether or not he wants to re-engage (not reinstate) the workers and that, in the absence of an agreement to the contrary, all accrued seniority rights are lost; (b) the strike may break the contract, with the result that the employer may, at his option, claim damages from the strikers or terminate their contracts or both, and, at least in some legal systems such as English law, claim damages in tort from anyone who induced the workers to strike,[7] and this may include a union or its officers; (c) the strike may suspend the contract with the result that while it lasts the employer cannot require the strikers to work nor can they claim wages; but at the end of the strike the contract still exists, the duties to work and to pay wages are automatically revived, and all seniority rights are preserved.

In all European countries the effect of the strike on the contractual relations between employers and employees has been a central problem of labour law since the Second World War, and to some extent even during the period between the Wars. The controversies surrounding this problem can only be understood if one realises that in all European countries most contracts of employment may be terminated only upon

7. The tort of inducing a breach of contract was invented in 1853: Lumley v. Gye, 2 E. and B. 216, 118 Eng. Rep. 749 (Q.B. 1853). For examples of liability for this tort in labour relations see: Taff Vale Ry. Co. v. Amalgamated Soc'y of Ry. Servants, [1901] A.C. 426; South Wales Miners' Fed. v. Glamorgan Coal Co., [1905] A.C. 239; Emerald Const. Co. v. Lowthian, [1966] 1 W.L.R. 691 (C.A.); Torquay Hotel v. Cousins, [1969] 2 Ch. 106. Liability for the tort was abolished by the Trade Disputes Act, 1906, 6 Edw. 7, c. 47, s. 3 for acts done in contemplation or furtherance of a trade dispute, provided the contract involved was a contract for employment. This provision was repealed by the Industrial Relations Act 1971, c. 72. It is now—in an extended form—re-enacted in the Trade Union and Labour Relations Act, 1974, c. 52, s. 13 as amended by the Trade Union and Labour Relations (Amendment) Oct. 1976 c. 7, s. 3. See further below.

the giving of a notice, the length of which is sometimes fixed by express individual agreement, but much more frequently by custom or collective agreement incorporated in the contracts of employment, or very often by statute. From the point of view of the law of contract an employer or employee who terminates or purports to terminate the contract without notice is in breach of it; legal systems differ on the point whether an unlawful termination is effective as an immediate termination, as in English law, or whether it is not so effective but terminates the contract as from the moment when a lawful notice would have expired, as in German law. This is more important if the employer is in breach of contract than if the employee is in breach. If the employer is in breach, the employee can, on the first of these alternatives, only claim damages, but on the second he can claim his wages and other contractual rights up to the moment of lawful termination. The employer can, in any event, only claim damages because no modern system of law allows him to obtain and enforce a judgment for specific performance against the employee.

The practical significance of the question – termination or suspension – is however at least as great as and probably much greater than that of the question – breach or no breach –. The problem is whether workers can only strike at the risk of losing their jobs or at least their seniority, or, more realistically, whether at the end of the strike the union has to bargain for reinstatement and maintenance of seniority or whether the law relieves it of this necessity.

A strike may be lawful or unlawful in the light of its purposes or of its methods or both. This is true whether the workers have a right to strike, as in France or Italy, or a mere freedom, as in England or in the United States. Even the right can be exercised only for certain objects and in certain ways. That which is known as a strike for political purposes, whatever this may mean in this context, is, despite the difference in traditions, as unlawful in the eyes of the French courts[8] as it is in the eyes of the German[9] courts. A go-slow is unlawful everywhere[10] and so is a sit-in.[11] The problem which, in relation to the contract of employment, has had to be solved all over Europe is this, – can a strike be a

8. Durand & Vitu, *supra* note 5, No. 269, at 769; leading case: Judgment of March 3, 1953, [1954] D. Jur. 89 (Cass. Soc.).

9. See, *e.g.*, the decision of the *Bundesgerichtshof* in the famous newspaper strike: Judgment of Sept. 9 , 1954, 14 BGHZ 347.

10. Judgment of March 5, 1953, 1953 *Droit Social* 226 (France); Judgment No. 1628 of June 7, 1952, 2 *Rivista di Diritto Internazionale e Comparato del Lavoro* 392 (1952) (Italy). See 2 A. Hueck & H.C. Nipperdey, *Lehrbuch des Arbeitsrechts* 892 (7th ed. 1970) [hereinafter cited as Hueck & Nipperdey].

11. See, *e.g.*, Sinay, *supra* note 5, at 226 ff.; R. Latournerie, *Le Droit Français de la Grève* 194 ff. (1972) [hereinafter cited as Latournerie] (France); G. Mazzoni, *I Rapporti Collettivi di Lavoro* 357 ff. (3d ed. Giuffré 1967) [hereinafter cited as Mazzoni] (Italy).

breach of contract although it is lawful in the light of its purposes and methods? Can a strike which is unlawful by reason of its purposes or methods nevertheless be a lawful termination or suspension of the contract? Do we, so to speak, look upon this problem of the legality of strikes through two different sets of spectacles, namely, that of the general law such as criminal law, and tort law, and that of the law of contract? Alternatively, does legality in one sphere automatically spell legality in the other?

It is here that, by comparing the development in France and in England, we can see how the distinction between the right and the mere freedom to strike produces consequences in practice. We can also see that the gulf can be bridged; a look at the developments both in England and in Germany may demonstrate this.

(a) Before 1939 the French courts generally took the view that the strikers either terminated or broke their contracts with the result that the employer could claim damages or dismiss all or some of the workers on strike.[12] A change was inaugurated by the *Cour Supérieure d'Arbitrage*[13] in an important decision of 19 May 1939. The decision was to the effect that, in the absence of an express or implied intention on the part of the strikers definitely to give up their jobs, the strike does not terminate the contracts. To see the reasons for this view, one has to turn to the submissions of the *Commissaire du Gouvernement,* M. Pierre Laroque. He referred to the *coutume ouvrière* which has established the strike as a normal weapon of defence and to a conclusion drawn from this premiss by Jean Jaurès to the effect that the strike, far from being the termination of the contract, is one of its *"clauses implicites et essentielles."* Here then we see the assumption that, quite apart from any constitutional guarantee (this issue was raised under the Third Republic whose Constitution said nothing about strikes), there exists a right to strike that is vested in the individual employee, and this right is implied in the contract.

The highest French Court did not change its attitude until 1951, i.e., after the coming into force of the Constitution of 1946, including its Preamble. It was on the basis of that Preamble that the *Cour de Cassation*[14] recognised the right to strike whose exercise merely suspends the contract. Like the *Cour Supérieure d'Arbitrage,* however, it ex-

12. See for this and for what follows the excellent analysis of the problem in Blanc-Jouvan, "The Effect of Industrial Action on the Status of the Individual Employee," in *Industrial Conflict, A Comparative Legal Survey* 176, 188 ff. (especially) (B. Aaron & K.W. Wedderburn eds. 1972) [hereinafter cited as Blanc-Jouvan]; Durand & Vitu, *supra* note 5, at 825, para. 289.

13. Judgment of May 19, 1939, [1939] 1 Gaz. Pal. 903.

14. Judgment of June 1, 1951, 1951 *Droit Social* 530 (Cass. Soc.); Judgment of June 18, 1951, 1951 *Droit Social* 532 (Cass. Soc.).

cluded cases of serious misconduct on the part of the strikers, and held that such misconduct may be found in the objects and methods of the strike itself. The general lawfulness or unlawfulness of the strike is made to determine its effect on the contract; if lawful it suspends the contract, if unlawful it terminates or, as was subsequently established, rather allows the employer to terminate it.[15] The principle was codified in 1950,[16] but the decisions of 1951 were based on the state of the law prior to the statute, by which *la grève ne rompt pas le contrat de travail, sauf faute lourde imputable au salarié.*

The exercise of a right which is implied in a contract cannot be regarded as its termination or as its breach. What is more, this right rests on considerations of public policy (*ordre public*). It cannot therefore be abrogated either by individual contract or collective agreement, but its exercise may be modified by the latter *e.g.*, through conciliation, arbitration, or cooling-off clauses.[17]

(b) Until 1875[18] there were few strikes in England which did not entail the risk of a prosecution for criminal conspiracy,[19] and until 1906 almost every strike could lead to an action for civil conspiracy or for an inducement to break contracts of employment. Statutes enacted in these two years established a number of immunities and privileges, much as the Norris-La Guardia Act did in the United States at a later date.[20] But at no time did this amount to a recognition of a right to strike. Until the 1960's it was generally understood that, if the contractual or statutory notices were given by the strikers, the strike terminated the contracts. This termination might be coupled with an offer of new contracts, often at higher wages. But, these being new contracts, seniority rights would be lost unless, as happened with regard to two decisively important statutes,[21] they were expressly preserved by legislation. If the strikers did not give the requisite notices each of them was in breach of contract and the employer could claim damages from each of them or dismiss all or some of them without notice. He could not, however, claim damages in tort for inducing his workers to break their contracts, provided the strike was "in contemplation or furtherance of a trade dispute," *i.e.*, broadly speaking, about employment

15. See Sinay, *supra* note 5, at 300 ff.; Latournerie, *supra* note 11, at 566.
16. Law of 11 Feb. 1950, art. 4, now replaced by the (consolidating) Code du Travail, 1974, Art. L. 521–1.
17. It should be noted that the word "rompt" means "terminates."
18. Conspiracy, and Protection of Property Act, 1875, 38 & 39 Vict., c. 86, s.3.
19. See 2 F. Stephen, *History of the Criminal Law of England* 218 (1883).
20. In 1932.
21. Contracts of Employment Act 1963, c. 49, now Contracts of Employment Act 1972, c. 53 (accrual of right to notice); Redudancy Payments Act 1965, c. 62 (accrual of redundancy payments).

or its terms.[22] This, therefore, was a purely individualistic approach to the strike as a social phenomenon, ignoring its collective character, and in sharp contrast to the view taken in France since 1951.

In the 1960's a number of English judges began to see the absurdity of this approach.[23] However, they did not see this absurdity in the failure to recognise a right to strike; they saw it in the faulty analysis of the intention of the strikers. Clearly, "[t]he strikers do not want to give up their job; they simply want to be paid more for it or to secure some other advantage in connection with it."[24] Hence, the strike notices are not notices to terminate the contracts, but notices "that the men will not come to work," *i.e.*, notices to break the contracts.[25] Thus in England the more realistic appraisal of the situation did not, as in France, result in a recognition of the right to strike as against the employer. On the contrary, if the view expounded in the judicial *obiter dicta* of the 1960's had been translated into positive law, every strike in England would necessarily have been unlawful, because every one of them—notice or no notice—would have resulted in breaches of contract. It would have been the end of the legal freedom to strike. This was seen by one of the judges to whose views I have referred, and in a case decided in 1968,[26] Lord Denning said that, though it was "difficult to see the logical flaw" in the argument "there must be something wrong with it: for if that argument were correct, it would do away with the right to strike in this country." Hence the notice to strike was a notice to suspend.

This, however, was but the view of one judge, and more recently the Employment Appeal Tribunal, which now[27] occupies a central position in these matters, dissociated itself from this *dictum*.[28] Under the short lived Industrial Relations Act, 1971,[29] the principle underlying it, was codified, but this provision disappeared when the 1971 Act was repealed in 1974,[30] and it was not replaced by subsequent legislation. Nevertheless, this recent legislation, i.e. the Trade Union and Labour Relations Acts, 1974 and 1976,[30] and the Employment Protection Act, 1975[31] has completely transformed the effect which a strike has on the

22. See note 7 *supra*.

23. Donovan, L.J., in Rookes v. Barnard, [1963] 1 Q.B. 623, 682 ff.; Lord Devlin in Rookes v. Barnard, [1964] A.C. 1129, 1204; Lord Denning M.R. in the Court of Appeal in Stratford v. Lindley, [1965] A.C. 269, 285.

24. Donovan, L.J., in Rookes v. Barnard, [1963] 1 Q.B. 623, 682.

25. Lord Denning in Stratford v. Lindley, [1965] A.C. 269, 285.

26. Morgan v. Fry, [1968] 2 Q.B. 710, 725.

27. Employment Protection Act, 1975, sect. 87, sect. 88.

28. *Simmons v. Hoover* 1976/I.C.R. 266, at 269.

29. Sec. 147.

30. Trade Union and Labour Relations Act, 1974, sect. 1.

31. Schedule 1, Paragraphs 4-15, as amended by the Trade Union and Labour Relations (Amendment) Act, 1976, and by the Employment Protection Act, 1975.

contracts of employment. It has done so without changing the common law rules on breach of contract. The result is that English law now provides a solution of this problem which, in its own way, is as original as that developed in France, and in other ways, in Germany, and completely different from both in form whilst similar in substance.

Since there is nothing in either statute or case law to remove or to restrict the impact which the common law has on the legal qualification of a strike as a breach of contract, English law seems still to use the "two sets of spectacles". Those who participate in a strike break their contracts, unquestionably if they do not give the prescribed notices, and very probably even if they do. A strike which is declared lawful for the purposes of the criminal law and of the law of torts, is nevertheless unlawful for those of the law of contract. The workers on strike can be dismissed. Even if dismissed, they are of course likely to be reengaged after the strike, but,—if there was nothing else,—this reengagement would be the making of new contracts of employment, and they would, even if they regained their jobs, have sacrificed their seniority. That statutory privileges or immunities protect them from criminal prosecution or action in tort does not mean that, in striking, they exercise a right which overrides, as it does in France, the employer's right to dismiss them without notice. If this was all, the conceptual scheme invented by Hohfeld would fit the situation perfectly.

But this is not by any means the whole story. To understand the situation, one must realise that, since the enactment of the Industrial Relations Act, 1971,[33] English law has adopted the principle of protection against unfair dismissal. The relevant provisions were, after the repeal of the 1971 Act, re-enacted in 1974[34] and decisively modified in 1975.[35] An employer who dismisses an employee may be compelled to re-instate him (i.e. to continue the contract of employment) or to re-engage him (i.e. to make a new contract) or to compensate him, unless he can prove that he had a substantial reason for dismissing him, and a substantial reason is one which refers to his capability, qualifications or conduct, or to the fact that he is redundant or that his further employment has become illegal. Normally it is for the employer to show "that (having regard to equity and the substantial merits of the case) he acted reasonably" in dismissing the employee.[36] If he does not, the dismissal is "unfair." But if it is not only "unfair," but discriminatory, that is, if its principal reason was actual or proposed union membership

32. Sections 71-80.

33. Sections 22-33.

34. i.e. in Schedule 1 of the 1974 Act.

35. The provisions mentioned in Note 32 have greatly enlarged the right to be reinstated or to be re-engaged.

36. Trade Union and Labour Relations Act, 1974, Schedule 1 Paragraph 6(1), (2), (8).

or activity, the reason for the dismissal is "inadmissible," and cannot on any grounds be justified.[37] Thus the new law of unfair dismissal serves the dual purpose of protecting job security and freedom of organisation.

This law of unfair dismissal has in practice revolutionised the impact of strikes on the contracts of employment. If the employer dismisses all those of his employees who are taking part in the strike and if, at the end of the strike, he does not offer to re-engage any one of them, he cannot be liable for unfair dismissal.[38] But this is a situation which is most unlikely to occur, except where the employer goes out of, or gives up a line of, business. If there is even one striker whom he does not dismiss, or,—which is much more significant,—even one whom he offers to take back when the strike is over, then all those whom he has dismissed or refused to re-engage can claim re-instatement, re-engagement or compensation.[39] Such selective dismissals or refusals to take back may often not only be "unfair," but "inadmissible" so that this becomes a remedy for the protection of active unionists. What matters here however is that in its practical effect the compulsion to re-instate with full seniority rights sets at nought the right to terminate the contract by reason of the breach involved in the strike. The power which the employer has to dismiss the strikers is formally unimpaired, but since in practice he will usually have to reinstate them after the strike, that power is in its social effect (though not in its legal form) reduced to a power to suspend. However different in their theoretical bases, French and English law are now very similar in their social impact in this matter. English law may—in the Hohfeldian sense—still give no more than a privilege or immunity where French law gives a true right to strike, but it makes up for it by giving (in the normal situation) a right to be re-instated after the strike, that is a "right" which Hohfeld would have recognised as such.

(c) The Bonn Basic Law of 1949, the Constitution of the Federal Republic of Germany, which guarantees the freedom of organisation,[40] mentions the freedom to strike only in an amendment of 1968 which protects the such freedom against certain emergency measures.[41] Nevertheless, it is generally thought that the guarantee of the freedom to strike is implied in these provisions.[42] One would, therefore, expect

37. *Ibid.* Paragraph 6 (4), (6), (7), (8).

38. *Ibid.* Paragraph 7, as amended by the Employment Protection Act, 1975.

39. *Ibid.* Paragraph 7 (2), (3), (4).

40. *Basic Law of the Federal Republic of Germany* art. 9. Whilst the constitution of the Federal Republic does not expressly guarantee the freedom to strike, that of the German Democratic Republic of October 7, 1949, purports to do so. (Art. 14).

41. *Basic Law* art. 9, para. 3, third sentence (added by law of June 24, 1968, [1968] BGBL. I 702.)

42. T. Maunz, G. Durig, & H. Herzog, *Kommentar zum Grundgesetz* art. 9, note 3 (1971).

that the German attitude would have developed along the same lines as the French. However, the remarkable thing is that whilst since 1955 the German courts have, in the matter here under discussion, arrived at the same result which the French *Cour de Cassation* adopted in 1951 (that a lawful strike merely suspends the contracts and that notices are irrelevant), they have done so on the basis of a general analysis of the relation between the collective and individual aspects of labour law and not, or certainly not primarily, on the basis of the Constitution. In other words, they have demonstrated that with more insight into social realities the English courts could, without the assistence of a statute, have liberated the freedom to strike from the shackles of the law of contract in the absence of a constitutional "right," just as the French *Cour Superieure d'Arbitrage* had done on the eve of the Second World War. In its fundamental decision of 28 January 1955 the Great Senate of the Federal Labour Court[43] cast away the "two sets of spectacles." Some of the words used by the Court deserve to be quoted:

> A labour dispute is an indivisible (*einheitliches*) event. It may not be treated otherwise in collective labour law than it is in individual labour law. One must not resign oneself to an allegedly irremovable collision between the law of labour disputes and the law of contract. A synthesis is impossible. Hence one of the two spheres must have priority.

It follows that a labour dispute which is legal as a dispute cannot be illegal in the law of contract, *i.e.*, a breach. It would be wrong to consider the same collective course of action as lawful in one branch of labour law and as unlawful in another. It follows further that if on general grounds the strike is unlawful (*e.g.*, by reason of its purpose or method) it is also a breach of contract, even if the notices have been given. But if it is lawful, it is not a breach, even in the absence of notice.

Moreover, a lawful strike does not terminate the contracts, but suspends them. This principle, however, was set at nought in practice by the Federal Labour Court itself because it was held that the employer was entitled to answer the strike with a lockout and that the lockout terminated the contracts (*Lösende Aussperrung*). In a second fundamental decision, that of 21 April 1971,[44] the Great Senate of the Federal Labour Court overruled its decision of 1955 on this point and on this point only. It held that the defensive lockout did not itself normally terminate the contracts of employment, but had a merely suspensive effect. In practice this means that if the strike is lawful, all the employer can do is to suspend those of his workers who are not on strike and thus cast off the burden of wage payments to non-strikers.

43. Decision of Jan. 28, 1955, 8 *Neue Juristische Wochenschrift* 882 (1955).
44. Decision of April 21, 1971, 24 *Neue Juristische Wochenschrift* 1668. (1971).

The well tried mechanism of "implied intentions," so highly developed in the common law, would have made it perfectly possible to do in England what was done in France, in Italy[45] and subsequently in Germany. In fact, the Swedish Labour Court had pointed the way decades before the Courts saw the light in the larger Continental countries further south.[46] The individualistic spirit of the Common Law may have prevented any such development in England; it is well known how difficult it is for lawyers trained in the Common Law to see the reality of collective phenomena in society.

In terms of our analysis, however, it appears that the recognition of a right to strike in the strict sense, whilst favouring the treatment of the strike as a suspension of the contracts, is not a necessity. It is merely a useful conceptual tool for this purpose. The purpose can be achieved through other means, as the English and German examples show, but this requires either a measure of judicial boldness which cannot be taken for granted, or the formulation of entirely new statutory remedies.

IV

The question as to who may strike arises no matter whether the ambiguous word *may* connotes a reference to a right or a reference to a mere privilege or immunity. In particular, each legal system must ask the question whether the right vests in the individual or in the union or in both, and whether the privileges and the immunities are objective (attaching to the nature of the act) or subjective (attaching to the person). This means asking whether the unofficial or wildcat strike is legal.

This problem of the attitude of the law towards the wildcat strike has gained an importance all over Europe, and here as always Europe includes the British Isles, which was undreamt of before the Second World War. The reasons are to be found in a very general crisis in the methods of collective bargaining, a crisis which was analysed in depth in the Report of the Royal Commission on Trade Unions and Employers' Associations of 1968,[47] and reflected very clearly in the French statute of 1968,[48] passed as a result of the events of May 1968, and of that of 1971.[49] The European system of territorial (district, national)

45. Mazzoni, *supra* note 11, at 362 ff.; Blanc-Jouvan, *supra* note 12, at 191-92.

46. F. Schmidt, *The Law of Labour Relations in Sweden* 203 (1962); Blanc-Jouvan, *supra* note 12, at 186.

47. *Cmnd.* 3623, especially chapters 3 and 4.

48. Law of December 27, 1968, (now consolidated in the Code du Travail, 1974) which had its political origin in the *"Protocole de Grenelle"* formulated at the end of the movement of May 1968. See G.H. Camerlynck & C. Lyon-Caen, *Droit du Travail* nos. 536 ff. (6th ed. 1973) [hereinafter cited as Camerlynck & Lyon-Caen].

49. Law of July 13, 1971; (now consolidated in the Code du Travail, 1974); Camerlynck & Lyon-Caen, *supra* note 48, nos. 555, 612-14.

bargaining was developed in an economic situation in which the supply in the labour market was assumed to exceed the demand and hence the employer had no inducement to pay wages that were higher or much higher than the minima fixed in the centrally concluded agreements. But in a market in which there was a scarcity of men rather than a scarcity of jobs the pressure for wages that were higher and conditions that were better than those fixed by territorial agreements increased at enterprise or plant level everywhere, and plant bargaining became the rule rather than the exception, so much so that the French law of 1950[50] which had sought to restrict plant bargaining was overtaken by events and amended by that of 1971. In England much bargaining was and is done through shop stewards who have no legal status, and in France they were given a statutory counterpart in 1968.[51] All this however meant that the spontenaous strike at plant level, the wildcat strike, became a common phenomenon. The scene of combat shifted with the scene of bargaining, and the legal question, namely, the question of the legality of the wildcat strike, became a vital problem.

Presently we shall see that the contrast in this respect between France and Germany is of special importance in our context, but it is of interest to cast a preliminary glance at Great Britain, where, for a number of years during the late 1960s and early 1970s the question of the legality of wildcat strikes was in the forefront of legislative events and led to a dramatic development. As we have seen, the freedom to strike has in Britain, been traditionally enshrined in a series of statutory immunities from criminal prosecution and from civil action in tort. These were formulated in statutes passed in 1875,[52] 1906,[53] and 1965.[54] The relevant provision of 1875 (which refers exclusively to the criminal law) is still in force, but the Acts of 1906 and of 1965 (which referred mainly to the law of tort) were repealed and, in a modified form, re-enacted by the Industrial Relations Act, 1971,[55] and, after the repeal of the statute, again re-enacted (in a much modified form) in the legislation of 1974 and of 1976.[56] This dry catalogue of enactments reflects a series of most intensive political battles. Thus the Act of 1875 was an outcome of a dramatic electoral victory of the Conservatives over the Liberals, that of 1906 resulted from an even more sensational victory of the Liberals over the Conservatives, and that of 1965 from an electoral ascendancy of the

50. Law of Feb. 11, 1950. (Now consolidated in the Code du Travail, 1974) See M. Despax, "Conventions Collectives," 7 *Traité de Droit du Travail* 411 ff. (G.H. Camerlynck ed. 1966).

51. By the law of December 27, 1968. See note 48 *supra*.

52. Conspiracy, and Protection of Property Act, 1875, 38 & 39 Vict., c. 86, s.3.

53. Trade Disputes Act, 1906, 6 Edw. 7, c. 47.

54. Trade Disputes Act 1965, c. 48.

55. Industrial Relations Act 1971, c. 72, s. 132.

56. Trade Union and Labour Relations Act, 1974, sect. 13, as amended by Trade Union and Labour Relations (Amendment) Act 1976, sect. 3 (2).

Labour Party. The Conservative majority in the House of Commons passed the 1971 Act against the embittered resistance of the Labour Party and of the trade unions, and the return of a (minority) Labour Government in 1974 led to the repeal of the 1971 Act by a statute some of whose provisions the minority Government had to accept unwillingly. After the second election of 1974 the Labour Party returned with a small majority, and the result of that was the Act of 1976 which removed some of the provisions of the 1974 Act and amended others. Among those amended in 1976 was one of the sections dealing with the immunities here under discussion. In a number of respects the immunity from tort liability was considerably enlarged by the Act of 1976.[57]

These kaleidoscopic changes in labour law may look bewildering. In fact, and subject to the ephemeral, but significant episode of the Industrial Relations Act 1971, the nature of the immunities from criminal prosecution and delictual action has undergone little change since they were first introduced in 1875 and in 1906. The scope of the civil immunities has been widened in the sense that new types of tortious action (e.g. certain types of intimidation) were brought within their orbit, but their nature remained until 1971 and became again after 1974 objective. They were, and they are now, enjoyed by whosoever acted or acts "in contemplation or furtherance of a trade dispute," no matter whether he does or does not act on behalf of or with the consent, or even against the express policy of a union. Quite clearly the freedom to strike, i.e. the immunity from prosecution and from delictual action was before 1971, and is now again, a freedom of the individual and not a privilege of the union. It is an immunity *ratione materiae* (the contemplation or furtherance of a trade dispute), not *ratione personae* (the union). There was under the 1906 Act and until 1971,[58] and there is now again under the Act of 1974[59] an additional trade union privilege. Important exceptions apart, a union as such is not liable in tort at all, no matter whether the tortious act is done or not done in contemplation or furtherance of a trade dispute. This, however, is of comparatively small importance in practice; if the liability, for e.g. conspiracy or inducing a breach of contract, is excluded on the ground that the act was done in contemplation or furtherance of a trade dispute, this

57. In that the privilege of freedom from tort liability has been extended to liability for inducing breaches of contract other than contracts of employment and also to any kind of interference with its performance or inducement of another person so to interfere. Equally the privilege of freedom from liability for threatening that a contract will be broken and from liability for threatening to induce another person to break it has been extended to contracts other than contracts of employment and to interference other than breach. These complex clauses are largely attempt to mend holes torn into the statutory immunity by a series of equally complex cases.

58. Sec. 4.

59. Sect. 14.

objective immunity protects the union in any event. If, on the other hand, the act itself is not so protected, and if consequently the representative of the union is individually liable, e.g. for defamation in the union newspaper, it is customary for the union to pay, and not to rely on its statutory privilege from the liability of its funds.

In sharp contrast to the law before 1971 and to the law since 1974, it was the policy of the Industrial Relations Act, 1971, to exclude wildcat strikers from the civil (not from the criminal) immunities. This it tried to do by creating new liabilities for what were called "unfair industrial practices." Thus, – and this was in practice the most important case, – a person other than a trade union registered under the Act or someone acting on its behalf, was liable if in contemplation or furtherance of an industrial dispute he induced or threatened to induce another person to break a contract.[60] The purpose of this was to mobilise the law of a new type of civil liability (including what was in fact, though not in name the threat of labour injunctions) against wildcat strikers, while leaving the immunities of the unions unaffected. This attempt to transform (in effect) an objective immunity into a subjective union privilege was based on the assumption that all or most unions would register under the Act, – only registered union were protected from this liability. Since however the unions (or their overwhelming majority) refused to register, the desire to reduce the number of wildcat strikes (which for other reasons has fallen in any event) resulted in a very serious encroachment of the freedom to strike in general. In this, as in other respects, the 1971 Act was a failure, an opinion which is now shared by all political parties.

In Britain it has for more than a century been a matter of tradition (interrupted only between 1971 and 1974) to link the freedom of strike with the nature of the act done in its course, irrespective of the person who does it, and there is no particular ideology discernable behind it. But the contrast in this respect between the French and German approaches is directly traceable to the conflicting ideologies to which I have referred. If, as is the case in France and in Italy, the right to strike is considered to be a fundamental civil liberty, then it must be obvious that the right is that of the individual.[61] This fact does not exclude the possibility that it may also be exercised by the union. Hence it is established law in, both France[62] and Italy,[63] that union approval is not required to make a strike lawful. More than that, the sharp distinction

60. Industrial Relations Act, 1971, sect. 96.

61. Note that, whilst in effect the freedom from strike was in France established in 1864 (when certain penal provisions of the Penal Code of 1810 were repealed), the freedom of organisation was only established in 1884, with the repeal of the Loi Le Chapelier of 1791.

62. Sinay, *supra* note 5, at 122; Latournerie, *supra* note 11, at 174.

63. Mazzoni, *supra* note 11, at 309-14. This was established by the Corte di Cassazione in Decision No. 1628 of June 7, 1952, 2 *Rivista di Diritto Internazionale e Comparato del Lavoro* 392 (1952).

between *official* and *unofficial* action, so decisive in Britain, America, Germany, Scandinavia, is scarcely understood in France and in Italy. Nor would it be likely to play a major role in practice if greater significance were attached to it in legal doctrine. The reason is that the practical implications of the legality of industrial action depend to a large extent on the financial status of the unions. In Germany and in the Scandinavian countries no less than in Britain and in the United States one major problem in labour law is whether the unions are liable, out of their funds, to pay damages or, in the common law countries, fines for contempt. This is a central issue in the law governing industrial conflict on the important though simply ground that in these countries the unions, or many of them, have funds, and some of them have considerable funds. This is not true of France and of Italy, and hence the emphasis on union liability which so largely explains the relevance of the distinction between unofficial and official action would have no practical meaning. The discussion in France and Italy centres not on the liability of the union, but on whether the individual stands to lose his job. This is especially true of France where most of the case law is a very voluminous gloss on the words "*sauf faute lourde imputable au salarié*," now in the Code du Travail of 1974, which indicate the outer limits of job protection in the case of a strike. Yet, since 1963[64] there has been on the French statute books a provision banning wildcat strikes in the public sector, a term which has been given a wide definition for this purpose. In the public sector strikes are lawful only if a strike notice has been given by a particular kind of union, known as a representative union.[65] This is an approach to the German attitude towards this problem, but it does not seem that, in practice, this provision has had a great effect on industrial practice.

Nowhere is the link between collective bargaining and the right to strike closer and stronger than in the German Federal Republic. Since the mid-1950's[66] the Federal Labour Court has developed the principle that a strike is an unlawful interference with business and hence a delictual (tortious) act,[67] unless it is conducted by a party capable of

64. Law No. 63-777 of July 31, 1963, on Strikes in the Public Services, art. 3, now consolidated in the Code du Travail of 1974.

65. The meaning of the term "*les organisations syndicales les plus représentatives*" was defined in the law of February 11, 1950, and now in the Code du Travail of 1974. See note 50 *supra*. See also J. M. Verdier, "Syndicats," 5 *Traité du Droit du Travail* 358 ff. (G.H. Camerlynck ed. 1965) and, with regard to the application of the law of 1963, Latournerie, *supra* note 11, at 665 ff.

66. See the decision of the Federal Labour Court of January 28, 1955, cited note 43 *supra* and generally Hueck & Nipperdey, *supra* note 10, at 990 ns. 11-12.

67. Civil Code section 823, paragraph 1, by which it is a tortious act, intentionally or negligently, and wrongfully, to violate, *inter alia*, "the property or another right" of another person. The courts have held for many years that an established business enterprise (*der eingerichtete und ausgeübte Gewerbebetrieb*) is "another right" in this sense. This is now the basis of the liabilty for unlawful strikes.

concluding a collective agreement (*i.e.*, a union) against a party so capable (*i.e.*, an employer or employers' association) with the object of achieving a collective agreement. This is a very logical conclusion from the premiss that the right to strike is complementary to collective bargaining. It is at the same time a very serious restriction of that right, probably the most serious restriction in the democratic countries of Western Europe. The principle has been underpinned by a number of general jurisprudential theories, *e.g.*, that to be lawful, a strike must be socially adequate,[68] and this presupposes that the strike satisfies the requirements referred to, or that, as a means to a social end, it must be *proportional,* which is a more modern variant of the same thought.[69] In any event, and this is all that matters here, the German ideological background (the link between collective bargaining and industrial action) produces the illegality of the wildcat strikes with the same necessity that in France and in Italy led from the fundamental human right background to the legality of the wildcat strike. The contrast in doctrine and in case law should not, however, induce anyone to think that the Federal Republic is blessed by an absence of wildcat strikes. In our subject, law and social fact are very different things. This is true in all countries known to the present writer.

V

The most telling effect of the contrast between the right (especially the constitutionally guaranteed right) to strike, based on the idea of the fundamental freedom of the individual, and the right to strike linked with the institutions of collective bargaining, is to be found in the German, French and Italian principles applied to industrial action in the public sector.

To see this contrast, one has to realise that the Continental countries, in which a sharp distinction is made between public and private law, have inherited from their constitutional past a division of public servants into two legally contrasted though outwardly indistinguishable categories. One is that of the ordinary employee who enters into a contract of employment with a public authority. The other is that of the *fonctionnaire* or *Beamter* who does not enter into a contract but owes his position to the conferment of a status. He is subject to a special duty of fidelity, based on this status of special subjection.[70] The words *fonctionnaire* or *Beamter* cannot be translated into the English language, because no such institution exists in any of the English

68. See case cited note 43 *supra*.
69. See case cited note 44 *supra*.
70. Hueck & Nipperdey, *supra* note 10, at 979 ff. give a summary of what is the unanimous view in practice and the predominant view in theory.

speaking countries, none of which have gone through the historical experience of absolute monarchy. It must be emphasised that the distinction has nothing to do with particular functions; a secretary in a government office may be a *Beamter* while his colleague at the opposite desk who does the same kind of work may be an employee. The distinction is hardly comprehensible rationally; however, especially in Germany, the idea of a *Beamtentum* is surrounded by an aura of romantic sanctity which gives it great political significance.

It is axiomatic in Germany that the duty of fidelity of the *Beamte* is incompatible with the right to strike; there are academic preachers in the wilderness who assert the opposite[71] without, it seems, any chance of making their voices heard. Quite apart from the duty of fidelity the fact that the salaries of *Beamte* are settled by statute would, on the grounds set out above, make a strike for better salaries unlawful.

France and Italy have the same concept and the same distinction; in France the relation between a *fonctionnaire* and his department is subject to public law and to the jurisdiction of the administrative courts, culminating in the *Conseil d'Etat*.

Nevertheless, in a decision of basic importance, it was held by the *Conseil d'Etat* in 1950[72] that the constitutional guarantee of the right to strike overrides the special principles applicable to *fonctionnaires* with the important qualification, however, that the right to strike must be restricted by administrative action in so far as is necessary to prevent abuse, and to protect vital public needs (*les nécessités de l'ordre public*), particularly the continuity of essential public services. All this, however, is placed under the control of the *Conseil d'Etat*. That this control is of vital importance was demonstrated in 1958 in another leading case[73] in which it was held that a restriction of the right to strike was justified only by reason of the function of officials, and not by reason of their status. Thus it was wrong to lay down that *fonctionnaires* above a certain point in the hierarchy were not permitted to strike.

A similar principle was applied by the Italian *Corte Costituzionale*[74] when it declared legislation inherited from the Fascist era[75] to be unconstitutional, as being contrary to article 40 of the Constitution, in so far as it purported to deprive public servants of the right to strike *en bloc*.

71. T. Ramm, *Das Koalitions-und Streikrecht der Beamten* (1970); W. Daubler, *Der Streik im öffentlichen Dienst* (1970).

72. The *Dehaene* Case of July 7, 1950, [1950] D. Jur. 263 (Conseil d'Etat).

73. The *Lepouse* Case of Nov. 28, 1958, [1958] D. Jur. 263.

74. Decision No. 31 of Dec. 17, 1969; G. Suppiej, *Fonti per lo Studio del Diritto Sindacale* 191 ff. (1970).

75. Penal Code art. 330 (1930).

VI

We can see how the difference in ideologies and the resulting differences in the concept of a right to strike have influenced the positive law in three directions: (1) the effect of the strike on the contract of employment; (2) the problem of the union monopoly of the right to strike; and, (3) the strike in the public sector.

It is, however, advisable in conclusion to point out that in other respects these differences have played no role or at least no significant role. Thus, as regards the definition of lawful and unlawful strike purposes and strike methods there exists a remarkable measure of consensus among the legal systems of Western Europe; the condemnation of the political strike is as common as the legality of sympathy strikes. The courts everywhere seem in one way or another to have set their faces against those contemporary sophisticated variations on the strike theme, such as the go-slow and the switch strike, which have been invented so as to saddle the employer with wages and overheads while depriving him of the benefit of the work. There are differences in nuances but the fundamental attitude is the same, and is compatible with both of the concepts of the right to strike that I have sought to distinguish.

This distinction between two different approaches to the right to strike exists within the framework of the European Economic Community and can continue so to exist because this is an area not directly touched by the Treaty of Rome. The only international obligation incurred by the nations whose laws have been under discussion is that based on article 6, paragraph 4 of the European Social Charter,[76] concluded by the Members of the Council of Europe and ratified by all the States to which reference has been made here. The Contracting Parties undertake "[w]ith a view to ensuring the effective exercise of the right to bargain collectively" to recognise "the right of workers and employers to [take] collective action . . . , including the right to strike." This provision is obviously based on the view that the right to strike is complementary to collective bargaining. A State can implement it whilst adopting either of the approaches that have been analysed in this article.

76. European Social Charter of October 18, 1961, in force since 1965, ratified entirely or in part by ten of the 18 States Members of the Council of Europe. Article 6, paragraph 4 has been ratified by nine Members.

INTERNATIONAL LAW AND THE DOMESTIC LAW OF CANADA

R. ST. J. MACDONALD

In this article I propose to explore the relationship between treaty law and domestic law in Canada. I will start with the familiar theory of the relationship between treaties and domestic law in England and in Canada and then move to less familiar areas of Canadian practice. An attempt will be made to investigate the rather murky area surrounding inter-departmental arrangements between Canada and sovereign states which are less than treaties but which do affect domestic law. I will attempt to raise, if not to answer, preliminary questions about the effectiveness of these procedures, the safeguards inherent in them, and their acceptability to the enlightened electorate of twentieth century Canada. These questions will lead to a few conclusions and some recommendations. The subject is one that interested Wolfgang Friedmann, to whose memory these remarks are dedicated.

I. CONVENTIONAL LAW AND MUNICIPAL LAW: THE THEORY

The law and the theory in England

The law in England is and has been for some time very clear that the power to make and ratify treaties lies with the Crown exclusively.[1] However, treaties so made and ratified cannot impose rights and duties on anyone in England except the Crown itself. If the ability to enjoy those rights and fulfill those duties lies within the royal prerogative that is the end of the matter; nothing further is required to implement the

R. ST. J. MACDONALD. Q.C. is Weldon Professor and Dean of the Faculty of Law, Dalhousie University, Halifax, Canada; Immediate Past President of the Canadian Council on International Law.

1. A. McNair, *The Law of Treaties* 78 (1961); 1 *Blackstone's Commentaries* 256 (14th ed.); 7 *Halsbury's Laws of England* 287 (3d ed. G. Simonds 1964).

treaty. If, on the other hand, the fulfillment of the treaty required actions outside the royal prerogative, then Parliamentary action is necessary to implement the treaty. To permit the Crown to exceed its powers in order to fulfill an obligation it has itself contracted would be to alter the basic constitutional law of England; that is an action indisputably beyond the power of the Crown acting alone.

It is in this light that Lord Atkin's dictum in the *Labour Convention Case* should be read: "Within the British Empire there is a well-established rule that the making of a treaty is an executive act, while the performance of its obligations, if they entail alteration of the existing domestic law, requires legislative action."[2] If it lies within the crown prerogative to make the requisite alterations in domestic law, no legislation is required; but if, as is generally the case, the required alterations in domestic law are beyond the crown prerogative, then legislation will be necessary.

Viewed in this way, the rule admits of no exceptions. There are simply situations where the royal prerogative suffices and situations where it does not, and McNair's famous exceptions to the rule that legislation is required become simple examples of the former situation. Thus, the Crown is acting within its prerogative when it seeks to enforce treaties it has ratified on rules for the conduct of war. This explains *Porter v. Freudenberg,* where it was held that the Hague Convention of 1907, which had not been implemented by legislation, could alter the common law rule that an enemy alien has no right to sue in English courts during hostilities.[3] Obviously, if Parliament has legislated on matters relating to the conduct of war, the Crown will be unable to modify the legislation.[4] Thus those parts of the Geneva Convention relating to prisoners of war which are implemented in the Geneva Conventions Act of 1957 are inviolable. By the same theory, F.A. Mann argues that the other provisions of the 1949 convention may also be in force in England.[5]

It would seem that the Crown has the power to cede its territory and that, although parliamentary approval has invariably been obtained, the Crown could have granted independence to its former colonies on its own. This power does not extend to territory within England nor does it extend to the property of English nationals. In a number of treaties, the Crown has purported to cede property rights located in a foreign

2. Attorney-General for Canada v. Attorney-General for Ontario, [1937] A.C. 326, 347 (P.C.) (Ont.).

3. Porter v. Freudenberg, [1915] 1 K.B. 857 (C.A.).

4. For example, the Crown's power to take land in wartime; *cf.* Attorney-General v. Dekeyser's Royal Hotel, [1920] A.C. 508.

5. Mann, "The Enforcement of Treaties by English Courts," 44 *The Grotius Society* 29, 39 (1958).

country. These treaties were made after the Second World War with Yugoslavia, Czechoslovakia, Poland, Bulgaria and Hungary, and the British Government declared "on their own behalf and on behalf of British nationals" that certain sums would be accepted "in full satisfactions and final discharge of all liability to British nationals."[6] It is submitted that if these provisions were sought to be enforced in English courts, they would fail. This area of the Crown Prerogative has given rise to what can only be described as a misinterpretation by Lord Sumner in *The Blonde,* where he said: "There can be no doubt that Germany was competent, on behalf of those nationals who were German subjects within the operation of the Treaty, to make cessions which would bind them and effect a transfer of their rights of property, as if the cession had been made personally by the owner concerned."[7] This view, which has been suggested in other Prize Court decisions, must be restricted to questions arising between nations and not between individuals. The Crown may also implement treaties of peace designed to end a war so long as these treaties impose no financial burden on the country. This power has created little controversy in England, although, as we shall see, there have been difficulties in Canada.

The common law rules on diplomatic and sovereign immunities provide an excellent opportunity to observe what the Crown can and cannot do. The Crown cannot create new immunities nor can it create new classes of persons entitled to these immunities; these actions require legislation. The Crown can, however, restrict the immunities given and it can determine who is and who is not a member of existing classes of persons who are entitled to these immunities; these actions are within its Prerogative.

The apparently opposing cases of *The Parlement Belge* and *Engelke v. Musmann* are illustrative of the Crown's power to determine membership in classes but not to create new classes. In the former case, the Crown opposed a motion for the arrest of a Belgian mailship on the ground that the Crown had signed a postal convention (not im-

6. Agreement between the United Kingdom and Yugoslavia Regarding Compensation for British Property, Rights and Interests Affected by Yugoslav Measures of Nationalisation, Expropriation, Dispossession and Liquidation, *done* Dec. 23, 1948, art. 2, [1949] Gr. Brit. T.S. No. 2 (CMD. 7600); Agreement between the United Kingdom and Czechoslovakia Regarding Compensation for British Property, Rights and Interests Affected by Czechoslovak Measures of Nationalization, Expropriation and Dispossession, *done* Sept. 28, 1949, art. III, [1949] Gr. Brit. T.S. No. 60 (CMD. 7797); Agreement between the United Kingdom and Hungary Relating to the Settlement of Financial Matters, *done* June 27, 1956, art. 5, [1956] Gr. Brit. T.S. No. 30 (CMD. 9820); Agreement between the United Kingdom and Bulgaria Relating to the Settlement of Financial Matters, *done* Sept. 22, 1955, art. 5, [1955] Gr. Brit. T.S. No. 79 (CMD. 9625); Agreement between the United Kingdom and Poland Regarding the Settlement of Financial Matters, *done* Nov. 11, 1954, art. 5, [1954] Gr. Brit. T.S. No. 77 (CMD. 9343).

7. The Blonde, [1922] 1 A.C. 313, 335 (P.C.).

plemented by legislation) to the effect that Belgian mailboats should be "treated [in British ports] . . . as vessels of war, and be there entitled to all the honours and privileges which the interests and importance of the service demand."[8] Sir Robert Phillimore held that the Crown did not have the power to, in effect, create immunities where none had heretofore existed:

> If the Crown without the authority of parliament, may by process of diplomacy, shelter a foreigner from the action of one of her Majesty's subjects who has suffered injury at his hands, I do not see why it might not also give a like privilege of immunity to a number of foreign merchant vessels or to a number of foreign individuals. The law of this country has indeed incorporated those portions of international law which give immunity and privileges to foreign ships of war and foreign ambassadors; but I do not think that it has therefore given the Crown authority to clothe with this immunity foreign vessels, which are really not vessels of war, or foreign persons, who are not really ambassadors.[9]

The Crown will not "clothe" non-members of the class with immunities belonging to that class.

In *Engelke,* the question was the status of a German cipher clerk, not the immunities to which he was entitled. The House of Lords accepted the Crown's statement, that it considered *Engelke* to be a member of a class to which immunities normally attach, as conclusive of that aspect of the case. Their lordships then dealt with the common law question of whether the immunities would attach in this case and what effect they might have. The Crown was thus permitted to define the membership of the class.[10] That the Crown may restrict the immunities granted is clear from *Fenton Textile v. Krassin,* where the official agents of the as-yet-unrecognized government of Soviet Russia were put in the class of diplomats for purposes of exemption from taxation, arrest and search.[11] The courts upheld this restriction of immunity on the principle that it represented a waiver of a foreign state's rights which the Crown could accept within its Prerogative.

Finally, the Crown may, by certain actions, such as a declaration of war, bring into operation a different set of common law rules. Although

8. The Parlement Belge, 4 P.D. 129, 132 (1879) and Engelke v. Musmann, [1928] A.C. 433.

9. 4 P.D. at 154-55.

10. *Cf.* Lord Buckmaster in Engelke v. Musmann, [1928] A.C. 433, 446. The case followed the ruling in Duff Development Co. v. Government of Kelantan, [1923] A.C. 395.

11. Fenton Textile v. Krassin, [1921] T.L.R. 259 (C.A.). This case is also support for the principle in the *Engelke* case.

this action has the effect of changing the law under which the country is governed, it is not an excess of the Crown's powers because the common law itself has provided for alternate sets of rules to govern in any event.

A treaty may be implemented by legislation in one of three ways: first, Parliament may translate the treaty into a number of statutes or amendments to existing statutes; second, it may enact a general law which uses the key terms of the treaty and is clearly designed to implement the treaty; finally, it may directly enact the treaty, with an appropriate preamble, into English law.

The latter two methods may give cause to the courts to go to the treaty itself and interpret it as an aid in the enforcement of the statute. In *Parke-Davis & Co. v. Comptroller-General of Patents, Designs & Trade Marks,* the government was defending its decisions on the ground that by the Patents Act, 1949 it could make "no order . . . at variance with any treaty."[12] To determine the question, the court felt obliged to interpret the International Convention for Protection of Industrial Property, 1934; in *Philippson v. Imperial Airways Ltd.,* the question arose in the interpretation of a contract as to whether the carriage in question was international. The conditions of carriage were based on the Warsaw Convention and the court looked to that convention to make its decision.[13] Of course, this case concerned a private contract and it was not suggested that the Warsaw Convention was the law of the land. Perhaps the classic example of the English courts' willingness to go to the treaty itself is to be found in *Stoeck v. Public Trustee,* where the question was whether or not Stoeck was an alien within the meaning of the Treaty of Paris Order, 1919. The order simply stated that certain parts of the Treaty of Paris were to have full force and effect. In examining the entire treaty with a view to determining the meaning of the relevant provisions, Russell J. said: "I apprehend it is the right of a litigant to assert before the Courts of this country, and the duty of those Courts to adjudicate upon, claims founded upon a consideration of the municipal law of this country, and not the less so because the law involved has been derived from, and has been enacted for the purpose of giving effect to, certain provisions of a document of an international character."[14]

The rule in English law, then, is clear that, apart from certain situations involving interpretation, a treaty which requires action outside the Crown's prerogative cannot be enforced without legislation. The constitutional theory behind this rule appears to be soundly based on the division of powers between the Crown and Parliament, but the

12. Parke-Davis & Co. v. Comptroller-General of Patents, Designs and Trade Marks, [1954] A.C. 321, 322.

13. Philippson v. Imperial Airways Ltd., [1939] A.C. 332.

14. Stoeck v. Public Trustee, [1921] 2 Ch. 67, 71.

rule itself leaves unanswered some questions as to the status of a ratified treaty requiring but not having implementing legislation. It might well be argued that, being solemn declarations of the Crown's policy and being binding upon Britain in the international community, these treaties ought to have some effect. This argument will be explored more fully after we have examined the Canadian cases.

The law and theory in Canada

Canadian courts have adopted substantially the same approach to conventional international law as have the English courts. Indeed, the principle quoted from the *Labour Conventions Case* as defining English law arose from an appeal to the Privy Council from a Supreme Court of Canada decision and is, to a certain extent, binding on Canadian courts. The principle had, in any case, been affirmed by the Supreme Court some five years earlier in the *Arrow River* case where the court held that "the Crown cannot alter the existing law by entering into a contract with a foreign power."[15]

The *Arrow River* case is illustrative of another aspect of the attitude of Canadian courts to treaties. The case arose when Ontario passed a statute which imposed a toll on lumber passing along certain rivers including the Pigeon River. Since the Pigeon River was an international boundary river, this toll would have violated the unimplemented Ashburton Treaty of 1842. The Court of Appeal of Ontario and the Supreme Court of Canada, by a majority of 3 to 2, while recognizing that the treaty, having no implementing legislation, could be overridden by a statute, were able to interpret the statute in such a way as to avoid conflict with the treaty. Riddell J. put the matter this way:

> The real argument is that the Treaty was made with Her Majesty, and is binding in honour upon Her Majesty's successor, his present Majesty, as it was upon his predecessor. Consequently, the Sovereign will not consider enacting anything that will conflict with his plain duty, unless the language employed in the statute is perfectly clear and explicit, admitting of no other interpretation . . . The King cannot be thought of as violating his agreement with the other contracting Power; and if the legislation can fairly be read in such a way as to reject any imputation of breaking faith, it must be so read.[16]

Thus the Ontario statute was read in such a way as to avoid violating the Ashburton Treaty. We shall return to this point presently.

15. Re Arrow River & Tributaries Slide & Boom Co., [1932] 2 D.L.R. 250, 260 (Sup. Ct. Can.).

16. Re Arrow River & Tributaries Slide & Boom Co., [1931] 2 D.L.R. 216, 217 (Ont. C.A.).

Although there have been few cases on the point in Canada, it is submitted that the English rule that the Crown can enforce a treaty without legislation so long as the actions required lie within its prerogative applies in Canada as well. In *Francis v. The Queen,* Rand J. of the Supreme Court of Canada gave support to this branch of the rule when he said that:

> Speaking generally, provisions that give recognition to incidents of sovereignty or deal with matters in exclusively sovereign aspects, do not require legislative confirmation: for example, the recognition of independence, the establishment of boundaries, and, in a treaty of .peace, the transfer of sovereignty over property, are deemed executed and the treaty becomes the muniment or evidence of the political or proprietary title.
>
> Except as to diplomatic status and certain immunities and to belligerent rights, treaty provisions affecting matters within the scope of municipal law, that is, which purport to change existing law or restrict the future action of the Legislature, including, under our Constitution, the participation of the Crown, and in the absence of a constitutional provision declaring the treaty itself to be the law of the state, as in the United States, must be supplemented by statutory action.[17]

It is submitted that this statement accurately reflects the rule in Canada with the caveat that one must read "the transfer of sovereignty over property" as restricted to the transfer of property to which Canada itself has title. A peace treaty could not transfer private property without legislation.

As a result of three *obiter dicta,* there has been some confusion about the status of treaties of peace in Canada. In *Secretary of State of Canada v. Alien Property Custodian of the United States,* Duff J. of the Supreme Court of Canada was dealing with the validity of the Treaty of Peace (Germany) Order of 1920.[18] The Order, passed pursuant to the Treaties of Peace Act, was, of course, valid, but Duff J. added that "[t]he treaty, it is to be observed, being a Treaty of Peace, had the effect of law quite independently of legislation."[19] In a subsequent case on the same point, *Ritcher v. The King,* Angers J. said that "[i]n passing, I will note that an Act was not necessary to bring into force the Treaty of Peace between the Allied and the Associated Powers and Germany in question in this case; a treaty of peace is law in itself, independently of any legislation on the subject."[20] he then cited the *Alien Property* case

17. Francis v. The Queen, [1956] 3 D.L.R.2d 641, 647 (Sup. Ct. Can.).
18. Secretary of State of Canada v. Alien Property Custodian of the United States, [1931] 1 D.L.R. 890 (Sup. Ct. Can.).
19. *Id.* at 902.
20. Ritcher v. The King, [1943] 3 D.L.R. 540, 545 (Ex.).

as authority. One year later, Thorson J. of the Exchequer Court was seized with the same question and, after quoting Duff J.'s dictum said:

> With the utmost respect, I venture the opinion that there is no authority for this statement and that it cannot be accepted without important qualifications. While a Treaty of Peace can be made only by the Crown, it still remains an Act of the Crown. While it is binding upon the subjects of the Crown without legislation in the sense that it terminates the state of war, it has never, so far as I have been able to ascertain, been decided or admitted that the Crown could by its own act in agreeing to the terms of a treaty alter the law of the land or affect the private rights of individuals.[21]

It is respectfully submitted that this last *dictum* is the correct statement of the law and that the two previous comments must be read subject to its qualifications.

The situation in Canada on the enforcement of treaties, while similar to that in England, is complicated by the federal nature of the Canadian constitution. The difficulties created by the *Labour Conventions Case*[22] and other decisions have been discussed elsewhere.[23] It is sufficient to quote Lord Atkin in the *Labour Conventions Reference:*

> But in a State where the Legislature does not posses absolute authority, in a federal State where legislative authority is limited by a constitutional document, or is divided up between different Legislatures in accordance with the classes of subject-matter submitted for legislation, the problem is complex. The obligations imposed by treaty may have to be performed, if at all, by several Legislatures; and the executive have the task of obtaining the legislative assent not of the one Parliament to whom they may be responsible, but possibly of several Parliaments to whom they stand in no direct relation. The question is not how is the obligation formed, that is the function of the executive; but how it is to be performed, and that depends upon the authority of the competent Legislature or Legislatures.[24]

The theory behind this proposition is that when Canada was created as a federal state within the British Empire, certain powers were

21. Bitter v. Secretary of State of Canada, [1944] 3 D.L.R. 482, 497-98 (Sup. Ct. Can.).

22. Attorney-General for Canada v. Attorney-General for Ontario, [1937] A.C. 326 (P.C.) (Ont.).

23. Rand, "Some Aspects of Canadian Constitutionalism," 38 *Can. B. Rev.* 135 (1960); Wright, "Rt. Hon. Sir Lyman Poore Duff, G.C.M.G., 1865-1955," 33 *Can. B. Rev.* 1123 (1955).

24. [1937] A.C. at 348.

conferred exclusively on the federal authorities and certain powers were conferred exclusively on the provincial authorities. As time passed and Canada acceded to the status of an independent and fully sovereign nation, the federal executive acquired new powers to discharge this new role. But, according to the theory, nothing in this transition affected the distribution of legislative powers between the dominion and the provinces. Hence, although the federal executive might bind Canada internationally, it might or might not be able to fulfill that commitment depending upon the nature of the subject matter of the international agreement. The concern underlying this theory is that provincial autonomy is threatened whenever the central government is permitted to legislate in areas that are exclusively provincial even if the purpose if to fulfil an international obligation. Thus, after the *Labour Conventions Case,* Canada was unable to live up to the agreement it signed and the federal authorities were forced to begin negotiations which, as we shall see, are still continuing with the provinces in an effort to induce them to implement the terms of the agreement.

This approach is consistent with strict federal theory but it fails to take into account the sweeping changes that have occurred in regard to Canada's status as an international person. When the British North America Act was drafted in 1867, it was thought that Canada's international obligations would arise only through membership in the British Empire. Section 132 of the Act provided the federal authorities with ample power to implement any treaty obligations so acquired; in other words, the Fathers of Confederation intended the central government to be able to discharge all of Canada's foreseeable international responsibilities.

As Canada began to make treaties in her own right and not as part of the Empire, section 132 of the Act became less and less relevant, until now it is obsolete. Canada is left in the difficult position of being a full international person, with the responsibilities that entails, and yet there is no one government that has the power to ensure compliance with international law, customary or conventional. Provincial autonomy, which would, in my opinion, have been protected by the doctrine of "colourable legislation," could have survived a reinterpretation of either section 132 or the federal general power under section 91 of the British North America Act permitting the federal authorities to legislate in provincial areas of competence in fulfillment of an international commitment.

In the *Offshore Minerals Reference,* the Supreme Court of Canada hinted that it might accept such an argument when it said, in support of its opinion that the Dominion owned the mineral rights in the continental shelf, that "it is Canada, not the Province of British Columbia, that will have to answer the claims of other members of the international community for breach of the obligations and responsibilities imposed by the Convention."[25] The Supreme Court has here demonstrated an awareness of the inadequacy of the present situation regarding the implementation of treaties, but it may take many more years before a proper case comes before it and, even then, the court may not overrule the previous decisions. The faster and surer way to change this situation is to take advantage of current efforts to revise the constitution and to introduce a modernized version of section 132. The federal government might have to pay for such a revision but in the long run the price would be cheap.

We have seen thus far that the rule in Canada and in England is similar; most treaties require implementing legislation in order to change domestic law. When we examined this rule in the English context, we found that it was justified by the theory of the separation of powers between Crown and Parliament. The same theory applies in Canada. It is an important principle of Canadian constitutional law that the Executive not be permitted to escape parliamentary control by doing by treaty what it could not otherwise do alone. Thus, in Canada, a treaty may be signed and ratified and yet have no effect internally as a result of either or both of two obstables: either Parliament does not implement it, or Parliament can not implement it. The treaty, to the extent that it was intended to operate internally, and many significant treaties of modern times are so intended, is rendered meaningless.

With due respect to the fundamental principles of separation and distribution of powers, may we not ask if such an approach to international relations is permissible? For example, after playing a role in the drafting of the International Convention on the Elimination of All Forms of Racial Discrimination of 1965, Canada waited until October 14th, 1970 before ratifying this treaty.[26] There has been no implementing legislation. The Canadian Bill of Rights which was assented to on August 10th, 1960 guarantees many of the freedoms called for in the Convention, but it has two basic weaknesses. First, it is a federal statute and applies only in areas of federal competence. While this does include criminal matters, for the most part it fails to cover the provincial areas of civil and property rights. Second, until rather recently, the Bill of Rights was not being accorded much weight in Canadian courts. In a number of apparently relevant situations, it was found inapplicable. The recent case of *R. v. Drybones* presents a notable exception to this trend and may signal a change in judicial thinking.[27]

25. Re Offshore Mineral Rights of British Columbia, [1967] S.C.R. 792, 821.

26. See Beesley & Bourne (eds.), "Canadian Practice in International Law during 1970 as Reflected Mainly in Public Correspondence and Statements of the Department of External Affairs," in 9 *Can. Y.B. Int'l L.* 300 (1971).

27. Regina v. Drybones, [1970] D.L.R.3d 473 (Sup. Ct. Can.).

The federal government, when questioned about the implementation of the civil and property rights portion of the 1965 Convention, has indicated that it believes that the provinces now provide a standard of civil rights sufficiently high to meet those of the Convention. Even if it is so now, will the provinces maintain those standards? If an individual is subjected to some form of discrimination and goes before a court, will it help his case to cite this Convention to the court, or to point out that Canada has ratified the treaty? Will it help him to inform the court that the federal government believes that civil rights in the provinces are protected at least to the extent required by the Convention? Surely, as the law is today, the answer is no.[28]

If we are to give some special status to the Convention, what might this status be? It is clear that we cannot simply permit the executive to bypass Parliament; nor does there appear to be a simple solution to the federal-provincial difficulty. In regard to the separation of powers, these could be adequately protected and, at the same time, recognition could be given to a solemn binding commitment of the federal executive, as an expression of official public policy, by granting ratified treaties a status higher than the common law but lower than statute law. In other words, a ratified treaty would be the law of Canada until and unless it conflicted with a statute passed by Parliament. Since, subject to some important exceptions to be discussed presently, treaties are submitted to Parliament for approval, the federal Parliament would be most certainly aware of these new laws and could, if it disapproved, pass a statute to overrule it. The check on the Executive would be maintained. But, unless such a law existed or was enacted the treaty would be law. This might also provide a solution to the separation of powers difficulty since the provincial Parliaments would have an opportunity to scrutinize the treaty and pass corrective legislation if they saw fit.

Another approach might be to provide that all treaties must be ratified by Parliament and then give them the force of law. This

28. It is interesting to note the brief history of such attempts in our judicial annals. In a series of prisoner-of-war cases, notably Regina v. Brosig, [1945] 2 D.L.R. 232 (Ont. C.A.), the courts appeared to hold that the Geneva Convention of 1929, although not implemented by legislation, was part of our law. There are, however, other explanations of these cases. There were two restrictive covenant cases which went both ways on the question of the force of the unimplemented San Francisco Charter and the Atlantic Charter: Re Drummond Wren, [1945] Ont. 778 (Ont. H.C.) and Re Noble, [1948] Ont. 579 (Ont. H.C.). In reversing the Ontario courts the Supreme Court of Canada, in Noble v. Alley, [1951] 1 D.L.R. 321 (Sup. Ct. Can.), did not mention either of the international instruments despite the fact that they were discussed at length by the lower courts. For a consideration of these cases as they relate to the matter under discussion see my essay "The Relationship Between International Law and Domestic Law in Canada," in *Canadian Perspectives on International Law and Organization* 88 (R. Macdonald, G. Morris & D. Johnston eds. 1974).

procedure might produce practical difficulties in that there is, as we shall see, some question about what is and what is not a treaty. The federal government has been, in recent years, signing agreements which it considers to be less than the type of treaty that customarily goes before Parliament for approval. Of course, this difficulty is overcome by the provision that, unless the treaty is ratified by Parliament, it has no legal effect except that which is already within the power of the executive. This approach also would avoid the separation of powers difficulty in that, if the subject matter of the treaty were provincial, the provincial legislatures would also have to ratify it. One can see immediately that there would be difficulties in this latter respect since one province might refuse to ratify. A better solution would probably be to allow the federal Parliament's ratification to implement the treaty and deal with the federal-provincial aspect in some other way.

The simplest solution, at least on the surface, to the division of powers question would be a reference to the Supreme Court on the treaty question. It has been suggested, here and elsewhere, that the Supreme Court might well be ready to overrule or refuse to follow the *Labour Conventions Case*. There are two difficulties here. First, the Supreme Court might decide against the federal government; and, second, even if the federal government was successful, it might not be politically feasible to take advantage of the victory. Such was the case with the *Offshore Minerals Reference*.[29] A better approach must be, as suggested earlier, to negotiate a modernization of section 132 with appropriate safeguards. Since the separation of powers problem will require a constitutional change in any case, it would be appropriate to consider all aspects of this issue at once.

We have seen that, in a sense, Canada is restricted as an international person in regard to treaties. The possible solutions to this problem, and only a few have been discussed, will probably be long in coming and, in the meantime, the federal and to a lesser extent the provincial governments have been working out methods of dealing internationally which avoid some of the more serious repercussions. These methods are best examined by studying Canadian practice, as opposed to theory, in dealing with international obligations.

29. This is not to deny that a favourable judgment allows Ottawa to bargain from strength, an important consideration in the federal government's overall strategy.

II. CONVENTIONAL LAW AND MUNICIPAL LAW: THE PRACTICE

Traditional Practice in Canada

The word treaty, as is well-known, is frequently used to describe a variety of binding international arrangements of differing degrees of formality and importance of subject matter, all of which come within the category of conventional international law. These include treaties themselves, conventions, protocols, agreements, declarations, final acts, and exchanges of notes. These arrangements may be contracted between heads of states, foreign ministers, and heads of administrative departments. Ratification and evidence that the contractor has full powers may or may not be required. Parliament may implement, ratify or approve them; or, they may not be put before Parliament at all. It is only in the light of these various possibilities that one can properly appreciate the difficulties and dangers of attempting to state anything like a rule, custom or even trend in the area of Canadian practice.

A.E. Gotlieb has examined discrete periods of Canada's treaty-making history since the Second World War, including the period 1965-1970, and concluded that, except for bilateral treaties with the United States, Canada has shown a tendency towards greater formality in its treaty-making in recent years. As he says, "it may be observed in the declining use of exchanges-of-notes in the bilateral field; in the emergence of a higher percentage of bilateral treaties subject to ratification than in late pre World War II years, and in an upswing in formal multilateral treaty-making."[30] He goes on to note that, although multilateral treaties are increasing in frequency, bilateral treaties with the United States, by far our most common treaty, have been for some time and continue to be informal. The exact nature of these informalities will be discussed later. It is difficult to draw any conclusions from Gotlieb's observations except to note that Canada appears to treat commitments with partners other than the United States with more caution.

There are few statutory provisions relating to the exercise of the treaty-making power in Canada, it being, for the most part governed by constitutional custom. The power itself is part of the royal prerogative which is, in Canada, exercised by the Governor General in Council. There is no obligation at law, therefore, to submit treaties, either before or after their signature to Parliament for its approval or otherwise.

30. A. Gotlieb, *Canadian Treaty Making: Informal Agreements and Inter-Departmental Arrangements* 13 (1968) [hereinafter cited as Gotlieb].

Ratification, in its strict international sense, refers to the competent constitutional organ of a state giving its definitive consent to be bound by the treaty. It is part of the treaty-making power and in Canada it too is exercised under the royal prerogative by the executive. There is, however, tradition in Canada, dating back at least to the 1920's, of submitting treaties for Parliamentary approval before ratification. Of course, this policy relates only to those treaties which do not require Parliamentary action to implement them. Those treaties requiring implementing legislation are approved when such legislation is passed or they have no effect.

On June 21, 1926, Mr. Mackenzie King, then Prime Minister, introduced a resolution approving the recommendations of the 1923 Imperial Conference regarding treaty making; this resolution said in part that "This House . . . considers . . . that before His Majesty's Canadian Minister advise ratification of a treaty or convention affecting Canada, or signify acceptance of any treaty, convention or agreement involving military or economic sanctions, the approval of the Parliament of Canada should be secured."[31] Mr. King had, in earlier speeches, indicated that this policy would apply to "important treaties" and "obligations involving any considerable financial outlays or active undertakings" as well as those involving "political considerations of a far-reaching character."[32] This approach was extended in 1941 when Mr. King said: "The present practice is that, except in the case of very unimportant agreements or in the case of great urgency, the Senate and House of Commons are asked to approve formal treaties, conventions and agreements, before they are ratified. . "[33] In recent years, however, there has been a backing off from this position and it may now be said that only in cases of very important treaties is Parliamentary approval sought. The renewal of the NORAD agreement, the ratification of the Treaty on the Non-Proliferation of Nuclear Weapons, and the ratification of the extradition treaties with Austria and Israel are all instances where no approval was sought and yet they would appear to come within even the early guidelines set down by Mr. King.

In addition, distinctions are being drawn between "treaties" and "agreements," Mr. King's guidelines being considered as referring to the former only. On September 30, 1963, after it had become apparent that the agreement between Canada and the United States to permit the deployment of nuclear warheads on Canadian territory would not be

31. Beesley (ed.), "Canadian Practice in International Law during 1969 as Reflected Mainly in Public Correspondence of the Department of External Affairs," in 8 *Can. Y.B. Int'l L.* 337, 367 (1970) [hereinafter cited as "1969 Canadian Practice"].

32. *Id.*

33. *Id.*

placed before Parliament, Mr. T.C. Douglas asked Prime Minister Pearson if and when Parliament would be permitted to scrutinize the agreement. Mr. Pearson replied that it would never be presented with that opportunity, justifying his position by saying that "[t]he agreement to which my hon. friend refers is not a treaty or a heads of state agreement, which would require ratification and the customary prior approval of the House of Commons. It is an executive agreement, an exchange of notes between governments."[34] A motion to table the agreement was defeated by a vote of 105 - 91.[35]

In 1966, the Minister of Industry, Mr. Drury, moved a resolution to approve the agreement on automotive products signed in Johnson City, Texas, on January 16, 1965 and implemented by Orders-in-Council on that day. When questioned by the Opposition about the fifteen-month delay and the implementation before approval, Mr. Drury replied that, if this were a treaty, it would clearly come within Mr. King's guidelines: "But in this case this is not a treaty. It is an agreement between the administrations of two countries governing the exercise of their normal administrative functions."[36] Other examples include the voluntary restraints on trade negotiated with Japan in 1964, the memorandum of the understanding reached between the governments of Canada and Hong Kong on restrictions of certain cotton textile exports to Canada in 1965, and the limits agreed to with the Government of Communist China regarding certain sensitive items as part of a wheat sale contract.

It can be seen then that as Canada's treaty-making becomes more sophisticated, there is a tendency away from Parliamentary scrutiny. Even where Parliament is called upon to approve a treaty, the terms of the treaty are not open for debate, only whether or not it should be ratified. In 1964, the Columbia River Treaty was before Parliament for approval and the New Democratic Party wished to amend the approving resolution to make it subject to Canada's negotiating a new protocol to the treaty clarifying certain clauses. The Speaker ruled this amendment out of order on the ground that, in putting the treaty before Parliament for approval, the government was not *ipso facto* relinquishing its prerogative in the realm of treaty-making. His ruling was upheld by a vote of the House.[37]

It is, however, the practice of the Secretary of State for External Affairs to table, in both the House and the Senate, the texts of almost all international agreements which would not otherwise come to the attention of Parliament. There is also a list, deposited periodically in Parliament by the Prime Minister, of all Orders-in-Council, including

34. 4 H.C. Deb. (Can.) 3028-29 (1963).
35. *Id.* at 3118-19.
36. 5 *id.* 4815-16 (1966).
37. 4 *id.* 3954 (1964).

those authorizing the conclusion of international agreements. Finally, there are the annual reports of the Department of External Affairs, the Department's bi-monthly bulletin, *International Perspectives,* and the Canada Treaty Series.

It is significant that even those treaties which are given the severest scrutiny - those for the ratification of which approval is sought - are not exposed to the possibility of amendment. And the others, that ever-growing category of "unimportant treaty" and "other than treaty," are simply published after the fact in a manner in which only those Members of Parliament with the greatest interest or time would have a chance to read let alone study them. Of course, even if they did study them, there would be no opportunity to discuss the matter in Parliament without the use of skillful tactics.

Reviewing momentarily what we have seen thus far in Canadian treaty practice, we find that the signing and ratifying of a treaty is within the power of the Executive. It is the Executive which decides upon the form and content of the treaty. If the treaty requires implementing legislation according to the *Arrow River* doctrine, the Executive will normally, before signing or at least before ratifying the treaty, place the implementing legislation before Parliament, and a full opportunity to debate the treaty will be afforded. If, however, implementing legislation is unnecessary, there is no legal requirement for the Executive even to inform Parliament of what it is doing. The individual members might, some time after the fact, glean from records and long lists of Orders-in-Council that something had happened, if their constituents had not notified them already. Even then, however, there would be no simple way to bring the matter before the House, save by using the intricate medium of the question period or by attaching it to other bills such as Motions for Supply.

Comments and Proposals on Practice in Canada

Recognizing the limitations of the existing system, Prime Minister King said in 1923 that "the day has passed when any government or executive should feel that they should take it upon themselves without the approval of parliament to commit a county to obligations . . . "[38] Were this the start of a binding custom, there could be no cause for concern at the lack of formal constitutional requirements. But, as we have seen, the custom if it ever was one, is falling into disuse. In addition, it has been decided that Parliament has only a minimal role in these resolutions of approval, although full debate is allowed.

Surely the day Mr. King was speaking of has passed. Can it be ac-

38. "1969 Canadian Practice," *supra* note 31, at 367.

ceptable in Canada today to have a treaty as important as the Automotive Products Agreement, with its important tariff changes, its far reaching economic impact, and its significant political implications, put into effect almost secretly? It is true that this was done legally, for these changes were made under powers that had been delegated to the Executive by Parliament at a time when such an Agreement was not even contemplated. And, of course, it is true that the agreement received a certain amount of publicity when it was signed. But these considerations cannot make up for the fact that the tariff changes were in effect for fifteen months before Parliament was given an opportunity to approve or disapprove them, there never being an opportunity to change them. Can this be justified by saying that the changes in Canadian law were made pursuant to an "agreement" and not a "treaty"?

If there were a constitutional requirement, either in written or unwritten form, that all treaties (using that word in its broadest meaning) of any significance, be it economic, military or political, be placed before Parliament for its approval before ratification or, if no ratification were required, before bringing them into force, most of the dangers, real and apparent, in the present system would be eliminated. Parliament would see the terms of the treaty as a body before Canada was bound to it and, since the terms of the treaty would themselves be up for approval, amendments could be proposed. The prospect of Parliament sending back approvals conditioned upon the negotiation of certain new terms may appear horrifying to the professional in foreign affairs, but we must have faith in Parliament's ability to grasp the difficulties which such a procedure would create. Obviously, in the case of multilateral agreements, it would have to be a take it or leave it approach.

Such a custom would also make more acceptable my earlier proposal about the status of a signed and ratified treaty. The suggestion was that such treaties, though lacking implementing legislation, should be considered as the law of the land until and unless contradicted by statutes of Parliament which would, of course, take precedence. There was a danger implicit in this suggestion that Parliament would not even know about these new "laws" until they were in force and, even then, would not hear of them as a body, but rather as individuals. It might be too difficult for opponents of the new treaty to organize a bill to change it.

Under my proposed approval system, any treaty which would affect our domestic law or make any economic, military or political commitments for Canada, whether or not implementing legislation was required, would be placed before Parliament in the form of a resolution approving its terms before Canada bound herself to it. Once the approving resolution was passed and Canada had bound herself internationally, the terms of the treaty would be Canadian law, having a status above the common law but below statute law. If implementing legislation were thought necessary, either for the sake of clarity or to override existing statutes, Parliament could then pass it. If none were required, the Executive could issue the requisite Orders-in-Council, if they were necessary, with the assurance that Parliament had already approved their actions.

At the same time, it would be helpful, to say the least, if the meaning of the term "treaty" could be cleared up. At present, there are many international commitments created between Canada and other countries, the United States in particular, which take the form of exchanges of notes between the heads of administrative departments or even simple exchanges of letters. These come to the attention of Parliament, if at all, only in the most indirect and off-hand manner. The theory behind these forms of agreements is that nothing is being agreed to that is not within the power of the administrator to do on his own already. That is, he is acquiring no new powers by virtue of the treaty and any changes he makes are pursuant to powers already delegated to him by some act of Parliament. Since he is acting for the Executive, he is in the same position as the Executive in not having to account to Parliament for its actions within its prerogative.

Several points come to mind. First, administrators do not have any prerogatives; they have, if Parliament has granted them, certain powers to make regulations through Orders-in-Council within predetermined guidelines. Second, when Parliament delegates this authority it has, generally speaking, few expectations that this authority is going to be used to commit Canada as a nation to international obligations. Third, the terms of these arrangements become obligations and those in Canada who are charged with administering various Acts of Parliament have their discretion fettered to the extent these obligations impinge upon their subject ares. Finally, these are international commitments with invariably widespread political consequences, consequences which may exceed the apparently minor nature of the subject matter, and consequences which Parliament should have an opportunity to consider beforehand.

The procedures for obtaining Parliamentary approval suggested above, then, should be applied to all treaties including any type of arrangement by which Canada becomes bound, whether legally or morally, to do certain things. This will assure that the people in Canada who will be affected by these obligations will, through their representatives, be given an opportunity to scrutinize them in advance.

The Special Problem of the Distribution of Legislative Powers: The Federal Government and the Provinces

The Canadian practice with regard to the problem of the distribution of legislative powers is interesting as well. A.E. Gotlieb in his *Canadian Treaty-Making* argues that the federal government has, through an informal and pragmatic approach, developed effective and simplified means for making treaties despite the apparent restrictions of the *Labour Conventions* doctrine.[39] In support of this argument he notes that many of the treaties Canada enters into require no implementing legislation. Of those treaties which do require implementing legislation, many lie within the federal sphere of competence. Treaties which have as their subject matter defence, trade, fishing, high seas and taxation make up some 85% of the formal treaties entered into by Canada and these all lie within federal competence.

Some treaties do require provincial legislation to implement them, however, and for these Canada has two choices. It can insist on the inclusion within the treaty of a so-called "federal state" clause by which Canada ratifies only such parts of the treaty as lie within the federal power and ratifies the other parts when and if the provinces pass the necessary legislation. This method has several obvious drawbacks, the most obvious being that Canada's treaty partners may be, and frequently are, unwilling to permit Canada to enjoy this special position. In addition, Canada's actual fulfillment of her international obligations becomes a rather amorphous quantity.

A more practical solution and one which Canada adopted after the legislation implementing the three I.L.O. Conventions was disallowed, is to have consultations between the various levels of government respecting the legislation or administrative changes required to implement a given treaty. The substantial success achieved by Canada in implementing these labour treaties is chronicled by E.A. Landy.[40] There have been, since that time, a number of I.L.O. conventions and the constitution of the I.L.O. requires that a member state bring a convention "before the authority or authorities within whose competence the matter lies for the enactment of legislation or other action." In 1964, the Minister of Labour, speaking of a convention respecting discrimination in employment said: "The Prime Minister (Mr. Pearson) wrote to each provincial premier to ask for confirmation that the province is pursuing . . . a policy of promotion of equality of opportunity . . . was positive."[41] Canada did not employ the "federal

39. Gotlieb, *supra* note 30, at 20.

40. E. Landy, *The Effectiveness of International Supervision: Thirty Years of I.L.O. Experience* 111-12 (1966).

41. 4 H.C. Deb. (Can.) 8993-94 (1964).

state" clause method when it signed the International Convention on the Elimination of all Forms of Racial Discrimination. Instead a series of communications and consultations were commenced which were reported in a communication from the Department of External Affairs replying to an inquiry about the status of the convention. "In this connection the Government is now entering a process of consultation with the provinces concerning those provisions of the Convention which fall within the provincial jurisdiction. The federal government, at the present time, is actively engaged in consulting the provinces about the possibility of Canada's ratifying several conventions which touch upon human rights.[42]

As we saw earlier, this Convention was ratified on October 14, 1970 and, since no legislation was passed in pursuance of the convention by most of the provinces, we are left to infer that these consultations yielded the response that the provinces were already meeting that standard. This is, in fact, the position of the Department of External Affairs and the weaknesses of this approach have been discussed earlier. These observations, which are applicable to the consultation approach generally, reduce to the simple proposition that, so long as implementing legislation is necessary to supplant the common law by a treaty provision, letters written to provincial premiers eliciting general replies are not fully satisfactory. The federal government will wish to put more substance behind its signature.

There are, of course, several substantial responses to the foregoing observations. It might well be suggested that even if Canada has no adequate method of fulfilling its obligations, it is still worthwhile signing these documents if only to lend what moral support we can to the principles contained in them. The argument would run that few countries do initially fulfil these conventions, which are designed to protect individuals within their own country; but, if we can at least get them to sign a document purporting to set these protections as goals, the reality might gradually move towards the form.

The second response might be that while it probably is unsatisfactory to be committing oneself to obligations one cannot properly fulfil, nevertheless if we did not do it this way, we could not sign any treaties at all. In the absence of substantial constitutional change (and it would have to be substantial since the types of treaties we are talking about concern basic civil rights and property rights issues) the only alternative would be massive prior consultations provincial representation at the negotiations, and provincial legislation passed and waiting to go into force before Canada could sign an agreement. This alternative

42. Gotlieb (ed.), "Canadian Practice in International Law during 1966 as Reflected Mainly in Correspondence and Statements of the Department of External Affairs," in 5 *Can. Y.B. Int'l L.* 253, 275-76 (1967).

appears so difficult that to articulate it is to reject it. We are, therefore, better off muddling through as we are than doing nothing.

In response to the first answer, that these treaties are useful even if only as ideals, I would have to agree. If it became clear that Canada's abilities to fulfil its obligations could in no way be strengthened, then it probably is better to sign anyway for moral support and in the hopes of gradual improvement. But, our moral support must be backed up by our ability to "deliver" within our own territory. As to the second argument, that muddling through is better than not moving, I can only partially agree. While this approach is, admittedly, in our Anglo-Canadian tradition and is even a source of pride among one school of political scientists, it does tend to avoid for a scandalous length of time fundamental questions and difficulties. It is not an answer to say that by a very pragmatic approach we are managing to get some things done. The true question ought to be: what could we do if the system were more finely tuned? It is by the standards set by the answer to that question that we must measure our present system.

Sooner or later we will have to face the reality that Canada, as a member, and more so, as one of the leaders, of the world community must have the power to change domestic law even in the sacred provincial rights areas popularly referred to as the sociological issues. This should be done sooner rather than later. These changes can be wrought by a reinterpretation of our present constitution or, better, by a modernization of section 132 of the British North America Act with appropriate safeguards against "colourable" interference.

CONCLUSION

In the area of conventional international law Canada has serious problems which affect us both domestically and internationally. There is the question of the status of a treaty duly signed and ratified but not implemented, the treaty which is not brought before Parliament, and the treaty which the federal government cannot implement even if it wanted to. None of these problems admits of any easy solution. The tentative suggestions put forward - the special status for an unimplemented but signed treaty, the requirement for Parliamentary approval, and the amending of our constitution - are all of them major changes. They may well carry with them the seeds of even greater difficulties. But they, along with other even more sweeping possibilities, such as a role for a provincially oriented Senate of Canada in treaty-ratifying or provincial treaty-making outside of the present "Umbrella Treaty" method now employed, must be considered if we are to begin to resolve these difficult questions.

SOME LEGAL ASPECTS OF INTERNATIONAL AND MULTINATIONAL ENTERPRISES

ROGER PINTO

Our friend and colleague Wolfgang Friedmann was one of the first lawyers to draw the attention of the academic world to those new entities in international relations which are so much now in the public eye—the international and multinational (or transnational) corporations and enterprises. The first item mentioned in a bibliography which I recently prepared for a graduate student seminar on multinationals refers to an article published in the *Modern Law Review* thirty years ago by Wolfgang Friedmann.[1] Probably one of his last publications on the subject appears in the *International Encyclopedia of Comparative Law*.[2]

In the last paragraph of his piece in the *Encyclopedia,* Wolfgang Friedmann makes a distinction between public international economic and financial organizations and international and multinational companies in which public and private enterprises may join hands. The public international economic and financial organizations (such as the World Bank and regional development banks) have international legal personality and status. On the other hand, since there is no international company law or register "the legal status and personality of such multinational companies must still be based on the commercial law of the country of incorporation."[3]

This view is shared by Schmithoff[4] who goes one step further in

ROGER PINTO is Professeur à la Faculté de Droit et des Sciences Economiques de Paris.

This article was completed in 1974 and thus cannot take into account developments which have taken place in the OECD and in the United Nations (*eg.* Commission and Center on Transnational Corporations) since then.

1. Friedmann, "International Public Corporation," 6 *Mod. L. Rev.* 185 (1943).

2. "International and Multinational Public Corporations" (section VIII), in Friedmann, "Governmental (Public) Enterprises" (chapter 13), in "Business and Private Corporations," 13 *International Encyclopedia of Comparative Law* 13-1, 13-25 (A. Conard ed. 1972).

3. *Id.* sec. 34.

4. The international company is a conception of public international law. The international company must not be confused with the multinational enterprise which

providing legal terminology with two distinct basic terms which in my opinion, if generally adopted would help to clear up existing confusion and ambiguities. The term "international" should be used exclusively to designate those organizations, enterprises or companies which are created by the collective decision of two or more States, acting under public international law processes. These might take the form of agreement, custom or parallel unilateral instruments whether or not the States parties to such a venture provide that such enterprise, or corporation is to be incorporated under the laws of one or more countries. On the other hand, the term "multinational" would be used exclusively to designate all other enterprises, companies or corporations which, under certain conditions to be dealt with later in this article, operate internationally but are not created under public international law. Such terminology is already widely used by lawyers; it is not merely a matter of convenience.

International enterprises may be public, mixed or private.[5] As noted earlier, at some point in the process of organizing the enterprise, two or more states will cooperate to define their purpose, status, powers, duties and privileges. The international enterprise is thus a concept of public international law. Schmitthoff has taken a somewhat more restrictive view of this concept. He seems to exclude any procedure other than formal treaty or agreement between States. It is true that international enterprises or corporations are generally created by treaty, but this is not always the case,[6] Informal procedures may be followed; the States concerned may approve the organization of an international company by parallel decisions granting privileges and requiring undertakings. As a result of negotiations between the States and the corporations concerned, an international corporation may be organized. A corporation might become international as a result of common conduct and practices. It may become international due to the participation in its capital of two or more States who would have acquired a joint controlling interest.

A common feature in all these international enterprises, whatever their formal organization, is that they are subject to the jurisdiction of

---

consists of a group of companies incorporated under different national laws. Obviously an international company can *only* be created by an international convention between governments. Schmithoff, "The Multinational Enterprise in the United Kingdom," in *Nationalism and the Multinational Enterprise* 22 (H. Hahlo, J. Smith, & R. Wright eds. 1973). See Goldman's penetrating study: "The Law of International Companies," 90 *J. Droit Int'l* 321 (1963) [hereinafter cited as Goldman].

5. Depending upon their legal structure they fall into the following categories: enterprises owned and operated by the states concerned directly or through an independent legal entity owned by the states concerned but operated by a private company; corporations with or without state participation in their capital.

6. Scandinavian Air Line System; Goldman, *supra* note 4, at 325 n. 7.

all the participating States acting *collectively*. International enterprises or corporations are subject to a common jurisdiction.[7] This is not the case with multinationals.

Multinational corporations are subject to the jurisdiction of two or more States, but these States act independently of each other; there is no common jurisdiction. It is precisely by playing one jurisdiction off against another and by occupying vacuums resulting from conflicting State jurisdictions that multinational corporations are able to create their own system of customary rules in their international operations. Such a system of rules is part of today's international law, whether "public" or "private" (if this distinction has a meaning other than a formal and procedural one).

In a report on Multinational Corporations in World Development published by the United Nations, the term is used "in the broad sense to cover all enterprises which control assets—factories, mines, sales offices and the like—in two or more countries."[8] Also one finds in a French report, a complementary definition to which this author subscribes: "a multinational is an enterprise, the operations of which transcend the borders and the regulations enacted by Nation States."[9]

From a legal point of view, two characteristics of multinationals emerge from such definition: subjection of the corporation to the parallel jurisdictions of two or more States, and the possibility for such a corporation to create an independent system of rules in its international operations. These two characteristics are sufficient criteria to classify an enterprise or a corporation as being multinational. Thus there is no need to discuss definitions of the multinational company based on economic, social or political factors. It is true that the gigantic, global,

7. This list does not take into account international enterprises organized by two or more socialist countries. This list is the following: (1) *Banking and financial establishments* (World Bank and its subsidiaries; Bank for International Settlements; European Bank of Investments; Bank for Economic Integration of Central America; Inter-American Development Bank; Asian Development Bank); (2) *Transportation* (Abidjan-Niger railroad system; Benin-Niger railroad system; Franco-Ethiopian Railroad Company; European Company for financing railroad equipment (Eurofima); Air Afrique; Scandinavian Airline System; Bale-Mulhouse Airport; Mont-Blanc Tunnel Company); (3) *Power* (Sarre-Lorraine Coal Union; Emossou (France-Switzerland); Central African Power Corporation; Franco-Belgian Nuclear Energy Company of the Ardennes (SENA); Société Internationale de la Moselle); and (4) *Telecommunications* (Intelsat (Comsat)). This is, of course, an incomplete list.

8. U.N. Doc. ST/ECA/190, at 5 (1973); *id.* annex II, Selected Definitions, at 118-21 [hereinafter cited as U.N. Report].

9. Decouflé, "Firmes Multinationales et Prospective du 'Système International,' " in *Les Firmes Multinationales* (Datar ed. 1973). Decouflé notes that his definition is quite close to that proposed by Stephen Hymer and Robert Rowthorn in "Multinational Corporations and International Oligopoly: the Non-American Challenge," in *The International Corporation* 57 (C. Kindleberger ed. 1970).

cosmo-corporation is the problem child. But it may well be that smaller multinationals lend themselves more easily to legal scrutiny and reveal the actual processes through which a new system of international rules is created and operates.

A legal analysis of the multinational corporation will cover the following fields: intra-multinational corporation rules, regulations and standards of conduct of the multinational corporation; relations of the multinational corporation with the various countries with which the multinational corporation has contacts, e.g., countries in which the multinational corporation is based, usually termed countries of origin or "home" countries, and countries in which the multinational corporation operates outside its main base, generally termed host countries; [10] relations between these countries with reference to the multinational corporation.

The most difficult problem is that of the intra-multinational corporation rules and standards of conduct. Whatever their practical importance and their world impact, these rules and standards are generally not considered to be lawyer's law. However, these rules and standards of conduct are those of some five hundred powerful multinational corporations as well as those, with certain limitations, of the several thousand corporations that are also classified as multinationals. It is difficult for the lawyer to dismiss them as non-law or infra-law.[11] A brief comment here will deal exclusively with the rules and standards of conduct of multinationals.

Among the intra-multinational corporation practices that respond to international operations, is the setting up of a parallel structure of power and line of command that bypasses the formal organization of subsidiaries of the multinational corporations. Regional headquarters, with management, sales, personnel, finance directors or controllers are organized to forward instructions and decisions to the subsidiaries and to supervise and control them. The requirements of local company laws are considered to be mere formalities and red-tape to be complied with on a routine basis. Generally, corporate documents are kept by law

10. These terms imply a specific and different tie with the various countries with which the multinational has contacts. However, whether the multinationals are patriotic, cosmopolitan, or egocentric, and whether the "home" country is just another "host" country, are questions of fact, which should not be solved by *a priori* labels.

11. The U.N. Report, *supra* note 8, at 127, lists some 650 of the largest industrial corporations and states that almost all are multinationals according to the definition adopted. To these must be added the largest nonindustrial multinational corporations. The total number of multinationals according to the U.N. Report (*id.* at 7) is 7,300. A 1966 United States survey uncovered 3,400 United States based multinationals with foreign affiliates. *Multinational Corporations,* Subcommittee on International Trade, Senate Committee on Finance, 93d Cong., 1st Sess. (Feb. 1973) [hereinafter cited as Senate Report on Multinationals].

firms; these documents formalize decisions taken outside the corporate structure in the form of other legal instruments. The local corporate structure becomes an empty shell.

Moreover, the officers (president, general manager, manager) of subsidiary companies, whatever their specific status under local laws, are considered to be employees of the multinational corporation. As it is not always possible to give them such an employee status by agreement with the subsidiary in which they have their position, an employment contract is executed with the parent corporation or one of its other subsidiaries. The legal status of these parallel structures, their interrelationship with the official structures in the various jurisdictions is part and parcel of the law of multinational corporations.

Central management, with the assistance of regional headquarters, attempts to hire and manage multinational corporation personnel all over the world, or at least regionally, under the same general terms and conditions. Standard employment contracts are enforceable when their terms are more favorable than the minimum required by local laws; this is generally the case. Otherwise when, in certain areas, provisions of local labour laws and collective agreements are mandatory; multinational corporation regulations cannot be maintained unless the multinational corporation avoids subjecting itself to such jurisdictions.

Multinational corporations also try to operate with streamlined standard forms of contracts for world-wide usage, without taking into account local systems of law. In fact, this is not possible without adjusting these contracts to local requirements. However, the multinational corporations usually attempt to limit these adjustments to regional levels. A study of multinational corporation commercial contracts (*e.g.*, license to manufacture, distributorship, agency), if it were at all possible to make such a study, would show uniform terms and conditions in the field of operations of multinational corporations which probably cover more ground and are more effective than uniform laws.[12]

International money management by multinational corporations has recently been subject to intensive scrutiny because of its cumulative effects on State investment and exchange controls as well as on the international monetary system. While it is true that only giant multinational corporations are capable of organizing a central management of their finances, the numerous other, multinational corporations are able to move their available funds under the guidance

12. The fact that these uniform practices and rules in employment and commercial contracts draw heavily on the United States legal system is not a problem for lawyers, but for trade-unionists, diplomats, politicians. Lawyers may note, however, that this process brings out the common features and core of competing legal systems and regional and local adjustments which in return influence United States legal practices.

of multinational banks all over the world.

The mass of funds at the disposal of multinationals was evaluated in 1971 at 268 billion dollars; it amounts to twice the volume of world reserves (US $121 billion) that existed at the end of that year. As a consequence, "an independent, largely uncontrolled monetary system has sprung within the world of domestic systems, central banks that manage them . . . and stocks of international reserves used to hold things steady until balance of payment "adjustments" can work themselves out."[13] Here again we find multinational corporations in a position, if not to change the monetary system, to at least install a parallel system. Legal instruments for such development have been multinational corporation practices and decisions on "leads and lags,"[14] intra-multinational corporation payments, contractual terms and conditions and forms provided for by multinational bankers and lawyers to create new international currencies (Euro-dollars, Euro-currencies, or more generally xeno-currencies), and offerings of loans and bond issues in these currencies outside the jurisdiction of national markets proper. Central Banks themselves have contributed to the operation of this parallel international monetary system by lending Euro-currencies through the Bank for International Settlements in Basle.[15]

Another technique for bypassing national jurisdictions, namely, transfer pricing, is available to multinational corporations for various purposes, including the following: to provide investment and cash flow to subsidiaries; to escape exchange controls; to circumvent price controls; to obtain protection against erosion of local currencies; to minimize tax bills and custom duties; and to conquer a given market. Such purposes do not lend themselves to unified practices and may well be contradictory. Moreover transfer pricing is well known to public authorities charged with responsibilities in areas such as customs, tax, anti-trust, exchange and investment controls in most jurisdictions where multinational corporations operate. Arm's-length transactions are

13. Senate Report on Multinationals, *supra* note 11, at 541.

14. Delaying and/or speeding intra-multinational corporation payments in the various countries where the multinationals operate. This technique may be used to transfer funds where they are needed and might not be easily available because of investment controls; to anticipate devaluation or re-evaluation of local currencies.

15. In 1971, European central banks decided not to loan dollars accumulated in reserves deposited with the BIS to commercial banks. At the end of 1971, Mr. Louis Camu, President of the Bank of Brussels, was not quite sure whether the central banks had lived up to their undertaking. *Banque,* Feb. 1972, at 118. Since then these central banks have been much stricter and have loaned most of their excess dollars to the United States Treasury. The general manager of the BIS, Mr. Larre, confirmed in April 1973 in Brussels that this was the case. *Banque,* june 1973, at 538. The "Xeno" dollar currencies market has outlived these restrictions because of dollar accumulation in oil producing countries of the Middle East and Latin America, and in Australia and Brazil.

generally a legal requirement but are not easy to define for purposes of enforcement of the law.

Multinational corporations are thus encouraged to establish a general policy and a set of rules for "inter-company" pricing which will be acceptable to all jurisdictions, and which are based on reasonable criteria. These rules are not publicized, and it is perfectly understandable that they should not be. However, the principles on which they are based are important in that they would provide some sort of a code of good conduct in pricing. If such a code became generally recognized, in each domestic jurisdiction, this would protect multinational corporations against conflicting decisions in the various countries where they operate and would also prevent dubious manipulations in pricing.

This normative activity of multinational corporations demonstrates that, though they are not legal entities as such, but rather groupings of legal entities, they act and operate *de facto* as if they were legal units which overlap several jurisdictions. Law cannot ignore continuing *de facto* situations. In many countries multinational corporations are now considered as single entities for certain purposes (*e.g.*, taxation, custom, anti-trust). However, these countries act independently of and in competition with each other, with all the conflicts, weaknesses and abuses inherent to such lack of coordination.

In the past, permanently structured international relations such as control of epidemics, carriage of mail, telephone and telegraph have been regulated, first by bilateral, then by multilateral treaties, and in certain cases through international organizations. Bilateral treaties are already in force in some economic fields (*e.g.*, taxation and customs). Consultations take place on a regular basis in other fields such as anti-trust. There are indications that the time is ripe for the multinational corporations to appear on the international scene in their own right. However, at this stage only comparatively modest schemes can be put forward. A general agreement on multinationals or chartering the multinational at the international level seems out of the question. An agreement, prepared under the auspices of the Organization for Economic Cooperation and Development (OECD), between the United States, Canada, the European Community, countries members of the Council of Europe, and perhaps Japan, is a possibility.

Under a possible arrangement, the OECD would provide for a secretariat. A list of multinational corporations would be established. It would be mandatory for multinational corporations to register if they possessed certain characteristics. Other multinationals could register voluntarily. Certain information would have to be supplied by listed multinationals. A committee of all States parties to the multinational agreement would, with the assistance of the secretariat, study, on a continuing basis, problems raised by multinational corporations, and would offer solutions. Panels would be organized to hear and report on any dispute between two or more State parties regarding a particular multinational corporation. Multinationals that would be listed would have access to such panels whenever, in a particular case, they were subject to conflicting decisions of two or more States. It remains an open question whether multinationals should have the right to apply to such panel in case of conflict with one State only.

Such system would tend to "internationalize" jurisdiction over multinational corporations; States parties would cooperate in the control and supervision of the multinational. Moreover, common regulations may be necessary in certain fields. To a certain extent, multinational corporations would become "international," in the sense given to this term at the beginning of this article.

PRINCIPLES OF INTERNATIONAL SOCIAL JUSTICE

OSCAR SCHACHTER

Wolfgang Friedmann's profound concern with problems of social justice and his strong support of international efforts on behalf of disadvantaged peoples make it especially fitting to address these related themes in an essay in his honour. His stimulating papers on unjust enrichment, his detailed inquiries into joint ventures and the administration of development aid, his advocacy of equitable sharing of ocean resources, his perceptive studies of international cooperative arrangements—these are not only lasting contributions to legal scholarship but also eloquent testimony of his dedication of the building of a just and decent social order for all peoples.

Although social justice has long been a common and reasonably well understood ideal in national political life, it has not generally been regarded as significantly applicable to the relations among nations or the distribution of resources among them. However in the present decade this is no longer the case. The demands of countries which are poor, weak or specially disadvantaged for measures to overcome their handicaps have become a prominent feature of international assemblies and international law-making. As in the case of analogous demands by disadvantaged groups within national States, the claims advanced in the international forums are usually justified on grounds of a commitment to equality or requirements of equity. These abstract ideals—which can be rhetorically combined in the conception of social justice—have come to be accepted by most countries as legitimate international goals whose meaning and application in particular contexts require further specification. In the process of specification, several concepts have emerged around which concrete grievances and claims can be

OSCAR SCHACHTER is Professor of Law, Columbia University School of Law; Member of the Institut de Droit International; past President of the American Society of International Law; and, former Director of the United Nations General Legal Division, and the United Nations Institute for Training and Research.

Many ideas in this paper and much of the text have been included in the author's book *Sharing the World's Resources* (Columbia University Press, 1977).

grouped. These concepts are often articulated as principles or as rights and duties, a process greatly facilitated by the growing practice of United Nations organs to adopt resolutions recognizing the demands of the developing countries. While the principles expressed in such resolutions generally do not purport to be legal prescriptions, their language and form suggest that governments regard them as *de lege ferenda* and in some cases as evidence of existing law. At any rate, their potential for international law-making whether through treaty or practice, is a significant factor in judging their importance.

In this article I shall discuss five such concepts of international social justice prominently asserted in the United Nations and other international assemblies which are likely to have an important effect on the development of international law and institutions in the next few years. These concepts are:

1. The Responsibility to Assist Needy Countries;
2. Just Prices;
3. World Food Security;
4. The Right to Benefit from Science and Technology;
5. Permanent Sovereignty over Natural Resources.

My aim in this paper is a modest one: to indicate the justification advanced for these concepts, to point out how they have been construed and applied and how they may influence international legal and institutional arrangements in the near future. The paper will be mainly analytical and only occasionally normative or recommendatory but my general bias in favour of a wider sharing of wealth and power will be evident. It seems to me important to clarify ideas and means for moving toward that objective. Moreover in doing so it is essential to consider realistically the conditions required for their acceptance by the principal segments of the international community. If such general acceptance is not achieved the concepts remain no more than vague exhortations or slogans which foster illusions of progress and, in the end, cynicism and apathy.

I. THE RESPONSIBILITY TO ASSIST NEEDY COUNTRIES

The responsibility of the rich countries to improve the lot ot the poor nations may be perceived either as a commonplace, if somewhat hazy, notion affirmed by nearly all countries or as a radical idea demanding the obligatory transfer of resources on a scale considerably beyond present trends. Clearly, in its weak form, responsibility has been accepted, not merely in declarations, but in practice since most of the affluent countries continue to provide assistance to the needy countries year after year.[1] This includes not only direct aid but also assymetrical trade arrangements which involve one-way transfers to poor countries on the basis of need and equity. Such assistance is generally justified by the donor countries on mixed grounds of self-interest and moral or humanitarian duty. At the same time, the donor countries have consistently rejected the proposition that they were under an international juridical obligation to transfer resources directly or through trade preferences. In their view, they have full discretion to determine in what circumstances, to what extent and in what way they would render assistance. Their continued and even predictable behavior in extending aid does not, as they see it, give rise to an obligation of a legal character since it is clearly understood by all that their actions are voluntary.

This position is rarely challenged, though from time to time spokesmen for the poor countries employ the language of law to express their view that aid is a matter of right and not a discretionary act.[2] Some world figures, for example Pope Paul, have taken similar positions.[3] It is perhaps arguable that a consistent practice over years by donor States furnishing assistance in one form or another, coupled with their own assertions of responsibility to do so, should be considered evidence of customary law but that "custom" is itself sufficiently flexible as to include a State's refusal to grant aid to a particular recipient or its decision to reduce the amount of aid. But it can be said that the expressions of responsibility by the Governments of rich countries, backed by continued grants have created a climate of opinion and expectations that tend to support their continuation and in that way, the line between voluntary and obligatory aid has begun to blur.[4] It may still be

1. International Commission on Development, *Partners in Development* ch. 7, tables 15-19 (1969) (the Pearson Report); J. Howe, *The U.S. and the Developing World: Agenda for Action 1974* statistical annexes D (1974). For an annual summary of practice in regard to assistance, see the reports of the United Nations on the review and appraisal of the international development strategy. The first "over-all review and appraisal" appeared in 1973 (U.N. Pub. Sales No. E.73.II.A.6).

2. See, for example, the proposals of developing countries for the draft Charter of the Economic Rights and Duties of States. UNCTAD Working Group on Draft Charter of the Economic Rights and Duties of States, *Reports,* U.N. Docs. TD/B/AC.12/2-4 (1973).

3. Pope Paul VI, *Populorum Progressio* paras. 23, 49 (1967) (Papal Encyclical of March 26, 1967) [hereinafter cited as Papal Encyclical]. See also Robert McNamara, Address to the Board of Governors of the International Bank for Reconstruction and Development, Sept. 25, 1972 [hereinafter cited as McNamara Address]; G. Myrdal, *The Challenge of World Poverty* 368 (1970) [hereinafter cited as Myrdal].

4. As conservative an international lawyer as Sir Gerald Fitzmaurice has referred to an "incipient recognition of an inchoate duty of samaritanism in international relations (aid to underdeveloped countries, etc.)." See his special report to the Institut de Droit International, *The Future of Public International Law* 129 (1973). For discussions of this "twilight zone" see Virally, "La Deuxième Décennie des Nations Unies pour le developpement—Essai d'interprétation para-juridique," 16 *Annuaire Français de Droit*

possible for donors to cut down an aid or introduce limitations of one kind or another but it has become much less likely that they will completely eliminate assistance.

Although the principle of responsibility may be considered as accepted (in the qualified form indicated), the basis and justification for such assistance continue to be highly controversial. Both in donor and recipient countries the question "why foreign aid?" gives rise to a variety of replies. Economists are as likely to differ as are politicians or the general public. The fact that the question has been debated for nearly three decades has not narrowed the differences, though the answers have become more sophisticated and less simplistic.[5] Moreover, with experience, the issues raised have acquired more practical significance. Each answer to the question "why aid?" can now be seen to have implications for the decisions of both donors and recipients and for the general principles that might be agreed on by the entire international community. An attempt to clarify the issues is therefore still of some importance even though the question has been with us a long time. In the brief remarks that follow, I shall point out some of the newer tendencies and their implications for policy. I shall consider first questions raised by the moral and humanitarian justification and second the questions of self-interest.

Notwithstanding the arguments of those who regard assistance as entirely or mainly motivated by self-interest, it is evident that a significant justification in the minds of many in the donor countries is essentially of a moral and humanitarian character.[6] This, I suggest, is not negated by the fact that grounds of self-interest may also be advanced. It would be a very austere moral doctrine that assumes the presence of self-interest precludes a sense of moral and humanitarian responsibility. Moreover, the relative importance of one or the other

---

International 9, 28-33 (1970); Fatouros, "The Participation of the New States in the International Legal Order of the Future," in 1 *The Future of the International Legal Order* 317, 364-368 (R. Falk & C. Black eds. 1969); Lasswell, "The Relevance of International Law to the Development Process," 60 *Proc. Am. Soc'y Int'l L. 1* (1966) Schachter, "The Evolving International Law of Development," 15 *Colum, J. Transnat'l Law 1* (1976).

5. See R. Asher, *Development Assistance in the Seventies* 19-38 (1970) [hereinafter cited as Asher]; "Discussion of Papers by Kenneth Boulding, Martin Pfaff and Chris Economides," in *The Gap between Rich and Poor Nations* 183 (G. Ranis ed. 1972) [the book edited by G. Ranis cited hereinafter as Ranis].

6. See OECD, *Development Co-operation, 1972 Review* (1972); U.S. Commission on International Trade and Investment Policy, *Report to the President on International Economic Policy in an Interdependent World* (1971) [hereinafter cited as *International Economic Policy Report*]; The Brookings Institution, *Reassessing North-South Economic Relations: A Tripartite Report by Thirteen Experts* (1972). For a negative view see T. Sumberg, *Foreign Aid as a Moral Obligation?* (1973); P. Bauer, *Dissent on Development* (1 The Washington Papers No. 10, 1972).

ground varies with cases and circumstances. It is hard to deny, for example, that in some cases, self-interest (whether or not well-founded) is the decisive motivation whereas in other cases, a significant and perhaps dominant element in the public opinion of the donor countries is that the action is called for by moral humanitarian considerations. The latter is probably more, rather than less, common as donor countries have become disillusioned about the direct benefits to them of their aid. There is in fact ample evidence that recipients tend to attribute unfavorable motives to donors and that efforts to utilize aid as a lever to influence recipient's political decisions often have backfired.[7] That experience is no doubt reflected in the fact the appeal in the donor countries increasingly tends to stress the moral tradition and the humanitarian sentiments of the country.

An important practical consequence of this type of justification is that it thrusts into prominence certain problems of moral choice. One such problem, often of great political significance, is whether the duty to assist the poor countries is limited by the needs of the disadvantaged groups in the donor countries themselves. What priority should be given the latter as a matter of morality and self interest? It might be supposed that from a global prespective, there should be no basic difference in moral principle between the needs of nationals and those of foreigners. As the Pope stated in his 1967 Encyclical "the rule which up to now held good for those nearest to us must today be applied to all the needy in the world."[8] Governments, obviously, cannot follow this injunction in its full implication; whatever the moral principle, they are compelled at least for prudential reasons to accord preference to their own nationals. Yet if they were to accord such preference in a full sense and seek to meet the need of their own disadvantaged nationals before aiding others, it is doubtful if in most cases they could justify any significant aid programme or preferences to foreign countries. In actuality, of course donor Governments do not follow the logic of either position; they do not place nationals and non-nationals on the same footing, yet they do provide assistance to foreigners even though that results in some deprivation to their own nationals.

To a certain extent the political costs of reduced benefits within the donor countries are sought to be reduced by maintaining that the national self-interest of the donor country is served by assistance to the

7. J. Nelson, *Aid, Influence and Foreign Policy* (1968); T. Geiger, *The Conflicted Relationship* (1967); J. Fulbright, "Suggested Basic Changes in Foreign Aid Programs," 112 *Congressional Record* 7464 (1966); Church, "A Farewell to Foreign Aid," Wash. Post, Nov. 7, 1971, sec. B at 1. For some highly critical views on the use of aid for political advantages of the donor countries see T. Hayter, *Aid as Imperialism* (1973); T. Mende, *From Aid to Recolonization* (1973) [hereinafter cited as Mende].

8. Papal Encyclical, *supra* note 3, para. 49.

poorer countries and that the losses to the domestic economy or special groups in the donor State are thereby justified by political gains or benefits in trade.[9] That argument thus turns the issue of aid into a question of calculating benefits and costs of the contributing Government, a calculation which may not always result in the conclusion that self-interest is served. Since experience has rather disillusioned donors as to their direct benefits, whether political or economic, a consequence has been to minimize calculated self-interest in aid and to stress the moral and humanitarian justification, but broadened to include "adjustment assistance" to those adversely affected in the donor countries.[10]

There is still another problem of principle raised by the moral justification of aid. If the essential element is the moral or humanitarian obligation to come to the aid of those in need, is it not crucial that the benefits of assistance accrue to the needy—that is, to the people in need? There is of course much evidence that in many countries foreign aid, whether bilateral or multilateral, has barely, if at all, benefited the poor and that the well-to-do and the Government have been the beneficiaries.[11] This has been the case not only where aid has been relatively ineffective in bringing about development but also in the relatively successful cases of countries which have greatly improved their economic base and increased their gross national product. The implications of this have not been lost on the donor countries which have based their aid on a moral duty to help the needy. Some of these countries are now tending to require assurances that their contributions will in fact improve the lot of the poor and achieve that within a reasonably short period. The implication is that aid will be cut off if its benefits do not appreciably reach the truly needy classes in the recipient countries.[12] Thus, social justice within the national economy is linked to international social justice.

However, that conclusion also encounters political and moral ob-

9. See Asher, *supra* note 5, at 27-33; *International Economic Policy Report, supra* note 6.

10. The difficulties of such adjustment assistance in market economies are considered by Robert Shaw. Shaw, "Foreign Investment and Global Labor Adjustments," in *Development Today* 216 (R. Hunter & J. Rielly eds. 1972). See also C. Frank, *Adjustment Assistance: American Jobs and Trade with the Developing Countries* (1973) (Paper 13 of the Overseas Development Council).

11. On unequal income distribution in less developed countries see I. Adelman & C. Morris, *Economic Growth and Social Equity in Developing Countries* (1973), a comprehensive and cogent analysis of the failure of "trickle down" in developing countries and of the concentration of benefits at the upper end of the income spectrum.

12. As Myrdal puts it, the "ordinary man" in the rich countries will ask "Why do they not tax their own rich and reform their own countries before they come to us with the begging bowl?". Myrdal, "The World Poverty Problem," in *Britannica Book of the Year 1972*, at 22, 34 (1972).

jections. Recipient countries, by and large, maintain that their internal economic and social arrangements are to be determined by them alone as sovereign and independent States and that it runs counter to that fundamental tenet to condition assistance on internal changes desired by donors. From this standpoint, their entitlement to aid rests mainly on grounds other than charity to the needy. One such ground might be summed up as the moral debt. The other, more general, is the idea of interdependence and solidarity. I shall consider both briefly.

The idea that there is an entitlement to aid based on a moral debt owed by the affluent countries has been widely advanced by spokesmen for the less developed countries and, in a not insignificant way, by some in the developed world. It has been reflected in various ways in resolutions of United Nations bodies. The thesis rests mainly on the argument that the industrialized countries have exploited the less developed countries, the primary producing countries, by usurping by far the greater share of increased productivity brought about by technology instead of sharing it with their trading partners through lower prices and free movement of labor and capital.[13] In support of this, it is argued that restrictive practices and oligopolistic controls by the industrialized countries kept up prices of industrial products artifically whereas they discriminated against the backward agricultural countries by keeping down prices of primary products and using subsidies and import restrictions to exclude many agricultural products. The terms of trade were thus said to turn against the primary producers.[14] A further point is that colonial rule (and neo-colonial domination) compelled the less developed countries to remain largely suppliers of cheap food and raw materials and consumers of industrial products.

It is not my aim to go into the validity of these arguments except to state that they are debatable. The question of whether rich countries "sell dear to, and buy cheap from," the less developed countries requires a great deal of clarification and analysis before it can be given a meaningful answer.[15] Or, one should say, meaningful answers since a

13. Economides, "Should the Rich Countries Help the Poor? How could they do so?," in Ranis, *suprra* note 5, at 171 [hereinafter cited as Economides]; Mende, *supra* note 7; A. Emmanuel, *L'échange inégal* (1969) [hereinafter cited as Emmanuel]; G. Haberler, *A Survey of International Trade Theory* ch. 4 (1961) [hereinafter cited as Haberler].

14. The United Nations Conference on Trade and Development (UNCTAD) has tended to accept this conclusion as almost axiomatic. See *Final Act, First UNCTAD* principle Seven (1964). The position was asserted in the Report of the Secretary-General of UNCTAD (Raoul Prebisch) entitled *Towards a New Trade Policy for Development* (1964) [hereinafter cited as Prebisch].

15. Haberler, *supra* note 13; Bhagwati, "Trade Policies for Development," in Ranis, *supra* note 5, at 245 [hereinafter cited as Bhagwati]; Statements of Professor Eastman, in "Discussion of Papers by Kenneth Boulding, Martin Pfaff and Chris Economides," in

whole series of questions and a great range of different situations need to be considered. However the belief that there has been unjust enrichment and usurpation by the industrialized countries is widely held in the less developed countries as well as in countries of Marxist ideology and there are appreciable segments of opinion in the other developed countries who assert a similar position. The idea that compensation is owed to the poor therefore plays a not insignificant role in the political positions taken by many Governments and by international assemblies.[16] It is expressed especially in demands for a just price for raw materials (which we shall discuss later) and in support of non-reciprocal trade preferences and aid for industrialization. Its appeal which is strong even in the industrialized countries is attributable not so much to arguments based on history or economic theory, as to the consciousness of the present gap between the rich and poor and the feelings of guilt in those who are relatively well-off. That psychological fact coupled with the resentment and frustrated expectations of the poor has given the limited juridical concept of unjust enrichment a new and wider significance as an international normative principle.

It would be wrong to assume from our discussion of the moral factors that aid is entirely divorced from motives of national interest. Obviously in some cases ties of alliance and specific quid-pro-quos are essential factors. But, as we have already noted, donors have been disillusioned as to the direct value of aid to them; buying support or a favorable political position through aid programmes has too often turned out to be a snare or a delusion. However the national interest of donor countries may also be perceived in wider terms and there are indications that a transformation in the rationale of aid has been taking place in many of the developed countries. The causes of this change are to be found not so much in moral idealism as in the troubles of the industrialized countries. The threat to the supply of energy, inflation and monetary crises, pollution and waste, terrorism are obvious examples of recent phenomena which have brought about an acute awareness of the

---

Ranis, *supra* note 5, at 183, 187-88; M. Atallah, *The Long-Term Movement of the Terms of Trade between Agricultural and Industrial Products* (1958) [hereinafter cited as Atallah].

16. The declaration adopted by the U.N. General Assembly at its sixth special session in May 1974 on the "establishment of a new international economic order" includes as a principle "[t]he right . . . to restitution and full compensation for the exploitation and depletion of . . . natural and . . . other resources of those States," territories and peoples under foreign occupation, alien or colonial domination or apartheid. G.A. Res. 3201, 6 Special Session U.N. GAOR, para. 4f, U.N. Doc. A/RES/3201 (1974) [hereinafter cited as Resolution 3201]. The entire declaration was adopted without vote, though some reservations were expressed by the developed market-economy countries. For analysis of philosophical and juridical assumptions, see O. Schachter, *Sharing the World's Resources* (1977).

limits of wealth and power and a sense of dependence on others. Thus the hard and disagreeable predicaments of advanced societies as well as those of the less developed world have fostered a new consciousness of global interdependence. The metaphors of the "global village" and the "space-ship earth" reflect objective conditions that have begun to create and intensify a sense of common destiny. We find this increasingly voiced in the language of recent United Nations resolutions and in the statements of authoritative spokesmen in rich as well as poor countries.[17]

To convert this new perspective into concrete action is a formidable task in a world of sovereign States and it would be fatuous to assume that an awareness of common interests is sufficient to overcome deep divisions. Yet there are manifestations of emerging international action directed toward improving the lot of the poor and disadvantaged countries which reflect a conception of mutual interests and common responsibility. That conception falls considerably short of requiring a radical modification of sovereign rights or the redistribution of the world's wealth on the basis of need or equity. Yet its thrust is clearly toward a wider sharing of power and wealth and it is to that end that new international norms and mechanisms are being devised in international assemblies. Some examples will now be considered.

II. JUST PRICES

A conspicuous feature of current demands for a more equitable economic order is the idea of "just prices" or more broadly a just relationship of prices.[18] Although the conception of a just price goes

17. See *id.* para. 3; K. Waldheim, *Introduction to the Report of the Secretary-General on the Work of the Organization,* U.N. Doc. A/9601/Add.1 (1974). See also the statements of Pope Paul VI. Papal Encyclical, *supra* note 3. See also Myrdal, *supra* note 3; McNamara Address, *supra* note 3.

18. See Resolution 3201, *supra* note 16, para. 4j; G.A. Res. 3202, 6 Special Session U.N. GAOR* para. 1d, U.N. Doc. A/RES/3202 (1974) [hereinafter cited as Resolution 3202]. Numerous references were made to the problem of just prices and equitable price relationships at the 1974 Special Session of the U.N. General Assembly on Raw Materials and Development [documents issued from the plenary meetings will be identified hereinafter as 1974 Special Session]. See, for example, statement of President Boumédiene of Algeria, in 1974 Special Session, *supra,* at 31-32, 37, U.N. Doc. A/PV 2208 [hereinafter cited as Boumédiene]; statement of J. Amouzegar of Iran, in 1974 Special Session, *supra,* at 103-10, U.N. Doc. A/PV 2209 [hereinafter cited as Amouzegar]; statement of M. Jobert of France, in 1974 Special Session, *supra,* at 36-42, U.N. Doc. A/PV 2209 [hereinafter cited as Jobert]; statement of M. Perez-Guerrero of Venezuela, in 1974 Special Session, *supra,* at 80 *et seq.,* U.N. Doc. A/PV 2213 [hereinafter cited as Perez-Guerrero]; statement of M. Stevens of Sierra-Leone, in 1974 Special Session, *supra,* at 6, U.N. Doc. A/PV 2212 [hereinafter cited as Stevens].

back to medieval philosophy, it has not acquired a generally accepted meaning in either economic or juridical thought and it certainly cannot be regarded as a technical term of art in international economic relations. Yet there is no doubt that the concept of the just price, as well as the closely related notion of a just relationship of prices, expresses political demands that are of considerable importance in the development of new international legal and institutional arrangements. It is particularly interesting to note that the concept which has long played a leading role in the grievances of the poor countries has recently received emphasis in the statements of spokesmen for the industrialized countries faced with the soaring prices of oil and minerals.[19] The idea of linking justice to prices may seem to some to be a vain effort to mingle ethical and economic factors, possibly with overtones of medieval metaphysics, but the political realities cannot be wished away and the demands for fairness and equity in international pricing will have to be faced.

This is not to say that pricing patterns will be determined by abstract considerations of justice or that economic strength will become a minor factor in fixing prices. Obviously governments and companies will continue to seek to maximize their benefits by taking advantage of strong positions and yielding when their positions are weak. Important as this is, it does not exclude the role of non-economic factors particularly as they affect the attitudes and positions of governments in undertaking collaboration and collective action. For one thing their perceptions of injustice as to economic returns generate tensions and demands which lead to political intervention on both a national and international level. On the international level, the necessity to win acceptance of States with diverse interests tends to increase the importance of non-economic factors and particularly in recent times the demand for more equitable distribution of goods in world trade.

It does not seem idle therefore to seek to clarify the conceptions of just prices which appear to be held by government spokesmen in international bodies. I shall attempt to do this largely on the basis of the debates in United Nations bodies which have focussed mainly on the demands of developing countries for a larger share in world trade and on the consequences of rapidly rising prices of raw materials in world trade. In the light of these debates (principally in 1974), we can perceive some of the principal ideas underlying the conception of just prices and their practical implications.

19. Statement of Secretary Kissinger, in 1974 Special Session, *supra* note 18, at 22-26, U.N. Doc. A/PV 2214 [hereinafter cited as Kissinger]; statement of Scheel of the Federal Republic of Germany, in 1974 Special Session, *supra* note 18, at 56-57, U.N. Doc. A/PV 2209; statement of Ennals of the United Kingdom, in 1974 Special Session, *supra* note 18, at 117, U.N. Doc. A/PV 2209 [hereinafter cited as Ennals].

In this analysis, it will be apparent that ideas of a fair price are largely addressed to specific and well-known grievances and that little effort is made in the political debates to formulate definitions of a theoretical kind. However, definitions are implicit in the arguments and it may help to clarify the issues by distinguishing the various senses in which the conception of just price is employed.

One such sense of the term is, of course, the classic economists' notion of the market price based on free trade and comparative advantage. (This, interestingly, is similar to the dominant medieval notion of the just price as one reached through free bargaining and full knowledge).[20] Within international bodies this conception receives implicit support in the attack made on restrictive practices and monopolistic or oligópolistic conditions. A widely-held thesis is that the international pricing of industrial products involves collusive practices, based on cartel arrangements and multinational company practices in restraint of free competition.[21] In contrast, it is maintained that agricultural products and raw materials are marketed under conditions of nearly perfect competition and often face discrimination in the markets of the industrialized world.[22] As we shall see below, recent developments in respect of petroleum and minerals have altered this thesis in some respects and have raised the issue of restraints on trade in an entirely different political context. However, the principal thrust against "monopolistic" and collusive arrangements is directed toward the industrial goods rather than primary products and against the private sector rather than governments. The pricing and restrictive agreements made by the governments of countries producing raw materials have been justified by most of the developing countries as necessary defensive measures which help to achieve a more equitable balance in the terms of trade.[23]

A somewhat related but more complex proposition asserts that the

20. Albertus Magnus and Thomas Aquinas were the leading proponents of this position. See de Roover, "Ancient and Medieval Thought," in 4 *Int'l Encyclopedia of Social Sciences* 430, 433 (D. Sills ed. 1968). For a detailed study see J. Baldwin, *The Medieval Theories of the Just Price* (1959).

21. See, for example, statement of the representative of Liberia, in 1974 Special Session, *supra* note 18, at 13-15, U.N. Doc. A/PV 2209; Stevens, *supra* note 18; statement of the representative of Peru, in 1974 Special Session, *supra* note 18, U.N. Doc. A/PV 2213; statement of the representative of Saudi Arabia, in 1974 Special Session, *supra* note 18, at 31, U.N. Doc. A/PV 2217.

22. References cited note 21 *supra*. See also Economides, *supra* note 13; Prebisch, *supra* note 14.

23. See Boumédienne, *supra* note 18, at 18-20; statement of the representative of Iraq, in 1974 Special Session, *supra* note 18, at 16, U.N. Doc. A/PV 2217; statement of the representative of Zambia, in 1974 Special Session, *supra* note 18, at 101-02, U.N. Doc. A/PV 2211. In UNCTAD, see the note by the Secretary-General, Mr. Corea, to the Board of Trade and Development, U.N. Doc TD/B (XIV)/Misc. 3 (1974).

structural features of the world economy tend toward a deterioration of the terms of trade against primary producers.[24] The terms of trade can be summarized as the index of the average price of a country's exports in terms of the average price of its imports. The gist of this analysis is that capital and technology are relatively scarce and therefore command an increasing economic rent which redounds to the benefit of the industrialized countries whereas the producers of agricultural goods and raw materials face competitive conditions and inelastic demand. Whether there has been a long-run downward trend in terms of trade of primary product is a matter of controversy among economists.[25] United Nations bodies have continued to treat the proposition as amply confirmed, though some historical studies and the rise in commodity prices in the past decade tend to throw doubt on its validity.[26] Even so, it seems clear that at least in recent years many of the less developed countries have been adversely affected by high costs in food, fertilizers and manufactures which they import from the developed countries. This is especially evident for the large group of countries with insufficient resources or with highly unfavourable demographic conditions, as in the Indian sub-continent, who have been severely prejudiced by such rising prices of imports without any equivalent rise in their export prices.[27] These current trends in price relationship which are particularly injurious to many poor countries though not all, have an important bearing on the complex idea of a just relationship between prices of goods bought and those sold.

They support the conclusion that just prices cannot be equated with market prices and that in many situations the desirable objective of an equitable relationship between prices of goods sold and bought can only be achieved by manipulating prices for the benefit of the less developed countries or providing for other compensatory arrangements. This seems quite clearly to be the position adopted by the United Nations, as indicated in recent resolutions.[28] It is not, of course, inconsistent with the view that monopolistic restraints and restrictive business practices

24. See G. Haberler, *A Survey of International Trade Theory* ch. 4 (1961); Haberler, "Terms of Trade and Economie Development," in *Economic Development for Latin America* 275 (Ellis & Wallich eds. 1961); see Emmanuel, *supra* note 13, for an analysis based on Marxist theory of value.

25. Many economists doubt that there has in fact been a downward trend in the terms on which primary products exchange with manufactures. For example see Atallah, *supra* note 15; Bhagwati, *supra* note 15.

26. Reports of the U.N. Secretary-General on the evolution of basic commodity prices since 1950 (U.N. Docs. A/9544, April 2, 1974 and A/9544 Add. 1, April 4, 1974).

27. Resolution 3202, *supra* note 18, notes that the countries which are most seriously affected by high prices are the least developed, the land-locked and those with low per capita income. A list of criteria of needs is set forth in part X of the resolution.

28. See *id.* Programme of Action, pt. I (on raw materials and primary commodities).

should be eliminated but it clearly implies a conception of the just price that is different from the ideal market price. It might be defined as the price necessary to cover the costs of production, including social costs of minimum welfare and development. The practical implication of this position in the present international situation is that concessionary arrangements, through prices or otherwise, are necessary to bring about equitable price relationships for the poorer countries. In effect this means a one-way transfer of resources to the poor countries and therefore subsumes the case for just prices under the general principle of responsibility to assist the more needy countries. Under that principle, the requirement of concessionary arrangements or direct aid should be applicable not only to industrialized countries but to some non-industrialized resource-rich countries which sell vital resources to the poor countries at relatively high prices.[29]

This last observation leads us to the highly controversial problem of just and fair prices for natural resource products, notably petroleum, natural gas and minerals, which enjoy a strong market position and have had spectacular price increases in the last few years. Not all raw materials are in this category and the weaker primary products present different problems of international pricing. However, as we shall suggest below, international solutions may require action on a range of commodities to obtain general acceptance and to achieve the objective of a just relationship between prices. Before discussing such solutions, I shall briefly summarize the issues of equity and justice that have been raised by the price rises of the strong commodities in the field of natural resources. My present concern with equity and justice does not of course imply that I consider the market and other economic factors (and in some respects political power) as of lesser importance. On the contrary, the issues of equity are raised in an economic and political context that sets the critical limits for choices. But it is also true that ethical and social values are involved and that attitudes as to what is fair and just create tensions and may influence choices.

As seen by the producing countries the equitable justification for the price increases of their natural resource products rests on several grounds, ranging from the moral "debt" for past exploitation to the obligation to meet the needs of future generations. What might be called the historical argument maintains that for several decades the importing countries through coercion had set prices at so low a figure that they usurped the lion's share of the economic rent of the natural resource. With the recent change in relative strength, arising from a combination of political, economic and technological factors, the

29. See, for example, statement of the representative of Kenya, in 1974 Special Session, *supra* note 18, at 8-10, U.N. Doc. A/PV 2224; statement of the representative of Thailand, in 1974 Special Session, *supra* note 18, at 47-50, U.N. Doc. A/PV 2220.

producing countries have been able to reverse the situation and obtain redress for past exploitation.[30] To have refrained from the exercise of their economic power would, in their view, have been to perpetuate the unjust relationship of the past. An answer to this line of argument, particularly as expressed by the companies and consumers of the purchasing countries, is that the technology and capital brought in by the importing countries made exploration and production possible and therefore were entitled to a commensurate share of the economic rent.[31] The issue thus joined has generated considerable emotion and rhetoric though it does not lead to any new solutions. As we shall see, the other equitable issues appear to be more suggestive of constructive action.

A second equitable justification advanced by the producers is that they have been faced with rapidly rising costs of imported goods and therefore that they were entitled on the basis of increased demand to raise their prices to keep pace with inflationary trends in industrial countries.[32] Although this line of reasoning has not been entirely persuasive to the consumers who compared the soaring prices of oil with lesser price increases of other goods, it has had an appeal to many of the poorer countries which have been especially hard hit by increases in their imports of manufactures, fertilizers, grains and other commodities. The argument has served to underline the importance of a balanced movement in price relationships and the linkages between various commodities. These factors have emerged as significant elements in the efforts for new international measures.

A third line of justification by the producers of petroleum and some other minearls is that the high prices operate to bring about a more rational use and allocation of relatively scarce energy resources, both for the present and future generations.[33] The thesis has cogency, particularly in the light of rapidly growing demands for energy and the consequential need to expand existing resources and to create feasible new sources. Without entering into the statistical data, there is good reason to believe that a relatively high plateau of prices will further more rational and less wasteful consumption and that it will almost certainly result in an appreciable acceleration of research, exploration and development of conventional and novel sources of energy.[34] While

30. See statements cited note 23 *supra*.

31. For a sophisticated discussion of this issue see R. Mikesell, *Foreign Investment in Petroleum and Mineral Industries* 435-36 (1971).

32. See Boumédiene, *supra* note 18; Amouzegar, *supra* note 18; Perez-Guerrero, *supra* note 18.

33. References cited note 32 *supra*. See also the statement of the representative of Indonesia, in 1974 Special Session, *supra* note 18, at 49-50, U.N. Doc. A/PV 2214.

34. See Amouzegar, *supra* note 18. See also the report of the OECD's Long-Term Energy Assessment summarized in "First Results of OECD's Long-term Energy Assessment," *OECD Observer*, June 1974, at 7.

this may be regarded as an economic justification, it also has an important element of equity since the welfare of disadvantaged peoples (as well as the unborn) requires the growth of productive capacity on a massive scale and this need may be accorded a higher priority in terms of justice than the losses involved in short-term dislocations and higher prices of consummers in affluent countries.

There are, of course, arguments of an equitable character against the price increases. As we have already noted, those increases have caused severe deprivations for many disadvantaged countries, most seriously in affecting fertilizer production and in consequence, food supply.[35] This has been a widely-recognized inequity of the sudden increase in oil prices and remedial measures have been undertaken but remain inadequate. A two-tier pricing system, with lower prices for the most disadvantaged countries, has not been acceptable to producers, nor commended by economists, and it seems clear that the relief must be sought through direct assistance and investments rather than through discriminatory pricing.[36]

It has also been argued by industrialized countries that the scale of oil price rises has produced a substantial risk of precipitating a world-wide depression which could have devastating consequences for nearly all countries including the producing countries.[37] Both the inflationary effect (adding to other forces) and the adverse consequences on balance of payments of importing countries create expectations of defensive measures that threaten reduce world trade, create massive unemployment, and lower production. Although this, too, is an economic argument, it presents questions as to the equities in bearing the costs and sacrifices that are involved in meeting the problems. The petroleum-producing countries have acknowledged their self-interest in avoiding a depression and have stressed the potential benefits of recycling their enlarged funds to productive use in their own and other countries.[38] International emergency programes for the poor countries and for the especially disadvantaged industrialized countries have been proposed and undertaken but thus far on a relatively modest scale and

35. UNCTAD, *The Impact of Recent and Prospective Price Changes on the Trade of Developing Countries,* U.N. Doc. UNCTAD/OSG/52/Add. 1 (1974).

36. See statement of the representative of New Zealand, in 1974 Special Session, *supra* note 18, at 56, U.N. Doc. A/PV 2211; statement of the representative of Kenya, in 1974 Special Session, *supra* note 18, at 8-10, U.N. Doc. A/PV 2224.

37. See President Gerald Ford's address to the U.N. General Assembly, in 1974 Special Session, *supra* note 18, U.N. Doc. A/PV 2234. See also Kissinger, *supra* note 19; statement of the representative of Hungary, in 1974 Special Session, *supra* note 18, at 27, U.N. Doc. A/PV 2213; statement of the representative of Italy, in 1974 Special Session, *supra* note 18, U.N. Doc. A/PV 2218; Ennals, *supra* note 19.

38. See Amouzegar, *supra* note 18. See also Levy, "World Oil Cooperation or International Chaos," 52 *Foreign Affairs* 690, 712 (1974).

less than adequate to meet the requirements. Some hope for more positive action may be found in the increased awareness in both rich and poor countries that inflation and recession endanger their social order and that the network of interdependencies demand international solutions. There is, also, a greater recognition of the need to meet considerations of justice and equity as well as economic requirements if international solutions are to be generally acceptable.

Some such international measures have already been alluded to in the previous comments but it may be appropriate to indicate briefly the principal lines of approach which seem feasible for international action in the near future. It will be seen that the measures suggested all involve the application or development of legal concepts and principles and the creation of new international procedures for their implementation.

One line of action would be concerted measures to eliminate or reduce restrictive practices by companies and cartels, whether private or public. It will be recalled that an effort of that kind aborted in the still-born Havana Charter of 1948.[39] In recent years however renewed attempts have been made under the United Nations to identify undesirable practices (such as territorial allocations, restrictive licensing provisions, transfer pricing policies, cartel arrangements) which have significantly adverse effects for developing countries and these efforts suggest the need for international guide-lines and possibly eventually a code of impermissible practices.[40] Presumably implementation would have to be left largely to national legislation and enforcement but that might be supplemented by international inquiry and consultation procedures. The concern over multinational companies and the recent developments in regional groups (such as the European Economic Community and the Andean group) tent to encourage the emergence of a new political consensus in favor of a continued international effort against restrictive practices. Although the producers associations in the developing countries fall into a special category and are strongly supported within the international bodies, suggestions have been made by various countries in both the developed and developing world that these associations should also conform to international standards directed against restraints on supply and trade of a discriminatory character.[41] There is reason to believe that this could more readily be

39. Havana Charter for an International Trade Organization, March 24, 1948, *reprinted in* U.S. Dept. of State, *Havana Charter for an International Trade Organization* 23 (1948); see United Nations Conference on Trade and Employment, *Final Act and Related Documents,* U.N. Doc. E/CONF. 2/78 (1948).

40. UNCTAD Committee of Experts on Restrictive Business Practices in Relations to the Trade and Development of Developing Countries, *Report,* U.N. Doc. TD/B/C.2/119 (1973) [hereinafter cited as Restrictive Business Practices Report].

41. See Gardner, "The Hard Road to World Order," 52 *Foreign Affairs* 556, 566 (1974). See also statement of the representative of the Philippines, in 1974 Special Session, *supra* note 18, at 66, U.N. Doc. A/PV 2221; statement of the representative of Italy, in 1974 Special Session, *supra* note 18, at 23-26, U.N. Doc. A/PV 2218.

achieved through separate arrangements on a commodity basis than through general rules but the acceptability of particular arrangements would be influenced not only by the specific quid-pro-quos by both sides but also in some degree by the general climate of opinion manifested in principles relating to restrictive and oligopolistic practices. The subject calls for extensive international study and consultation.

A second category of measures would be multilateral commodity arrangements which are aimed at achieving stability for a particular commodity or perhaps a class of related commodities. Such commodity arrangements have traditionally been addressed to situations of price instability which were particularly hard on the producers of primary commodities.[42] No doubt it is still easier to begin with these weak commodities. However, even for the strong commodities high prices and interruptions in supply tend to make it economically feasible for buyers to exploit alternative sources and also for producers to expand the scale of production of the commodity in question or substitutes for it. As a consequence, producing countries of some strong commodities might gain from international arrangements which would be directed toward slowing the upward trend of the development of new sources and the downward trend in the need for old sources. Apart from this factor, both sides have an interest in smoothing out the heights and depths in commodity prices and production which affect all producers and consumers and in an arrangement which would achieve a flexible adaptation to supply and demand.[43] International market regulation for these purposes requires a set of procedures for exchange of information and consultation on conditions which determine the price of the commodity in question (as, for example, supply and demand, stocks and reserves, replacement costs and feasibility of replacement). It would also require agreement on procedures for negotiations based, to the extent possible, on agreed criteria for assuring a flow of supply and a reasonable return to producers. In some cases, buffer stocks may be a critical feature of the arrangement. Under commodity agreements with adequate information on market conditions and costs available to both sides a negotiated price might be as close to a "just" price as one could expect in international trade.

The impact of inflation on the poorer countries has given impetus to proposals for an international price indexing system under which increases in price of the imported goods into the poor countries would be matched by increases in their export price. In effect, this would constitute an extension to the international level of such national techniques as parity pricing schemes in agriculture and cost-of-living

42. See 2 UNCTAD, *Proceedings, The Development of International Commodity Policy,* U.N. Doc. TD/113 (1973).

43. See the report of the Secretary-General of UNCTAD to the Sixth Special Session of the General Assembly, U.N. Doc. TD/B/488 (1974).

clauses in wage contracts. Ideally a general system of price indexation should be attractive to both developed and developing countries particularly in the light of the widespread inflation, but its practical implementation on a world scale is a formidable undertaking under present political and economic conditions. Indexation may however prove viable for a limited number of commodities in world trade.[44] They would probably have to be commodities whose supply could be controlled as for example by buffer stocks, production regulation, or export controls depending on the particular commodity. Such supply control can be more easily achieved for commodities with relatively price-inelastic demand. International commodity agreements would be the preferred instruments for indexation arrangements but long-term contracts and producers associations may also be used in some cases. Proponents of indexing claim that by reducing short-term instability of prices, it could bring about an improved international allocation of resources and might lead to a more economical use of non-renewable resources. It has also been noted that indexation of primary commodity prices may provide a stimulus to the developed market countries to reduce their rates of domestic inflation since the prices of their commodity imports would decline as a result of reductions in the prices of their export goods. However there may also be rigidities of the price structure casued by indexation which need to be counteracted, but these are not believed to create serious difficulties provided the price structure is kept under review.

The term "indirect" or "passive" indexation has also been devised to refer to arrangements for financial transfers from developed importing countries to developing exporting countries designed to compensate them for adverse movements in the flow of trade. As proposed such compensatory transfers would be made on a country basis; they would be automatic, on shortfalls from agreed export norms and on satisfaction of other agreed criteria.[45] It is maintained that this type of indirect indexation would be a necessary supplement to direct indexation since the latter could, as we indicated, only be used for a limited number of commodities.

A much more modest step would be the establishment of a world economic monitoring center under the aegis of the United Nations which would make world markets more "transparent".[46] Such tran-

44. See UNCTAD studies on the indexation of prices in U.N. Doc. TD/B/503, Aug. 6, 1974; U.N. Doc. TD/B/503/Supp. 1, July 30, 1974; U.N. Doc. TD/B/503/Supp. 1/Add. 1, July 5, 1974.

45. A somewhat related scheme of the International Monetary Fund provides for compensatory financing to compensate for shortfalls in exports, but this is in the form of short-term repayable loans.

46. A proposal to this effect was made by the Foreign Minister of France. Jobert, *supra* note 18.

sparency could be attained by recording prices and publishing "a weighted mean price, as a world reference known and agreed to by all",[47] for every commodity in world trade. It is hoped by its sponsors that international action of this kind leading to a comprehensive global economic intelligence system on commodity prices would in itself help to bring about a balance between prices of raw materials and industrial products and facilitate international regulatory machinery for a range of commodities. The fact that various proposals for market regulation including indexation were made by governments of developed and developing countries in the United Nations suggests that new types of price-control arrangements will be explored. Whether they can be achieved probably depends on the threat, or the actuality, of world depression and severe inflation.[48] At any rate, it seems almost certain that the demand for a just relationship of prices will remain in the forefront of international concern and that the search for solutions will extend to the development of new legal concepts and mechanisms on the lines indicated above.

III. WORLD FOOD SECURITY

The problem of providing food to those in need may be seen as a special case of the general responsibility to extend aid to the disadvantaged. However, food security has distinctive aspects which raise rather more sharply than other subjects problems of a normative character that merit discussion. It seems incredible that the age-old gulf between the well-fed and the starving still persists despite miracle grains and advanced technology for agriculture. The response to famine has been nearly always too little and too late to alleviate large-scale starvation. The shortage of water, the creeping "desertification", soil erosion, vulnerable monocultures and other threats to food supply indicate continued and probably greater shortages. The growth of population and the trend toward food consumption at the higher levels of the food chain (that is, in animal protein) represent further dangers. The countries most endangered are those which are otherwise most adversely affected by present trends - particularly, countries with severe population pressures (the Indian subcontinent) and lacking in sufficient resources or technology to exploit those which exist. For these countries, an adequate supply of food demands more than the usual trade arrangements, even on a concessionary basis and with "just" prices. Nor

47. *Id.* See also Perez-Guerrero, *supra* note 18.

48. The threat of inflation and particularly high oil prices and the danger of world depression were strongly stressed by President Ford in his address to the World Energy Conference in which he called for a "global strategy" of international cooperation in regard to energy and resources. N.Y. Times, Sept. 24, 1974, at 12, col. 2.

can their needs be met by the customary forms of transfer of technology or technical co-operation. Adequate food supplies to meet the large-scale threat of famine may only be provided if the more prosperous countries make changes in their agricultural policy and probably also in their dietary patterns.[49]

That is why the problem of food, more than any other, involves acceptance of a common responsibility that rests on a sense of global community. For one cannot easily base the requisite action on economic trade-offs beneficial to both sides. It requires a long-range conception of global needs and solidarity that extends beyond national interests as they are generally perceived. The idea of a common responsibility for meeting food needs has been formulated and accepted in general terms by the governments of the world in recent assemblies and conferences. On the basis of that responsibility, subsidiary principles have been proposed together with multinational institutional mechanisms for their implementation. Thus we can now discern the main elements of an emerging global mechanism which would include a set of new norms and co-operative procedures designed to eliminate or substantially reduce the risk of starvation and widespread malnutrition.

One of the central features of that scheme is an undertaking by the countries of the world to build up and maintain national stocks of cereals including reserves on the basis of internationally determined requirements.[50] The Food and Agriculture Organization would assess world needs and supplies and it would lay down guidelines for the reserves to be maintained by all countries, not only for their own domestic needs but also for export to others in case of crop failure or national disaster.[51] These actions would be supported by procedures for consultation on the adequacy of national stocks of grain and as to required action to meet any difficulty. To give these collective efforts an adequate factual foundation, the countries would undertake to furnish information on crop conditions, stock levels and prospective exports and imports. In addition, a whole series of international measures would be taken to assist countries, especially in the developing world. This would include, particularly, expansion of fertilizer production,

49. United Nations World Food Conference, *Assessment of the World Food Conference,* "Assessment of the World Food Situation," section II, U.N. Doc. E/CONF.65/3 (1974) [hereinafter cited as World Food Report]. See also Brown & Eckholm, "Food: Growing Global Insecurity," in *The United States and the Developing World: Agenda for Action 1974* (J.W. Howe ed. 1974).

50. An international undertaking on world food security was endorsed in principle by the Council of the Food and Agriculture Organization at its 63d Session in July 1974, and was reaffirmed by the World Food Conference in November 1974. For the text of the undertaking (as proposed to the World Food Conference) see U.N. Doc. E/CONF.65/4 (1974), at 177-81 [hereinafter cited as Food Conference Undertaking].

51. *Id.* at 178.

improvement of water supply, and technical assistance in all phases of agriculture.[52]

A system of food security based on reserves would also benefit the developed countries. The creation of reserves could be used to promote stability and moderate wide swings in prices and supplies in those countries.[53] The existence of reserve stocks governed by international negotiation could help in reducing agricultural protectionism (by lowering assumed requirements of sufficiency) and liberalize trade in agriculture to the benefit of the poorer countries. These are highly complex matters in actuality and one should not overestimate the importance of a scheme of national reserves to meet the likely scarcities in food. But the acceptance of a general responsibility to meet the needs of the food-deficit countries is at least a step toward a whole series of international actions that may serve the national interests of the developed countries as well as those of the poorer areas.

However, to attain "world food security", it seems essential to go far beyond a scheme of reserves toward a restructuring of agriculture on a world scale. The wide use of agricultural support systems imposes high costs on consumers without significantly providing means for modernizing agricultural production. Moreover, the necessity for technology and capital in agriculture (especially in new and less productive areas) also means that food crops are increasingly more costly, with adverse consequences for small producers as well as for consumers. In addition, recent events reveal ecological deterioration resulting from the infusion of technology in agriculture which, has not been adapted to local conditions and needs. The inter-relationship of these various factors - technology, ecology, markets and prices, social organization - are still not fully understood but it is clear that improvements in food production on a world scale require policies and measures that take account of the linkages. The problem of food scarcities can no longer be solved by technical specialists working on fragmented segments of the total task. It is for this reason that international structures need to be adapted (or created) for multidimensional assessment and prescription.[54] They should be in a position to discern and evaluate the variety of conditioning factors and goals, to clarify the trade-offs involved in action and to suggest combinations of social mechanisms that might be employed. This is not to say that disaster relief is unimportant or that technical assistance should be dropped; they both have an essential place in meeting the continuous threat of famine. But the effort to achieve minimal food security requires a far more complex in-

52. See World Food Report, *supra* note 49, at 267-323.

53. See Food Conference Undertaking, *supra* note 50, at 199-207.

54. *Id.* at 219-37.

ternational effort whose dimensions we are only just beginning to perceive.

IV. THE RIGHT TO BENEFIT FROM SCIENCE AND TECHNOLOGY

The claims of the less developed States to the fruits of science and technology has been increasingly emphasized in international assemblies. While this may be considered a special case of assistance to those in need, it also reflects the idea that scientific knowledge and technology are common property of mankind and that all peoples should have access to such knowledge and the opportunity to develop the skills to use it. The industrialized States may not be prepared to agree to a formal recognition of a right to technology but they appear to accept, in principle at least, an obligation to facilitate access to and transfer of technology to the less developed world.

But the fact remains that by and large technology is not a commodity like others which can be freely purchased in open markets. There are restraints on transfer that are deeply imbedded in the economic and legal conditions governing the operation of the enterprises (whether private or public) that actually control the most important sectors of technology relevant to development.[55] Moreover, the disparities in social systems, education, skill and values between donor and recipient countries give rise to constraints and ambivalences that inhibit the transplanting of techniques and lead to feelings of frustration and exploitation by would-be recipients.[56]

The general objective of facilitating transfer through international action can be broken down into the following four tasks

1) to assist the recipient countries in developing their capabilities for appraisal and selection of appropriate technology (which may be very different from advanced technology);

2) to reduce the restraints imposed by patents and other forms of industrial property restrictions;

3) to facilitate access to the large amount of technology in the public domain;

4) to facilitate transfers by multinational companies under

55. See W. Chudson, *The International Transfer of Commercial Technology to Developing Countries* (UNITAR Research Report No. 13, 1971); J. Baranson, *International Transfer of Automotive Technology to Developing Countries* (UNITAR Research Report No. 8, 1971); *The Technology Factor in International Trade* (R. Vernon ed. 1970).

56. UNCTAD Intergovernmental Committee on Transfer of Technology, *Report,* U.N. Doc. TD/B/424 (1973).

arrangements that would leave to the recipient the major decisions concerning production and distribution.

The idea of a code of conduct for technology transfer has been proposed by representatives of the developing countries and efforts toward this end are now under way in the United Nations.[57] In addition to stating general objectives a code would set standards defining obligation of suppliers and recipients with the aim of strengthening the bargaining position of the developing countries. Some examples of provisions that have been suggested as obligations of the supplier include:[58] (1) informing the recipient of and supplying him with all improvements to the technology involved during the period of the agreement; (2) providing adequate training to indigenous personnel in the operation of a technology; (3) assuring delivery of spare parts and capital goods required during an agreed period of time; (4) the automatic extension of more favourable terms to prior licensees if granted in subsequent licenses.

It has also been suggested that the code of conduct provide for preferential treatment to developing countries as, for example, scaling down the charges for technology in proportion to the size of the recipient's market and providing untied credit for the purchase of components, spare parts and other goods needed for use of the technology. The code would also include standards of behaviour for the recipient as for example a duty to maintain quality standards where the supplier's trademark or name is used. Its proponents suggest that the code might be adopted by the United Nations initially as a set of guidelines and eventually as an international agreement. Implementation would be left to national action but international investigation and discussion would be utilized to assist in bringing about compliance.

Apart from the elaboration of the code, it is proposed that institutional steps be taken to strengthen the capability of recipient countries to select and negotiate for technology and to obtain the requisite information through international agencies. Another task of practical importance is to identify or create agencies which can be used to mobilize the various elements (*e.g.* financial, labour, engineering) which are required for effective transplantation of technology in a less

57. UNCTAD Intergovernmental Group on the Transfer of Technology, Third Session, *Report* paras. 95-127, U.N. Doc. TD/B/520 (1974). Resolution 3202, *supra* note 18, also called for an international code of conduct for the transfer of technology to meet needs of the developing countries.

58. A draft code (U.N. Doc. TD/B/AC.11/L.12) prepared by a working group of the Pugwash Conference was circulated to the UNCTAD Intergovernmental Group. References in the text to proposed provisions are drawn from this draft.

developed country. Still another and more general task to which we have previously referred is the elimination of restrictive practices which limit the use of the transferred technology as for example through import and export restrictions, limitations on sub-licensing or production allocation arrangements within companies.[59]

Although the wider dissemination of science and technology is desired by the less developed countries, they have also displayed concern that scientific research and technical fact-finding may be detrimental to their interests, particularly when it involves access to data about their resources. This concern has taken the form of claims of sovereign rights to impose limits on scientific activity involving their resources. Some of the developing countries have maintained that oceanographic research in adjacent coastal resource zone (economic or patrimonial zones) beyond the territorial sea should require prior consent of the coastal State and compliance with its conditions.[60] To the great concern of the ocean scientific community, that new position seems likely to receive wide support. It may be that a less stringent solution would emerge under which the requirement of advance consent would be dropped in return for obligations by the researcher to safeguard coastal interests. This might include advance notification, coastal State participation, sharing of data and samples with the coastal State and assistance to the coastal State in assessing the implications of the research for its interests. A system of sharing would seem to meet the interests of both researcher and coastal State.

A similar claim of sovereign rights has been asserted in regard to information obtained by the earth resource satellites which photograph the territory of States from outer space. Several of the countries photographed have asserted that the photographs and data should not be made available to any third party,[61] objecting to the present policy of the United States under which the information obtained by its satellites is made freely available to all. A treaty has been proposed to safeguard this new variant of an international right of privacy and it seems probably that it will be favoured by many of the countries involved. The concern of developing countries that outsiders will take advantage of the availability of data about their resources and utilize it to their prejudice does not seem to rest on any specific evidence that this has occurred but it reflects a fear that access to information on resources could in the future be employed for commercial or military advantage. The developed countries which may derive some benefit from knowledge of agricultural or mineral resources in the less developed

59. Restrictive Business Practices Report, *supra* note 40.

60. See Stevenson & Oxman, "The Preparations for the Law of the Sea Conference," 68 *Am. J. Int'l L.* 1, 28-30 (1974).

61. U.N. Committee on the Peaceful Uses of Outer Space, *Report by Working Group on Remote Sensing of the Earth by Satellites* para. 80, U.N. Doc. A/AC.105/125 (1972).

countries would probably favour having all such data in the public domain, though they would not be prepared to do that in respect of their own patented technology. It still seems a long way to realization of the ideal of free dissemination of scientific and technological information.

V. PERMANENT SOVEREIGNTY OVER NATURAL RESOURCES

No normative principle has been more vigorously asserted by the less developed countries in recent years than that of "permanent sovereignty over natural resources", a concept generally defined by its proponents as the "inalienable" right of each State to the full exercise of its authority over its natural wealth and the correlative right to dispose of its resources fully and freely.[62] For many developing countries this right is regarded as an essential condition of their national independence and of their ability to decide on their basic political and economic arrangements. The main thrust of the demand for permanent sovereignty, both in rhetoric and in practice, has been to justify the nationalization of foreign firms or their transfer of ownership to nationals of the host countries especially in the extractive industries. In its strong form the principle is asserted to legitimize the refusal of States to submit to international standards or international tribunals disputes relating to nationalization or other take-overs.[63] In a somewhat weaker form, the concept of permanent sovereignty serves to provide justification for a variety of national measures which impose limits and duties on foreign firms, as for example, requiring them to employ nationals of the country in managerial capacities, to meet local supply needs first, to give up repatriation of profits, and to renegotiate contracts prior to their agreed expiry.[64] On the international level, the

62. G.A. Res. 1803, 17 U.N. GAOR Supp. 17, at 15, U.N. Doc. A/5217 (1962); G.A. Res. 3016, 27 U.N. GAOR Supp. 30, at 48, U.N. Doc. A/8730 (1972); G.A. Res. 2692, 25 U.N. GAOR Supp. 28, at 63, U.N. Doc. A/8028 (1970); Resolution 3201, *supra* note 16, para. 4e; Resolution 3202, *supra* note 18, section VIII.

63. Resolution 3201, *supra* note 16, refers to "the right to nationalization or transfer of ownership to its nationals, this right being an expression of the full permanent sovereignty of the State." It adds: "No State may be subjected to economic, political or any other type of coercion to prevent the free and full exercise of this inalienable right." *Id.* Representatives of the market industrialized countries expressed their reservations to this clause, laying stress on the requirements of international law with respect to the grounds of nationalization and the obligation to pay compensation.

64. Summaries of national measures can be found in a series of reports by the Secretary-General on Permanent Sovereignty over National Resources. See, *e.g.*, U.N. Doc. E/5425 (1973); U.N. Doc. E/5170 (1972); U.N. Doc. A/9716 (1974) [hereinafter cited as U.N. Doc. A/9716]. For discussions of problems of national control see R. Vernon, *Sovereignty at Bay* (1971); Fatouros, "The Computer and the Mud Hut: Notes on Multinational Enterprise in Developing Countries," 10 *Colum. J. Transnat'l L.* 325 (1971).

principle of permanent sovereignty has become the focal normative conception used by States to justify their right to exercise control over production and distribution arrangements without being hampered by the international law of State responsibility as it had been traditionally interpreted by the capital exporting countries.[65]

It is not denied that the national measures of control and expropriation may have the effect of impeding foreign investment and in that way, contributing to the economic handicaps of the poorer States. On the other hand, in many cases the hard reality of the need for capital and technology brings about agreements based on quid pro quos satisfactory to both sides and giving the foreign investor at least a short-range assurance of an adequate return on and recovery of his investments. Consequently, the actual significance of the concept of permanent sovereignty in reducing economic inequality can be determined only in the context of particular cases and the rather complicated circumstances of each national economy. But it is plain enough that the emphasis placed on that concept by almost the entire community of have-not States reveals their concern over the economic penetration by the transnational companies.[66] Such economic penetration is considered in many cases as a threat to internal measures of social justice, income distribution, or greater participation of disadvantaged groups in the national political process.[67] It should also be noted that several of the industrialized countries have placed importance on their sovereignty over resources to reject what they regard as excessive economic penetration by multinational companies.[68]

These concerns indicate that the fact that the economic world has become more interdependent has not reduced the demand for national autonomy; on the contrary, the reality of interdependence probably has intensified the subjective feelings against excessive dependence on others. It would therefore be a mistake to consider the concept of permanent sovereignty over resources simply as nationalistic rhetoric. It is deeply rooted in the popular aspiration for self-rule and greater

65. For an analysis of the present position in international law see Orrego Vicuña, "Some International Law Problems Posed by the Nationalization of the Copper Industry by Chile," 67 *Am J. Int'l L.* 711 (1973); Schachter, "The Evolving International Law of Development," *supra* note 4 at 7-9.

66. U.N. "Group of Eminent Persons," *The Impact of Multinational Corporations on the Development Process and on International Relations,* U.N. Doc. E/5500/Add.1 (1974) [hereinafter cited as Report on Multinationals].

67. See, *e.g.*, Sunkel, "Big Business and 'Dependencia,'" 50 *Foreign Affairs* 517 (1972).

68. See Task Force on the Structure of Canadian Industry, *Foreign Ownership and the Structure of Canadian Industry* (1968); J. Servan-Schreiber, *Le Défi Américain* (1967); J. Behrman, *National Interests and Multinational Companies; Tensions among the North Atlantic Countries* (1970).

equality. One cannot forget, in the words of a perceptive United Nations official that "the historical circumstances of decolonization, memories of exploitation, and the persistence of unequal bargaining powers have created the atmosphere in which foreign investment is now being judged".[69] At the same time, as he notes, the principle of sovereignty over resources needs to be reconciled with the inescapable fact that non-renewable "resources acquire value largely through international markets and that they can be exploited only through the most complex technological and logistic operations".[70] These facts underlie the ambivalence in the attitudes and legislation of many of the developing countries: their desire for unhampered control on the one hand and, on the other, the incentives they offer to attract foreign capital. The apparent contradiction in their position cannot be dismissed as irrational; it should be understood as reflecting a polarity inherent in the objective circumstances and in that sense as a challenge to seek a reconciliation that would, to the extent possible, maximize the competing values.

In considering specific measures toward that end, it is important to take into account the changing relationship of host country and foreign investor in a typical resource development project. In the first stage, the government of a developing country, anxious to develop its natural resources, is conscious of its lack of capital, knowledge, and skilled personnel. It has to induce an investor to make a substantial outlay under conditions of considerable uncertainty, with a return to him not possible until large sums of money have been sunk into the operation and a high degree of production achieved. The risk is increased by the fact that fixed costs are relatively high and there is little opportunity to adjust output in operations. In such circumstances, the bargaining power is heavily weighted on the side of the foreign investor and generally inducements are offered by host countries to attract him. But the psychological relationship changes when the investment proves successful and the uncertainty and the risk disappear. At that point the original terms of the concession seem excessively favourable to the investor and the host government views its long-range commitment as a mistake.[71] As experience in Latin America and Middle East indicates, it

69. De Seynes, "United Nations Study of the Multinational Corporations," in Southwestern Legal Foundation, *Private Investors Abroad—Problems and Solutions in International Business in 1974* 181, 184 (1975), U.N. Doc. OPI/CESI Note /254, at 3 (address by the U.N. Under Secretary-General for Economic and Social Affairs on June 13, 1974).

70. *Id.* at 4.

71. For descriptions of this process see Moran, "Politics of Economic Nationalism and the Evolution of Concession Agreements," 66 *Proc. Am. Soc'y Int'l L.* 216 (1972); Moran, "Evolution of Concession Agreements in Underdeveloped Countries," 7 *Vand. J. Transnat'l L.* 315 (1974). For a more general account see R. Vernon, *Sovereignty at Bay* (1971).

then feels impelled to increase its share of taxes or royalties or to nationalize the company or compel transfer ownership to local nationals.[72] The issue of "sanctity of contract" versus national sovereignty comes to the forefront and produces tension and a sense of injustice in both parties.

One solution is to modify the traditional concession agreement so as to meet the likely evolution of the relationship and the shift in bargaining power. Concretely, this could be done by providing for a gradual reduction of the holdings of the foreign investor.[73] A policy of such gradual "divestment" built into the contracts would tend to avoid the impasse that occurs when a government feels impelled to make radical changes in an existing agreement. If provisions for compensation are agreed to in advance and if assurance is given that such compensation would be paid (perhaps by creating an escrow fund held in an independent party) the investor would feel sufficiently protected to undertake the venture on a relatively short-term basis. It should be noted that divestment would not necessarily help the host country in a financial sense or in its development programme, since it may induce investors to lay stress on quick returns and to reduce their input of technology. Moreover the host country might have to provide new capital at high cost and to assume risks of failure. But as against these disadvantages to the host country there would generally be a gain in avoiding situations of sudden expropriation and confrontation which could substantially reduce the flow of foreign capital and technology.

Similar trade-offs are also involved in arrangements under which foreign technical assistance is provided through service contracts or management contracts without foreign equity ownership. Such arrangements do not invite the criticisms that are associated with ownership, though they may not necessarily be more economic for the host country. Still other techniques are useful to raise capital for natural resource development without direct ownership: for example, financial institutions have raised funds for developing countries through various types of factoring by selling collection rights to long-term contracts. In other cases processors or customers have advanced money for contracts in return for an assured supply during an agreed period of operation. In all these cases, the tensions that arise from foreign control are

72. See *Foreign Investment in the Petroleum and Mineral Industries* (R. Mikesell ed.); E. Penrose, *The Large International Firm in Developing Countries* (1969); Moran, "The Politics of Oil (1) Coups and Costs," *Foreign Policy,* Fall 1972, at 129; U.N. Doc. A/9716, *supra* note 64.

73. See Report on Multinationals, *supra* note 66, at 22. See also A. Hirschman, *How to Divest in Latin America in a Bias for Hope: Essays on Development and Latin America* (1971).

eliminated or reduced significantly. There does not appear to be any threat to sovereignty over resources.

The ability of host countries to deal on an equal basis with large foreign enterprises and protect their interest is also a function of knowledge and skill, particularly in dealing with highly technical engineering, accounting and legal matters. Recent United Nations reports have placed considerable stress on the potential role of international institutions in providing information to host countries in order to strengthen their position in dealing with multinational corporations.[74] This would call not only for data and analysis but also for training of experts in negotiation and administration and providing technical advisory teams to governments of the developing countries. Beyond such fairly obvious assistance (which is not as easy to carry out as it may seem) proposals have been made for international procedures involving disclosure and evaluation of multinational company practices and agreements.

These proposals, like those involving technical advice, would require a high level of technical expertise in the international organizations concerned; they would also call for the maintenance of exemplary standards of integrity and impartiality to safeguard the confidentiality and fairness of the information gathering system.[75] It is understandable that questions may arise as to whether these conditions can be met in an international organization that is intensely political in its legislative organs and bureaucratic in its administration. One must conclude that in this, as in the other matters we have discussed, the objective of international social justice demands not only the development of new obligations and of new procedures, but also of an expanded international public service composed of persons of talent, vigour and dedication. Despite frustrations, that does not seem an unrealistic goal.[76] Its realization will be made more likely by gifted teachers who like Professor Wolfgang Friedmann can provide intellectual vision and personal inspiration.

74. Report on Multinationals, *supra* note 66, at 36-38, 80-82.

75. See *id*. pt. II, at 91, 99 (comments by Senator Javits); *id*. pt. II, at 115 (comments by Irwin Miller).

76. See Schachter, "Some Reflections on International Officialdom," in *International Organization: Law in Movement* (J. Fawcett & R. Higgins eds. 1974).

VOTING PROCEDURE IN INTERNATIONAL CONFERENCES FOR THE CODIFICATION OF INTERNATIONAL LAW, 1864-1930

LOUIS B. SOHN

The question of voting procedure applicable in international conferences for the codification of international law has been troubling lawyers and diplomats for many years. The question became important in the United Nations in view of the increase in the pace of codification of international law, especially in connection with the law of the sea.[1] It might be desirable, therefore, to see how the rules on the subject developed in pre-United Nations practice, and to explore reasons for both the basic unanimity rule and the actual departures from it in practice.

The paper is limited to voting rules of international codification conferences; and only incidental references will be made to the related topics of voting rules in other types of international conferences or in international organizations.[2] The paper covers the period from 1864 to 1930, when the issue was hotly debated at a number of international conferences, and in connection with the preparation of general rules for international conferences.

LOUIS B. SOHN is Bemis Professor of International Law, Harvard Law School; member of the United States Delegation to the Third U.N. Law of the Sea Conference, 1973-1977; and, formerly Counselor on International Law, Department of State (1970-1971).

1. For a discussion of the United Nations approach to the question of voting procedure of international codification conferences see Sohn, "Voting Procedures in United Nations Conferences for the Codification of International Law," 69 *Am. J. Int'l L.* 310 (1975) [hereinafter cited as Sohn].

2. There is an extensive literature on these subjects. For works dealing primarily with United Nations rules see Sohn, *supra* note 1, at 310 n. 1. Among the earlier writings, the following might be usefully consulted: F. Dunn, *The Practice and Procedure of International Conferences* 123-31, 202 (1929); Greaves, "International Voting Procedures," 18 *Political Q.* 331 (1947); N. Hill, *The Public International Conference* 187-94 (1929); W. Koo, *Voting Procedures in International Political Organizations* 26-114 (1947); C. Riches, *The Unanimity Rule and the League of Nations* 37-166 (1933); C. Riches, *Majority Rule in International Organization* 1-306 (1940); L. Woolf, *International Government* 108-223 (1916).

I. FIRST GENEVA RED CROSS CONFERENCES

The issue seems to have arisen first at the 1864 Geneva Conference for the Amelioration of the Condition of Soldiers Wounded in Armies in the Field, which prepared the first codification of the laws of war. At the first meeting of that Conference there was a discussion concerning the system of voting to be used, especially whether the voting should be by States or by heads, some countries being represented by several delegates. The first French delegate, Mr. Jagerschmidt then observed that "there cannot be any votes on the articles, as the majority can never bind the minority, however small it may be."[3] Satow, the great international expert on diplomatic practice, commented on this statement that "[w]ithout doubt this is the correct international doctrine."[4]

The question was reopened at the Geneva Conference of 1868, called to amend the 1864 Convention, where a more complicated solution was adopted: "As far as voting was concerned, it was agreed that with respect to anything relating to the internal order (*régime*) [of the Conference] voting shall be by heads; but with respect to adoption, or rejection, or merely the taking under consideration, of any subject which in any manner might impose an obligation on the High Contracting Parties, voting shall be by States. It was agreed further that majority shall be sufficient for putting a subject on the agenda for discussion, but for final adoption [of a provision] unanimity shall be required."[5] Thus a distinction seems to have been made, for the first time, between matters of substance and questions of procedure,[6] and

3. Protocols of the International Conferences held in Geneva in 1864, 20 Martens Nouveau Recueil Général de Traités (1st ser.) 375, 380 (1875) [hereinafter cited as Martens]. Riches ascribes this statement wrongly to General Dufour. C. Riches, *Majority Rule in International Organization* 10 (1940).

4. 2 E. Satow, *A Guide to Diplomatic Practice 133* (2d ed. 1922) [hereinafter cited as Satow].

5. Protocols of the International Conferences held in Geneva in 1868, Martens, *supra* note 3, at 400, 403. See also 2 Satow, *supra* note 4, at 125.

6. It may be noted that at the Congress of Berlin in 1878 dealing with the Balkan Question, Prince Bismarck, the President of the Congress pointed out that it was "an incontestable principle that the minority of the Congress cannot be obliged to submit to a vote by the majority." He added that it would be nevertheless useful for expediting the work of the Congress "if resolutions adopted by the majority with respect to procedure, without touching the substance, could be regarded as decisions of the Congress in all cases in which the minority did not find it necessary to register a formal protest." The Congress unanimously accepted this suggestion. Protocols of Berlin Congress, 69, *British and Foreign State Papers* 862, 892 (1885). See also *id.* at 904-06, 918, 957-58. An issue of substance may sometimes be disguised as an issue of procedure, as happened at the Algeciras Conference in 1906. E. Satow, *International Conferences and Congresses* 3-5 (United Kingdom, Historical Section of the Foreign Office, Peace Handbooks No. 151, 1920); A. Tardieu, *La Conférence d'Algésiras* 268-71 (1907).

between preliminary and final decisions.[7]

II. HAGUE PEACE CONFERENCES

The two Hague Conferences of 1899 and 1907 were the first major codificatory conferences, dealing with several important areas of international law. While the first of them was still limited in membership, the second one included most of the States of the world. In both of them, the smaller powers were admitted on the footing of equality and they insisted that the traditional rule of unanimity—that nobody can be bound without his consent—should apply across the board to all the proceedings of the Conferences. But it became quickly apparent that a strict application of the unanimity rule would make practically impossible any decisions whatever, and ways had to be found to get around this difficulty.

The record of the First Hague Conference shows that in subcommissions and commissions decisions were made by a majority vote.[8] This seems to have been done on the understanding that "the delegates are supposed to be expressing simply their personal opinions and by no means to be committing their respective Governments;"[9] and that "the votes cast" by them "do not positively pledge their respective Governments."[10] When it came to the final votes in the plenary meetings, the strict unanimity rule was not in fact adhered to, as some documents were adopted "unanimously less two votes (United States of America and Great Britain)" or "unanimously with the exception of two votes (United States and Great Britain) and one abstention (Portugal)."[11] During the discussion of the Final Act of the Conference, it was pointed

7. At the 1906 Geneva Conference concerning the revision of the 1864 Convention relating to the Amelioration of the Conditions of Soldiers Wounded in Armies in the Field, though the rules of procedure contained no provision on the subject, majority rule seems to have prevailed in the commissions of the Conference. All plenary decisions seem to have been adopted by unanimity, except for a *voeu* on arbitration. See, *e.g.*, Convention de Genève, *Actes de la Conférence de Revision* 50, 73, 100, 125, 153, 300 (1906).

The 1929 Geneva Conference on the same subject (and on the treatment of prisoners of war) adopted, without objection, the rule that "decisions of both the Conference and the Commissions shall be taken by an absolute majority of votes." *Actes de la Conférence Diplomatique de Genève de 1929*, at 37, 64 (1930); E. Satow, *A Guide to Diplomatic Practice* 315 (3d ed. 1932). The Rules of Procedure of the 1949 Geneva Conference for the Protection of War Victims provided even more leniently that "[a]ll decisions of the Conference and Committees shall be taken by a simple majority . . . of members present and voting." 3 *Final Record of the Diplomatic Conference of Geneva of 1949*, at 13, 19 (1950). Amendments to these draft rules of procedure (relating to questions other than voting) were adopted by majority votes. 2 *id.* at 28, 41.

8. See, *e.g.*, *The Proceedings of the Hague Peace Conferences, The Conference of 1899*, at 89, 274, 279, 287, 451, 495 (J. Scott ed. 1920). But see *id.* at 394-95.

9. *Id.* at 480.

10. *Id.* at 365.

11. *Id.* at 79, 87.

out, however, that "it was not thought wise to mention the votes upon the Conventions and Declarations. The reason for this is that the Final Act states only that they were adopted and in no way implies that they were approved. It appeared inadvisable therefore to mention whether the Conventions and Declarations received a unanimous vote or not. The Powers have at their disposal a very simple means of showing their approval or disapproval by signing or not signing."[12]

The much larger 1907 Hague Conference seems to have invented the principle of near unanimity or quasi-unanimity,[13] which "is necessary to give a sufficient moral authority to a deliberation."[14] The crucial issue before the First Commission related to obligatory arbitration, and as various proposals received "only a large majority" and not the necessary "unanimity or near unanimity," the Austrian-Hungarian delegation suggested that a further study of the subject be conducted after the close of the Conference.[15] The United States delegate (Mr. Choate) disagreed, pointing out that the Commission expressed its will by an overwhelming majority of 31 votes to 5, with 8 abstentions.[16] He asked rhetorically: "Can five votes nullify the will of the thirty-one?"[17] He claimed that "approximate unanimity" should be sufficient for Commission and Conference action; and that the record of the two Hague Conferences showed that absolute unanimity had been abandoned in favor of two more flexible rules which were subject to the determination of the Conference, i.e. that "the rule of absolute unanimity 'generally' holds," and that the vote "must be unanimous or 'nearly so'."[18] The delegate of Austria-Hungary replied ironically that there seemed to be a confusion whether the delegates were present at an international conference or in a parliament. While in a parliament the majority decides, the basic principle of an international conference is that "all that is unanimously accepted, stays, and all that is not accepted by everyone, disappears."[19] The President of the Conference (Mr. Nelidow, Russia) concurred that "the first principle of any conference is that of unanimity," as "each delegation represents a different State, equally sovereign, and has no right to accept a decision of the majority contrary to the will of its Government."[20] The United States delegate then explained that he was evidently misunderstood, as he did not mean to imply that the will of the majority should be imposed upon

12. *Id.* at 103-04.

13. 2 *The Proceedings of the Hague Peace Conferences, The Conference of 1907,* at 95, 118, 119, 166, 495, 566 (J. Scott ed. 1920) [hereinafter cited as Scott].

14. 2 *id.* at 562.

15. 2 *id.* at 166, 903.

16. See 2 *id.* at 165. Another important vote, in favor of an Anglo-American proposal, was 32 to 9, with 3 abstentions. 2 *id.* at 119.

17. 2 *id.* at 168-69.

18. 2 *id.* at 169-70.

19. 2 *id.* at 170-71.

20. 2 *id.* at 171.

the minority. What he meant to say was that "when a large majority of the Conference desires to conclude an agreement with regard to obligatory arbitration, an agreement in which those who may wish to do so are to take part, and an agreement that leaves it free to the rest to abstain if it seems best to them, it has the right to do so and to do so under . . . the 'flag of the Conference'." The contrary proposition would subject not only the majority but the whole Conference, minus one member, "to the dominating and destructive will of this solitary member."[21] The Belgian delegate defended the principle of unanimity not only as an expression of the principle of "perfect equality" of States but also on the basis that the very purpose of the Conference was to "define the common ground on which their varying views may meet." Otherwise irreducible groups may develop, and once a large majority gains confidence in its stability, the spirit of concession will vanish.[22] The United States delegate disagreed that the rule of unanimity was the basic rule, as at the first Hague Conference the decisions relating to the use of asphyxiating gas and the dumdum bullets had been inserted in the Final Act of the Conference and had become "a part of the law of the world," in the face of the earnest protest by Great Britain and the United States. Similarly, at the second Conference a decision was made with respect to the international prize court despite the negative vote of Brazil.[23] The President of the Conference explained that the 1899 decisions related to purely technical questions, while the Brazilian delegate did not object to the project relating to the prize court appearing in the Final Act so that "in this hypothesis moral unanimity was not lacking."[24] After the Austrian-Hungarian proposal was defeated by 24 votes to 14, with 6 abstentions, a drafting committee was appointed to find a formula acceptable to everyone; the declaration prepared by it, couched in general terms, was approved unanimously, with 4 abstentions (Haiti, Japan, Turkey and the United States).[25]

As far as the final decisions of the 1907 Conference were concerned, they were adopted unanimously, with various delegations recording

21. 2 *id.* For other references to the right of a majority to sign between themselves a special treaty, see 2 *id.* at 135, 165, 448-49. Fried endorses this approach as a way of avoiding the dilemmas caused by the unanimity rule. A Fried, *Die zweite Haager Konferenz* 162-64 (1907).

22. 2 Scott, *supra* note 13, at 171-72.

23. 2 *id.* at 173.

24. 2 *id.*

25. 2 *id.* at 176-77, 191-93. For another account of this debate see the report of Baron Guillaume, 1 *id.* 395, at 542-47. The Reporter pointed out that a "strong and homogenous majority" elaborated a proposal based on the Anglo-American proposition, but it should not ignore "the convictions of a loyal minority"; it is better to postpone "the realization of projects, the premature execution of which might compromise the principle of unanimity, which is the basis of every international conference." The adoption of the compromise declaration, made possible by four abstentions, enabled the rights of all to be safeguarded in "a spirit of concord and wise conciliation." 1 *id.* at 546-47.

their reservations or abstaining.[26] Various writers have drawn different conclusions from the record of the Hague Conferences. While Zorn concluded that the rule of "quasi-unanimity" was applied there,[27] Huber insisted that each outvoted State has a right to an absolute veto but for political reasons might decide not to make use of it for the purpose of opposing the inclusion of the document in the Final Act.[28] Satow noted that[29]

> There was much uncertainty as to the effect of a negative vote. Sometimes complete unanimity was held to be necessary, on other occasions a majority was regarded as sufficient to entitle a proposal to be recorded as part of the proceedings.

One of the chief historians of the Hague Conferences, James Brown Scott, summarized the general rules in the following manner: [30]

> Majorities show undoubtedly the trend of international feeling; but, each nation, being independent and charged with the preservation of its own existence, must judge for itself

26. 1 *id.* at 87, 168 (Brazil voting against), 232, 274, 279, 328-32. Though the Final Act of the Conference notes that the resolution on obligatory arbitration was adopted unanimously, "while reserving to each of the Powers represented full liberty of action as regards voting," and notes that another resolution was adopted unanimously, it does not mention the vote on the *voeux* embodied in the Final Act. There is, however, a list of reservations made, including the statement by Switzerland that it does not accept the *voeu* relating to the Court of Arbitral Justice. 1 *id.* at 678, at 689, 700-03.

27. Zorn, "Zur neuesten Entwicklung des Völkerrechts," in *Festgabe für Karl Güterbock* 195, 207-10 (1910). Schucking agrees with Zorn, but prefers three-fourths majority to quasi-unanimity. W. Schucking, *The International Union of the Hague Conferences* 209-22 (1918). Nippold also notes that the Hague Conferences rejected all types of majority vote and adhered unconditionally to "the principle of unanimity or at least near unanimity." 2 O. Nippold, *Die zweite Haager Friedenskonferenz* 255 (1911). Later, Nippold abandoned unanimity and quasi-unanimity in favor of a special league of like-minded States to carry out a progressive program of international law. O. Nippold, *The Development of International Law after the World War* 28-33 (1923).

28. Huber, "Die Fortbildung des Völkerrechts auf dem Gebiete des Prozess- und Landkriegsrechts durch die II. internationale Friedenskonferenz im Haag 1907," 2 *Jahrbuch des öffentlichen Rechts* 470, 475-77 (1908). Fauchille reaches similar conclusions. 1 P. Fauchille, *Traité de droit international public* 245-48 (1926). As Hill notes,

> where conferences have subscribed to the rule of unanimity in principle its application has been distorted by a weighing of the votes of dissenting nations, and, where feasible, agreeing upon a course of action in spite of a small amount of opposition, leaving the obstructing states to decide for themselves whether they will fall in line or discontinue their participation.

N. Hill, *The Public International Conference: Its Function, Organization and Procedure* 193 (1929). See also 3 R. Genet, *Traité de diplomatie et de droit diplomatique* 257 (1932).

29. 2 E. Satow, *supra* note 4, at 172.

30. 1 J. Scott, *The Hague Peace Conference of 1899 and 1907,* at 35-39 (1909). See also L. Oppenheim, *The Future of International Law* 19-21, 30-31 (1921); F. Dunn, *The Practice and Procedure of International Conferences* 123-31 (1929).

> whether the conclusion of the majority is advantageous or detrimental either to its existence or legitimate interests. The majority may give pause and cause a State in the minority to reconsider its position in order to see whether what the many desire is not also desirable for the few. Majorities, therefore, exist, but they exercise a moral influence; they do not coerce. At most the decree or resolution of a majority binds the majority; it does not, and, under existing conditions, it can not well control an individual State. . . . .
>
> The purpose of a conference is to reconcile divergent views, and, by conciliation and renunciation if necessary, to produce substantial agreement. This often means that progressive measures are discarded for more moderate formulas, just as the advanced guard of an army halts that the laggard may catch up; for the purpose is not to secure the assent of the few but to bind the many, and it is better to make haste slowly than by an excessive zeal to make no progress. The result of a conference, therefore, is often strangely at variance with its program. The sweeping reforms of the enthusiast are brushed aside, and in their place tentative measures, timid measures perhaps, appear; but we must not forget that a step in advance is still a step in advance, and that the failure of today is the success of the morrow.

Fifty years later Tammes reached similar conclusions. He pointed out first that the maojrity has two means at its disposal. It may threaten a separate agreement among the majority alone (which, one might add, can be paralleled by an agreement among the minority), or it may assert itself "by seduction, rather than pressure." He explained the second method as follows:[31]

> Unanimity is reached by making the retreat for dissenting delegations easier. They are permitted to have their objections fully recorded in the minutes. They are exempted from the rigid alternative of either subscribing to what is hardly acceptable to them, or defeating what may present itself as the hope of Mankind. It will not be considered irregular, therefore, if they abstain from the vote. Abstentions not being counted in ascertaining whether there is common acquiescence, the principle of unanimity is outwardly saved, but under that veil, as was the case in mediaeval communities, majority decision is virtually introduced.
>
> Often the majority works through the gradualness of the

31. Tammes, "Decisions of International Organs as a Source of International Law," 94 Académie de Droit International, *Recueil des Cours* 261, 287 (1958). See also B. Broms, *The Doctrine of Equality of States as Applied to International Organizations* 108-09 (1959).

decision-making process. In the early stages, in the sub-committee, in the study-group, a draft may be adopted even by simple majority vote. The definite voting in plenary meeting is still far away and, in the meantime, several opportunities will present themselves to a minority to take a firmer stand. Yet, when something substantial has emerged from the early discussions, when amendments have been added and compromises inserted in order to meet the opposition, the final product is the work of the whole, rather than of the majority, and minorities may find it more and more difficult completely to deny or reject that product when, in the course of the successive legislative stages, it gains in weight and approval.

III. PARIS PEACE CONFERENCE

It is in the light of the experience of previous conferences that the French Government proposed the following rule for the Paris Peace Conference in 1919: [32]

> 14. All decisions are to be taken unanimously; the minority, therefore, will not be bound to submit [to] a majority vote.
>
> Nevertheless, the resolutions of the majority which are concerned with questions of procedure, but do not involve main issues, are to be regarded as decisions of the Conference, in any cases where the minority may not deem it necessary to lodge a formal protest.

When this draft was discussed by the Council of Ten on 15 January 1919, the voting provision was completely suppressed. The records contain only the following cryptic summary of the discussion which then took place: [33]

> Section 14. Mr. WILSON inquired whether those present were ready to adopt such a rule. Would it not enable a small

32. [1919] 1 *Foreign Rel. U.S.* 392, 396 (1942). For prior French drafts and United States comments see 1 *id.* at 347, 352, 364, 367, 405.

33. 3 *id.* at 575 (1943). When the issue was raised later concerning the rules which should govern the discussions relating to the League of Nations, President Wilson pointed out that it had been agreed that there should be no voting. Mr. Lloyd George replied that "the delegations would not be asked to vote. The small Powers would only be entitled to record their dissent. The Great Powers need merely say that they would take note of any suggestions or dissent and consider it latter. The Great Powers must reserve the great decisions to themselves." 3 *id.* at 681. A similar view was presented during a discussion of the voting rule in the Council of the League of Nations, where President Wilson thought that small powers may attend but should not vote, while Lord Robert Cecil noted that all "international decisions must by the nature of things be unanimous." 1 D. Miller, *The Drafting of the Covenant* 161 (1928) [hereinafter cited as Miller].

minority to hold up the proceedings? He also pointed out that this would be a body of sovereign powers, and as they could not be bound by such a regulation, why not omit the whole section? His proposal was accepted.

Consequently, when the rules of procedure were presented to the Peace Conference on 18 January 1919, they contained no provision on voting.[34] On one occasion, when a vote on a Japanese proposal on race equality could not be avoided in the Commission on the League of Nations, President Wilson ruled that the proposal was rejected as it had not received the unanimous approval of the Commission and the States opposing the provision insisted on their objection and were not willing to have the provision incorporated with a reservation on their part.[35]

The Covenant of the League of Nations, inserted by the Peace Conference in all the peace treaties, provided in Article 5 that "decisions . . . of the Assembly or of the Council shall require the agreement of all the Members of the League represented at the meeting," but that all matters of procedure, including the appointment of Committees to investigate particular matters, may be decided by a majority of the Members of the League represented at the meeting.[36] In commenting on this provision, the Permanent Court of International Justice stated that this rule of unanimity was "in accordance with the unvarying tradition of all diplomatic meetings or conferences," and noted that in such a body as the Council of the League, "observance of the rule of unanimity is naturally and even necessarily indicated." It explained that:[37]

34. [1919] 3 *Foreign Rel. U.S.* 169, 172-75 (1943) (text of the rules). See also F. Marston, *The Peace Conference of 1919: Organization and Procedure* 264-67 (1944).

35. 1 Miller, *supra* note 33, at 461-66; 2 *id.* at 387-92.

36. Covenant of the League of Nations, *done* June 28, 1919, in 1 *International Legislation* 1, 5 (M. Hudson ed. 1931). The practice of the League developed various devices for getting around the severity of this provision. See C. Riches, *The Unanimity Rule and the League of Nations* 37-157 (1933); W. Koo, *Voting Procedures in International Political Organizations* 96-114 (1947). With respect to a proposed amendment to Article 5 of the covenant for a two-thirds majority concerning decisions relating to the development in practice of the principles laid down in the Covenant, see League of Nations, Committee on Amendments to the Covenant, *First Report of the Committee to the Council,* L. N. Doc. A.24.1921.V, C.110.M.62.1921.V, at 12-13 (1921); League of Nations, *Records of the 2nd Assembly, Committee Meetings* 94-98, 177-79 (1921). Concerning voting on amendments to the Covenant see *id.* at 43-68, 88-92, 157-65. See also Hudson, "Amendment of the Covenant of the League of Nations," 38 *Harv. L. Rev.* 903, 910-11, 924-25 (1925).

The procedure of quasi-unanimity was followed also at the Washington Conference on the Limitation of Armament in 1922, where a resolution relating to the Chinese Eastern Railway was adopted unanimously "by the Powers other than China." United States Department of State, *Conference on the Limitation of Armament* 316-24 (1922).

37. Advisory Opinion concerning Article 3, Paragraph 2, of the Treaty of Lausanne (Frontier between Turkey and Iraq), [1925] P.C.I.J. ser. B, No. 12, at 29-30.

only if the decisions of the Council have the support of the unanimous consent of the Powers composing it, will they possess the degree of authority which they must have: the very prestige of the League might be imperilled if it were admitted, in the absence of an express provision to that effect, that decisions on important questions could be taken by a majority. Moreover, it is hardly conceivable that resolutions on questions affecting the peace of the world could be adopted against the will of those amongst the Members of the Council who, although in a minority, would, by reason of their political position, have to bear the larger share of the responsibilities and consequences ensuing therefrom.

IV. CODIFICATION OF INTERNATIONAL LAW UNDER THE AUSPICES OF THE LEAGUE OF NATIONS

A Committee of Experts for the Progressive Codification of International Law was established by the Council of the League in 1924, pursuant to a resolution of the Assembly of the same date.[38] At its first session in 1925 the Committee decided to appoint a Sub-Committee to "examine the possibility of formulating rules to be recommended for the procedure of international conferences, and the conclusion and drafting of treaties, and what such rules should be."[39] When this proposal was adopted, it was explained that at large international conferences "considerable time was lost in useless discussions, which were often little likely to result in an agreement, in regard to the procedure to be followed within the conference," especially with respect to "the question of unanimity or a majority vote," and the question "whether an act might be regarded as an act of the conference when it commanded the support of only a majority of its members." It would, therefore, be advantageous to lay down "rules which would not have a compulsory character but which might be presented to the Governments as a guide," analogous to the Hague rules governing arbitration.[40]

The second session of the Committee had before it a report by Mr. Mastny (Czechoslovakia), assisted by Mr. Rundstein (Poland), which

38. Assembly Resolution of 22 September 1924; *League of Nations Off. J., Spec. Supp.* 21, at 10.

39. Committee of Experts for the Progressive Codification of International Law, *Minutes of the First Session,* L.N. Doc. C.P.D.I./1st Session/P.V., at 49, para. g (1925). [hereinafter cited as "Committee of Experts"].

40. *Id.* at 37, 44. For a discussion of the question whether the Committee itself should operate on the basis of the unanimity principle see *id.* at 33-34. For an early suggestion by the Chairman of the Committee, Mr. Hjalmar L. Hammarskjold (Sweden), that the Committee consider the question of international legislative conferences and whether the voting should be unanimous or quasi-unanimous, see L.N. Doc. C.P.D.I. 10, at 2 (1925).

proposed the codification of certain general principles of procedure for all international conferences, including the question of voting.[41] As approved by the Committee, the questionnaire sent to Member States included the following question: "Necessity of Unanimity. Absolute Majority. Specified Majority."[42]

The Committee pointed out that there was no question of attempting to prepare "a body of rules which would be binding obligatorily upon the various States; " it was marely sought to put at the disposal of States "rules which could be modified as they chose in each concrete case but whose existence might save them much discussion, doubt and delay."[43]

Twenty-seven Governments replied to the questionnaire: fourteen were in favor of immediate codification; six expressed some reservations; and eight replied in the negative.[44] Only Finland noted that "as certain branches of international law come to be codified, it becomes a matter of urgency and importance to know whether, as regards the particular branch codified, an amendment requires an absolute majority or whether departures from this strict principle should be allowed."[45] Egypt suggested that the Secretariat of the League of Nations should draw up model regulations, which the States would usually follow unless there were good reason for departing from them; "in this way the rules would ultimately become established by dint of constant observance."[46] Sweden also considered codification unnecessary, as certain definite customs were growing up in connection with the conferences convened by the League of Nations.[47] The reporter (Mr. Rundstein, Poland), nevertheless concluded that a codification of the "rules to be recommended for the procedure of international conferences" would be "desirable and realisable," it being understood that such rules "would not be binding obligatorily upon the signatory parties."[48]

41. Committee of Experts, *Questionnaire No. 5: Procedure of International Conferences and Procedure for the Conclusion and Drafting of Treaties,* L.N. Doc. C.47.M.24.1926.V, C.P.D.I.57, L.N. Pub. 1926.V.4, at 4-5 (1926) [hereinafter cited as *Questionnaire No. 5*]; Committee of Experts, *Report to the Council . . . Adopted . . . at its Third Session,* L.N. Doc. C.196.M.70.1927.V., C.P.D.I.95 (2), L.N. Pub. 1927.V.1, at 105, 108-09 (1927) [hereinafter cited as Committee of Experts, *Report*]; 20 *Am. J. Int'l L. Spec. Supp.* 204, 210, 212 (1926).

42. *Questionnaire No. 5, supra* note 41, at 11; Committee of Experts, *Report, supra* note 41, at 114-15; 20 *Am. J. Int'l L. Spec. Supp.* 204, 220 (1926).

43. *Questionnaire No. 5, supra* note 41, at 1; Committee of Experts, *Report, supra* note 41, at 105; 20 *Am. J. Int'l L. Spec. Supp.* 204 (1926).

44. Committee of Experts, *Report, supra* note 41, at 271-73.

45. *Id.* at 163.

46. *Id.* at 259.

47. *Id.* at 238.

48. Committee of Experts, *Minutes of the Third Session,* L.N. Doc. C.P.D.I./3rd Session/P.V., at 94 (1927).

When the question was discussed by the Committee of Experts, it was noted that a set of rules was as desirable here as with respect to arbitral procedure, in both instances parties being free to make any changes necessitated by each particular case. Experience has shown that because of the lack of such guiding principles, at many international conferences "whole days had been passed in discussing rules which were finally found to be identical to those employed by other conferences."[49] Following a suggestion by McNair (Great Britain), the Committee decided to recommend to the Council of the League that this "highly technical" question should be further examined by a small committee of experts, who might prepare model rules which a conference could adopt en bloc, thus preventing the loss of time entailed by detailed discussions concerning the procedure to be followed. Even should these drafts be accepted by a codificatory conference they "would simply be in the nature of *droit dispositif,* that is, of rules which would leave the parties concerned quite free to come to some different arrangement."[50]

When this recommendation was presented to the Council of the League, the Council's rapporteur on this subject (Zaleski, Poland) suggested that the matter was in no sense urgent and that it might be sufficient to ask the Secretary-General to consider the preparation by the Secretariat of the League of "a study of the methods of conference," which might be "submitted to criticism by international organizations and Governments having special experience of the holding of general conferences."[51] This proposal was endorsed by the Assembly, which, on the basis of a report by Politis (Greece), requested the Council to instruct the Secretariat to collect all available precedents, to obtain information from Governments as to their practice, and to encourage research on the subject by specialists in various countries.[52] This study was promptly authorized by the Council.[53]

Even before this general matter of conference procedure was settled in this rather cursory manner, the Assembly had to face the practical question of the voting procedure of the forthcoming Codification Conference, which was to discuss three important topics—nationality, territorial waters and responsibility of States.[54] Politis pointed out in the

49. *Id.* at 42-43.

50. *Id.* at 42-44, 72. See also L.N. Doc. C. 198. M.72.1927.V, C.P.D.I.94 (1), L.N. Pub. 1927.V.3.

51. 8 *League of nations Off. J.* 749, 754 (1927). This report was approved by the Council. *Id.* at 756-57.

52. Records of the 8th Ordinary Session of the Assembly, Minutes of the First Committee, *League of Nations Off. J., Spec. Supp.* 55, at 54, 57 (1927) [hereinafter cited as Records]; Resolutions . . . Adopted by the Assembly during Its 8th Ordinary Session, *League of Nations Off. J., Spec. Supp.* 53, at 9 (1927) [hereinafter cited as Resolutions].

53. 9*League of Nations Off. J.* 123 (1928).

54. Resolutions, *supra* note 52, at 9.

First Committee of the Assembly that the first point to be considered in dealing with the procedure of that Conference was "the unanimity rule." He noted that:

> At the last Hague Conference the question had been raised, not whether the majority could bind the minority—that was inconceivable—but whether countries that did not wish to accept a convention agreed upon almost unanimously by the Conference should prevent the other countries binding themselves among themselves at that Conference.
>
> It was essential that before the first Codification Conference was held this important point should be settled, and that it should be understood that, though no country could be directly or indirectly bound against its will, the other countries could bind themselves by a convention concluded at that same Conference.

He suggested that one way of dealing with this problem might be to consider "the possibility of a comprehensive general convention embracing all the questions to be submitted to the Conference, this convention embodying only certain principles, and being consequently acceptable to all parties. Then, within the framework of this general convention there would be more limited and detailed conventions."[55] Following his suggestions, the Committee approved a report of a Sub-Committee which contained the following two rules:[56]

> (a) *Rule of Unanimous Vote or Majority.*—Although it is desirable that the Conference's decisions should be unanimous, and every effort should be made to attain this result, it must be clearly understood that, where unanimity is impossible, the majority of the participating States, if disposed to accept as among themselves a rule to which some other States are not prepared to consent, cannot be prevented from doing so by the mere opposition of the minority.
>
> (b) *Rule of the Scope of the Engagements entered into.*—In such matters as may lend themselves to this, it would be useful to provide for the possibility of concluding two kinds of conventions: a very comprehensive convention on the general rules of the subject, likely to be accepted by all States; and a more restricted convention, which, while keeping within the framework of the other convention, would include special rules

55. Records, *supra* note 52, at 16. Lange (Norway) also recalled that at the Hague Conference the issue was raised whether "the rule of unanimity should be interpreted to mean that one or more Powers might place an absolute veto on any action on the part of the rest;" and warned that to "demand absolute unanimity would condemn the work to sterility." *Id.* at 17.

56. *Id.* at 56.

> binding only upon such States as might be prepared to accept them.

The Assembly endorsed these rules in its resolution relating to the convening of the Conference, and asked the Council to include in the draft regulations for the Conference provisions with regard to: [57]

> (a) The possibility, if occasion should arise, of the States represented at the Conference adopting amongst themselves rules accepted by a majority vote;
>
> (b) The possibility of drawing up, in respect of such subjects as may lend themselves thereto, a comprehensive convention and, within the framework of that convention, other more restricted conventions.

The Council referred the task of preparing the rules to the Preparatory Committee for the Codification Conference in the light of "the possibilities open to the Conference."[58] The Committee, in framing the rules, "drew upon the Regulations adopted by a number of recent Conferences and upon the Rules of the Assembly."[59] Its draft contained the following provisions on voting: [60]

> XVIII.—Within the Committees, each provision shall be voted upon separately. The vote shall only be valid if the proposal is supported by a majority of the delegations present at the meeting.
>
> If, however, a majority of the delegations represented on the Committee was not present when the vote was taken, a new vote shall be taken should this be asked for by ten delegations.
>
> XIX.—If the Chairman of a Committee considers that modifications of certain provisions adopted by that Committee are likely to facilitate a unanimous agreement, he may request the Committee to discuss such modifications.
>
> XX.—If the Committee cannot reach unanimous agreement on all points, it shall incorporate the provisions upon which it has unanimously agreed in a special instrument.
>
> The Committee shall also formulate the provisions which have obtained the assent of the majority of the delegations.
>
> It may also establish the terms of a Declaration setting forth the principles regarded at least by a majority of the delegations represented on the Committee as the expression of existing international law.

57. Resolutions, *supra* note 52, at 9-10.
58. 10 *League of Nations Off. J.* 534, 535 (1929).
59. *Id.* at 1108.
60. *Id.* at 1111-12.

XXI. — Each Committee shall forward to the Conference the results of its work, backed by a report. In particular, it shall state whether it regards certain drafts as final or whether it recommends that certain questions or drafts should be submitted for fresh examination by Governments.

XXII. — The Conference shall pronounce upon proposals submitted to it by the Committees.

XXIII. — In so far as the Conference arrives at a unanimous agreement, the act embodying such agreement shall be signed by all the delegations subject to ratification; it shall be open for the accession of any State.

Reservations to the unanimous act may be made by individual signatories. Such reservations may either imply the exclusion of a particular article or may consist of a declaration that the provisions of the act are insufficient, but they may not relate to any other point, for example, the interpretation of the act. The said act shall indicate the extent to which reservations may accompany accession. It shall also specify the period of its validity and, if necessary, the method of revision.

XXIV. — In the absence of or in addition to a unanimous agreement, conventions may be signed, as acts of the Conference, provided that the object of the convention comes within the competence of the Conference and provided they are finally adopted by a vote of the majority of the Members of the League of Nations and non-member States represented on the Committee in which the draft was prepared. Each of these conventions shall be open to accession by any State; the period of validity and, if necessary, the method of revision shall be specified in the convention.

XXV. — Declarations by which the signatory Governments will recognise certain principles as being sanctioned by existing international law may also be signed as acts of the Conference, provided the said Declarations have been finally adopted by a vote of a majority of the Members of the League of Nations and non-member States represented on the Committee in which the draft was prepared. These Declarations, which shall be subject to ratification, shall be open for accession; they shall not specify any period of validity or contain any denunciation clause, and they shall lapse if the rules which they enunciate cease to form part of international law.

The Committee explained these provisions as follows: [61]

61. *Id.* at 1109. The Council asked the Secretary-General to transmit these rules and the report of the Committee to Governments invited to the Conference. *Id.* at 995-96. The rules were communicated to the Governments in L.N. Doc. C.190(1).M.93.1929.V, L.N. Pub. 1929.V.7, at 2-4 (1929). For a comment on these rules, see Redonensis, "La procédure de la première Conférence de Codification: Les caractères des accords envisagés," 57 *J. Droit Int'l* 16-63 (1930).

> As regards the use to be made of the majority rule, the draft is based on the idea that this rule should merely be adopted for the successive votes which may have to be taken when the various parts of a draft proposal are being framed in a Committee. The matter is more delicate when the question of the final adoption of a draft is involved. The Preparatory Committee is of opinion that the Conference should do everything in its power to secure unanimous agreement, and that, where agreement is reached, it should be definitely placed on record. Moreover, in conformity with the Assembly resolution, the draft Rules recognise as being an act of the Conference any convention concluded by a majority of the States represented. Finally, it provides for a declaration, also representing the views of the majority and indicating what the States which subscribe to it regard as constituting existing international law.

In the 1929 Assembly some doubts were expressed about the meaning of these provisions; it was felt, in particular, that the "two forms of convention or declaration, both of which were represented as liable to be either unanimous or limited to a certain number of States, seemed to overlap to some extent."[62]

When the Hague Conference for the Codification of International Law met in 1930, the President of the Conference (Heemskerk, the Netherlands) introduced the draft rules of procedure with the statement that "we should maintain the principle that we must adopt unanimous resolutions;" and that "[u]nless we do so, we cannot have any codification of international law."[63] While Politis (Greece) agreed that it was undoubtedly the wish of all to take unanimous decisions, he pointed out that certain States claimed in the past "the right to prevent the vast majority of a Conference from taking a decision on behalf of the Conference;" it was generally agreed during the preparatory work for the Conference that "these difficulties should not be allowed to recur in the future." It must be understood, he added, that "no State or minority group of States will be permitted at this Conference to prevent the majority from embodying the results of its deliberations in a diplomatic instrument."[64]

The matter was referred to the Bureau of the Conference, which in turn referred it to the Central Drafting Committee. That Committee presented its report only near the end of the Conference; in it the Committee expressed the view that "it would not be proper to give to any of the documents embodying the results of the Conference the form of 'Declarations'," and suggested the deletion of provisions relating to

62. *League of Nations Off. J., Spec. Supp.* 76 at 20 (1929).

63. 1 *Acts of the Conference for the Codification of International Law, Plenary Meetings,* L.N. Doc. C. 351.M.145.1930.V, L.N. Pub. 1930. V.14, at 21 (1930).

64. *Id.* at 22.

Declarations (Rules XX(3) and XXV).[65] The Drafting Committee recommended a two-thirds majority for decisions of the Committees, and a simple majority for final decisions of the Conference.[66] There was a bitter debate in the Conference concerning the question whether a two-thirds majority should be required also for embodying in a special protocol provisions accepted by a simple majority. In arguing against the need for a two-thirds vote in this limited situation, Politis contended that a minority has been formed that was resolved to prevent a part of the Conference's work from being carried through, and that the work of the Conference could be saved only by allowing a simple majority to authorize the preparation of a special protocol embodying provisions agreed to by members of that majority. He remonstrated that: [67]

> We should be offering the world a lamentable spectacle if, after a month's work, when a great many countries have already taken a decision and many concessions have been made to reach unanimity as far as possible — in any case to secure almost complete unanimity in committee — we were to lay before you in a few days' time texts containing mere shadows of obligations; and if, after all, even when these texts have been whittled away, curtailed, deprived of their force, they were not only not signed (it is the right and sovereign prerogative of every State to withhold its signature) but if States that are prepared to subscribe to these instruments were prevented from doing so. That would be an example of international intolerance which I am sure would be criticised and stigmatised by public opinion.

The amendment proposed by him was adopted by 18 votes to 17.[68] On the other hand, an amendment by Guerrero (El Salvador) to require a two-thirds majority for the final decisions of the Conference was rejected.[69] Consequently, the revised rules read as follows: [70]

> XVIII. — Within the Committees, each provision shall be voted upon separately. The vote shall only be valid if the proposal is supported by a majority of the delegations present at the meeting.
>
> If, however, a majority of the delegations represented on the Committee was not present when the vote was taken, a new vote shall be taken should this be asked for by ten delegations.
>
> XIX. — If the Chairman of a Committee considers that

65. *Id.* at 29, 65.
66. *Id.* at 66.
67. *Id.* at 34.
68. *Id.* at 35. For text, see Rule XX(3).
69. *Id.* at 37.
70. *Id.* at 64.

modifications of certain provisions adopted by that Committee are likely to facilitate a unanimous agreement, he may request the Committee to discuss such modifications.

XX.—Each Committee may draw up one or more draft conventions or protocols and may formulate recommendations or *voeux*.

A Committee may embody in the draft conventions or protocols any provisions which have been finally voted by a majority containing at least two-thirds of the delegations present at the meeting at which the vote takes place.

In the case of provisions which have secured only a simple majority, a Committee, at the request of at least five delegations, may decide by a simple majority whether such provisions are to be made the object of a special protocol open for signature or accession.

The provisions referred to in the two preceding paragraphs, if they are not embodied in a draft convention or protocol, shall be inserted in the Final Act of the Conference.

Each convention or protocol shall contain a provision expressly showing whether reservations are permitted, and, if so, what are the articles in regard to which reservations may be made.

Recommendations and *voeux* may be adopted by a simple majority.

XXI.—Each Committee shall forward to the Conference the results of its work, accompanied by a report in which special mention shall be made of those provisions which have been unanimously adopted. The report shall further indicate the points on the Committee's agenda which it has not discussed, and, in general, every question which the Committee considers it desirable to bring to the attention of the Governments.

XXII.—The Conference shall pronounce upon proposals submitted to it by the Committees.

XXIII.—The draft conventions and protocols, recommendations and *voeux* presented by the Committees may be adopted by the Conference by the vote of the simple majority of the delegations present at the meeting at which the vote takes place.

The final documents of the Conference were adopted by varying majorities, ranging from 40 for and 1 against to 20 for and 11 against; a few recommendations and the Final Act were adopted unanimously.[71]

71. *Id.* at 41-43, 54-55. Commenting on these decisions, Hudson noted that this "departure from the usual requirements of unanimity in diplomatic conferences has set a useful precedent." Hudson, "The First Conference for the Codification of International Law," 24 *Am. J. Int'l L.* 447, 449 (1930). But see J. Guerrero, *La Codification du Droit International: La Première Conférence* 23-28 (1930).

V. CONCLUSIONS

This short excursion into the history of the voting rules of international codification conferences shows that the unanimity rule prevailed absolutely only in the early part of the period studied here, though already in 1868 distinction was established between matters of substance and questions of procedure, as well as between preliminary and final decisions. Once the conferences became larger, absolute unanimity could not be easily adhered to; and the Hague Conferences seem to have proceeded on the basis of near unanimity or quasi-unanimity.

When the League of Nations embarked on the process of codification, it found it difficult to agree on precise voting rules; and the voting rules of the Hague Codification Conference led to bitter debates. A complicated set of rules was finally adopted, some decisions requiring a simple majority, other a two-thirds majority, with a predilection for unanimous agreement lurking in the background.

The results of the Conference were not an unmitigated success; agreement was reached on only one of the three codification subjects and the cause of codification suffered a serious defeat. Consequently, when the United Nations decided to renew the codification process, the question of the best method of procedure and voting had to be considered in the light of this discouraging experience. While the rule of unanimity was to some extent discarded, a new rule of consensus emerged, quite similar to the 1907 rule of quasi-unanimity. *Plus ça change, plus c'est la même chose.*[72]

72. For United Nations developments see Sohn, *supra* note 1.

CONSCIENCE, LAW, FORCE AND THE GENERAL ASSEMBLY

JULIUS STONE

The design of this paper is to examine the legal and moral bases of the pretensions of the General Assembly as an arbiter of global issues, against three backgrounds. The first of these is the classical publicist position on the duties of law and conscience between sovereigns, especially as regards treaties of peace between victor and vanquished (Section I). The second is the modern reagitation and "solution" of this issue, together with the issue of "unequal" treaties generally, in the work of the International Law Commission and the resultant Article 52 of the Vienna Convention of the Law of Treaties (Sections II and III). The third is the treatment of these same matters manifest in the Security Council resolution of November 22, 1967 concerning the basis for settlement of the Arab-Israel conflict (Sections IV and V), and in the General Assembly resolutions on the "Palestinian" question of November 22, 1974 (Section VI). Against these backgrounds I have then presented my views of the legal status of resolutions of the General Assembly, in relation to the contemporary crisis dominated by use of the weapon of the oil boycott (Section VII), and also in general (Sections VIII and IX).

I. LAW AND CONSCIENCE

International law as a nominate legal order arose on a rationale which served also as a measure for its own self-criticism. The reference, of course, is to its natural law foundations pegged out by Vitoria and laid, as firmly as they may be said to have been laid at all hitherto, by

JULIUS STONE is Distinguished Professor of Jurisprudence and International Law, University of California, Hastings College of the Law; Professor of Law, University of New South Wales; and formerly Visiting Professor of Law at Columbia University, and Bemis Visiting Professor of International Law, Harvard Law School.

The text of this article was closed in 1975 and it has not been possible to make a further revision within the time table exigencies of the production of the present volume.

Grotius. Granted the contrast between former centuries of Monarch-Sovereigns, and our modern world of State-Sovereigns, the double role of natural law, and the related "conscience" notion, as both progenitor of international law and its precepts, and as the censor of the justice of these, merits attention as a model of approach to the notion of international justice. It deserves early consideration because of its successes, and also because of its failures when confronted by sheer force. The failures help us to see, in particular, not only the limits of that particular approach, but also some limits which affect any approach whatsoever to both international law and international justice.

The fact that modern States first emerged as the personal domains of more or less absolute monarchs bears both on the formation of technical international law and on the criticism of that law and its operation by the norms of justice.[1] Insofar as the systematic exposition of its rules by Grotius and his successors in fact went (as it obviously did) beyond the mere discovery of rules already binding on States, it was using the notion of the conscience of the monarchical head of State in a broad sense as a source of substantive technical law-making. In that broad sense even bodies of rules which have long ceased to be the center of serious frictions, like the immunities of heads of States and their representatives, the principle of exclusive jurisdiction of the territorial sovereign, the law and procedure of treaty-making, were accredited for state acceptance by the dictates of conscience. While the emerging idea of the State was still personified in the monarchical sovereign, we were still quite far from the present reification of state entities, in which the politically organized community and its apparatus of government are seen as transcending any particular persons, even though access and communication must be through persons holding particular status in it. Even to begin to understand the notion of conscience in early international law we have to remember thus to dismantle our present more abstract notions of the state entity into its developing phases.

Concurrent, however, with this use of the appeal to conscience for "discovery" of rules of law as already technically binding, there was the continuing use of the notion as a channel of criticism of these rules.[2] Students of English legal history will here recall the analogy of the operations of the English chancellor as "keeper of the King's con-

1. See Julius Stone, *Legal Controls of International Conflict* 7-18 (1954, 2 impr. with supplement, 1959) [hereinafter cited as Stone, *Legal Controls*], and the literature there cited; see especially Lauterpacht, "The Grotian Tradition in International Law," 23 *Brit. Y. B. Int'l L.* 1 (1946).

2. The assertions in this and the preceding paragraph concern the dominant moods of publicist discourse, rather than any *invariable* usage by the writers concerned, and (of course) rather than the historical state of affairs in post-medieval Western societies.

science."[3] On this basis he not only developed the comprehensive body of binding legal principles known as "equity," but also maintained a continuing, interstitial criticism of the operation of the rules of both common law and equity.[4] The role of "conscience" and of related natural law ideas down to the end of the eighteenth century certainly parallels this; but it also has aspects (here of close interest) which go beyond this analogy. For the appeal to the monarch's conscience also served in early international law thinking the function of protest and *cri de coeur* in face of injustices which the publicists, owing to inescapable facts of international life, saw no possible means of alleviating by law. There is, perhaps, no better illustration of this than the long, tortuous, and agonizing body of thought, from Grotius down to the contemporary work of the International Law Commission, on the effect of duress (and in particular of the duress of war), upon treaty undertakings thereby imposed.[5]

Even the common law, which gave no civil action for duress, recognized (like the Roman law and its civil law successors) that a transaction entered into under duress can be held void at the instance of the oppressed party. A treaty entered into by a sovereign after military defeat, or to escape military defeat, obviously manifests duress of a very extreme kind. It was to be expected, therefore, that from its beginnings the pioneers of international law were deeply perplexed by the question whether such treaties were binding under the principle *pacta sunt servanda*. The principal writers concluded that such treaties were binding and could not be avoided. But they usually accompanied this with solemn denunciations of oppressions by one sovereign against another, and (more significantly for our purpose) sometimes by the affirmation that it was in conscience the duty of the dominant monarch to renegotiate the treaty so as to remove its oppressive features. Vattel's exposition on this point, as on so many others, sharpens all the contrasts involved.[6] On the binding force of peace treaties he opens with the

3. *Cf.* from the standpoint of "reason," "humanism" and "socialist" principles, Johnson, "The Age of Terror," 88 *New Statesman* 763 (1974); and from a different standpoint the comment, "Terrorism and the U.N.," *Wall Street J.*, Nov. 20, 1974, at 26, col. 1.

4. On this see J. Stone, *Human Law and Human Justice* 77-78 (1965); J. Stone, *Social Dimensions of Law and Justice* 54-56 (1966) [hereinafter cited as Stone, *Social Dimensions*].

5. See Stone, "Approaches to the Notion of International Justice," in 1 *The Future of the International Legal Order, Trends and Patterns* 372, 381-90 (R. Falk & C. Black eds. 1969), of which I have with kind permission of Princeton University Press used a number of passages here. On the I.L.C. *travaux* there is a rather fuller account in Stone, "*De Victoribus Victis:* The International Law Commission and Imposed Treaties of Peace," 8 *Va. J. Int'l L.* 356 (1968).

6. The text follows Vattel's general analysis in Book IV, Chapter IV, of his celebrated treatise, *The Law of Nations or Principles of Natural Law* (1768), translated in 3 *Classics of International Law* (J.B. Scott ed. 1916). The Chapter is entitled "The Observance and the Breach of the Treaty of Peace."

assertion not only that they are binding but that it is "always disgraceful and absurd" for the weaker party to plead either fear or constraint. He thought that the fairness of such treaties must be judged, not in terms of peacetime relations, but in terms of the alternative evils which confront a state faced with the prospects of defeat and destruction. From this aspect the burdens of treaties of peace on the weaker party must be supported by the law, and he thought finally that "common safety and welfare of Nations" required this.

The main legal position thus clear, Vattel proceeded to exhort sovereigns on matters of conscience and justice. They must not, for example, confuse genuine treaties of peace with treaties of oppression, as when an "ambitious and unjust conqueror subdues a nation, and forces it to accept hard, disgraceful, and unendurable terms of peace."[7] Necessity may constrain the nation to submit to them. But this show of peace is not real peace; it is oppression of the constrained nation, which "endures" such a treaty only "so long as it lacks the means to free itself . . ."[8]

Morally inspiring as this at first seems, close examination quickly suggests cautions as to its effect on law. One is that Vattel remains to the end ambiguous as to whether he is saying that in law such a treaty of peace is void, or merely that in fact such a treaty will not endure since the oppressed sovereign will repudiate it at the first opportunity. The second caution is that, even if he did mean the former, the range of treaties of peace which would be voidable for oppression would be narrow and also very difficult for the victim to establish. Since he is emphatic that it is even "disgraceful and absurd" for a defeated sovereign to complain that he was forced to accept onerous terms, at what point, and how, exactly, can the victim prove, as Vattel's account would require him to prove, that terms are "contrary to justice and to all the duties of humanity," and that they violate "all" the principles of natural law, and are mere "oppression"? So sophisticated a thinker must have known that such requirements for overcoming the binding force of treaties entered into under duress could rarely if ever be met, even if there had been an impartial forum (which, of course, there was not) with power to determine the applicability of such critical precepts.[9]

Finally, it has to be recognized that this whole problem of imposed treaties of peace represents what we have elsewhere described as a limit-situation for international law.[10] We have now to add the possibility

7. *Id.* book IV, ch. IV, sec. 37, at 356.

8. *Id.*

9. Vattel's discussion of unequal treaties generally follows in essence the structure above analyzed, and is open to similar comment. See *id.* book II, ch. XII, secs. 180-181, at 169.

10. See J. Stone, *Quest for Survival* 63-71 (1961), from which this treatment is substantially derived.

that it represents a limit-situation also for any quickly approachable notion of international justice. And it is because a Vattel as well as a Grotius and their classical colleagues were already aware of this that they resorted to this kind of approach, on the dual level of clear rule of law and eloquent admonishment of conscience.

The question posed usually arises when there has been a war between States, and one State bears the guilt of war-making. If that guilty State was defeated and had unfavorable terms imposed on it there is little problem (at any rate for present purposes). The State got no fruits from its wrong, only burdens and penalties possibly according to its deserts. This is clear on principle, and it is now quite explicit in Article 75 of the 1969 Vienna Convention on the Law of Treaties[11] which will also be later referred to in Section V. That Article declares that the avoiding provisions of the Convention do not "prejudice . . . any obligation in relation to a treaty which may arise for an aggressor State in consequence of measures taken in conformity with the Charter of the United Nations with reference to that State's aggression." Treaties between a State which was the victim of aggression and an aggressor whose aggression it succeeded in defeating are clearly valid, under these provisions. But if the guilty State is the victor, it will usually stipulate for benefits from the defeated State, often involving deep suffering on that State's people.

We are all agreed that it is morally outrageous for the law to give effect to such a treaty. But our question is, how is the law to avoid giving effect to it? By hypothesis, since the beneficiary is the victor, he has the power to compel observance of the terms. By the same token no other States have been willing to engage the victor in a trial of force while the war is on; and *a fortiori* no other State is likely to begin a separate war to prevent enforcement of the terms after the peace treaty is signed. Apart from anything law might do, therefore, the equitable revision of the terms of the wicked treaty of peace must wait until the power relations of victor and vanquished have changed. This may take only a few years, as when Italy was expelled from Ethiopia or Germany from the Sudetenland and Czechoslovakia, on their defeat in World War II, or it may take generations, as did the liberation of Poland from the partitioning powers in World War I, or it may remain uncertain into our own times, as with the Soviet seizure of the Baltic States, and of paramountcy over Finland early in World War II.

This is the harsh and naked truth which Washington recognized when it stopped dead in the tracks of a campaign for the "liberation" of satellite Europe on the very occasions when in East Germany and in

11. *Open for signature* May 23, 1969, United Nations Conference on the Law of Treaties, *Official Records* 289, U.N. Doc. A/CONF.39/27 (1971) [hereinafter cited as Vienna Convention].

Hungary, the opportunity to give effect to the programme was offered to it, for it was offered only at a cost which might involve a general war. This, too, was the harsh and naked truth of Mr. Khrushchev's observation a month or two before the abortive Summit Conference of 1960, that the present arrangements in Europe (meaning satellite Europe) were produced by war (an observation reasserted just as clearly, though perhaps less offensively, by Prime Minister Kosygin on February 9, 1967), and it could only be changed by war. "War" here includes such a confrontation by changing power relations as makes it not worthwhile for the erstwhile victor to try and maintain his gains by war. In substance, this was precisely Vattel's point, that the victim of a "treaty of oppression" will "endure" it only so long as it lacks means to throw it off.

The power situation created by military victory being itself the firm anchorage of the terms of the treaty of peace, what attitudes can the law adopt as to the legality of these terms? Suppose the law says, in conformity with our sense of justice as men, that these terms are null and void, and no other State must recognize that they have any legal effect. Can this deprive the victor of the fruits of these terms? Conceivably it might have a certain nuisance value, and it might even constitute a degree of moral pressure against the victor. Yet the basic fruits will usually be placed by the terms of peace within his actual grasp, which no mere nuisance tactics will relax; and as an aggressor he is unlikely to be sensitive to moral pressure. In substance even if the legal rule squarely denied his titles under the peace treaty, he would still continue to enjoy the fruits, as Japan continued to do in Manchuria, despite the refusal of members of the League to recognize her title.

But the story would not end there. For whatever view be taken of the Japanese conquest of Manchuria, many other states in the world still had need to maintain legal relations of some sort with both Manchuria and Japan. If they, on the one hand, were not prepared by force to undo the Japanese conquest, and international law, on the other hand, forbade them to have any dealings on the basis of the *status quo,* then Japan and Manchuria would cease *pro tanto* to be within the international legal order at all. And this result might be as harmful to the rest of the world as it was to Japan. And since over a recent generation many States and areas of the world have become involved in such forcible changes, international law might find itself in the position of not extending at a particular time to a substantial number of the States and peoples of the world.

These are some of the reasons why international law as well as the practice of States on which it is based have continued, even into our own age, to recognize the validity of the terms of a treaty of peace imposed by victor on vanquished. The lawyers have continued to express emphatically that the imposition of such terms violates natural justice, good conscience, and fairness. They have sometimes declared that the only way in which the victor can purge himself of the sin was to enter upon negotiations for a new treaty, on the basis of freedom and equality, with the defeated party. They shared, therefore, the general sense of moral outrage. But they saw no way in their world, any more than we can see one in ours, whereby international law can take unto itself sufficient power to defeat every victor at the moment of his victory. In a world in which militarily strong States remain the supreme depositories of wordly power and collective organs wield only feeble power, and that only by the grace of those States, military victory by a State is a limit-situation for international law, as it is for the vanquished.

But the choice before international law is in one way more difficult than the choice before the vanquished. For the vanquished it may be counted noble and even wise if, in the name of justice or some other high principle, they reject all terms and choose the path of self-immolation. But for international law there is really no alternative to accommodation with the victor as to his terms for the vanquished. The victor will have whatever way his power, tempered by his conscience gives him, whatever international law may do. The effect of refusing the limited accommodation will thus be but to destroy in whole or in part the international legal order generally. And in the case of a war in which the greatest military States are involved, this would but make it all the easier for the victor to impose on the world a whole new legal order tailor-made to suit his own interests. Insofar as the international legal order exists to mitigate as far as possible the rigors of life among States, and not for its own sake, there can be neither virtue, wisdom, nor nobility in destroying itself in a polite and futile protest against those rigors and injustices which it cannot mitigate. It has neither the right nor the duty to commit suicide, when suicide can only increase the rigors on States and peoples

It is only rarely, in most national societies, that the forces of marginal demands reach dimensions which the public force cannot overwhelm. When this happens, the stable and robust national legal order breaks. A new legal order is substituted, whether by a dictator, a constituent assembly, or other revolutionary instrument. This breach in the continuity of the legal order is what we mean in the strictest sense by revolution, because the public monopoly of force is so critical in a national legal order that, when this monopoly is broken, the legal order is also broken. When we move over to the international legal order all is topsy-turvy. Here we have an order not flexible under the hand of a legislator, but held rigid in the grip of States whose joint consent is necessary for change. Here we have, instead of a stability and robustness founded on a public monopoly of force, an absence of any substantial public force and the persistence of great concentrations of military power in the private hands of States. Here at a pinch the public force cannot prevail over the private force wielded by any of a substantial number of the members of the community; it can attempt at the most to marshal some of these private forces against others for public ends. This being so, the international legal order is frequently confronted in hostile fashion by a superior force of its own members. If, therefore, the pattern of the national legal order were here followed, the international legal order, and any norms of justice which support it, would have a moth-like existence, fluttering inevitably and precariously year by year into the destructive flame of power. To avoid so shiftless an existence, the international legal order takes the extraordinary course of providing by its own rules for its collision with overwhelming power. The municipal legal system breaks under these strains; the international legal system is not broken, it merely operates, incorporating into it the net result of what otherwise would be an extra-legal, or even an illegal, revolution.

The doctrine of "the just war" as formulated by St. Augustine and incorporated by Grotius into his design for a modern international law, has been the repository into our own times of many noble aspirations for a righteous and peaceful world order. But as regards the limit-situations here under discussion, the criteria of the justness or unjustness of war, whether offered as doctrines of the law of God or of the law of nature and nations, could not be sustained as either religious or social or specifically legal controls.[12] Even if the doctrine were to establish itself as a part of international law, as some still think it may and should, its effectiveness for the control of violence between individual States would remain problematic.[13] It has been ably suggested, indeed, in recent notable reexaminations by Robert W. Tucker, that forms of the just-war doctrine are implicit in the policies and conduct of the nuclear giant states of our own times, and that as expounded and practiced by them, the actual tendency of use of the doctrine may be to increase rather than decrease both the number of occasions and the level of violence. And it has also been thought that the doctrine, as now addressed impartially to secular states by the second Vatican Council, with all its great religious and ethical prestige, cannot even yet be stated

12. On this see Stone, *Legal Controls, supra* note 1, at (especially) 13-14, 16-17; and generally J. Stone, *Aggression and World Order* (1958) [hereinafter cited as Stone, *Aggression*] and *The Just War* (R.W. Tucker ed. 1960); R.W. Tucker, *The Just War and Vatican Council II: A Critique* (1966) [hereinafter cited as Tucker]. See also Miller, "The Contemporary Significance of the Doctrine of Just War," 16 *World Politics* 254 (1963).

13. See Stone, *Legal Controls, supra* note 1, at 331-34, 381-82; Stone, *Aggression, supra* note 12, *passim.*

precisely enough to exclude each State's freedom to interpret the requirements of justice in a manner as likely as not to continue the escalation.[14]

To challenge the implications of such an analysis would pre-require that we can somehow reverse the menacing tendency of State power to mold to its purposes the nationally acceptable versions of truth and justice which underlie conflicting interpretations of the "justness" of particular causes of war. But even if, as all of us must devoutly hope, such a pre-requirement could be met, this would still leave most difficult problems to be faced in an effort to exclude gross injustices from being tolerated in international law. That law would still from time to time be confronted with limit-situations in which it would have to choose, as we have seen, between three alternatives so dour that only the third remains as a kind of Hobson's choice. First, it might choose to immolate itself in resistance to the will of the victory, with little prospect of gain for mankind. Or, second, it might choose to seek desperately for sufficient power to defeat every victor at the moment of victory. Or, third, it might choose, as it has done hitherto, to incorporate the victor's terms into the body of international law, thus preserving at any rate the rest of its own rules and the possibility of its own future growth.

II. ARTICLE 52 OF THE VIENNA CONVENTION ON THE LAW OF TREATIES

Despite redoubtable efforts, the International Law Commission, led by its eminent Special Rapporteurs on the Law of Treaties, Sir Hersch Lauterpacht (1953), Sir Gerald Fitzmaurice (1958), and Sir Humphrey Waldock (1963), tracked no clear legal path through this limit-situation for international law and justice created by the obstinate facts of power.[15] Sir Gerald Fitzmaurice's draft respected these facts, and on this ground, while it provided for the case of duress exercised against a State's negotiations, it offered no provision as to duress exercised against the State itself. He observed rather cogently that "the same compulsion . . . that procured the conclusion of the treaty will ensure its execution; and by the time, if ever, that circumstances permit of its repudiation, it will have been carried out, and many steps taken under it will be

14. See Tucker, *supra* note 12; and P. Ramsey's attempted rebuttal of Tucker's critique in *id.* at 68.

15. See, respectively, "Law of Treaties," [1953] 2 *Y.B. Int'l L. Comm'n* 90, 147-52 (Lauterpacht) [hereinafter cited as 1953 Report]; "Law of Treaties," [1958] 2 *Y.B. Int'l L. Comm'n* 20, 26, 38-39 (Fitzmaurice) [hereinafter cited as 1958 Report]; "Law of Treaties," [1963] 2 *Y.B. Int'l L. Comm'n* 1, 50-52 [hereinafter cited as Second 1963 Waldock Report]; *id.* at 197-98 [hereinafter cited as Third 1963 Waldock Report]; "Draft Articles on the Law of Treaties and Commentaries," 21 U.N. GAOR, Supp. 9, U.N. Doc. A/6309/Rev. 1, *reprinted in* 61 *Am. J. Int'l L.* 285, 406-09, 438-41 (1967) [hereinafter cited as 1966 Report].

irreversible or reversible, if at all, only by further acts of violence." Basically this conforms to classical publicist positions, and respects the differences between the international and municipal orders which have just been sketched.

It was, however, the supposedly conflicting view of the other two Rapporteurs which is generally thought to have prevailed, and which was finally embodied in Article 52 of the Vienna Convention on Treaties,[16] which now provides: "A treaty is void if its conclusion has been procured by the threat or use of force in violation of the principles of international law embodied in the Charter of the United Nations."

Sir Hersch proposed that treaties "imposed" by threat or use of force "in violation of the principles of the Charter of the United Nations are invalid if so declared by the International Court of Justice at the request of any State."[17] While admitting that experience "shows that the nullification of treaties imposed by force takes place not in pursuance of a judicial verdict but of a political action taken in conformity with changed conditions of power," he was content to assert the above as the correct legal principle regardless of the practicalities of implementation. Nor was he concerned to solve the problem of how to ensure that the Court had jurisdiction to make this declaration, in view of the fact that victors, vanquished, as well as any intervening third State would have to give consent.

Sir Humphrey Waldock's positions underwent various vicissitudes, moving to the view that a tainted treaty is null *ab initio,* even if the coerced State does not ask and does not even wish for this. He shared with Sir Hersch, of course, the view that principle required such a treaty to be void. Yet since he, unlike Sir Hersch, provided no forum for determining when a treaty is null,[18] the net effect would surely be to

16. Note 11 *supra.*

17. See 1953 Report, *supra* note 15, at 147; and Sir Humphrey's summation of Sir Hersch's view in Second 1963 Waldock Report, *supra* note 15, at 53.

18. Article 65 of the Vienna Convention, *supra* note 11, concerning procedures of notice and the like for cases involving *inter alia* "invalidity" and "termination" of a treaty, has little or no bearing on this point. Not only do procedures involving notice seem irrelevant to the case of treaties whose voidness was declared, with extreme emphasis, to be *ab initio.* The Rapporteur's emphasis (it is recalled) was carried so far as to say that even if the victim state did not wish to void the treaty and indeed desired its continuance, the treaty would still be void. The victim would (he said) have to negotiate a new one with similar terms. It would certainly be inconsistent with this to say that voidness for duress under Article 52 is in some way conditional on fulfillment of the procedures of Article 65.

Moreover, if voidness under Article 52 were subject to the procedures of Article 65 this would also not affect the critique in the text. For the procedures of Article 65, paragraphs 1 and 2, even if they applied, do but set into motion processes which can only go beyond mere bilateral or multilateral diplomatic negotiation if all the parties so agree. Such mere negotiation would be an available recourse, even without Article 65; and its outcome would, under Article 62, depend on the realities of power just as much as under the traditional rule by which imposed treaties were valid, and changeable only by negotiation

leave the burden on the victim State of choosing whether to raise or not to raise the plea of nullity. This *solution,* which is what became fully embodied in Article 52 of the Vienna Convention, still leaves unsolved the practical problem which had engaged the classical publicists, that the victim's willingness and success in asserting nullity depends on his relative power position.

This problem is, of course, the more intractable since these Rapporteurs, and now Article 52 itself, insist that voidness is conditioned, not on any simple presence of threat or use of force, which might be comparatively self-evident, but also violation thereby of the principles of the Charter. It is no doubt correct that Article 2(4) prohibits the threat or use of force. It may also be said that this is a "clear-cut" prohibition, as the Rapporteur seemed to say in para. 1 of his Comment, within whatever may be the scope of Article 2, paragraph 4. Sir Humphrey himself drew attention however (1966, paragraph 3 of Comment to Article 49) to the doubts surrounding the question whether the prohibition therein extends to less obvious forms of coercion than the merely physical, for example to "economic strangulation." And he should perhaps also have referred to even graver, as well as sharper and more complex, legal controversies as to the range of circumstances in which that prohibition operates, and therefore the entire application of Article 2(4) to concrete cases of use of force. In the light of these doubts it must be said that the scope of avoidance of treaties under his new Article (now Article 52 of the Vienna Treaty), far from being "clear-cut", is really profoundly obscure.

This obscurity represents a veritable Achilles' heel. Insofar as it exists, a cloud of doubt lies over a wide range of treaties, with no forum usually available either to clear it up or to precipitate it into legal nullity. All the more, insofar as this last is so, would it usually fall to the allegedly coerced State to determine whether to confront its alleged oppressor with the plea of nullity. Its decision on this matter would necessarily be determined, in existing international condition, by considerations of power relations. The actual effects would not be significantly different

of a new treaty. Nor does Article 65, paragraph 3, providing for recourse to Article 33 of the United Nations Charter, thereby afford any forum capable of deciding the issue independently of the *ad hoc* consent of all parties at variance.

Finally, Article 65, paragraph 4, seems to make clear in so many words that the procedures described in that Article shall *not* affect (not merely, be it noted, shall not *prejudice*) "rights and obligations" of the parties with regard to "settlement of disputes" under "*any* provisions in force." So that even if we could plausibly read some designation of a competent forum into the preceding paragraphs (which we cannot) paragraph 4 would destroy this plausibility, and leave us still confronted by the difficulties raised in the text.

from those operative under customary law where the imposed treaty is valid but will, if the power relations change sufficiently, be renegotiated or denounced.[19]

III. "UNEQUAL" TREATIES

Another irony is manifest at this point. This relates to current theses that merely "unequal" or "leonine" treaties also void, without specification as to either degree of "unequalness", or the illegality of the means of inducement, when they are juxtaposed with the principle concerning treaties imposed by duress. In relation to the latter, all three Rapporteurs, despite their deeply divergent philosophies, seemed to agree in one respect, namely, that the risks to general stability of treaty relations by a rule nullifying duress-induced treaties would be least in the case of the extreme physical duress of military defeat. Correspondingly, they seemed to agree that risks become greater as lesser types of pressure and coercion, such as economic and political ones become involved. Sir Gerald Fitzmaurice's statement went straight to this point. The argument for nullification, he thought, "must evidently be confined to the use or threat of *physical* force, since there are all too numerous ways in which a State might allege that it had been induced to enter into a treaty by pressure of *some* kind (for example, economic)."[20] If it were extended to the latter less gross situations "a dangerously wide door to the invalidation of treaties, and hence a threat to the stability of the treaty-making process, would be opened."[21] Hence, if introduction of a nullity rule should be considered at all, it should "obviously" be "confined to the gross situations."

The deepest point of the current irony is reached when Soviet representatives and writers concurrently argue that treaties which are entered into under coercion, which are of an "enslaving" or "economic" nature, which otherwise disregard the principle of equality, or which do not correspond to a State's "real will", are thereby void under in-

19. Beside these rather old-fashioned difficulties, the points of real novelty in the 1966 Report are insignificant, even if technically interesting. One is that the Article was not to affect the validity *ab initio* of a coerced treaty entered into before "the modern law regarding the threat or use of force" was established. This "modern law" at the latest came into effect with Article 2(4) of the Charter; but the Special Rapporteur left it open as to whether it might not have come into effect earlier, and if so, when. On this most controversial issue see Stone, *Legal Controls, supra* note 1, at 298-300, 324-27; J. Stone, *Aggression, supra,* note 12, (especially) 1-103 (1959), and literature there cited.

20. 1958 Report. *supra* note 15, para. 62, at 38.

21. *Id.*

ternational law.[22] Soviet leaders have also insisted on the binding force of treaties of peace imposed with the extreme of coercion and inequality involved in military defeat. No doubt it could be argued in resolution of the apparent conflict that the settlements which Khrushchev and Kosygin, for example, have admitted were imposed by force and insisted could only be changed by force were not imposed by *unlawful* force. It could also be said that even such settlements as were based on clearly or arguably "unlawful" use of force, like the "absorption" of the Baltic States by the Soviet Union, were at the relevant time, that is, prior to the coming into force of the United Nations Charter, not technically unlawful. Neither of these arguments, however, would dispose of problems of violation of the Kellogg-Briand Pact or the League Covenant itself, by such clear suppressions by force of both the territorial integrity and political independence of the States concerned. Nor do they dispose of the paradox that "unequal" treaties can be void regardless of the presence of other illegality. The most dramatic point is that the imposed treaty of peace, on the validity of which Soviet practice rather indiscriminately insists, generally manifests both inequality and coercion in extreme forms. Thus, no objective criterion based on the mere degree of either or both of these elements can really explain the Soviet position.

In this state of the matter earnest writers[23] have proposed, in effect, giving the General Assembly a roving commission to determine voidness with respect to practically all treaties, for treaties are almost always, like contracts in municipal society, open to the charge that one party got the better bargain. So momentous a role directs our attention to the grave dangers raised by any extension of the legal authority of the General Assembly in present international conditions.[24] In addition to my own position as to the limit-situations with which imposed treaties of peace confront both international law and justice, three other comments need to be made. One is that in international society as in municipal societies, we cannot base the judgment of justice on equality alone. Another is that the time is obviously distant when any important group of States, except perhaps and for obvious reasons some of the newer African States, would ever grant to the General Assembly or any other

22. See the valuable discussion in Ingrid Detter, "The Problem of Unequal Treaties, 15 *Int'l & Comp. L.Q.* 1068, 1081-85 [hereinafter cited as Detter, "Unequal Treaties"]. Many of the comments of the Soviet Union and other Socialist countries were directed to the extension (or even translation) of the coercion article into terms of "leonine" treaties, *e.g.*, certain ones accompanying grant of independence or economic aid. See, *e.g.*, U.S.S.R., Bulgaria, Byelorussia, Czechoslovakia in U.N. Doc. A/CN 4/183 Add. 1, at 3, 6, 9. *Cf.* these same states in U.N. Doc. A/CN 4/175, at 236, 264.

23. Detter, "Unequal Treaties," *supra* note 22, at 1086-89.

24. See sections VI-IX *infra*.

United Nations organ such a roving commission to probe and declare void any treaty they have made. Nor is it pleasant to contemplate the mixture of pandemonium and Tower of Babel which would occur if such a miracle did in fact take place.[25]

In view of all this we may finally have to recognize that this particular gross and lamentable conflict of international legal binding effect with justice[26] has thus proved insoluble by merely legal invention.[27] The heart of the matter lies not in technical niceties regarding the effect of duress in vitiating treaties, but in the overall problem of regulating the use of coercion in international relations.[28] The key to the containment of coercion, including threats of major coercion, still lies, however regrettably, in international politics rather than in international law.[29] Correspondingly, it is prudent to expect that the use of *principles* offered to resolve questions of voidness of treaties induced by *unlawful* force, or entered into as *unequal* treaties, will manifest itself in the raucous operations of political warfare rather than the quiet processes of adjudication, or the drafting and conclusion of treaties.

25. The above critique is directed to the general concepts thus far offered to delimit treaties to be declared void. It does not exclude the possibility of delimiting more concrete classes of treaties to be void or voidable, *per se,* as it were. Such might be (without offering these as necessarily warranted, or adequately drafted) post-colonial treaties limiting a new State's opportunities of developing its overseas trade or conducting its foreign relations freely; or treaties involving a substantially total alienation (for instance under pressure of immediate distress) of a nation's economic assets; or concessions to a foreign state or other entity, manifesting what Roman law would have called *laesio enormis,* or gross inadequacy of the *quid pro quo*. Such precepts, by concreteness in their framing, could avoid both futile attempts to control uncontrollable limit-situations of power, and criteria (such as "unequal") which cast an excessive cloud over treaty law generally.

26. On equality and justice in municipal legal orders see J. Stone, *Human Law and Human Justice* 325-35 (1965).

27. Even if the thesis of J.W. Burton, *International Relations* (1965) as to the inadequacy of "power" as the main focus of concern had some general, long-term validity, it could not affect the present point. Nor can the noblest pacificism subdue it; see recently from a reflecting pacifist standpoint, Folliet, "A Dissection of Pacificism," 2 *World Justice* 162 (1960). And see sections VI ff. *infra.*

28. This point was clearly made by Sir Gerald Fitzmaurice in his 1958 Report, *supra* note 15; and see Sir Humphrey Waldock's summation of it in the Second 1963 Waldock Report, *supra* note 15.

29. See in general Stone, *Aggression, supra* note 12; Stone, "What Price Effectiveness," 50 *Proc.* Am. Soc'y Int'l L. 198 (1956); Stone, "Realistic-Compliance Goals," 58 *Proc. Am. Soc'y Int'l L.* 24 (1964). The issues arising from Article 51 of the Vienna Convention *supra,* note 11, rendering of no effect consent given on behalf of states by individual representatives coerced by "acts or threats directed against" them are, of course, different and have not in the past been subject to the same difficulties. On the meaning of "acts or threats" under Article 51, see Sir Humphrey Waldock, Second 1963 Waldock Report, *supra* note 15.

IV. OCCUPATION AND SECURITY COUNCIL RESOLUTION OF NOVEMBER 22, 1967

It is a main conclusion of the analysis set forth above that attempts to push legal controls beyond the limit-situations created by war contribute to the protraction and exacerbation of conflict by political warfare rather than to settlement, and to the abuse rather than to the use of legal resources. The impotence of law in such situations is, at present, only too well illustrated by the mounting threats of force by "front-line" Arab States against the State of Israel, now reinforced with ancillary pressures by OPEC Arab States against the economic existence of most industrialized States. It is interesting to ask what attention is being paid in this conflict to the criterion given by Article 52 of the Vienna Convention on Treaties whereby threat or use of force "in violation of the principles of the United Nations Charter" is what invalidates a treaty procured by force. Though there may be debate as to what constitutes such a violation, it must be clear that a treaty induced by force without such violation would obviously not be caught by this invalidating rule. *A fortiori* it should follow that a military occupation resulting from hostilities resorted to in self-defense, would not be caught by any emanation from Article 52.

Insofar as it is not caught within article 52, or the United Nations Charter, there was no legal ground on which the Israeli occupation following the 1967 War can be impugned. The matter rests with general international law, whose pertinent provisions are very clear. These are that a belligerent who controls territory at the moment of cease-fire is entitled to remain, *uti possidetis,* until he is ousted by a renewal of hostilities, or until a peace is negotiated. And this peace might, and frequently does, embrace territorial adjustments. Whether and how far this legal position has been changed under the Charter is the present question. On this issue, the ambivalence of recent doctrinal statements is matched by that of the well-known Security Council resolution[30] of November 22, 1967.[31] This Resolution was adopted on the motion of the United Kingdom representative, Lord Caradon, after prolonged and meticulous negotiations with all the parties concerned.[32] On no points were these negotiations more prolonged and painfully meticulous than on Principle I(i) of "withdrawal of Israel armed forces from territories occupied in the recent conflict," and the recital in the Preamble of the "inadmissibility of the acquisition of territory by war,"

30. Security Council Res. 242, in *Resolutions and Records of the Security Council, 1967,* at 8.
31. *Cf.* on this matter J. Stone, *No Peace—No War in the Middle East* (1969); J. Stone, *Of Law and Nations* 436-41 (1974).
32. This part of the story is well told by Arthur Lall, *The United Nations and the Suez Crisis* 260-63 (1967).

both of them linked with Principle I(ii) asserting the right of "every State in the area . . . to live in peace within secure and recognized boundaries. . . ." And the most painful and painstaking negotiation of all centered on the deliberate refusal to insert the word "the" into the phrase: "withdrawal of Israel armed forces from territories occupied. . . ."

Lord Caradon withstood formidable pressures from Arab and other States to adopt the formulation *"all the* territories." He also resisted an Indian argument, supported by threat of a Russian veto, that a projected expression of the Indian view that the Resolution was to be understood as embodying the definite article, would create a *binding* Council understanding to that effect. It was after Lord Caradon indicated that he would, for his part, respond to such an Indian move by declaring that "the Indian interpretation is not binding on the Council," that the Indian delegate joined in the unanimous vote. In the result, Lord Caradon merely declared that "it will be recognized that it is only the Resolution that will bind us, and we regard its wording as clear." Ambassador Goldberg made a similar declaration and, of course, it is clear in any case that the adoption of a resolution consists not of diverse views and policies of individual members, but of the meaning attributable to its actual contents. And despite a rather successful intervening campaign by Arab and Communist State spokesmen to spread a contrary impression, the United Kingdom Government reaffirmed in the House of Commons, as recently as late as 1969, that the November Resolution it had drafted and sponsored did not necessarily require withdrawal from *"all the* territories" occupied by Israel in the 1967 war. Lord Caradon himself reconfirmed this history in a speech in Jerusalem in February 1975.[33]

In the absence of a negotiated peace, then, what can be said concerning the final disposition of the territories which fell under Israeli administration after the 1967 war?

Were the charge that Israel entered the occupied territories by an unlawful resort to war well-founded, then insistence on Israeli withdrawal would have substance. This would then flow from the assumed unlawfulness of the resort to war from which the occupation ensued, and from the application of the principle *ex iniuria non oritur ius* to the facts as thus hypothetically assumed. Even this, however, would seem to be negated, as to Jerusalem and the West Bank and as to Gaza, by the

33. Jerusalem Post Weekly, Feb. 13, 1973. Contrary expressions forced from the United Kingdom, other European countries and Japan, by Arab threats to cut off oil in 1973, were made under duress probably caught by Article 52 of the Vienna Convention, *supra* note 11.

fact that Jordan and Egypt themselves appear to have no title to these lands, save that of former occupants arising from illegal resorts to force in the 1948 war.[34]

Of course, the actual facts of the June war were *not* as assumed in the last paragraph. Even according to criteria of aggression long adopted and disseminated by the Soviet Union itself, unlawful forceful initiatives were taken by Arab States before any Israeli move across their respective frontiers on June 5. These included naval blockade of the Straits of Tiran, and shellings from the Gaza Strip by Egypt, the air runs over Israel by Syria, and the bombardment of West Jerusalem by Jordan. All this was apart from the massive mobilisation of armies and aircraft on all her frontiers, which also on some views left her no choice but to act in self-defense.[35] The view of Members of the Security Council was indicated in the fact that by a majority of eleven (including all the other Permanent Members) against four the Soviet draft resolution seeking to declare Israel the aggressor in the June hostilities, failed of adoption. And substantial majorities of the General Assembly, after prolonged debate and an adjourned session, also later refused to pass any of several similar resolutions. The majorities (including abstentions in each case) were of the order of 88 against 32, 98 against 22, 81 against 36 and 78 against 36. It seems clear, on this record, that the principle *ex iniuria non oritur ius* cannot be applied against Israel. If the matter were then left, as in the present view it finally must, to the relevant rule of traditional international law, the rule applicable would be that of *uti possidetis,* leaving the final territorial outcome to the negotiation of peace, and offering no principle justifying any particular change in the meantime.

However, we are still confronted with ambivalences of the November Resolution, the meaning of which on the point, though it is probably only a non-magisterial decision, may still offer some evidence of State practice. What then, first of all, of the preambulatory recital of the "inadmissibility of the acquisition of territory by war?" Its apparent simple clarity fails immediately at a second glance. One possibility is that it declares an absolute rule of restoration of the *status quo ante,* even in favour of an aggressor and regardless of the merely aggressive function of the territory concerned. This would supersede *pro tanto* the

34. See also for fuller analyses J. Stone, *No Peace—No War in the Middle East* 38-40 (1970); Blum, "The Missing Reversioner," 3 *Israel L. Rev.* 279 (1968).

35. *Cf.* the similar conclusions in Schwebel, "What Weight to Conquest?" 64 *Am. J. Int'l L.* 344 (1970); O'Brien, "International Law and the Outbreak of War in the Middle East, 1967," 11 *Orbis* 692, 722-23 (1967). E. Lauterpacht, *Jerusalem and the Holy Places* 52 (1968); R.A. Falk, Letter to the Editor, in 64 *Am. J. Int'l L.* 162, 163 (1970). N. Feinberg has collected and quoted views of Henri Rolin, Charles Chaumont, T.M. Franck and others in his *On an Arab Jurist's Approach to the State of Israel* 98 ff. (1971).

maxim *ex iniuria non oritur ius,* and would bar acquisition "by war" even if the entry was, as in the case of Israel, lawful. This is a first possible meaning; but a second, and even a third meaning, are more likely. The second is that the recital was merely recalling, in the eloquently ambiguous style apt in a preamble for reconciling diverse standpoints, the *ex iniuria* principle as this applies to war. The third possibility, similarly plausible and motivated, is that the recital was merely stating the rather technical and commonplace principle, but one formerly debated, that mere military occupation or conquest does not transfer title, this requiring some further act in the law such as formal annexation or cession under a negotiated treaty of peace.

Only the first of these meanings, if it were correct, would give a ready-made answer for the territorial settlement in the Middle East; it would require full withdrawal from all the territories. The second meaning, when we remember the above facts and the voting positions of the majority of Members both of the Security Council and the General Assembly in 1967, would leave the customary *uti possidetis* rule applicable. The territorial settlement would still have to be negotiated. The third approach would leave the disposition of the matter virtually to the occupier's discretion. As between these three meanings, only the second presents the substance of existing law, while the third constitutes a kind of procedural rider to it. The first is inconsistent by its breadth with any existing law, unless we are to assume, as we surely cannot, that this recital in the Preamble constituted in itself a radical piece of innovative legislation.

It may be said, as to this last, that a *via media* would be to treat the recital, not as a legislative innovation, but as a declaration of policy. So treated, the recital would be asserting *de lege ferenda* that an occupier ought to withdraw even before peace terms are agreed, even if as in the instant case he entered lawfully in self-defense against an aggressor. This is, indeed, worth very serious examination. A rule presented *de lege ferenda* must *ex hypothesi* be a rule of which the consequences are regarded as desirable for members of the community generally. But would not *this particular proposed rule* be disastrously *undesirable?* It would certainly assure every prospective aggressor that, should he fail, any territory of his own which he lost in the course of his unlawful adventures, would be restored to him. It would do this even if he still openly reserved the liberty to renew his aggressive designs, and even if, as with some parts of the territory involved here, the areas involved are geopolitically appropriated for the aggressive activity, and little else. Professor Baxter's reference to "ease" of administration of a simple *status quo ante* rule seems inadvertent to these effects of underwriting unconditionally the aggressor's risks of loss from any planned aggression.[36] Such a proposed rule would shift international law from its present position which sets out, by means of the *ex iniuria* principle, to discourage aggressors, onto a course of encouraging aggressors by reinsuring them in advance against the principal risks of defeat. It would be strange, other meanings being available, to choose a meaning with so novel and grotesque a result.[37]

The conclusion that the preambular recital in no way affects the existing international law principle applicable to acquisition of territory, and that this still is *ex iniuria non oritur ius,* is now confirmed beyond serious doubt by the terms of the definition of *aggression* finally adopted by consensus at the twenty-ninth General Assembly on December 14, 1974 in Resolution 3314 (XXIX).[38] Spectacularly equivocal as that definition is on many critical points, its terms are quite beyond doubt on the point that the legal consequences of the use of force still depend on whether the resort to force was unlawful.[39] Even in the reference to this matter in the Preamble to the Resoluion, the continuation of this rule, which conforms to basic principles of international law as well as to common sense and international policy, is maintained.

However speciously attractive maxims like "no weight to conquest!" may sound, they should thus not be mistaken for either actual or desirable international law. Such a maxim must be read, as a distinguished international lawyer has observed,[40] along with the legal principles that no legal right springs from a wrong, and that United Nations Members are required to refrain from the threat or use of force against the territorial integrity and political independence of any State. This leads Professor Schwebel to three basic points as to the existing international law concerning conquest. First, it remains lawful today for a State, when lawfully exercising self-defense, to seize and hold territory of the State attacking it, when this is necessary for its self-defense. Second, such an occupying State may stipulate, as a precondition to its withdrawal, the institution of measures to give it

36. Baxter, "The Legal Consequences of the Unlawful Use of Force under the Charter," 62 *Proc. Am. Soc'y Int'l L.* 68 (1968) [hereinafter cited as Baxter]. See note 42 *infra* and accompanying text.

37. It may perhaps be added that Soviet and Arab voting patterns in the West Irian and Goan affairs showed no particular support for a norm barring *simpliciter* acquisition of territory by force. See Halderman, "Some International Constitutional Aspects of the Palestine Case," 33 *Law & Contempt. Prob.* 78, (especially) 89-90 (1968), in the Symposium edited by him, "The Middle East Crisis: Test of International Law," *id.* at 1.

38. "Definition of Aggression," G.A. Res. 3314, 29 U.S. GAOR, Supp. 31, vol. 1, at 142, U.N. Doc. A/9631 [hereinafter cited as Definition of Aggression].

39. See, *e.g., id.* preamble (5th, 6th, & 7th paras.), arts. 1, 2, 6. For this writer's elaboration of this and other aspects of the 1974 Concenous Definition of Aggression, see now J. Stone, *Conflict through Consensus* (1977).

40. Schwebel, "What Weight to Conquest," 64 *Am. J. Int'l L.* 344 (1970).

reasonable assurance that the territory shall not again be used as a base for attack on itself. Third, and no less important, where the prior possession by the ousted State itself arose from unlawful seizure, then the State which has now entered lawfully in course of self-defense has, in any case, a better legal title than the ousted State. He concludes, not without persuasiveness, that, since the possession by Egypt and Jordan of Gaza and the West Bank from 1948 to 1967 was itself by unlawful occupation and since the Israeli actions of self-defense were lawful in both 1948 and 1967, Israel already holds those territories by a legal title superior to any claimable by the former illegal occupiers.

V. ISRAEL'S RIGHTS OVER OCCUPIED TERRITORIES

It is certainly the case that the Israeli military occupation after 1967 pending a negotiated settlement is perfectly lawful under international law. Principles of law have been canvassed by distinguished writers, quite recently, from which it is more than arguable that the constant use of these territories in the decades preceding 1967 as bases for unlawful armed attacks against Israel would legally entitle Israel, should it so choose, to annex them. Professor R.R. Baxter, in a 1970 symposium on the legal status of war, noted the difficulties as to forum and applicable standards for determining which side's resort to force is unlawful, and also observed that "[i]t is conceivable that in some instances the complete subjugation of a persistent aggressor may be the only way to maintain the territorial integrity and political independence of the State attacked."[41] Mr. Lauterpacht, on the same matter, has submitted that the limits of proportionality in self-defense, which in his thesis must replace the "state of war," called for measures to restore the *status quo ante,* and also "perhaps to exclude the renewal of aggressive measures." It did not much clarify the ambiguity of this, as applied to post-war territorial settlements, for him to add that the self-defending state is "not, for example, entitled to annex *the whole* of the attacker's territory."[42]

These positions, Delphic as they are, have an obvious importance for the current Middle East crisis. The Golan Heights were openly used for almost twenty years by Syria, in violation of the Armistice Agreement of the Charter, as a base for attacks on the adjacent territory of Israel. Egyptian occupation of Gaza was used as a forward offensive base remote from metropolitan Egypt, pointing towards the main cities of Israel only forty miles away, and threatening to bisect that state, in 1967, at the narrow neck of only twenty miles dividing Egyptian forces

41. Baxter, *supra* note 36, at 74.

42. Lauterpacht, "The Legal Irrelevance of the 'State of War,' " 62 *Proc. Am. Soc'y Int'l L.* 58, 64 (1968). (Emphasis added).

from their Jordanian allies. It was thence that on Egyptian demand, on May 18, 1967, the United Nations Force was removed in view of Egypt's projected land operations, shortly before her actual initiation of hostilities by closure of the Tiran Straits on May 26, 1967. The "bulge" of territory held under Jordanian military occupation, south of Jerusalem, forbidding access to Jerusalem except by a corridor of only five to ten miles invested on all sides by Jordanian forces, raised similar problems, complicated, however, by the presence of centres of population such as Bethlehem and Jericho.

The actuality and the difficulty of the question call, perhaps, for brief consideration here in terms going beyond generalities about what it might be "easy" for the organs of the United Nations to administer. Mr. Lauterpacht's propositions that a self-defending State is not entitled "to annex the whole of the attacker's territory,"[43] but also that steps may be justified "to exclude the renewal of aggressive measures,"[44] leave open whether *some* territorial changes can be made, for the latter purpose. Professor Baxter indicates that it is comparatively easy for the United Nations organs to require the Parties, regardless of who is the aggressor and who is the victim, to return to their original boundaries. Yet this, when read with his recognition on the same page that there may be circumstances in which "complete subjugation of a persistent aggressor may be the only way to maintain the territorial integrity and political independence of the State attacked,"[45] obviously also leaves that same question rather open. In fact, of course, the State of Israel has not as yet attempted to avail itself of that legal possibility.

The view regarding this matter under general international law asserted by Professor Baxter is now implicitly reaffirmed by Article 75 of the Vienna Convention. As already mentioned,[46] this provides that "[t]he provisions of the present Convention are without prejudice to any obligation in relation to a treaty which may arise for an aggressor State in consequence of measures taken in conformity with the Charter of the United Nations with reference to that State's aggression." Insofar as Article 51 of the Charter scrupulously preserves the legality of self-defense against armed attack, nothing in Article 52 of the Vienna Convention or any other relevant legal principle could impeach the validity of territorial adjustments by treaty between Israel and the Arab States involved in the 1967 or 1973 armed attacks. And it is difficult to see, if this is so, any legal basis for questioning the interim rights of Israel as a military occupier pending the conclusion of the customary treaties of peace.

43. *Id.*
44. *Id.*
45. Baxter, *supra* note 36, at 74.
46. See note 11 *supra* and accompanying text.

VI. THE GENERAL ASSEMBLY RESOLUTION OF NOVEMBER 22, 1974

Insofar, then, as general international law and the Charter could be expected to operate in this area, it was also to be expected that the continued hostilities of the Arab States against Israel should have been censured by the appropriate United Nations organs, especially after the gross and flagrant Egyptian and Syrian breaches of the cease-fire agreements in 1969-1970 and 1973. *A fortiori* one should expect that in an arena supposed to be governed by the principles of international law, examined in Sections IV and V above, the steady and open support of terrorist group operations against Israel by Lebanon, Egypt, Syria and Iraq, under the acknowledged aegis of the Palestine Liberation Organization, would be the objects of at least censure by United Nations organs. The facts, of course, are a startling perversion of all these expectations, turning them dismayingly upside down.

Within the overall frame of the Arab States' political use of the weapons of oil boycott, of the Soviet and French rearming of front-line Arab States, of the power-political drives of Soviet policy, and of the multiplication of United Nations Members aligned in log-rolling voting blocs with Communist and Arab Members, the Security Council showed itself impotent through the October war of 1973 to give effect to either legal or political principles. No move was made, for example, to arrest the treacherous attacks by Egypt and Syria in October 1973, as long as they had any chance of succeeding. In 1974 the General Assembly, with the Arab States' oil weapon poised over its Membership, passed successive resolutions which, in respects I shall shortly detail, seem a travesty of relevant basic principles of both the Charter and international law. No one can tell how the voting on the merits of those resolutions would have gone, had not the Damocles' sword of the extreme coercion of the oil boycott hung over the proceedings—"a stranglehold" British Foreign Secretary Callaghan termed it, in a television interview on November 21, 1974. Such operations in the General Assembly reflect neither law, justice nor morality; they threaten, on the contrary, by the dishonesty of judgments pronounced in such a context, the most elementary bases of all of these, together with, I must submit, the survival of the United Nations and the growth of a more stable international community.

First, the General Assembly, in the main resolution of November 22, 1974,[47] purported (by a vote of 89 against 8, with 37 abstentions and 4 States absent) to recognize the Palestine Liberation Front as a claimant to rather unspecified parts of "Palestine." By this it impliedly endorsed

47. "Question of Palestine," G.A. Res. 3236, 29 U.N. GAOR, Supp. 31, vol. 1, at 4, U.N. Doc. A/9631 (1974).

past years of terrorist activities through various "fronts" and "groups" deliberately aimed, not only at the State of Israel, but at civilian men, women and children, as well as at the citizens, airports and aircraft of States not involved in the Middle East dispute. And by the same token, it seems to offer dispensation for the continuation of such activities.

Second, the resolution also violated other legal principles and legal rights vested under international law, and under longstanding United Nations resolutions. Thus, by its blanket endorsement of the Palestinian Organization's aspirations, which have since that Organization's inception openly included that of destroying the State of Israel, the resolution violated Israel's rights of sovereign equality under Article 2, para. 1 of the Charter, not to speak of its rights to be free of threat or use of force and armed attack under Article 2(4) and Article 51.

Third, it contradicted the assurance given by Security Council Resolution 242[48] of 1967 of Israel's right to "live in peace within secure and recognized boundaries free from threats or acts of force."[49]

Fourth, by rexffirming that it calls "the inalienable rights of the Palestinian people *in Palestine,*" with no geographical limitation on those last two words, it contradicted the United Nations Partition Resolution,[50] which Israel accepted, but against which the Arab States unsuccessfully waged their first unlawful war. Historic and geographic "Palestine" includes not only the West Bank, but also the whole of Israel, Gaza and Jordan. The Jordanian representative in the debate made clear his country's view that Israel was in the "Palestine" claimed for the Palestinians, but presumably that Jordan was not. The fact remains that of the 118,440 square kilometres of Palestine, 97,740 (or almost four-fifths) are the State of Jordan, that most of Jordan's citizens are Palestinians, constituting with Palestinians on the West Bank the great majority of all Palestinians. Is Jordan not already a State for Palestinian Arabs?

Fifth, with like irresponsibility, the 1974 resolution implicitly contradicted the General Assembly's deliberate and well considered recognition of the rightfulness of the creation of the State of Israel, though, of course, the *legal* existence of Israel does not depend on such recognition.

Sixth, while the General Assembly in 1947 requested the Security Council to treat the use of force against Partition as "a threat to the peace, breach of the peace or act of aggression," the General Assembly in 1974 lent itself to the role of a cat'spaw or even an accomplice in generating renewal of such unlawful use of force by Arab States and the Palestinian groups.

48. Note 30 *supra.*
49. *Id.* para. 1 (ii).
50. G.A. Res. 181, U.N. Doc. A/519 at 131 (1947).

Seventh, this regrettable role taken by the General Assembly is underlined by the resolution's express approval of the use of "*all means*" by the Palestine Liberation Organization to achieve its ends, despite the continuing record of unlawful violence of its constituent elements, and by its appeal to all States and international organizations to assist with such means. The succeeding words "in accordance with the Purposes and Principles of the Charter" are quite ambivalent as to whether any limits are to be read into this licentious endorsement of "all means."

This General Assembly action was quickly followed by the Palestinian attack on civilians at Beth Shean within the boundaries of the State of Israel, by the air hijacking of the British VC 10 with scores of passengers on board in Dubai, and a grenade attack in a Tel Aviv cinema, a sequence which suggests that at least the first and last of the points made in the preceding pages of this article should here be expanded. Naturally, Mr. Arafat in seeking the General Assembly's ligitimation of the claims of the Palestinian Liberation Organization did not highlight terrorist attacks against civilians, including the aircraft and civilians of other States as well as Israel. And after the General Assembly's resolutions he made verbal disavowals of violence against other then Israeli military targets, and even requested that the Dubai hijackers be handed over to his Organization for discipline. But words do not in themselves change facts. The fact that the General Assembly found it unnecessary to express any limits to "the means" which the P.L.O. was authorized to pursue, must be understood in the context of the record of its military groups right up to that moment and continuing thereafter. Seen in this light the resolutions remind us that the General Assembly, far from being an indicator for either law or conscience on the world scene, is proving itself capable of condoning and apparently offering support to the most clearly lawless activities of certain groups and States, against selected target States.

It is certainly a clear principle of international law, and a fundamental one, that every State shall be held legally responsible for the harm to other States brought about by use of violence in and from its territory, with its knowledge and acquiescence, and according to some views, even by its neglect. On the basis of this undoubted principle of international law the State of Israel has insisted on demanding that a number of Arab States should cease organizing, harbouring, or aiding terrorist groups for attacks against her territory, population and aircraft. But power-political alignments in the organs of the United Nations, now reinforced by the coercive "clout" of the oil weapon, have ridden roughshod over this principle, to the climactic point, in the General Assembly's "Palestinian" resolutions of November 1974, of encouraging implicitly the spread and intensification of violations of the principle.[51]

Until the phase of indiscriminate sabotage of civilian aircraft early in 1970, third States also were disposed to overlook, if not to condone, the flouting of this principle. We should no doubt remember, in mitigation of this, fear of the hostility of Arab States controlling great natural resources. The States showed themselves ready to exert open pressure even on judicial trials, as in the case of the Arab terrorists charged in the Greek courts with crimes arising from the aircraft attack at Athens airport in 1969. No doubt, too, reactions were also confused by the very proliferation of splinter terrorist groups under the aegis of El Fatah, the military wing of the Palestine Liberation Organization, and their claims to be "credited" with particular terrorist acts. But the crime which led to the Swissair Coronado crash of February 21, 1970, in which a passenger aircraft with all on board perished, and the clear sabotage against an Austrian commercial aircraft on the same day, reinforced the need for insisting on the principle of responsibility of the host sovereign State, precisely in face of these difficulties. The attacks of February 1970 followed a savagely reckless bomb-throwing at Munich airport on February 11, 1970, in the name of "the Action Committee for the Freeing of Palestine." As security measures against simple hijacking were improved, terrorist tactics moved (as at Athens and Munich) to grenade or bomb attacks against passenger lounges and buses, and (in the Austrian and Swissair cases) to the indiscriminate treachery, as the official inquiries revealed, of putting delayed action explosive devices into the international airmail and cargo channels.

Before the Swissair disaster, no Arab Govern.ment had expressed disapproval of such acts. After it, on February 23, 1970, a Jordanian spokesman officially expressed regret to Switzerland. But even while he was declaring it "unthinkable that it could have been an Arab act in any way," the leader of the Popular Front for the Liberation of Palestine,

51. A similar tendency is apparent in the claims made by a number of states (though flatly rejected by others) as to the relation between Article 3(g) (acting as host to armed bands), and Article 7 (saving clause for self-determination), of the 1974 Definition of Aggression, *supra* note 38. See, *e.g.*, among the conflicting pronouncements Siage (Syria) U.N. Doc. A/C 6/SR 1475, at 9; Wehry (Netherlands) U.N. Doc. A/C 6/SR 1473, at 5; Lee (Canada) U.N. Doc. A/C 6/SR 1473, at 9; Petric (Yugoslavia) U.N. Doc. A/C 6/SR 1479, at 5; Obadi (Dem. Yemen) U.S. Doc. A/C 6/SR 1479, at 10; Boulbina (Algeria) U.N. Doc. A/C 6/SR 1479, at 11; Alvarez Tabio (Cuba) U.N. Doc. A/C 6/SR 1479, at 14; Kakotoson (Madagascar) U.N. Doc. A/C 6/SR 1474, at 13; Steel (U.K.) U.N. Doc. A/C 6/SR 1477, at 9-10; Hassouna (Egypt) U.N. Doc. A/C 6/SR 1483; Bracklo (West Germany) U.N. Doc. A/C 6/SR 1478 (Oct. 16, 1974); Martens (Portugal) U.N. Doc. A/C 6/SR 1478, at 8 (Oct. 16, 1974).

George Habash, with headquarters in Amman, was telling foreign newsmen in Amman that his organization's attack on American and Israeli planes all over the world would continue, and that his group had already carried out eight operations in Europe. Prior to this, Beirut radio had broadcast a claim that George Habash's "Popular Front" had sabotaged the Swissair Coronado plane.

King Hussein's Government continued for some time thereafter to host the Habash organization. It scarcely in this light removed Jordanian responsibility, that El Fatah leader Arafat denied, on March 14, 1970, any part in the Swiss and Austrian explosions, and claimed that Arab terrorists "were careful not to endanger the safety of civilians." Jordanian responsibility was engaged by harbouring and encouraging the group responsible, regardless of how many other groups are also involved.

There is no need to exhaust the list of terrorist acts to make the point that they called urgently for vindication of the traditional basic principles of responsibility of States, quite apart from the Middle East conflict. The deliberate mass massacres at Lod and Rome airports, at the Munich Olympics, the mass killing of school children as a Maalot and elsewhere, the murder of peaceful villagers and townspeople in markets, cinemas and in their homes, are examples too well known. It is well to emphasize, however, that the deliberate targets have regularly included not merely Israeli civilians and civil aircraft, but those of many other nations, and that credit for most of them was claimed by groups within the military arm of the P.L.O., from the capital of some Arab State harbouring and supporting the groups involved, and sometimes their very headquarters. The special hazards of attacks on aircraft emphasized rather than concealed the gravity of all breaches of this principle of State Responsibility.[52]

It was in face of the urgent need to vindicate such basic legal principles, that the General Assembly adopted the 1974 resolutions. With only slight ambiguity, these offered a colour of legitimacy to such terrorist acts, and thus aimed a serious blow at the very foundations of the international legal order. It is but a slight mitigation of this, and no comfort at all for legal ordering, that the General Assembly action concerned was obviously taken under the sponsorship and pressure of a small group of Arab rulers wielding the oil weapon, and its vast attendant financial power. Verbal disavowals and other gestures, made in the time context of the P.L.O.'s bid for legitimation, cannot conceal

52. For the rather abortive attempts, thus far, to secure action through technical bodies see I.C.A.O. Legal Committee, Draft Convention on Unlawful Seizure of Aircraft, I.C.A.O. Doc. 8865, LC/159, March 16, 1970. For an admirable summation see E. McWhinney, "Hijacking of Aircraft," [1971] 1 *Annuaire de l'Institut de Droit International* 520 [hereinafter cited as McWhinney].

the facts that El Fatah is the military arm of the Organization, that the Arab terrorist groups involved are part of this military arm, that these groups have a consistent record over many years of such terrorist activities supported by the P.L.O., and a number of Arab States, and that against this background the General Assembly has now authorized the P.L.O. to use "all means" towards its ends.

VII. THE OIL BOYCOTT AND THE GENERAL ASSEMBLY

The present writer observed, nineteen years ago, that the General Assembly's claim to represent "the conscience of mankind" could become "a protective shield for predatory and imperialist designs against them, and an execution chamber for any State that tried to defend itself against these designs." This would be inevitable, I said, if "through a regular stacking of votes regardless of the merits, it committed a *détournement* of the moral authority of that body."[53] These trends were apparent even before the gross *coup d'état* of the oil boycott in support of the aggressive surprise attack by Egypt and Syria on Israel in October 1973. The question I thus raised in 1958 for the long term future has now become the most urgent and important question for the immediate future. How long can Western States continue to permit or even assist in strengthening a General Assembly which has become a protective shield for predatory and imperialist designs against them, and an execution chamber for any State that tries to defend itself against these designs? The issue is not merely whether the Western States should continue to assume the major financial burden of maintaining a United Nations which has turned into a committee to execute the will of the Soviet, African and Asian blocs, steered by the Arab oil-producing States. That is a sufficiently grave issue; but at this stage it is minor compared with the issue, whether the West will continue to be led, one by one, issue by issue, step by step, like sheep to the slaughter.

No doubt, the abject submissiveness of Western States thus far has been mostly due to their immediate helplessness in face of the threat of a kind of economic aggression. In part, however, it also has been due to the notion that even measures of economic coercion as extreme as the oil boycott are immune not only from any legal restraints applicable to strictly military coercion, but also from any legal liberties of legitimate defense of the victims. It has been a main theme of my own work, however, from the books, *Legal Controls of International Conflict* (1954) and *Aggression and World Order* (1958) onwards, that this notion is confused and erroneous, and that it can lead, if persisted in,

53. Stone, *Agression, supra* note 12, at 161-65 (especially 164-65).

only to chaos and disaster. I continue to believe that the notion is not based in law, and is indefensible in policy in two respects. First, it grossly overstates the range of restraint on the use of military force under international law, including the Charter. Second, it also overstates the legal immunity of States, which use non-military means of coercion and other invasions of rights, from military response by the victims.

On the extreme coercion of the oil boycott itself, I addressed the following letter to the Editor of the *Washington Post* on November 26, 1973:

> The Arab States which have imposed an oil embargo on States with which they are ostensibly at peace, have not bothered to conceal their aim. This is to compel third States to assist them in achieving the objectives which Syria and Egypt failed to achieve by military aggression.
>
> Have international law and the United Nations Charter nothing to say about all this? After all, it is, on its face, a carefully calculated conspiracy, timed for the approach of winter, in which oil cutbacks, price rises and embargoes against neutral States were coordinated with a large scale surprise military attack by Syria and Egypt against Israel, so as to add the "oil weapon" to the more conventional weapons of aggressive war.
>
> There are solid grounds, too little noticed, for indicting the gross violations by Arab oil duress of both international law and the U.N. Charter, as well as of basic political morality.
>
> 1. Article 53 of the U.N. Charter expressly commands that "no enforcement action shall be taken under regional arrangements, or by regional agencies without the authorization of the Security Council." This is exactly what present Arab State oil measures against the U.S., Netherlands, Japan and other States amounts to, even if their demands conformed (which they do not) to the Security Council Resolutions involved.
>
> 2. The extreme coercion of the concerted oil measures, arising from the near monopoly power involved, may also constitute a threat or use of force, forbidden by Art. 2(4) of the Charter. *There is a great difference between this degree of economic coercion, and mere embargoes by one State against another when a monopolistic position of a group of conspiring States in the particular commodity is not involved.*
>
> 3. Many U.N. Members have taken the view in U.N. debates regarding the definition of "agression" that this international crime includes "economic aggression," and that the victims of such aggression may lawfully take appropriate measures of self-defense.

4. This kind of unauthorized concerted plan by a group of Members to cripple the economies of other Members for collateral political ends obviously flouts the "Purposes" and "Principles" of Articles one and two of the Charter, as well as the Declaration on the Principles of Friendly Relations of States unanimously adopted by the U.N. General Assembly.

5. The extreme coerciveness and dubious legality of the Arab oil boycott under Article 53 of the Charter would also seem to constitute "a threat or use of force in violation of the principles of the Charter" under Article 52 of the Vienna Convention on Treaties of 1969.

6. The calculated attempt by a group of Members to use their monopoly of a vital resource against other Members, amounts to an attempt to exploit the United Nations and its Members as mere catspaws of intransigent Arab policies.

Unless the United Nations and its Members resist this attempt by all possible means, that organization is doomed.

What is more, failure to resist will lead to a kind of colonialism. The blackmailer's appetite grows with what it feeds on. The rapacity of the Arab bloc, as the history of expropriations and arbitrary price rises shows, did not begin with the Syrian-Egyptian attack on Israel in 1973. And unless it is resisted and defeated it will set a precedent leading to a vast escalation of attacks on Western and other industrialized States, long after Arab-Israel issues are settled.

In a real sense these Arab tactics seek to translate the reckless anarchism of terrorist hijacking of commercial aircraft onto the critical level of the world economic and political order. They should be denounced and resisted as such, and met by collective action of all potential victims.[54]

It is to be noted in elaboration of the above points that the oil boycott of 1973 went far beyond any plausible use merely to advance the foreign policies of the oil-producing States concerned favouring return of *Arab lands* and the cause of the Palestinians. The boycott was an attempt to force terms of settlement on Israel, by coercing third States to change their own foreign policies, and even to compel them to take coercive measures against Israel. It openly inflicted severe coercion as punishment against States classified as "supporting Israel." It aimed explicitly to force third States to sever diplomatic and trade relations with Israel, as well as to extend military and economic aid to Arab States. In all these respects it was an invasion of the sovereign prerogatives of the third States by the use of coercion quite as extreme as most threats of conventional military measures.

54. Washington Post, Dec. 8, 1973, sec. A, at 19, col. 2.

I add here that the present writer's rejection of the notion that such severe economic coercion is legally immune from self-defensive response by its victims, and from United Nations condemnation, is no mere *ad hoc* invention for the protection of Western interests. The Soviet Union's own definition of aggression pressed on the Special Committee on that subject in 1956 provided that a State is guilty of economic aggression if it:

> (a) Takes against another State measures of economic pressure violating its sovereignty and economic independence and threatening the basis of its economic life.
> (c) Subjects another State to an economic blockade.

There could scarcely have been a clearer case of aggression, in these terms, than the oil boycott as applied to Japan and other States in October 1973, in order to enforce their condoning, and indeed verbal approval, of the Syrian-Egyptian military aggression against Israel in the October war. And, as recently as the Diplomatic Conference on the Law of Treaties at Vienna in 1968, the Committee of the Whole adopted a draft declaration, to be included in the Final Act, condemning "the threat or use of pressure in any form, whether military, political, or economic, by any State in order to coerce another State to perform any act relating to the conclusion of a treaty in violation of the principles of sovereign equality of States and freedom of consent . . . "[55]

Richard N. Gardner also pointed out, in testimony before the Subcommittee of Inter-National Economics of the Joint Economic Committee of the U.S. Congress on December 13, 1973,[56] that the oil boycott violated a series of bilateral treaties between the United States and Saudi Arabia, Oman and Iraq, as well as the United Nations *Declaration on Principles of International Law Concerning Friendly Relations and Cooperation Among States in Accordance with the Charter of the United Nations.*[57] This provides: "No State may use or encourage the use of economic, political or any other type of measures to coerce another State in order to obtain from it the subordination of the exercise of its sovereign rights and to secure from it advantages of any kind."[58] This part of the Declaration was pressed for acceptance particularly by the Afro-Asian nations, including the Arab countries whose use of the oil embargo against the West so obviously flouted it.

55. United Nations Conference on the Law of Treaties, *Official Records* 285 (1971).
56. New York Times, Dec. 19, 1973, at 12, col. 2.
57. G.A. Res. 2625, 25 U.N. GAOR, Supp. 28, at 121, U.N. Doc. A/8028 (1970).
58. *Id.* at 123, col. 2.

VIII. TENSIONS WITHIN THE GENERAL ASSEMBLY

I share the astonishment and indignation with which Professor Gardner has noted that "not a single voice has been raised in the United Nations to cite this authoritative Declaration of the General Assembly since the Arab oil embargo began." This silence is eloquent of the subjugation of the United Nations and its principles by a combination of power groups antagonistic to those Western States which bear the greatest burdens of maintaining the Organization.

Such issues are at least as important to the future of the world as those of Taiwan, Rhodesia, apartheid in South Africa, or which was the legitimate Government of Cambodia before the military success of the Khmer Rouge, or the adoption of declarations about friendly relations or cooperation among States. And, of course, the Palestinian resolutions are only a recent instance of a series of precedents threatening both the legal and working structure of the United Nations, and the basic interests of any Member against which the votes of Arab, African, Asian and Communist Members are targeted. While, for instance, under Articles 5 and 6 of the Charter, suspension or expulsion of a Member requires a Security Council recommendation, the General Assembly asserted in 1974 an illicit power of producing similar effects by its own majority vote alone. Far from such issues engaging the attention of the Twenty-Ninth Session of the General Assembly, the work of that Assembly indicates that this body is becoming increasingly a supine agent for the legitimation and extension of economic and political warfare against all Western or Western-oriented States. When, as in the October 1973 crisis, this economic and political warfare is resorted to in flagrant support of military attacks by or against such a target-State, the General Assembly becomes a supine agent also of *military* aggression. In such circumstances a number of important States may well find it the lesser of threatening evils for the sake of peace, as well as the survival of Western democratic States, to strip away the façade by which the General Assembly pretends to speak impartially for mankind, while behind it selfish, sinister and irresponsible warfare is being waged by bloc alliances against selected target States. It is tragic that such a dismantling of the political machinery of the United Nations is thus forced into contemplation. Yet it is clear enough that mere verbal protests, even in the strong terms used by U.S. Ambassador Scali on December 6, 1974, are not adequate to the situation. How far this emergency also afflicts the Specialized Agencies will depend on whether the bloc alliances concerned are willing to desist at least from the power-political manipulations which abort the true function of the Agencies. The groundless exclusion of Israel by the 1974 UNESCO

General Conference from the educational, scientific and cultural work of UNESCO is not reassuring in this regard.

IX. THE EFFECTS OF RECENT CHANGES IN THE COMPOSITION OF THE GENERAL ASSEMBLY

One striking aspect of the Twenty-Ninth Session of the General Assembly was, of course, an ironic turning of the tables on the Western Powers. In the first decade of the United Nations, before the first "package deal" for extended membership and the flood of new Members arising from decolonization, the Western Powers and in particular the United States, were disposed to extend the functions of General Assembly majorities which they felt able to control. Western sponsorship of the Uniting for Peace Resolutions was a fruit of this period, although, as has been shown elsewhere,[59] these Powers were careful, even then, not to attribute to the General Assembly powers to impose legal binding obligations on Members. By the 1956 Suez Crisis those halcyon years were over, though President Eisenhower and his Secretary of State acted in that crisis as if they were still in full flow. The entry of new Asian and African States leading to more than a doubling of the total membership of the General Assembly ushered in a period when Western States and their policies have come to be put increasingly on the defensive, and the majorities they could win increasingly hazardous.

In the decade which followed, the General Assembly was able to promote a number of developments, notably the decolonization of most dependent territories, by measures which were often sponsored by Soviet, Asian and African bloc Members, but also mostly cooperatively received by Western States. Though voting power in the General Assembly had swung drastically against Western interests, a certain approximation to restraint and law-abidingness of outcome was assured by the continued economic independence and relative power of the Western States. The challenge of assuring international economic aid for raising to tolerable levels the standard of life of the poorer nations, compelled a degree of deliberation and give and take on both sides. This fruitful balance has now been drastically disturbed, over and beyond the sheer predominance in numbers of the Communist, Asian and African blocs, by the financial and economic crises affecting even the stronger Western Powers, aggravated by the drastic rise in energy costs, the shift of unprecedented financial power to a few sparsely populated OAPEC States, and the continuing threat of sudden oil boycott. The tables have in a sense been turned, both as to voting majorities and as to economic vulnerability.

59. *Cf.* J. Stone, *Of Law and Nations* 349-72, (especially) 353-58 (1974).

Correspondingly, the restraint and give and take which kept the General Assembly's activities within reasonably lawful and fruitful bounds in the 'sixties, have given way. States struggling with long-term economic crises are no longer promising contributors to funds for the aid of poorer nations whose votes dominate the General Assembly. We may hope that the oil-exporting States of Asia and Africa will finally be persuaded to assume a major part of this role on a scale commensurate with their wealth. But unless the grounds for this hope become much firmer than they are, the plight of poorer nations such as India must become desperate indeed, even without the doomsday projections of the Club of Rome. If that hope fails, the divisions between the OAPEC "have" nations, and the poorer African and Asian nations (the old "Third World") may once again change the voting alignments in the General Assembly; but that is for the longer run.

In the meanwhile, the combination of the voting power of the Communist, Asian and African blocs with the "persuasive" power of the OAPEC States dominating the political activities of the General Assembly, has led to the present crisis, recently signalled by the Palestinian resolutions of the Twenty-Ninth Session. The immediate task is to prevent the manipulation of that important body as a hostile instrument over the whole range of Western interests. Unless this is done the General Assembly will rapidly become an arena in which vital interests of great States are set at peril, raising tensions and frustrations to levels that would pose great dangers to peace.

We should not allow bemusement with the ironies of the reversal of Western positions in the General Assembly to conceal the substantial differences between the situation in the first decade of the United Nations, and that which now casts its shadow over the fourth decade. One of these, as already observed, is that the former Western-led majorities did not attempt to arrogate to the Assembly powers of binding decision, that is, of imposing legal obligations on Members. Second, even the recommendatory or hortatory power of the General Assembly was invoked for the most part with a certain restraint and give and take, and with attention paid to general principles *vis-a-vis* Communist bloc, and Asian and African bloc interests. Had not the United States and other Western countries shown this moderation it is difficult to see how the very growth of membership which has matured into the present situation could ever have taken place. The process of decolonization under General Assembly auspices owes as much to American anti-colonialist ideals as to Soviet self-interested initiatives. Third, at no point did the United States or other Western countries use the kind of extreme coercive power for wholesale control of votes which is now manifest in the operations of OAPEC. While such a power was theoretically open to the United States in the years preceding the Soviet nuclear breakthrough, it was neither used nor, as a practical matter, was it available for "lining-up" votes in the way now made familiar by OAPEC. Fourth, and related to this, Western interests never asserted the assured power of marshalling automatic majorities regardless of the merits, now asserted by the OAPEC-Soviet alliance. On this account, too, the present problem is unprecedented.

It remains, therefore, both proper and necessary to call attention to the fact that the present phase of tyranny of manipulated majorities in the General Assembly, creates unprecedented dangers for some of its Members and for most of the principles of the United Nations, not to speak of international law. The harsh arbitrariness of present and looming uses of unprecedented coercive power have created a new situation. Moreover, the stakes are momentous, not only in terms of the control by the Western Powers of their own destiny, but of the recovery of the West to a point at which it will again be capable of contributing to the economic advancement of the developing nations. Thus, however their interests may appear in the short run, the poorer States of the developing world have, on a slightly longer view, a heavy involvement in these same stakes.

In these circumstances, withdrawal from participation in and budgetary support of the General Assembly would not represent mere petulance or frustration; nor would it spell rejection of any peaceful means of settlement of the matters at issue which may be available, or any greater chance than already exists of resort to force by some side or other. The issues in question are now so clear, and the alignments hostile to the West in the General Assembly so implacably predictable, that the usurpation of authority by that body has become a main strategic weapon in the diplomatic struggle. To neutralize this weapon is important, of course, to the threatened States; it may also be a way of reducing or at least slowing the rise of tension.

This last possibility, despite the touch of paradox, is of great importance. In speaking a few years ago of the principle involved, I observed that "to press on with hopelessly locked negotiations is not necessarily better than ending them. Repeated confrontation of irreconcilable antagonisms can itself maintain or even increase tension, so that mutual withdrawal may be a positive step toward relaxation." The Great Power veto in the Security Council was an early institutional expression of this principle. The insistence of the veto by both Moscow and Washington was based on recognition that the choice was not between an international security organization with the veto and one without the veto, but between an international security organization with a veto and no international security organization at all. The lack of authority of the General Assembly, with a few express exceptions of marginal importance to international security, to take decisions legally binding on members was a corollary of this same principle for a body in which voting is by majority or even two-thirds majority.

Insofar as the General Assembly now seeks to arrogate such authority to itself, it also imperils its merely hortatory role in international security matters. Edward McWhinney has written recently of the "increasing institutional propensity in the United Nations for self-inflicted wounds in the form of often irresponsible *ad hoc* decisions that reflect the pursuit, by the countries immediately concerned, of temporary political advantage and the scoring of cheap debating points at the expense of long-range principle."[60] With some delicacy he sees regional security and cooperation arrangements transcending ideological differences as "a major stabilizing factor in an ever less certain world." We may hope that this positive inference will not prove too optimistic. The negative inference seems indisputable, that the General Assembly is not likely to be permitted to consolidate its usurpation of powers so irresponsibly claimed and exercised.

The movement of Washington-Moscow relations into a phase of *détente*—even if still hesitant- if anything, confirms this point. So do the efforts, though still rather nebulous, to transcend ideological difference by regional security and cooperation arrangements in Europe. And the main point, that withdrawal from blocked negotiations may sometimes provide the best hope of progress toward settlement, is the more apposite to the General Assembly, for not merely reduction of contacts is involved, as it was between Moscow and Washington in the 'sixties, but the removal from the hands of their adversaries by the important States concerned of a General Assembly which has become an illicit weapon of certain power blocs.

This point is related also to that of peaceful settlement. The economic and financial "stranglehold", in Foreign Secretary Callaghan's terms, of the States which manipulate majorities in the Assembly is in itself severe enough. To allow the General Assembly to be used to limit the political options of the threatened States still further by usurpation of legislative or quasi-legislative powers may well make peaceful settlement even more remote than it is presently, and increase rather than reduce the risks of military responses. No one, of course, can predict with assurance what the outcome will be of the grave conflicts now dominating the international scene; will they be settled peacefully or by war? Yet this very fact should deter us from facile acceptance of such unsubstantiated assertions as those that: the General Assembly, as it nears universality, becomes the Town Meeting of the World, expressing Human Conscience; or that as long as

60. McWhinney, *supra* note 52.

representatives of States meet in New York, their armies and missiles will not be unleashed; or, that what is good for the General Assembly is good for the United Nations, or even for all Mankind.

How far any of these assertions is true depends on the actual behaviour patterns of Member States in the context of the actual constellation of power within the General Assembly. Present patterns, in the actual constellation of power, are turning that body into an ever more dangerous weapon against the vital interests of Western States, consolidating rather than resolving hostile alignments, hardening rather than tempering negotiating positions, and depriving States subject to its pressures of any but military alternatives. Even in terms of avoiding military confrontation, it may therefore be necessary to arrest, as soon as possible, the operation of current patterns in the General Assembly. Collective withdrawal by the threatened States may be the only practical step to this end, not only because of the importance of their budgetary contributions,[61] but because continued participation by the target States themselves is an important source of the legitimacy which the blocs manipulating the General Assembly seek for their actions.

The United States Senate Foreign Relations Committee, on November 26, 1974, unanimously recommended the cutting off of United States contributions to UNESCO until that body reversed the action of its General Conference, led by Soviet and Arab blocs, in virtually excluding Israel from participation in UNESCO activities. While this may be seen as an example in miniature of appropriate response to arbitrary use of majority voting in international agencies, it is important to note the differences in the nature and scale of response which may be necessary to curb the General Assembly. The whole range of United States interests is vulnerable to usurped authority of the General Assembly, and not merely (as with UNESCO) marginal interests in that body's work for education, science and culture. Insofar as usurped power in these areas is allowed to operate, the General Assembly is substituting its processes for those of the Security Council, depriving the United States of the veto power which has always been both a legal and political condition of its participation. It is true that all the permanent members would also be thus deprived, but the threat involved points only at the United States and other Western States and interests. The alignment of the Soviet bloc with the dominant majority blocs sufficiently assures Soviet interests for the foreseeable future.

Correspondingly, mere symbolic financial protests, which may suffice

61. The United States alone pays 25 percent ($60 million) of the United Nations budget; the United Kingdom, France, U.S.S.R. and China another 25 percent. The OAPEC states contributed less than 0.8 percent, and 45 of the 72 states which sponsored the November 22, 1974 Resolutions contributed together only 0.9 percent.

for dealing with *détournements de pouvoir* in specialized Agencies, are not enough to deal with the dangers from the General Assembly. What is at issue is not the reversal of particular acts but the check and arrest of the broad-based bid of the aligned blocs for global domination. Insofar as the General Assembly becomes basically an instrument of this bid for power, flouting both international law and the Charter itself, the required responses are likely to include a sufficient withdrawal of the prospective victims to expose clearly the illegitimacy of this misappropriation.

IX. CONCLUSIONS

The general problems involved in these developments are central to the international law and politics of the next decade. They raise issues of how any framework of international relations can survive the substitution of wishful fantasies for reality, of pseudo-mechanical legal artifacts for the wisdom and agonized conscience of good statesmanship, and of slogans and stacked votes of self-propagating majorities in the General Assembly for adjustment mechanisms which work.

In terms of the limit-situations traditionally handled through the treaty of peace, I have show, in Section II above, that the vast legal and political energies invested in what now stands as Article 52 of the Vienna Convention yield few dividends for theory or practice not already available under general international law. In relation to "unequal" treaties the supposedly innovative doctrine spells no beneficent expulsion of power from such areas, but rather a covert and meretricious effort to enthrone a new set of power-wielders. Is not an undertaking from certain States extracted by a threat to cut off oil within the Afro-Asian doctrine regarding unequal treaties or even treaties induced by "force"? Moreover, the "principles," self-righteously promoted by the new aspirants for power may savour of justice even less than those of the old. For example, such doctrines as "wars of liberation," and "self-determination" lack even the formal merit of equal application by and to all States which fall within their terms. And even when their *ex parte* nature and operation are not explicit, these become manifest in the stacking of votes in the General Assembly regardless of the merits of the particular issue. A resolution that the earth is flat, once sponsored by a representative group of Soviet bloc and African and Asian States, will have its majority *ruat coelum*.

If we can talk of a marketplace of ideas in what some think to have become "the global village," there might nevertheless be something to be said for all States and peoples regarding with equanimity resolutions of the import that the earth is flat in Miltonian or Holmesian faith that truth anyhow will finally emerge from the clash of ideas. There are several reasons why the world, at any rate the Western world, may not wait for emergence along this path.

One reason is that many pronouncements of the General Assembly, even when purporting to be "declaring" or "interpreting" law, are operations of power politics rather than explorations of truth. In old Concert of Europe power politics, as between the Great Powers and their clients, the ambitions of at least each major party were checked by those of some other On the one-State, one-vote basis of General Assembly operations, the Soviet bloc's alliance with the multitude of new Asian and African States dispenses pronunciamentos free from any such salutary check. A second reason is that the coercive oil embargo power wielded by a few States, diminutive in population but formidable in ambitions, might inhibit Members who might wish to vote no, or even to abstain, on resolutions which might seek to pronounce that, for example, the United States is a racist State, that the United Kingdom violates the principle of self-determination and that the rights of "Liberation Organizations" in Wales and in Scotland respectively be recognized, that the limits on immigration into Australia violate the Charter of the United Nations and that levels of immigration there from overpopulated countries elsewhere be laid down by the Economic and Social Council. A third reason is the rather indiscriminate doctrinal fashion, in the aftermath of decolonization, of endorsing and even promoting assertions made in the name of international law, merely because they seem "progressive" in the sense of constricting the legal rights of Western States. Such positions are usually take in sincerity, even when they represent a naive view of international politics, sometimes to the point of self-contradiction. Thinkers can be found who take stern restrictive views of the range of prohibition of force by States, while insisting, with no sense of the incongruity of their position, on the liberty of States to wage "wars of liberation," presumably against any targets of their own choice, provided that the numerically preponderant blocs in the General Assembly will go along.

This "softening" of hard-headed publicist doctrine which had been a mainstay of Western statecraft since before the Peace of Westphalia, is not due merely to changing power-constellations, cultural styles, ideological commitments, or to guilt feelings accompanying and following decolonization. It is also in part due to the skill, political imagination, and energy with which non-Western publicists have given juristic shape to their revolutionary demands against the existing legal order. The result, whatever the causes, has been that too many Western publicists have failed to meet the challenges of keeping international law as a viable working system reflecting in a stable manner the existing constellations of power, and the aspirations which these constellations can tolerate.

This would be dangerous enough, even if it rested in mere default. When, however, doctrines are allowed to grow virtually unchallenged, filling the vacuum of authority with whatever precepts serve the interests of States positioned to stack votes in the General Assembly, the survival of both the United Nations and the general international legal order is risked. The growing literature now seeking to attribute binding force to resolutions of the General Assembly may represent in Freudian terms a yearning for authoritative shelter from the storms of legal and political change. Beside the compulsions of such a yearning, it might seem a small matter that to confer such legal force and the legislative authority this would presuppose are clearly at odds with the Charter, its amendment provisions, and the *travaux preparatoires* for these. Yet such fantasies, however helpful to the publicist psyche, do not change the hard facts of the relations of States; to try to convert them into international law may be so to distort the law as to foreclose any chance of more adequate development of it, and to invite political and military disasters as well.

The publication of Professor Gaetano Arangio-Ruiz's work, *The Normative Role of the General Assembly of the United Nations and the Declaration of Principles of Friendly Relations*[62] is to be hailed as a potential rallying point for return to the less "soft" publicist traditions which have given three centuries of viability to the law of nations. Professor Arangio-Ruiz has diligently assembled, scrupulously explicated, patiently organized and critically analyzed, the growing literature which seeks to explain or support the pretensions of the United Nations General Assembly to exercise legislative or quasi-legislative power, beyond the few well-known cases of binding decision explicitly authorized by the Charter. Anyone who has discussed this matter, or may yet wish to do so, will, if he values juristic and intellectual integrity more than mere fashion and ideology, ignore at his peril the exquisite reasoning and balanced conclusions of this definitive work.

Professor Arangio-Ruiz ranges over all the bewildering apologiae for claims of magisterial authority of the General Assembly: the supposed legitimation by the Charter or other contractual rule; a supposedly authorizing rule of customary law; the supposed "will" of the "Organized International Community"; the supposed binding force of particular resolutions seen as the practice of States maturing into custom, or seen as "treaty" obligations based on "consensus", or as "declaring" "principles of international law," or as "determining" or "interpreting" international law.[63] As to every such ground, Professor

62. 137 Académie de Droit International, *Recueil des Cours* 419 (1972) [hereinafter cited as Arangio-Ruiz].
63. *Id.* at 431-518.

Arangio-Ruiz's fair and painstaking analysis leads to the conclusion that the General Assembly is devoid of legal authority either to exact or to "declare," or "determine" or "interpret" international law so as legally to bind States by such acts, whether these States be Members of the United Nations or not, and whether these States voted for or against or abstained from voting on the resolution in question.

By this critical analysis the learned author is led to observe upon the "futility of grandiloquent theories" as manifest, for example, in the General Assembly's "Declaration of Principles of Friendly Relations among States" of 1970,[64] and upon the dangers *de lege lata* as well as *de lege ferenda,* which may accompany this futility.[65] His demonstration of the General Assembly's lack of legally binding power save where the Charter expressly provides, is cogent for such projects of abstract "declaration." Recognition of its equal cogency may become a matter of life and death, especially for the embattled minority States of the West, in areas where the General Assembly seeks to usurp the power of making "determinations" on matters as to which States are at legal variance.

Professor Arangio-Ruiz summons his fellow-publicists to resist and reject what he calls the "soft-law method," building on "notions like the Organized International Community or the constitutional nature of the Charter of the United Nations and . . . the General Assembly's 'legislative' or 'quasi-legislative' powers." The present writer begs leave to join in this call because indulgence of such methods leads to an endless fantasmagoria of useless doctrine related neither to law nor to the objective facts and also because the resulting legal chaos is a perfect medium for subjugating the United Nations and some of its Members to the extraneous power-political drives of the predominant voting blocs. It would be disingenuous, of course, for Western statesmen and jurists to ignore that, inevitably, power politics are played within the General Assembly. But, by the same token, it would approach suicidal madness to ignore steady erosions of international law and of the Charter provisions which would empower numerically dominant blocs in that body to pass *legally binding* sentences, step by step and one by one, on those States with whose foreign policies they disagree.

When the argument is seriously made, as it has been, that repetition of an alleged rule in preambles to General Assembly resolutions can make that rule into customary law, it is necessary to take an emphatic stand, on the legal level as well as on the political level. Professor Gaetano Arangio-Ruiz, in a rare departure from scholarly understatement provides a fitting peroration:

64. Note 57 *supra.*

65. Arangio-Ruiz, *supra* note 62, at 624-25.

It would be too easy if the "shouting out" of rules through General Assembly resolutions were to be law-making simply as a matter of "times" shouted and size of the choir. By all means, we would urge that one let the General Assembly shout as often and as loud as it is able and willing to shout. However, for the shouted rule to be customary law there still remains to consider the conduct and the attitudes of States with regard to the actual behaviour, positive or negative, contemplated as due by the rule.[66]

66. *Id.*

THE NEW SYSTEM OF INTERNATIONAL LAW

GREGORY I. TUNKIN

The unprecedented tempo of scientific and technological development and social change are characteristic features of our time.

How have these transformations affected international law? Where are we with respect to this social institution and what can we expect of it in satisfying the deepest hopes of mankind for international peace and cooperation, "to promote social progress and better standards of life in larger freedom?"[1]

These are problems of great theoretical and practical importance to which the late Professor Wolfgang Friedmann devoted much attention. His writings and especially his fundamental treatise *The Changing Structure of International Law* were an inspiration even to those, such as this author, who often disagreed with him.

I. PROFOUND CHANGES IN THE WORLD AND INTERNATIONAL LAW

What are major transformations in the world that have decisively influenced the development of international law in the course of the last half-century?

According to the Marxist-Leninist theory international law is an element of superstructure. The basis of societal development constitutes the development of the mode of production of material means of life. The mode of production is a sum total of two elements: forces of production (including means of production and men using them) and relations among men in the process of production—relations of production. The evolution of the forces of production renders relations of production inadequate at a certain stage. Then social revolution comes and changes these relations of production to make them correspond to the level of development of the forces of production. This makes inevitable a drastic change in the whole superstructure: state, law, social sciences. A new socio-economic system or, in other words, a

. GREGORY I. TUNKIN is Professor of International Law at Moscow University.

1. *U.N. Charter* preamble.

new socio-economic formation emerges. This is the basic law of societal development. It found its confirmation in the Socialist revolution of 1917 in Russia and later on in Socialist revolutions in a number of other States.

History never stands still. Today the development of productive forces is greatly accelerated as a result of the revolution in science and technology. One of the immediate results of it is a further deepening of the international division of labour, on regional as well as on global levels. There is, therefore, a widening of economic ties between states and growing economic interdependence between nations despite fundamental differences in their socio-economic systems.

It is on this economic plane that internationalization of other spheres of human activities is taking place. Problems such as those of maintaining international peace and security, the preservation of the environment and some others have already acquired global character. These new tendencies have also resulted in an enormous growth in international organisations. All these changes in society influence international law not directly but through actions of States which create rules of international law.

Certainly the Great October Socialist Revolution exercised the greatest influence on the development of international law. It brought into international relations new ideas—the ideas of socialism. It created a new socio-economic system and States of a new nature, which have ever since been actively struggling for the introduction into international law of new principles and norms reflecting the ideas of socialism. It started a chain reaction, the principal results of which have been the emergence of new socialist States, mighty upheavals of national liberation movements, the collapse of the colonial system and formation of new independent states as a result of the liberation of colonies.[2]

These events coupled with other changes in society have altered the relation of forces in the world in favour of forces of socialism and peace and have brought about basic changes in international law.

There is considerable difference of opinion, first of all between international lawyers of socialist countries and those of capitalist countries, as to the extent various factors have affected international law. But almost all international lawyers agree that profound transformations have taken place in international law in the course of recent decades.

Professor Friedmann was one of those Western scholars who stressed the importance of these changes. In his preface to *The Changing Structure of International Law* he wrote: "The present book is an

2. For more detail see G. Tunkin, *Theory of International Law* (1974).

attempt to analyse, in their respective importance and interdependence, the many profound changes that have affected contemporary international law to such an extent that it is today something very different even from what it was a generation ago."[3]

International law, however, is not a mirror reflection of international realities. It is a system of legal norms, formed in international intercourse; it is, however, a distinct social phenomenon, having a certain degree of independence from international relations. In its development international law may lag behind international relations, it may advance in a parallel fashion, or it may even be ahead of international relations. In this last role, international law may function as an instrument for creating new international relations in certain spheres.

If we consider international relations and international law as a system, international law is a regulating sub-system. Because of the interaction between international relations and international law, the study of international law should not be divorced from that of international relations, and conversely international relations should not be studied, as is often the case, without taking international law into consideration. The system "International relations—international law" depends on its environment as it constitutes a part of a wider system. Therefore, the study of causes and of the essence of transformations which have taken place in international law requires the analysis of interactions not only inside the system "International relations—international law" but also of interactions between this system and its environment. By applying this method we can explain why and how profound changes in the world have influenced international law.

The thoery of coordination of the wills of States proposed by the present author and widely accepted in the Soviet doctrine offers adequate explanation of the processes through which changes that take place in the world influence international law.[4] According to this theory norms of international law are created, modified or abrogated by the coordination (by agreement) of the wills of subjects of international law concerning the contents of the rules of conduct and the recognition of such rules as norms of international law. Primary norms, that is norms of general international law, are created by States only.

The will of a State is the will of its ruling class, *i.e.* the class that occupies the dominant position in the economic and political life. The content of this will is determined by conditions in which the ruling class finds itself at a certain moment. In the sum total of those conditions the major role is played by economic conditions, or, in other words, by the

3. W. Friedmann, *The Changing Structure of International Law* vii (1964) [hereinafter cited as Friedmann].

4. See G. Tunkin, *Fundamentals of Contemporary International Law* (1956); G. Tunkin, *Theory of International Law* (1974).

económic structure of society at a certain stage of its development. The defence of this economic structure, of which the most important part is the system of property that ensures dominant position of the ruling class, plays the decisive role in determining the content of the will of this class, and therefore, the will of the State.

The influence of the economic structure on the will of the State is, in the final analysis, a decisive one.[5] However, in addition to the economic structure the will of State is determined by many other social phenomena such as class struggle, municipal law, political, legal and philosophical theories, and religion.

The fundamental changes that have taken place in the world since the Great October Socialist Revolution, and that have determined the content of the wills of various States have had a decisive influence on the results of the coordination of those wills, that is, the norms of international law.

Various natural law theories proceed from the assumption that there are legal rules which spring from a number of factors such as the nature of man, the nature of international society, and reason, independently of the wills of States. It is probably not superfluous to briefly explain that the Marxist-Leninist theory of international law is not a natural law theory as it has been suggested sometimes.[6] According to the Marxist-Leninist theory the development of society is a "natural historical process."[7] This means that there are laws of development of society that people are unable to change, but these laws are not legal rules. We have already stated that rules of international law come into being as a result of the coordination of the wills of States. Through these wills laws of societal development, which find their realisation in conditions determining the contents of those wills, exercise a decisive influence on international law.

II. TRANSFORMATION OF INTERNATIONAL LAW

Of the many transformations that have taken place in international law since the Great October Socialist Revolution, the most important, in our opinion, are those relating to the preservation of peace, international cooperation, equality and the self-determination of peoples, and human rights. These changes have determined the general character of contemporary international law.

5. See 37 K. Marx & F. Engels, *Works* 394-95 (in Russian).

6. See for instance, Quadri, "Cours général de droit international public," 113 Académie de Droit International, Recueil des cours 237, 276-77 (1964).

7. 1 V.I. Lenin, *Complete Works* 139 [hereinafter cited as Lenin].

Resort to War

According to international law in force before the October Revolution the use of force and even the resort to war in international relations were permitted. Treaties obligating contracting parties not to wage war against each other or to resort to war only under definite conditions had existed for centuries; but these were not based on the prohibition of aggressive war as a principle of general international law, binding *erga omnes.* A corollary of the right of the State to resort to war was the right of a victorious State to impose its conditions upon a vanquished State and even to eliminate it altogether by annexing its territory. The old international law was, in effect, a law of the powerful; it permitted the use of force by a State against another State and gave its blessing to what was obtained by force.

Contemporary international law prohibits the resort to war, and the threat or use of force in international relations. The Soviet Socialist State has taken a firm position against aggressive wars since the first days of its existence. In its first decree—The Decree on Peace of 8 November 1917—The Soviet State proposed to immediately stop the imperialist war and declared: "To continue this war for the purpose of redistributing among powerful and rich nations spheres of domination over weak nations the Government considers the greatest crime against humanity . . . ."[8]

The concept of the criminal character of aggressive wars has found its expression in principles and norms of contemporary international law. As stated in the 1970 Declaration on *Principles of International Law Concerning Friendly Relations and Co-operation Among States in accordance with the Chater of the United Nations*[9] (hereinafter 1970 Declaration on Principles of International Law), "[a] war of aggression constitutes a crime against the peace, for which there is responsibility under international law."[10] The waging of an aggressive war is now a major international crime; there is also criminal international responsibility for individuals guilty of preparing, unleashing and waging a war of aggression.

A state of war is no longer a "normal" state of relations between States. According to present-day international law parties to an armed conflict, although equally bound to observe the rules of warfare, are not in the same legal position; an aggressor State commits a major international crime by starting and waging war of aggression, whereas the

8. 1 *Documents of the USSR Foreign Policy* 12 (in Russian) [hereinafter cited as *USSR Documents*].

9. G.A. Res. 2625, 25 U.N. GAOR Supp. 28, at 121, U.N. Doc. A/8028 (1970) [hereinafter cited as 1970 Declaration].

10. *Id.* at 122.

other party acts in self-defence, and therefore in accordance with international law.

The abrogation of the right of the State to resort to war and the emergence of the principle of the prohibition of aggressive war and of the prohibition of the threat and use of force, have meant the end of concept that the victorious State acquire rights derived from its victory. A victory gives no rights as such. The rights of the Allied countries over Germany and Japan and their allies were not based on their victory over these States. They resulted from the responsibility of Nazi Germany and Japan for the preparation, unleashing and waging aggressive war and for the crimes against mankind in general, as set forth in the Charters and Judgments of the Nürnberg and Tokyo international Military Tribunals.

Self-determination and human rights

The old international law was an instrument of colonial domination. It sanctioned the acquisition by the use of force of territories inhabited by "coloured peoples," colonial oppression, and exploitation of these peoples. In its Decree on Peace the Soviet Socialist State took a firm stand against the colonial system. It proclaimed the right of all nations and peoples to freely settle their own affairs and, in particular, to determine their political status, regardless of the degree of their economic development. The Decree stressed that this right should be ensured to colonial and dependent peoples of all continents.[11]

The principle of equality and self-determination of peoples was enshrined in the Charter of the United Nations and later on in a more extensive formulation in the 1970 Declaration on Principles of International Law.

According to the Declaration "all peoples have the right freely to determine, without external interference, their political status and to pursue their economic, social and cultural development, and every State has the duty to respect this right in accordance with the provisions of the Charter,"[12] States are bound to promote the realization of the principles of equal rights and self-determination of peoples in order to bring a speedy end to colonialism. The subjection of peoples to alien rule, domination and exploitation constitutes a violation of the principle as well as a denial of fundamental human rights, and is contrary to the Charter of the United Nations.

A remarkable feature of recent developments in international law is,

11. 1 *USSR Documents, supra* note 8, at 12.
12. 1970 Declaration, *supra* note 9, at 123.

as was ably shown by Professor Friedmann, the growing number of principles and norms of international law setting forth rules on the obligations of States to cooperate in various fields.[13] This is a direct consequence of the rapid growth of cooperation among States.

The 1970 Declaration on Principles of International Law stresses one specific principle of international law, the principle of cooperation. According to the Declaration, "States have the duty to co-operate with one another, irrespective of the differences in their political, economic and social systems, in the various spheres of international relations, in order to maintain international peace and security and to promote international economic stability and progress, the general welfare of nations, and international co-operation free from discrimination based on such differences."[14] It should be stressed that States are bound to co-operate with one another "irrespective of the differences in their political, economic and social systems," and that such cooperation should be "free from discrimination based on such differences." The number of legal norms regulating and enhancing cooperation between states is growing at all levels in international law, that is, general, regional and bilateral, as well as in all branches of international law.

The Great October Socialist Revolution marked a new era in the history of the struggle against oppression and exploitation and for human dignity and human rights. The collapse of the colonial system has been a new important step in this direction. The progressive forces of the world have intensified their struggle for the recognition of and respect for human rights without distinction as to race, sex, material position or religion.

International law has to some extent reflected these developments. The number of norms relating to international protection of human rights is constantly growing. The coming into force of international covenants on human rights will be a considerable step forward. In this connection attention should be drawn to a widely entertained illusion that international action is called upon to play a decisive role in ensuring respect for human rights, In fact, the scope of human rights and their realisation are generally determined by the socio-economic and political system of the State, which is where the principal work in the struggle for human rights takes place. The international protection of human rights, though important, is still a secondary means for ensuring these rights.

13. Friedmann, *supra* note 3, at 60-74.
14. 1970 Declaration, *supra* note 9, at 123.

Peaceful Coexistence

The emergence in international law of the principle of the peaceful coexistence of States, irrespective of their socio-economic systems, is of major importance. This is a very broad principle that reflects the essence of contemporary general international law and which has been slowly penetrating into international law. The Soviet understanding of this principle includes two things: the inevitable struggle between States must be pursued by peaceful means only; and, co-operation, normal relations and, as far as possible, friendly relations between States belonging to different socio-economic systems must be developed.

The principle of peaceful coexistence was put forward by V.I. Lenin and has been embodied in Soviet foreign policy. The Decree on Peace and the first statements by Lenin as head of the Soviet Government contained proposals concerning cooperation between the Socialist State and capitalist countries for the purpose of restoring peace and of developing peaceful relations. In his concluding remarks on the Decree on Peace at the Second All-Russian Congress of Soviets on November 8, 1917, Lenin, speaking of the treaties of Russia with other countries, said: "We are not bound by these treaties. We shall not permit to impose them upon us. We reject all provisions, intended to subjugate and exploit other people, but we shall willingly accept all good-neighbouring provisions as well as economic agreements . . . ."[15] At the end of the armed intervention of the imperialist powers against Soviet Russia, Lenin again called for establishing normal and even friendly relations between States with different socio-economic systems. In his statement to the correspondents of the *Observer* and *Manchester Guardian* in 1922 Lenin said: "We consider that friendly relations with both powers [France and England] are quite possible and constitute our objective."[16]

The principle of peaceful coexistence has been gaining recognition in international law very slowly mainly because the ruling classes in the West had for a long time cherished hopes for ending of the Socialist socio-economic system. In the course of World War II cooperation between States of the two opposing systems, developed in the framework

15. 35 Lenin, *supra* note 7, at 20 (in Russian).

16. 45 *id.* at 237 (in Russian). Since Lenin the principle of peaceful coexistence has ever been one of the leading principles of the Soviet foreign policy. A widely known Soviet Peace Programme, formulated in a report presented by the General Secretary of the Central Committee of the C.P.S.U. L.I. Breshnev and approved by the XXIV Congress of the Communist Party of the Soviet Union is an embodiment of the policy of peaceful coexistence. The Congress stated in its decision: "The Congress instructs the CC of CPSU consistently to continue carrying forward into practice the principle of peaceful coexistence, to extend mutually advantageous relations with the capitalist countries." 24th Congress of the C.P.S.U., *Proceedings* 217 (1971).

of the Anti-Nazi coalition, went much further than it had been considered possible by either side. As a result of this, the principle of peaceful coexistence was embodied in the Charter of the United Nations, which, in its preamble, declares the obligation of States "to practice tolerance and live together in peace with one another as good neighbours." However, it required a quarter of a century more to bring the most powerful nation of the capitalist world to recognise *expressis verbis* this principle. "They will proceed from the common determination that in the nuclear age there is no alternative to conducting their mutual relations on the basis of peaceful coexistence," stated General Secretary of the C.P.S.U. Breshnev and President Nixon of the United States in the Basic Principles of Mutual Relations signed by them in Moscow, on May 29, 1972.

The principle of peaceful coexistence has been embodied in many decisions of United Nations organs and above all in the 1970 Declaration on Principles of International Law. The Declaration stipulates the development of friendly relations among nations, irrespective of their political, economic and social systems, and the duty of States to cooperate with one another irrespective of the differences in their political, economic and social systems.

Structural and substantive changes in International Law

The structure of international law has become much more complex than it was fifty years ago. There are today very great differences in the nature of various components of the system of international law. Norms of general international law based on the co-ordination of the wills of States belonging to different socio-economic systems, are of a general democratic nature. However, there are a growing number of socialist principles and norms in the context of relations among socialist States. There are other regional principles and norms the social nature of which is also different from that of general international law.

The growth of international organizations has introduced essential changes in the structure of international relations and international law. It has considerably changed norm-creating processes in international law as well as modes of ensuring compliance with and application of international law.

The emergence of the principles of *jus cogens* (a specific group of principles from which states can not derogate by agreement) is of considerable importance. These principles are a reflection in international law of a new situation when the growing internationalization of economic and other spheres of human activities has transformed many international problems into global problems affecting interests of all states. The principles of *jus cogens* express the idea that in view of such general interest in these problems their legal regulation should be uniform.[17]

The late Professor Charles de Visscher stated that Article 53 of the Vienna Convention on the Law of Treaties of 1969 concerning *jus cogens* was the most remarkable innovation.[18] Article 53 of the Vienna Convention is undoubtedly a remarkable step forward; it constitutes a clear cut recognition by the majority of states of the existence of the principles *jus cogens* in contemporary international law.

The norms of general international law can be created, as in the past, only by agreement between States. However, with the advent of international organizations there have appeared various new types of international legal norms. These consist of legal norms created by agreements concluded by international intergovernmental organizations, and legal norms existing within every international organization. Another new type of international norm consists of the recommendations of international organizations. Such recommendations are of different legal nature and have a different relation to the general processes of creating norms of international law.

Many new branches of public international law that reflect the expansion of human activities and the emergence of new international problems have emerged or are in the process of formation. These include the law of international organizations, the law of outer space, the law of environment, and international economic law. There is no sphere of international law which has not undergone some substantial changes. We may safely say that contemporary international law differs substantially from the old international law ("classical international law") and it should be considered to be a new international law. The thesis presented by Sir Gerald Fitzmaurice in his report to the Institute of International Law that "traditional international law" is "the foundation for the future" and that there has been a "change for the worse but not always"[19] was not proved by him; this author believes that such a thesis cannot be proved since it seems to be completely removed from reality.

17. See Tunkin, "Jus Cogens in Contemporary International Law," 1971 *U. Toledo L. Rev.* 107.

18. De Visscher, "Stages in the Codification of International Law The Hague 1930—Geneva 1958—Vienna 1969," in *Transnational Law in a Changing Society* Essays in Honor of Philip C. Jessup 17, 29 (W. Friedmann, L. Henkin, & O. Lissitzyn eds. 1972).

19. G. Fitzmaurice, *The Future of Public International Law and of the International Legal System in the Circumstances of Today* paras. 19, 20 (1973) (special report for the Institut de droit international).

III. FUNCTIONS OF CONTEMPORARY INTERNATIOHAL LAW

It is generally and rightly agreed that international law fulfils two social functions: a stabilizing one when international law gives its blessing to existing relations; a creative one when international law is used to create new relations among states. These functions are parallel and often interrelated. If the stabilizing function is very often spoken of, the creative function is sometimes not taken into consideration at all. Thus, it is easy to present international law as a system of rules hindering the development of international relations, a kind of "strait jacket," to use George Kennan's words.[20]

Careful study of contemporary international relations shows that, in an era of accelerated tempo of development, the role of the creative function of international law has increased considerably. The old international law developed mainly as customary law; however, beginning with the second half of the 19th century the part played by the treaty has increased to the point where today the treaty is the primary instrument for creating norms of international law.[21]

In 1959 twelve States were working in Washington on an Antarctic treaty; this author took part in the negotiations as a delegate for the Soviet Union. The parties to the negotiations intended to change, at least to some degree, the existing situation and to create new relations among themselves with respect to Antarctica. These new relations were set forth in the norms of the Antarctic Treaty.[22] At its inception the Treaty's function was principally a creative one. When the new relations had been created the primary function of the Treaty became a stabilizing one.

When the Charter of the United Nations was signed there was no international organization in existence. The legal norms of this treaty encompassed such matters as the structure of the organization, the functions and competences of its organs, and the relationships between its members. The first task of the norms of the Charter was to fulfil the creative function. After the Organization has been created, the Charter became the legal basis for its activities, and has been fulfilling principally a stabilizing function.

Norms of international law can also play a creative role in bilateral relations among states. The Soviet Union and the United States have

20. G. Kennan, *American Diplomacy 1900-1950,* at 98 (1951).

21. International customary law follows the practice of States, whereas a treaty can move ahead of practice and pave the way for new relations between States. When States come to an understanding to legally fix an existing situation or to create new relationships among themselves, they embody their agreement in an international legal norm (treaty) to make it legally binding. A treaty creating new relations embodies them in its provisions; they will then be put into practice by the parties to the treaty.

22. *Done* Dec. 1, 1959, 402 U.N.T.S. 71.

recently concluded many agreements on political, economic, scientific and technical questions. Most of those agreements were intended to create either completely new or substantially new relations between the two States.

Recognition of the creative function of international law does not amount to the acceptance of the theories according to which societal relations develop on the basis of law. According to the Marxist-Leninist theory the content and form of law are determined in the last analysis by the economic structure of society at a certain stage of its development. At the same time, because law is a part of a social system, and is in constant interaction with other social phenomena and influenced by them, it exercises an influence upon them and to a certain degree can be used as an instrument for changing existing societal relations or for creating new ones.

International law has always played creative and stabilizing roles but the social character of these functions has changed from era to era. The social character of these functions, or in other words, the social aims that these functions serve at a certain moment of human history, depend on the character of the international law of the particular period and on the social environment within which such international law operates. Thus, the social character of the functions that are essentially different from those fulfilled by international law as it existed before the Great October Socialist Revolution.

International law of a certain socio-economic type, together with socio-economic conditions that had given birth to this law, inevitably becomes a hindrance to the development of society and is replaced by a new international law. Such was the case with feudal international law, which was replaced by bourgeois international law, and which in its turn has gradually given way to contemporary international law. This law is neither bourgeois nor socialist; it is general—democratic.

The social character of the functions of contemporary international law are directed mainly at strengthening international peace and the peaceful coexistence and cooperation of States irrespective of their socio-economic systems, and at ensuring the freedom and independence of peoples and respect for human rights. Given these functions of international law, and given the fact that in our era the settlement of international global problems and, above all, the problem of maintaining international peace here become a *conditio sine qua non* to the progress and even the very existence of mankind, to demand strict compliance with international law is to defend objectively the interest of the entire human race.

A BIBLIOGRAPHY OF THE WRITINGS OF WOLFGANG FRIEDMANN*

ADMINISTRATIVE AND PUBLIC LAW

Books and Pamphlets

Administrative Law in a Changing World (Presented to the Indian Institute of Public Administration, 1962) 11 pp.

Government Enterprise: A Comparative Symposium (London 1970) 351 pp. (ed. with J. Garner).

Principles of Australian Administrative Law (1st ed., Melbourne 1950) 118 pp.; (2nd ed., Sydney 1962) 368 pp. (with D. Benjafield).

The Public Corporation: A Comparative Symposium (Toronto 1954) 612 pp. (ed.).

State and the Rule of Law In a Mixed Economy (London 1971) 103 pp.

Articles and Casenote

Autonomie und Staatskontrolle im Sozial-und Wirtschaftsrecht, *Mitteilungen des wirtschaftwissenschaftlichen Instituts der Gewerkschaftèn,* no. 11, at 228 (1952).

Constitutionalism and the Corporate Order, in 3 *The Business System:*

*This bibliography is based on "Wolfgang Gaston Friedmann: A Selective Bibliography" which was published in the *10th Anniversary Issue of The Columbia Journal of Transnational Law,* dedicated to Professor Friedmann, 10 *Colum. J. Transnat'l L.* 32 (1971). The bibliography has been expanded and brought up to date. Approval of the use of the bibliography has been obtained from the editors of the *Columbia Journal of Transnational Law.*

Readings in Ideas and Concepts 1697 (C. Walton & R. Eells eds. 1966).

Declaratory Judgment and Injunction as Public Law remedies, 22 *Austl. L. J.* 446 (1949).

Forms and Functions of Public Enterprise—A Comparative Survey, in 22 *Current Legal Problems* 79 (G. Keeton & G. Schwarzenberger eds. 1969).

French Administrative Law and the Common-Law World, 9 *U. Toronto L. J.* 143 (1953).

Government Enterprise: A Comparative Analysis, in *Government Enterprise* 303 (W. Friedmann & J. Garner eds. 1970).

Governmental (Public) Enterprise, in 13 *International Encyclopedia of Comparative Law* ch. 13 (A. Conard ed. 1972).

Incorporated and Unincorporated Bodies (Wurzel v. Houghton Main Delivery Services and Wurzel v. Atkinson, 1 K. B. 380 [1937]), 1 *Modern L. Rev.* 76 (1937).

Status of Incorporated Public Authorities, 22 *Austl. L. J.* 7 (1948).

The Legal Status and Organization of the Public Corporation, 16 *L. & Contemp. Prob.* 576 (1951).

The New Public Corporation and the Law (pt. 1-2), 10 *Modern L. Rev.* 233 and 377 (1947).

Public and Private Enterprise in Mixed Economies, in 13 *International Encyclopedia of Comparative Law* (A. Conard ed. 1974).

Public Law Problems in Recent English Decisions, in 4 *Current Legal Problems* 370 (G. Keeton & G. Schwarzenberger eds. 1951).

Public Welfare Offences, Statutory Duties, and the Legal Status of the Crown, 13 *Modern L. Rev.* 24 (1950).

The Shield of the Crown, 24 *Austl. L. J.* 275 (1950).

Statutory Powers and Legal Duties of Local Authorities, 8 *Modern L. Rev.* 31 (1945).

Technical Assistance: A Challenge for Corporations: A Round Table, 8 *J. Public L.* 173 (1959).

A Theory of Public Industrial Enterprise, in *Public Enterprise* 11 (A. Hanson ed. 1955).

BOOK REVIEWS

Jewkes: *Public and Private Enterprise* (1965), 1969 *Wisc. L. Rev.* 362 (1969).

Schwartz: *French Administrative Law and the Common Law World* (1954), 11 *U. Toronto L. J.* 143 (1955).

Schwartz: *Le droit administratif Américain: notions générales* (1952), 31 *Can. B. Rev.* 1061 (1953).

ANTITRUST LAW

BOOKS

ANTI-TRUST LAWS: A COMPARATIVE SYMPOSIUM (Toronto 1956) 635 pp. (ed.).

ARTICLES

Anti-Monopoly Law—Some Comparative Observations, in 1 *Festschrift für Ernst Rabel, Rechtsvergleichung und Internationales Privatrecht* 453 (Tübingen 1954).

The Harris Tweed Case and Freedom of Trade, 6 *Modern L. Rev.* 1 (1942).

International Aspects of Anti-Trust Law, 1956 *Am. Soc'y Int'l L. Proc.* 1 (Pacific Northwest Regional Meeting on the International Implications of United States and Canadian Anti-Trust Laws) (Bulletin No. 12, Part 1).

Monopoly, Reasonableness and Public Interest in the Canadian Anti-Combines Law, 33 *Can. B. Rev.* 133 (1955).

Book Reviews

Brewster: *Antitrust and American Business Abroad* (1958), 58 *Colum. L. Rev.* 1311 (1958).

Dix, Evelyn & Mills: *Law Relating to Competitive Trading* (1937), 21 *J. Comp. Legislation* 301 (1939).

Papandreou & Wheeler: *Competition and Its Regulation* (1954), 12 *U. Toronto L.J.* 144 (1957).

CONTRACT LAW

Articles and Casenotes

Changing Functions of Contract in the Common Law, 9 *U. Toronto L. J.* 15 (1951).

Effect of Nullity Decree, Mistake of Fact, Unjust Enrichment (*Re* Eaves, 56 T. L. R. 110 [1939]), 3 *Modern L. Rev.* 232 (1940).

Nature of Quasi Contractual Liability (Brook's Wharf and Bull Wharf Ltd. v. Goodman Bros., 1 K. B. 534 [1937]), 53 *L. Q. Rev.* 449 (1937).

Quasi-Contract—Quantum Meruit (Craven-Ellis v. Canons, 2 K. B. 403 [1936]), 1 *Modern L. Rev.* 76 (1937).

The Principle of Unjust Enrichment in English Law, 16 *Can. B. Rev.* 243 (1938).

Unjust Enrichment (*Re* Cleadon Trust, 55 T. L. R. 154 [1938]), 2 *Modern L. Rev.* 315 (1939).

Unjust Enrichment as a Defence (Ayres v. Moore, 56 T. L. R. [1940]), 4 *Modern L. Rev.* 236 (1940).

BOOK REVIEWS

Anson: *Principles of the Law of Contract* (18th ed. Miles & Brierly 1937), 2 *Modern L. Rev.* 173 (1938).

Challies: *Doctrine of Unjustified Enrichment in the Law of the Province of Quebec* (1952), 30 *Can. B. Rev.* 851 (1952).

FOREIGN AND COMPARATIVE LAW

BOOKS

DIE BEREICHERUNGSHAFTUNG IM ANGLO-AMERIKANISCHEN RECHTSKREIS IN VERGLEICHUNG MIT DEM DEUTSCHEN BÜRGERLICHEN RECHT (Berlin 1930) 148 pp.

MATRIMONIAL PROPERTY LAW: A COMPARATIVE SYMPOSIUM (Toronto 1955) 472 pp. (ed.).

ARTICLES

Australian Legal Education: Further Observations, 9 *J. Legal Ed.* 495 (1957).

The British Commonwealth: Its Problems as a Coordinated Legal System, 9 *Am. J. Comp. L.* 349 (1960).

Common Principles of Law in the Western Family of Nations, 12 *J. Int'l Aff.* 193 (1958).

Comparative Law Course at Melbourne University, 1 *J. Soc'y Pub.* 274 (n. s. 1949).

The Interpretation of Statutes in Modern British Law, 3 *Vand. L. Rev.* 365 (1950).

Modern Trends in Soviet Law, 10 *U. Toronto L. J.* 87 (1953).

A Re-examination of the Relations Between English, American and Continental Jurisprudence, 20 *Can. B. Rev.* 175 (1942).

Some Observations on Legal Education, 1 *U. West. Austl. L. Rev.* 93 (1948-50).

Stare Decisis at Common Law and Under the Civil Code of Quebec, 31 *Can. B. Rev.* 723 (1953).

Teaching and Research in Comparative Law: Recent Developments at the University of Toronto Law School, 10 *U. Toronto L. J.* 245 (1954).

The Teaching of Comparative Law, 1 *U. West. Austl. Rev.* 90 (1948-50).

Tendances de la common law en matière de résponsabilité civile, 11 *Themis Revue Juridique* 130 (Montreal 1954).

Book Reviews

1 *Annuaire Européen* (1955), 70 Harv. L. Rev. 396(1956).

Baudouin: *Le droit civil de la province de Québec: modèle vivant de droit computé* (1953), 10 U. *Toronto L.J.* 229 (1953-54).

Brady: *Democracy in the Dominions: A Comparative Study in Institutions* (2nd ed. 1952), 9 *Int'l J.* 144 (1954).

Cohn & Wolff: 1 *Manual of German Law* (1950), *U. Toronto L. J.* 152 (1951).

Dix: *In the Eyes of the Law* (1937), 20 *J. Comp. Legislation 301* (1939).

Eder: *A Comparative Survey of Anglo-Saxon and Latin-American Law* (1950), 10 *U. Toronto L. J.* 162 (1953-54).

Grzybowski: *The Socialist Commonwealth of Nations—Organizations and Institutions* (1964), 17 *Stan. L. Rev.* 1204 (1965).

Hamson: *Executive Discretion and Judicial Control: An Aspect of the French Conseil d'Etat* (1954), 12 *U. Toronto L. J.* 140 (1957).

Hazard: *Law and Social Change in the U.S.S.R.* (1953), 32 *Can. B. Rev.* 1056 (1954).

Hazard & Weisberg: *Cases and Readings on Soviet Law* (1950), 9 *U. Toronto L. J.* 164 (1951).

Lloyd: *Public Policy: A Comparative Study in English and French Law* (1953), 10 *U. Toronto L. J.* 291 (1954).

2 *Manual of German Law: Private International Law, Civil Procedure, Criminal Law, Criminal Procedure* (1952), 10 *U. Toronto L. J.* 161 (1953-54).

Mitchell: *Contracts of Public Authorities; A Comparative Study* (1954), 11 *U. Toronto L. J.* 330 (1956).

New Zealand: *The Development of its Laws and Constitution* (J. Robson ed. 1954), 19 *Modern L. Rev.* 441 (1956).

Potter: *The National Insurance Act, 1946* (1946), 11 *Modern L. Rev.* 126 (1948).

Sawer: *Cases on the Constitution of the Commonwealth of Australia* (1957), 57 *Colum. L. Rev.* 1195 (1957).

Schlesinger: *Comparative Law: Cases and Materials* (1950), 9 *U. Toronto L. J.* 162 (1951-52).

Schlesinger: *Comparative Law: Cases and Materials* (1950), 19 *U. Kan. City L. Rev.* 124 (1950-51).

V *Soviet Legal Philosophy* (1951), 38 *Va. L. Rev.* 563 (1952).

Street: *Governmental Liability—A Comparative Study* (1953), 54 *Colum. L. Rev.* 151 (1954).

Szladits: *Bibliography of Foreign and Comparative Law* (1955), 50 *Am. J. Int'l L.* 458 (1956).

Szladits: *Guide to Foreign Legal Materials; French, German, Swiss* (1959), 55 *Am. J. Int'l L.* 203 (1961).

United Kingdom: *The Development of its Laws and Constitutions* (G. Keeton & D. Lloyd eds. 1955), 72 *L. Q. Rev.* 578 (1956).

Von Mehren: *Civil Law System: Cases and Materials for the Comparative Study of Law* (1957), 11 J. Legal Ed. 122 (1958).

HUMOR

ARTICLES

Reviewmanship: How to be Successful in Reviewing Law Books Without Really Trying, 14 *J. Legal Ed.* 508 (1962). Reprinted in *Juristenzeitung,* December 11, 1965, at 373.

INTERNATIONAL LAW

BOOKS AND PAMPHLETS

CASES AND MATERIALS ON INTERNATIONAL LAW (St. Paul 1969) 1205 pp. (with O.J. Lissitzyn & R.C. Pugh eds.).

THE CHANGING STRUCTURE OF INTERNATIONAL LAW (New York 1964) 410 pp. LA NUEVA ESTRUCTURA DEL DERECHO INTERNACIONAL (F. Trillas ed., Mexico 1967) 481 pp. Abridged Edition (L. M. Friedmann ed. 1969).

THE CONTRIBUTION OF ENGLISH EQUITY TO THE IDEA OF AN INTERNATIONAL EQUITY TRIBUNAL (1935) 84 pp.

DE L'EFFICACITÉ DES INSTITUTIONS INTERNATIONALES (Paris 1970) 199 pp.

THE FUTURE OF THE OCEANS (New York 1971) 132 pp.

GENERAL COURSE IN PUBLIC INTERNATIONAL LAW (The Hague Academy of International Law, Recueil des Cours, vol. II, Leyden 1969) 246 pp.

INTERNATIONAL LAW AND THE PRESENT WAR (Transactions of the Grotius Society, London 1941) 23 pp.

INTERNATIONAL PUBLIC CORPORATIONS AS AGENCIES OF RECONSTRUCTION (World Unity Booklet No. 2, London 1946).

NATO — SHIELD OF FREEDOM (Canadian Institute of International Affairs, Vol. 12, No. 4, 1952) 17 pp.

TRANSNATIONAL LAW IN A CHANGING SOCIETY, ESSAYS IN HONOR OF PHILIP C. JESSUP (New York and London 1972) 324 pp. (with L. Henkin & O.J. Lissitzyn eds).

WHAT'S WRONG WITH INTERNATIONAL LAW? (London 1941) 48 pp.

ARTICLES

Act of State: Sabbatino in the Courts and in Congress, 3 *Colum. J. Transnat'l L.* 99 (1965).

Cambios en la Extension y Objetivos de las Relaciones Interestatales, 15 *Rev. de la Facultad de Derecho de Mex.* 357 (Mexico 1965).

Canada and the international Legal Order: An Outside Perspective, in *Canadian Perspectives on International Law and Organization* (R. St. J. MacDonald, J. Morris & D. Johnston eds. 1974).

Canadian Approaches to International Law, 19 *Int'l J.* 77 (1963-64).

The Changing Dimensions of International Law, 62 *Colum L. Rev.* 1147 (1962). Reprinted in Essays on International Law 95 (*Colum. L. Rev.* ed. 1965).

Changing Social Arrangements in State-Trading States and Their Effect on International Law, 24 *L. & Contemp. Prob.* 350 (1959).

Comment 4, in *Law and Civil War in the Modern World* 574 (J. N. Moore ed. 1974).

Comments on the Legality of the United States Action in Cambodia; Symposium on United States Action in Cambodia, 65 *Am. J. Int'l L.* 77 (1971).

Disintegration of European Civilisation and the Future of International Law, 2 *Modern L. Rev.* 194 (1938).

Droit de coexistence et droit de coopération. Quelques observations sur la structure changeante du droit international, 6 *Revue Belge du Droit International* 1 (1970).

Foreword, 2 *The Strategy of World Order* v (R. Falk & S. Mendlovitz eds. 1966).

The Growth of State Control Over the Individual and its Effect Upon the Rules of International State Responsibility, 19 *Brit. Y. B. Int'l L.* 118 (1938).

Half a Century of International Law, 50 *Va. L. Rev.* 1333 (1964).

Human Welfare and International Law—A Reordering of Priorities, in *Transnational Law in a Changing Society, Essays in Honor of Philip C. Jessup* (W. Friedmann, L. Henkin, & O. Lissitzyn eds. 1972).

The International Court of Justice and the Evolution of International Law, 14 *Archiv des Völkerrechts* 305 (Tübingen 1970).

International Law and the Present War, 3 *Modern L. Rev.* 177 (1940).

International Public Corporations, 6 *Modern L. Rev.* 185 (1943).

Intervention and International Law, 25 *Internationale Spectator* 40 (Netherlands 1971).

Intervention, Civil War and the Role of International Law, 59 *Am. Soc'y Int'l L. Proc.* 67 (1965). Reprinted in 2 *The Vietnam War and International Law* 151 (Falk ed. 1968) and in *International Law in the Twentieth Century* 724 (1969).

Law and Politics in the Vietnamese War: A Comment, 61 *Am. J. Int'l L.* 775 (1967). Reprinted in 1 *The Vietnam War and International Law* 292 (Falk ed. 1968).

Legal and Political Aspects of the Berlin Crisis, 1 *Colum. J. Transnat'l L.* 1 (1961).

National Courts and the International Legal Order: Projections on the Implications of the Sabbatino Case, 34 *Geo. Wash. L. Rev.* 443 (1966).

National Sovereignty, International Cooperation, and the Reality of International Law, 10 *U.C.L.A. L. Rev.* 739 (1963). Reprinted in 3 *The Strategy of World Order* 508 (R. Falk & S. Mendlovitz eds. 1966).

New Tasks for NATO, 11 *Int'l J.* 157 (1956).

The North Sea Continental Shelf Cases—A Critique, 64 *Am. J. Int'l. L.* 229 (1970).

The Position of Underdeveloped Countries and the Universality of International Law, 2 *Colum. J. Transnat'l L.* 78 (1963).

The Race to the Bottom of the Sea, 12 *Columbia Forum* 18 (1969).

The Reality of International Law—A Reappraisal, 10 *Colum. J. Transnat'l L.* 46 (1971).

The Role of International Law in the Conduct of International Affairs, 20 *Int'l J.* 158 (1965).

Selden *Redivivus* —Towards a Partition of the Seas?, 65 *Am. J. Int'l L.* 757 (1971).

Sir Hersch Lauterpacht and the International Court, 45 *Va. L. Rev.* 407 (1959).

Some Impacts of Social Organization on International Law, 50 *Am. J. Int'l L.* 457 (1956).

The Tennessee Valley Authority and International Public Enterprise, 11 *World Aff.* 35 (1945).

Textbook Myth on International Law, 4 *Modern L. Rev.* 299 (1941).

The United Nations Administrative Tribunal, 2 *Int'l Organ.* 13 (1957) (with A. A. Fatouros).

The United Nations and National Loyalties, 8 *Int'l J.* 17 (1952-53).

The United Nations and the Development of International Law, 25 *Int'l J.* 272 (1970).

United States Policy and the Crisis of International Law: Some

Reflections on the State of International Law in "International Co-operation Year," 59 *Am. J. Int'l L.* 857 (1965).

The Uses of "General Principles" in the Development of International Law, 57 *Am. J. Int'l L.* 279 (1963). Reprinted in *International Law in the Twentieth Century* 246 (1969).

Book Reviews

Adam: *I & II, Les organismes internationaux spécialisés. Contribution à la théorie générale des établissements publics internationaux* (1965), 60 *Am. J. Int'l L.* 606 (1966).

Bentwich & Martin: *A Commentary on the Charter of the United Nations* (1950), 6 *Int'l J.* 169 (1951).

Bishop: *General Course of Public International Law* (1965), 66 *Mich. L. Rev.* 409 (1967).

Brierly: *The Outlook for International Law* (1944), 8 *Modern L. Rev.* 168 (1945).

Briggs: *The Law of Nations* (2nd ed. 1952), 7 *Int'l J.* 233 (1952).

British Yearbook of International Law (1937), 1 *Modern L. Rev.* 255 (1937).

Cheng: *General Principles of Law as Applied by International Courts and Tribunals* (1953), 10 *Int'l J.* 230 (1955).

Cheng: *General Principles of Law as Applied by International Courts and Tribunals* (1953), 12 *U. Toronto L. J.* 106 (1957).

Clark & Sohn: *World Peace Through World Law* (1958), 107 *U. Pa. L. Rev.* 746 (1959).

The Evolution of International Organization (Luard ed. 1966), 83 *Pol. Sci. Q.* 114 (1968).

Finer: *The T.V.A. Lessons for International Application* (1944), 8 *Modern L. Rev.* 91 (1945).

Grant-Bailey: *The Law of Neutrality* (1944), 7 *Modern L. Rev.* 251 (1944).

Higgins & Colombos: *The International Law of the Sea* (1943), 7 *Modern L. Rev.* 250 (1944).

International Labour Code (1939/1941), 7 *Modern L. Rev.* 96 (1944).

International Labour Office: Constitutional Provisions Concerning Social and Economic Policy (1944), 8 *Modern L. Rev.* 91 (1945).

International Law. The Collected Papers of Sir Cecil J. B. Hurst, G.C.M.G., K.C.B., K.C. (1950), 6 *Int'l J.* 260 (1951).

Jacobs: *The Policy of Neutrality and the Practical Alternative* (1943), 7 *Modern L. Rev.* 253 (1944).

Jenks: *The Prospects of International Adjudication* (1964), 10 *N.Y.U. L. Forum* 441 (1964).

Kaplan & Katzenbach: *The Political Foundations of International Law* (1961), 62 *Colum. L. Rev.* 195 (1962).

Keeton & Schwarzenberger: *Making International Law Work* (2nd ed. 1946), 10 *Modern L. Rev.* 440 (1947).

Lissitzyn: *The International Court of Justice* (1951), 7 *Int'l J.* 165 (1952).

Lissitzyn: *International Law in a Divided World* (1963), 3 *Colum. J. Transnat'l L.* 87 (1964).

Litchfield: *Governing Postwar Germany* (1953), 14 *L. Guild Rev.* 141 (1954).

McDougal & Burke: *The Public Order of the Oceans: A Contemporary International Law of the Sea* (1962), 64 *Colum. L. Rev.* 606 (1964).

McDougal & Feliciano: *Law and Minimum World Public Order: The Legal Regulation of International Coercion* (1961), 64 *Colum. L. Rev.* 606 (1964).

McDougal, Lasswell & Miller: *The Interpretation of Agreements and World Public Order: Principles of Content and Procedure* 1967), 7 *Colum. J. Transnat'l L.* 354 (1968).

3 *The New Nations in International Law and Diplomacy* (W. O'Brien ed. 1965), 21 *Int'l J.* 125 (1965-66).

Nicholas: *The United Nations as a Political Institution* (1959), 16 *Int'l J.* 80 (1960-61).

Nussbaum: *A Concise History of the Law of Nations* (rev. ed. 1954), 9 *Int'l J.* 324 (1954).

Oppenheim: 1 *International Law* (5th ed. Lauterpacht 1937), 2 *Modern L. Rev.* 81 (1938).

Schwarzenberger: *A Manual of International Law* (1952), 9 *Int'l J.* 71 (1954).

Sohn: *Cases and Other Materials on World Law: The Interpretation and Application of the Charter of the United Nations and of the Constitutions of Other Agencies of the World Council* (1950), 9 *U. Toronto L. J.* 163 (1951-52).

Soward & McInnis: *Canada and the United Nations* (1956), 12 *Int'l J.* 309 (1957).

Sprecher: *III Trials of War Criminals Before the Nuernberg Military Tribunals Under Control Council Law No. 10* (1951), 67 *Harv. L. Rev.* 1284 (1954).

Stone: *Legal Controls of International Conflict* (1954), 15 *L. Guild Rev.* 31 (1955).

Weinfeld: *Towards a United States of Europe* (1942), 6 *Modern L. Rev.* 254 (1943).

II *Wheaton's International Law* (7th ed. Keith 1944), 7 *Modern L. Rev.* 251 (1944).

INTERNATIONAL POLITICS

Books and Pamphlets

The Allied Military Government of Germany (London 1947) 362 pp.

THE CRISIS OF THE NATIONAL STATE (London 1943) 197 pp.

GERMAN IMMIGRATION INTO CANADA (Published under the auspices of the Canadian Institute of International Affairs) (Contemporary Affairs No. 23, Toronto 1952) 63 pp.

AN INTRODUCTION TO WORLD POLITICS (1st ed., London 1951) 313 pp.; (2nd ed., London 1953) 384 pp.; (Japanese ed. 1954) 322 pp.; PENGANTAR ILMU POLITIK DUNIA (Indonesian ed., Bandung 1954) 374 pp.; (3rd ed., London 1956) 454 pp.; (4th ed., London 1960) 384 pp.; (5th ed., London · ıd New York 1965) 497 pp.

WORLD REVOLUTION AND THE FUTURE OF THE WEST (London 1942) 118 pp.

ARTICLES

The Arm of Germany's Trade Unions, 172 *Fortnightly* 291 (n.s. 1952).

Australia Faces the Future, 165 *Fortnightly* 236 (1949).

Australian Foreign Policy, 27 *Int'l Aff.* 312 (London 1951).

Auswanderung nach Australien und Kanada, *Englische Rundschau,* no. 32, at 387 (1952).

Betrachtungen zur Berlin-Krise, *Blätter für Deutsche und Internationale Politik* 174 (1959).

Britain's Crisis and the Commonwealth, 166 *Fortnightly* 289 (1949).

Canada at the Crossroads, 170 *Fortnightly* 717 (n.s. 1951).

The Changing Commonwealth, 58 *Queen's Q.* 465 (1951-52).

Comments in *The Dominican Republic Crisis* 1965, at 87 (The Hammarskjold Forum, C. J. Carey ed., Dobbs Ferry 1967).

Commentary on United States Intervention: Doctrine and Practice, 3 *Stan. J. Int'l Studies* 107 (1968). Reprinted in 2 *The Vietnam War and International Law* 1027 (R. Falk ed. 1969).

Consequences and Alternatives to American Interventionism, 5 *New University Thought* 46 (1966-67).

The European Coal and Steel Community, 10 *Int'l J.* 12 (1954-55).

A Foreign Policy for Australia, 4 *World Aff.* 72 (n.s. London 1949).

The International Organization of Security and the Use of Force: "Indirect" Aggression, National Sovereignty, and Collective Security, in 2 *The Strategy of World Order* 325 (R. Falk and S. Mendlovitz eds. 1966).

Intervention and the Developing Countries, 10 *Va. J. Int'l* 205 (1970).

Interventionism, Liberalism, and Power-Politics: The Unfinished Revolution in International Thinking, 83 *Pol. Sci. Q.* 169 (1968).

The Legal and Constitutional Position of Germany under Allied Military Government, 3 *Res Judicatae* 133 (Melbourne 1947).

The Limits of Functionalism in International Organization, 10 *Yearbook of World Affairs* 256 (1956).

Meeting of East and West, 14 *Int'l J.* 235 (1959).

Migration and World Politics, 7 *Int'l J.* 96 (1952).

Planning for Freedom, 24 *Modern L. Rev.* 208 (1961).

Some Reflections on the Anti-Communist Act, 1 *U. West. Austl. L. Rev.* 516 (1948-50).

The Suez Canal Crisis of 1956, in *International Law and Political Crisis* 91 (L. Scheinman & D. Wilkinson eds. 1968) (with L. Collins).

The U-2 and Outer Space Control, 39 *Foreign Policy Bull.* 157 (1960).

United States Involvement in Vietnam, in *Judaism and World Peace: Focus Vietnam* 32 (Synagogue Council of America, New York 1966).

Western Policy at the Crossroads, 168 *Fortnightly* 141 (1950).

Book Reviews

Lall: *Modern International Negotiations: Principles and Practice* (1966), 83 *Pol. Sci. Q.* 435 (1968).

Manning: *Peaceful Change. An International Problem* (1937), 1 *Modern L. Rev.* 174 (1937).

Northrop: *European Union and United States Foreign Policy, A Study in Sociological Jurisprudence* (1954), 64 *Yale L. J.* 469 (1955).

Pinto: *La crise de l'état aux Etats-Unis* (1951), 7 *Int'l J.* 238 (1955).

Vickers: *The Art of Judgment: A Study of Policy Making* (1965), 66 *Colum. L. Rev.* 1381 (1966).

LEGAL PHILOSOPHY

Books and Pamphlets

Law and Social Change in Contemporary Britain (London 1951) 322 pp.

Law In a Changing Society (1st ed., London 1959) 552 pp.; Penguin abridged edition (England 1964) 475 pp.; El Derecho En una Sociedad en Transformacion (Spanish ed., Mexico 1964) 546 pp.; Recht Und Sozialer Wandel (German ed., Frankfurt 1969) 452 pp.; Penguin 2nd edition (London 1971).

Legal Theory (1st ed., London 1947) 448 pp.; (2nd ed., London 1949) 470 pp.; (3rd ed., London 1953) 520 pp.; (4th ed., London 1960) 564 pp.; Théorie Générale du Droit (French ed., Paris 1965) 566 pp.; (5th ed., London 1967) 607 pp.

Sociology of Law: A Trend Report and Bibliography (Oxford 1963) 34 pp.

ARTICLES

American Legal Education, 2 *Oxford Lawyer* 7 (1959).

Arthur Nussbaum, A Tribute, 57 *Colum. L. Rev.* 1 (1957).

Bentham's Limits of Jurisprudence Defined, 64 *L. Q. Rev.* 341 (1948).

Changes in Property Relations, 2 *Third World Congress Sociology* 175 (1956).

The Changing Content of Public Interest: Some Comments on Harold D. Lasswell, in *Nomos V: The Public Interest* 80 (C. J. Friedrich ed. 1962).

Contemporary Tasks for Legal Theory, 4 *West. Ontario L. Rev.* 90 (1965).

Corporate Power, Government by Private Groups and the Law, 57 *Colum L. Rev.* 155 (1957).

Fenomenologia e scienza del diritto, 48 *Rivista Internazionale di Filifosio del Diritto* 327 (1971).

Gustav Radbruch, 7 *The Encyclopedia of Philosophy* 61 (P. Edwards ed. 1967).

Gustav Radbruch, 14 *Vand. L. Rev.* 191 (1960).

Hugo Grotius, 3 *The Encyclopedia of Philosophy* 393 (P. Edwards ed. 1967).

Interference with Human Life: Some Jurisprudential Reflections, 70 *Colum. L. Rev.* 1058 (1970).

Jeremy Bentham and the Law, in *Bentham And Modern Legal Thought* 233 (G. Keeton & G. Schwarzenberger eds. 1948).

Judges, Politics, and the Law, 29 Can. B. Rev. 811 (1951).

Judicial Law Making in England: Some Jurisprudential Reflections on the House of Lords, in *Law, Justice & Equity* 9 (Code-Holland & G. Schwarzenberger eds. 1967).

Jurisprudence, 8 *Chamber's Encyclopedia* 157 (rev. ed. 1967).

The Jurisprudential Implications of the South West Africa Case, 6 *Colum. J. Transnat'l L.* 1 (1967).

Law, 8 *Chamber's Encyclopedia* 406 (rev. ed. 1967).

The Lawyers in a Changing World, 5 *Alberta L. Rev.* 401 (1960).

Legal Theory, 8 *Chamber's Encyclopedia* 448 (rev. ed. 1967).

Legal Theory and the Practical Lawyer, 5 *Modern L. Rev.* 103 (1941).

Legal Philosophy and Judicial Law Making, 61 *Colum. L. Rev.* 821 (1961). Reprinted in *Essays on Jurisprudence* 101 *Colum. L. Rev.* ed. 1963).

Limits of Judicial Lawmaking and Prospective Overruling, 29 *Modern L. Rev.* 593 (1966).

Phenomenological and Legal Science, in *Phenomenology and Legal Theory* (M. Natanson ed. 1971).

The Planned State and the Rule of Law, 22 *Austl. L. J.* 162 (1948).

Property, Freedom, Security and the Supreme Court of the United States, 19 *Modern L. Rev.* 461 (1956).

Public and Private Law Thinking: The Need for Synthesis, 5 *Wayne L. Rev.* 291 (1959).

Quelques réflexions sur l'état de la philosophie du droit contemporain, 15 *Archives de philosophie du droit* 197 (1970).

The Role of Law and the Function of the Lawyer in Developing Countries, 17 *Vand. L. Rev.* 181 (1963).

Roscoe Pound, *Rabels Zeitschrift für ausländisches und internationales Privatrecht,* no. 2, at 225 (1965).

Sociology of Law, in *A Dictionary of the Social Sciences* 681 (J. Gould & W. L. Kolb eds. 1964).

Some Reflections on Status and Freedom, in *Essays in Jurisprudence in Honor of Roscoe Pound* 222 (P. Sayre ed. 1962).

Statute Law and Its Interpretation in the Modern State, 26 *Can. B. Rev.* 1277 (1948).

Teaching of Comparative Jurisprudence, 4 *Res Judicatae* 74 (Melbourne 1949).

Theory of Justice: A Lawyer's Critique, 11 *Colum. J. Transnat'l L.* 369 (1972).

Trethowan's Case, Parliamentary Sovereignty, and the Limits of Legal Change, 24 *Austl. L. J.* 103 (1950).

Vitalizing the Teaching of Jurisprudence, 4 *J. Legal Ed.* 392 (1952).

Western and German Legal Thought, Community or Cleavage?, 58 *L. Q. Rev.* 257 (1942).

Übergesetzliche Rechtsgrundsätze und die Lösung von Rechtsproblemen, in *Naturrecht oder Rechtspositivismus?* 405 (W. Maihofer ed., Bad Homburg 1962), and in 41 *Archiv für Rechts und Sozialphilosophie* 348 (1954-55).

Book Reviews

Allen: *Law in the Making* (1939), 3 *Modern L. Rev.* 244 (1940).

Allen: *Law in the Making* (5th ed. 1951), 15 *Modern L. Rev.* 386 (1952).

Austin: *The Province of Jurisprudence Determined* (1954), 18 *Modern L. Rev.* 306 (1955).

Bienenfeld: *Rediscovery of Justice* (1947), 65 *L. Q. Rev.* 91 (1949).

Black: *The People and the Court* (1960), 77 *L. Q. Rev.* 451 (1961).

Buckland: *Some Reflections on Jurisprudence* (1945), 63 *L. Q. Rev.* 375 (1947).

Cahn: *The Moral Decision: Right and Wrong in the Light of American Law* (1955), 31 *Ind. L. J.* 545 (1956).

Cahn: *Sense of Injustice: Anthropocentric View of Law* (1949), 25 *N.Y.U. L. Forum* 935 (1950).

Cairns: *Legal Philosophy From Plato to Hegel* (1949), 28 *Can. B. Rev.* 359 (1950).

Cohen & Cohen: *Readings in Jurisprudence and Legal Philosophy* (1951), 40 *Calif. L. Rev.* 325 (1952).

Current Legal Problems 1954 (Keeton & Schwarzenberger eds. 1954), 12 *U. Toronto L. J.* 145 (1954).

Del Vecchio: *General Principles of Law* (1956), 3 *Natural L. F.* 208 (1958).

Del Vecchio: *Justice—Droit—Etat* (1939), 3 *Modern L. Rev.* 80 (1939).

Denning: The Changing Law (1953), 10 *U. Toronto L. J.* 301 (1954).

DuPasquier: *Introduction à la théorie générale et la philosophie du droit* (1939), 3 Modern L. Rev. 30 (1939).

Ebenstein: *Die Rechtsphilosophische Schule der reinen Rechtslehre* (1938), 3 *Modern L. Rev.* 80 (1939).

Ebenstein: *The Pure Theory of Law* (1945), 62 *L. Q. Rev.* 98 (1946).

Ehrenzweig: *Psychological Jurisprudence* (1971), 60 *Cal. L. Rev.* 1718 (1972).

Eisenmann: *University Teaching of Social Sciences: Law* (1954), 8 *J. Legal Ed.* 253 (1955).

Esser: *Grundsatz und Norm in der richterlichen Fortbildung des Privatretchts* (1956), 57 *Colum. L. Rev.* 449 (1957).

Ginsberg: *On Justice in Society* (1965), 66 *Colum. L. Rev.* 992 (1966).

Hagerstrom: *Inquiries Into the Nature of Law and Morals* (1953), 12 *U. Toronto L. J.* 107 (1957).

Hall: *Readings in Jurisprudence* (1938), 3 *Modern L. Rev.* 80 (1939).

Hall: *Studies in Jurisprudence and Criminal Theory* (1958) 74 *Pol. Sci. Q.* 302 (1959).

Hamburger: *The Awakening of Western Legal Thought* (1942), 59 *L. Q. Rev.* 94 (1943).

Hart: *Law, Liberty, and Morality* (1963), 9 *Natural L. F.* 151 (1964).

Hobbes: *Leviathan* (Oakeshott ed. 1964), 11 *Modern L. Rev.* 108 (1948).

Hoebel: *The Law of Primitive Man: A Study of Comparative Legal Dynamics* (1954), 31 *N.Y.U. L. Rev.* 248 (1956).

Interpretations of Modern Legal Philosophies: Essays in Honor of Roscoe Pound (Sayre ed. 1947), 64 *L. Q. Rev.* 545 (1948).

Jenks: *The Common Law of Mankind* (1958), 59 *Colum. L. Rev.* 533 (1959).

Jones: *Historical Introduction to the Theory of Law* (1940), 4 *Modern L. Rev.* 313 (1941).

Kelsen: *What is Justice? Justice, Law and Politics in the Mirror of Science* (1957) 9 *Stan. L. Rev.* 844 (1957).

Kruse: *The Right of Property* (1953), 17 *Modern L. Rev.* 589 (1954).

Lachmann: *Renaissance of the Individual* (1947), 65 *L. Q. Rev.* 91 (1949).

Law in a Changing America (Hazard ed. 1968), 44 *Notre Dame Lawyer* 299 (1968).

Law, State and International Legal Order: Essays in Honor of Hans Kelsen (Engel and Métall eds. 1964), 16 *U. Toronto L. J.* 465 (1966)

Lawson, *The Rational Strength of English Law* (1951), 10 *U. Toronto L. J.* 132 (1953-54).

Llewellyn: *Jurisprudence: Realism in Theory and Practice* (1962), 15 *U. Toronto L. J.* 476 (1963-64).

Lloyd: *Introduction to Jurisprudence* (1959), 60 *Colum. L, Rev.* 1203 (1960).

Macmillan: *A Man of Law's Tale* (1952), 48 *Nw. U. L. Rev.* 661 (1953).

Maitland: *Selected Essays* (Hazeltine, Lapsley & Winfield eds. 1936), 1 *Modern L. Rev.* 93 (1937).

Nomos II: Community (Friedrich ed. 1959), 3 *Modern L. Rev.* 252 (1960).

O'Sullivan: *The Inheritance of the Common Law* (1950), 7 *Int'l J.* 241 (1952).

Osborn's Law Dictionary (2nd ed. Osborn 1937), 3 *Modern L. Rev.* (1940).

Oxford Essays in Jurisprudence (Guest ed. 1961), 76 *Pol. Sci. Q.* 615 (1961).

Patterson: *Jurisprudence: Men and Ideas of the Law* (1953), 28 *N.Y.U. L. Rev.* 1340 (1953).

Petrazycki: *Law and Morality* (1955), 33 *Can. B. Rev.* 970 (1955).

Potter: *The Quest of Justice* (1951), 10 *U. Toronto L. J.* 154 (1953-54).

Pound: *The Formative Era of American Law* (1938), 4 *Modern L. Rev.* 157 (1940).

Renner: *The Institutions of Private Law and their Social Functions* (Kahn-Freund ed. 1949), 1 *Brit. J. Sociology* 240 (1950).

Reuschlein: *Jurisprudence—Its American Prophets* (1951), 4 *J. Legal Ed.* 506 (1952).

Stone: *Legal System and Lawyer's Reasonings* (1964); *Human Law and Human Justice* (1956); *Social Dimensions of Law and Justice* (1966), 67 *Colum. L. Rev.* 1344 (1967).

Stone: *The Province and Function of Law* (1947), 11 *Modern L. Rev.* 235 (1948).

Vanderbilt: *The Challenge of Law Reform* (1955), 20 *Modern L. Rev.* 292 (1957).

Weber on Law in Economy and Society (1954), 7 *Stan. L. Rev.* 306 (1955).

Wharton's Law Lexicon (14th ed. Oppé 3 *Modern L. Rev.* 252 (1940).

LAW OF INTERNATIONAL INVESTMENT AND ECONOMIC DEVELOPMENT

Books and Pamphlets

International Financial Aid (New York 1966) 498 pp. (with G. Kalmanoff & R. Meagher).

International Transactions in Less Developed Countries (New York 1966) 3 parts.

Joint Business Ventures of Yugoslav Enterprises and Foreign Firms (Belgrade 1968) 192 pp. (ed. with L. Mates).

Joint Fishery Ventures in the Indian Ocean Area (Rome 1972) 14 pp.

Joint International Business Ventures (New York 1961) 558 pp. (with G. Kalmanoff); (Japanese ed. 1964) 662 pp.

Joint International Business Ventures in Developing Countries: Case Studies and Analysis (New York 1971) 448 pp. (with J. Béguin).

Legal Aspects of Foreign Investment (Boston 1959) 812 pp. (ed. with R.C. Pugh ass't ed.).

Methods and Policies of Principal Donor Countries in Public International Development Financing: A Preliminary Appraisal (New York 1962) 49 pp.

The State and the Rule of Law in the Mixed Economy (Tagore Law Lectures) (London 1971) 104 pp.

ARTICLES

Antitrust Law and Joint International Business Ventures in Economically Underdeveloped Countries, 60 *Colum. L. Rev.* 780 (1960).

Arbitration Between Governments and Foreign Private Firms, 55 *Am. Soc'y Int'l L. Proc.* 69 (1961).

Comparative Analysis in *Legal Aspects of Foreign Investment* 734 (W. Friedmann ed. & R. Pugh ass't ed. 1959) (with R. Pugh).

Economic Development and Foreign Investment—Role of Law, 5 *Int'l & Comp. L. Bull.* 24 (A.B.A. Sect. 1961) (with Hyde, Castañeda, Sohn & Stokes).

Foreign Investment Planning and Economic Development: Forward, 17 *Rutgers L. Rev.* 251 (1963).

Foreign Investment and Restrictive Trade Practices, *J. Bus. L.* 144 (London 1960).

Foreword to Law and Economic Development: A Symposium 10 Colum. J. Transnat'l L. 195 (1971).

Freedom and Planning in Yugoslavia's Economic System, 25 *Slavic Rev.* 630 (1966).

The Future of International Development Aid, 40 *Forensic Quarterly* 321 (1966) (with G. Kalmanoff and R. Meagher).

Legal Problems in Foreign Investment, 14 *Bus. Lawyer* 746 (1959).

Problems of Doing Business Abroad, 1956 *Am. Soc'y Int'l L. Proc.* 5 (Pacific Northwest Regional Meeting on the International Implications of United States and Canadian Anti-Trust Laws) (Bulletin No. 12, Part 1).

The Relevance of International Law to the Processes of Economic and Social Development, in 2 *The Future of the International Legal Order* 3 (R. Falk & C. Black eds. 1970).

Seminar on Problems of International Law and Economic Development, University College of Law, Dar Es Salaam, Tanzania, 60 *Am. J. Int'l L.* 367 (1966).

Social Conflict and the Protection of Foreign Investment, 57 *Am. Soc'y Int'l L. Proc.* 117 (1963).

BOOK REVIEWS

American Enterprise in the European Common Market (Stein & Nicholson eds. 1960), 61 *Colum. L. Rev.* 1534 (1961).

Anderson: *Changing Law in Developing Countries* (1963), 13 *Int'l & Comp. L. Q.* 362 (1964).

Berle: *Twentieth Century Capitalist Revolution* (1954), 12 *U. Toronto L. J.* 135 (1957).

Gardner: *Sterling-Dollar Diplomacy* (1956), 51 *Am. J. Int'l L.* 854 (1957).

Lister: *Europe's Coal and Steel Community: An Experiment in Economic Union* (1960), 55 *Am. J. Int'l L.* 517 (1961).

Newman: *Public Control of Business: An International Approach* (1956), 53 *Am. J. Int'l L.* 735 (1959).

Nussbaum: *Money in the Law, National and International: A Comparative Study in the Borderline of Law and Economics* (1950), 10 *U. Toronto L. J.* 146 (1953-54).

Pearson: *Partners in Development: The Report of the Commission on International Development* (1969), 8 *Colum. J. Transnat'l L.* 334 (1969).

Tindenburg: *Shaping the World Economy. Suggestions for an International Economic Policy* (1962), 58 *Am. J. Int'l L.* 546 (1964).

Wilson: *The United States Commercial Treaties and International Law* (1960), 56 *Am. J. Int'l L.* 228 (1962).

TORT LAW

Articles

Incidence of Liability in Nuisance, 59 *L. Q. Rev.* 63 (1943).

Law Revision Commission Eighth Report (Contributory Negligence), 3 *Modern L. Rev.* 154 (1939) (with other members of the editorial committee).

Liability of Highway Authorities, 5 *Res Judicatae* 21 (Melbourne 1951).

Liability of Visitors to Premises, 61 *So. Afr. L. J.* 418 (1944).

Liability to Visitors of Premises, 21 *Can. B. Rev.* 79 (1943).

Modern Trends in the Law of Torts, 1 *Modern L. Rev.* 39 (1937).

Principles of Tort Liability and the Growth of Insurance, 1956 *Internationales Versicherungsrecht* 25 (Karlsruhe 1956).

Social Insurance and Principles of Tort Liability, 63 *Harv. L. Rev.* 241 (1949). Reprinted in *Selected Harvard Essays in the Law of Torts* 239 (Harv. L. Rev. ed. 1964).

Social Security and Some Recent Developments in the Common Law, 21 *Can. B. Rev.* 369 (1943).

Casenotes

Contributory Negligence—The Last Opportunity (*The Eurymedon,* 1 All E.R. 122 [1938], 1 *Modern L. Rev.* 318 (1938).

Duty of Occupier of Premises Adjoining the Highway (Wringe v. Cohen, 1 K.B. 229 [1940]), 56 *L. Q. Rev.* 140 (1940).

Employer's Duty to Provide a Safe System—Rule in Wilson's & Clyde Coal Co. v. English (Speed v. Thomas Swift & Co., 1 All E. R. 539 [1943]), 7 *Modern L. Rev.* 77 (1944).

Incidence of Liability for Nuisance (Sedleigh-Denfield v. St. Joseph Society for Foreign Missions, 3 All E. R. 349 [1940]), 4 *Modern L. Rev.* 139 (1940).

Landlord Liability to Tenant's Visitors—Responsibility for Negligence of Independent Contractors—Repairers and the Principle of Donoghue v. Stevenson (Haseldine v. Daw, 3 All E. R. 156 [1941]), 5 *Modern L. Rev.* 242 (1942).

Liability for Dangerous Activities Carried Out by Public Order (Read v. Lyons, 1 All E. R. 106 [1945]), 8 *Modern L. Rev.* 248 (1945).

Liability for Independent Contractors (S. S. Pass of Ballater v. Cardiff Channel Dry Docks & Pontoon Co., Ltd., 2 All E. R. 79 [1942]), 6 *Modern L. Rev.* 83 (1942).

Liability of Local Authorities for Defective Air-raid Shelter (Baker v. Mayor of Bethnal Green, 1 All E. R. 135 [1945]), 8 *Modern L. Rev.* 162 (1945).

The Manchester Regiment—Chain of Causation—Alternative Danger (*The Oropesa* [1943]), 6 *Modern L. Rev.* 237 (1943).

Motor Cars as Dangerous Things, Opportunity of Inspection (Herschthal v. Stewart & Anderson, Ltd., 56 T.L.R. 48 [1939]), 3 *Modern L. Rev.* 235 (1940).

Nuisance and Negligence Again (Heap v. Independent Coope & Allsop, Ltd., 3 All E. R. 643 [1940]; Slator v. Worthington Stores, 1 All E. R. 245 [1941]; Cushing v. Walker & Son, 2 All E. R. 93 [1941]), 5 *Modern L. Rev.* 240 (1942).

Nuisance, Negligence and the Overlapping of Torts (Wringe v. Cohn, 56 T.L.R. 101), 3 *Modern L. Rev.* 305 (1940).

Once More—Overlapping of Torts and Rationalisation of the Law (Hanson v. Wearmonth Coal Co., 55 T.L.R. 747), 4 *Modern L. Rev.* 308 (1941).

The Rule in Donoghue v. Stevenson (East Suffolk Rivers Catchment Board v. Kent and Another, 4 All E. R. 257 [1940]), 5 *Modern L. Rev.* 142 (1941).

Rylands v. Fletcher—Statutory Liability (Makin v. L. & N.E. Railway, 1 All E. R. 645 [1943]), 7 *Modern L. Rev.* 235 (1944).

Statutory Duties and Contributory Negligence of Pedestrians—Interpretation of Statutory Regulations (Sparkes v. Edward Ashe, Ltd., 1 All E. R. 1 [1943]), 6 *Modern L. Rev.* 235 (1943).

Tort—Negligence—Professional or Administrative Functions (Lindsey C. C. v. Marshall, [1937] A. C. 97), 1 *Modern L. Rev.* 77 (1937).

BOOK REVIEWS

Fleming: *Law of Torts* (1957), 58 *Colum. L. Rev.* 918 (1958).

Lawson: *Negligence in the Civil Law* (1950), 9 *U. Toronto L. J.* 142 (1951).

Street: *The Law of Torts* (1955), 57 *Colum. L. Rev.* 145 (1957).

Underhill: *Underhill's Law of Torts* (13th ed. Sutton 1937), 2 *Modern L. Rev.* 92 (1938).

Winfield on Tort: A Textbook of the Law of Tort (Lewis ed. 1954), 33 *Can. B. Rev.* 244 (1955).

LETTERS AND ARTICLES IN NEW YORK TIMES

Dec. 9, 1951, § IV, at 10, col. 5 (*urging that the United States cooperate with all European governments, including socialist governments*).

Dec. 28, 1952, § IV, at 6, col. 5 (*concerning European Defense Community, Germany, and NATO*).

June 13, 1954, § IV, at 8, col. 6 (*concerning the United States—United Kingdom policy split on the Far East*).

Sept. 26, 1954, § IV, at 8, col. 6 (*urging political and economic integration in Europe through a stronger NATO and the creation of a supernational authority in various economic fields*).

Feb. 26, 1956, § IV, at 10, col. 6 (*deploring United States' reluctance to participate in the United Nations and other international pacts and convention*).

Aug. 12, 1956, § IV, at 8, col. 2 (*Egyptian nationalization of the Suez Canal seen not as clearly objectionable legally as politically*).

Nov. 20, 1956, at 36, col. 6 (*urging a stronger United Nations role in the Middle East*).

Oct. 27, 1957, § IV, at 8, col. 6 (*urgency of closer political and economic integration in Europe through NATO*).

Nov. 3, 1957, § IV, at 16 (*article*) (*importance of aiding underdeveloped nations without the attachment of political strings; importance of a private role in cooperation with government aid*).

Aug. 11, 1958, at 20, col. 4 (*danger, with reference to the Middle East, in United States promises to aid any state against indirect aggression*).

Jan. 17, 1959, at 18, col. 5 (*urges a more flexible Western approach to the German reunification issue*).

Dec. 11, 1959, at 32, col. 5 (*lauds the open discussion of the issue of birth control*).

May 15, 1960, § IV, at 10, col. 4 (*U-2 incident as violation of U.S.S.R. air sovereignty*).

May 1, 1961, at 28, col. 6 (*United States position on Castro's Cuba as an affirmation of United States national interests over restraints of international law*).

Dec. 31, 1961, § IV, at 8, col. 5 (*international law problems raised by private ownership of communications satellite systems*).

April 21, 1963, § IV, at 4, col. 2 (*foreign aid*).

Feb. 16, 1964, § IV, at 8, col. 4 (*criticism of United States economic boycott of Cuba*).

Sept. 25, 1964, at 40, col. 2 (*General Airline & Film Corporation—Interhandel settlement motivated by desire to resolve disputes with Switzerland*).

March 13, 1965, at 29, col. 2 (*urges continued foreign economic aid*).

May 9, 1965, at 13, col. 1 (*the Johnson "doctrine," with reference to Vietnam, imperils the application of international law*).

Dec. 21, 1965, at 2, col. 4 (*movement into Cambodia as a violation of international law unless the country is being used as a military staging area by North Vietnam or the Vietcong*).

March 26, 1966, at 3, col. 1 (*letter with seven other international law professors criticizing United States proposal to mine Haiphong harbor as a virtual declaration of war*).

July 28, 1966, at 32, col. 3 (*deploring United States foreign aid cuts*).

Jan. 8, 1967, § IV, at 13, col. 4 (*deploring United States decision to suspend food aid to Yugoslavia because of Yugoslavian aid to North Vietnam and Cuba; political significance of 1948 Yugoslavia breakaway from the Communist bloc*).

Oct. 8, 1967, § IV, at 11, col. 1 (*concerning the administration rationale for the United States Vietnam role*).

Aug. 11, 1968, § IV, at 11, col. 1 (*criticizes Papal Encyclical Humanae Vitae ("Of Human Life") for intellectual failings*).

March 25, 1970, at 46, col. 4 (*criticizing United States statement on the continuing United States bombing of Laos as a violation of international law*),

April 19, 1970, § IV, at 17, col. 2 (*criticizes United States claims to resources of continental shelf as leading to uncontrolled exploitation by other nations; discussion of continental shelf doctrine, stating that oceans will become less open and more polluted if national limits are expanded*).

Feb. 3, 1971, at 36, col. 3 (*expansion of territorial claims will destroy freedom of the sea; lauds United States proposal to confine the continental shelf, to establish an international seabed authority, and to give coastal states the right to administer an intermediate zone*).

Feb. 21, 1971, § IV, at 10, col. 3 (*latter with two other law professors criticizing United States incursions into Laos and Cambodia*).

May 16, 1971, § IV, at 12, col. 3 (*suggesting a United States strategy which would probably result in the seating of the Communist Chinese in the United Nations and the expulsion of Taiwan).*

Nov. 12, 1971, at 47, col. 3 (*article*) (*challenging, on moral and legal grounds, Professor Milton Friedman's criticism of wage and price controls as illegal and immoral*).

April 25, 1972, at 42, col. 4 (*warning that United States blockade or mining of Haiphong harbor could lead to direct confrontation between the U.S.S.R., Communist China, and other nations*).

MIX
Papier aus verantwortungsvollen Quellen
Paper from responsible sources
FSC® C105338

If you have any concerns about our products,
you can contact us on
ProductSafety@springernature.com

In case Publisher is established outside the EU,
the EU authorized representative is:
Springer Nature Customer Service Center GmbH
Europaplatz 3, 69115 Heidelberg, Germany

Printed by Libri Plureos GmbH
in Hamburg, Germany